Letters of Brigham Young to His Sons

THE MORMON HERITAGE SERIES · LEONARD J. ARRINGTON, GENERAL EDITOR · VOLUME ONE

BRIGHAM YOUNG

Letters of Brigham Young to His Sons

Edited and Introduced by Dean C. Jessee

With a Foreword by J. H. Adamson

Published by Deseret Book Company
In Collaboration with the
Historical Department of
The Church of Jesus Christ of Latter-day Saints
Salt Lake City, Utah, 1974

Copyright, 1974, by Deseret Book Company
Library of Congress Catalog Number 74-80041
ISBN No. 0-87747-522-9
Printed in the United States of America

To my own sons:
Lyle, David, Ronald, Gordon,
Merrill and Jonathan Jessee

General Editor's Preface

The archives of The Church of Jesus Christ of Latter-day Saints have a rich collection of papers related to the life and activities of Brigham Young. A member of the Church since 1832 and an apostle after 1835, Brigham Young served as president of the Council of Twelve Apostles after the death of Joseph Smith in 1844 and in January 1848 was sustained as president of The Church of Jesus Christ of Latter-day Saints. Brigham Young served as president until his death on August 29, 1877.

The Church Archives has approximately 150 boxes of Brigham Young materials, including a 50,000-page manuscript history of Brigham Young, four diaries written in Brigham Young's own hand during the years 1837 to 1844, and thousands of pages of office journals, correspondence, speeches, and other material of like nature.

Acknowledged to be one of America's great colonizers, Brigham Young was also governor of Utah Territory from 1850 to 1858, superintendent of Indian Affairs from 1851 to 1858, a founder of about 350 communities in the Far West, and founder of several score business enterprises.

A believer in the principle of plural marriage practiced by the Mormons during his lifetime, Brigham Young was the head of one of America's largest families. Sixteen of his wives bore him fifty-seven children. Of these children, forty-six grew to maturity, including seventeen sons and twenty-nine daughters. The Church Archives has more than one hundred letters written by Brigham Young to his children, including letters written to sons while they were away on proselyting missions for the Church, others written to sons who studied in eastern universities, still others written to sons away on business trips, and letters to two sons who were in the military service. The importance of Brigham Young as a letter writer has not previously been appreciated.

The Church Archives has the responsibility of collecting and preserving manuscript materials related to the history of the Mormon people. It also has the responsibility of making available materials in the archives that would be edifying and informative. Among the most interesting of these are Brigham Young's letters to his sons that are presented in this volume. Enjoying a warm relationship with his sons, Brigham Young gave them fatherly counsel through these letters. Much of this advice is as relevant today as it was when written a century ago.

Leonard J. Arrington
General Editor

Salt Lake City, Utah

 Contents

General Editor's Preface   vi
List of Illustrations   x
Foreword by J. H. Adamson   xi
Introduction   xxi
Editorial Procedure and Acknowledgments   xlii
Brigham Young's Letters to His Sons, with Biographical
    Introductions
        Joseph Angell Young   3
        Brigham Young, Jr.   19
        John Willard Young   91
        Brigham Heber Young   127
        Oscar Brigham Young   143
        Hyrum Smith Young (biography only)   149
        Ernest Irving Young   151
        Willard Young   161
        Mahonri Moriancumer Young (biography only)   213
        Alfales Young   217
        Brigham Morris Young   241
        Arta De Christa Young   253
        Joseph Don Carlos Young   263
        Lorenzo Dow Young   283
        Feramorz Little Young   295
        Alonzo Young (biography only)   317
        Phineas Howe Young (biography only)   319
Notes   322
Biographical Appendix   334
Appendix A: Chronology of Events in the Life of
    Brigham Young   352
Appendix B: Brigham Young's Family   357
Appendix C: Chronology of Brigham Young's Children   359
Chronological List of Letters   360
Index   362

Illustrations

Brigham Young   ii

Joseph Angell Young   2

Brigham Young's Handwriting   17

Brigham Young, Jr.   18

John Willard Young   90

Brigham Heber Young   126

Oscar Brigham Young   142

Hyrum Smith Young   148

Ernest Irving Young   150

Willard Young   160

Mahonri Moriancumer Young   212

Alfales Young   216

Brigham Morris Young   240

Arta De Christa Young   252

Joseph Don Carlos Young   262

Lorenzo Dow Young   282

Feramorz Little Young   294

Alonzo Young   316

Phineas Howe Young   318

Foreword

J. H. Adamson

If you wish to know the oak-rooted values of any ruler, read his letters to his sons. Brigham Young was, for a time, the ruler of a vast territory and a small people who had no intention of remaining small, who were determined that Utah would some day be known for more than its landscape. Utah was to be the heart of the Kingdom, and its people would first embody and then represent to the world the virtues of that kingdom.

Brigham was not overtly dynastic; perhaps he had too many sons for that. Never does he say to one of his boys, If you please your father, you may inherit a kingdom someday. Perhaps he was too wise in the annals of history, knowing that Ulysses is usually followed by Telemachus, that kingdom builders beget sons who may inherit their features but not their effectiveness.

But if Brigham's boys had ears to hear, their father's letters carried always one eloquent plea: here is what I have lived by. This is what formed my character. This is what you must live by if you would succeed me, succeed me as a man that is, for whether they should succeed him as a leader could wait. That was God's decision.

As a boy Brigham received almost no formal schooling. Perhaps he was exaggerating a bit, but he always said that he had no schooling until he "got into Mormonism," and if so he was then thirty-one years of age. What had he learned before that time? He

> had the privilege of picking up brush, chopping down trees, rolling logs, and working amongst the roots, and of getting . . . shins, feet, and toes bruised. . . . I learned to make bread, wash dishes, milk the cows and make butter. . . .
> Those are about all the advantages I gained in my youth.

One senses the wry humor, the confident self-deprecation of the man who is assured of his status, but also there is that continual defensiveness in his writings and speeches: "I have not the advantage of language. However . . . I rise to do the best I can."

Not the advantage of languages. Brigham must have been remembering the time back in Kirtland, Ohio, when Brother Joseph had sought out a Hebrew with a storied name, Joshua Seixas, and asked him to teach the sacred language to the School of the Prophets. Joseph himself, a very apt student, was soon reading aloud to the pleasure and delight of his teacher; but the stocky carpenter with the big shoulders could never puzzle out those exotic words, and the English Bible that he loved became more alien, more strange and forbidding with every lesson. Soon Joseph, perceiving Brigham's distaste for book learning, suggested that he paint the temple and take care of the other things that the more ethereal natures seemed to have no time for.

The early Mormon pioneers had an almost sacred thirst for education. The First Presidency at this time was no exception: Brigham Young, Heber C. Kimball, and Jedediah Grant each had a kinsman, son or brother, on a mission in England at the same time, and each was enormously proud that his relative had received an education, that the family was "improving." Each of these men was always self-conscious about his own lack of formal training. Brigham once said,

> . . . when I began to speak in public, I was about as destitute of language as a man could well be. . . . How I have had the headache, when I had ideas to lay before the people, and not words to express them; but I was so gritty that I always tried my best.

But Heber C. Kimball, speaking for all three fathers, said it best. Writing to his son William, he nostalgically recalled the time when he had been called by the Prophet Joseph to open the door of proclamation to England, the Church's first overseas mission.

> I did not at that time have the education that you have, neither did I know and understand one tenth part of what you did previous to your going on your mission. I was illiterate and unlearned, weak and feeble, and felt as though I was the weakest of all. Many times I thought to myself, why should I, so weak an instrument, be called to such an important work, while there were many who were learned and could speak with all the eloquence of artificial education.

As the frontiersman pondered this paradox, why a man with hard hands should have been chosen by the Lord when there were clerks available who knew how to spell, how to keep the tenses straight, and how to sprinkle their speech with the devices of rhetoric, Heber found an answer. It was the same answer his friends Brigham and Jedediah had also found. A man who can do none of the clerkish things feels weak, uncertain, confused, vulnerable to satiric attack, to the condescension of other men who write and speak with an acquired grace. In this wavering state, the man for whom the beginning has always been a deed rather than a word can only fall back on his God, can only ask the Holy Ghost to speak through him and for him. Ten words from such a man are worth more than ten thousand words from those who pride themselves on their learning and who have a "pretty language." Prettiness does not go far in this world; truth does. Give truth her ten words; say those words for her, and then be silent. Allow the mouth more than ten words and the muscles relax, the resolution wavers, the voice goes on talking, tickling, brushing the ear like a feather while the guts of the enterprise turn to water.

Brigham and Heber had both known the pain of traveling backward in time to England where their people had come from, to England where men spoke the speech of Shakespeare. And among those sophisticates of the word they had felt smaller than a bean, smaller than a pea. So what could they do? They would avoid the university towns or the fashionable resorts; they would not seek out the sleek women or the smiling men. They would go rather to some place where they had to travel thirty miles out and thirty miles back and say their ten words. Never mind the shoe leather; that was the shoemaker's worry. Let the humble men find the humble place and begin to preach. "Out there" people would gather around who would find their scrambled tenses and provincial pronunciations natural and familiar; out there, thirty miles from anywhere, Brigham could write "all things are going pertiwell," and no one would smile for they wrote that way too. Out there, whether in England or America, he could write of the greatest tragedy he had ever known,

> It has ben a time of morning the day that Joseph and Hyram ware braught from Cartheg to Nauvoo. It was Judged by menny boath in and out of the church that there was more then 5 barels of tears shead. I cannot bare to think enny thing a bout it

and such a letter would bring more tears to those who read it.

And so in England Brigham had gone to the cities and villages to tell the people about the Kingdom. Salvation after death was well enough, he would disturb no beliefs about that, but here and now there was a new and holy land, an empty land waiting for its people. Brigham spoke about that land, sketching a bright dream full of hope for women who, with their babies, were huddled in the blight of milltowns, for men in villages whose lives were forever mortgaged to the landlord. These were the people whom an untaught missionary could touch and melt and send walking, sailing, river-boating to Zion. Zion where the devil wants to kick and make a fuss but the Saints won't let him. Out in Zion, says Brigham, the Saints are happy; it is the devil who has the blues. Remember that, boys: in Zion the Saints are happy. Some of them were people who had called happiness a lie, who had given up on life, who never knew health for sickness, who thought more about death than life, who couldn't taste any sweetness because the sour was always on their tongues. But they were happy now in Zion where the devil had the blues.

But unschooled men have their blind spots, just as clerks do. Brigham's mistrust of the men of words, his perception of the limitation of clerks, sometimes led him into strange positions. For example, he mistrusted both the writers and readers of novels. That was odd in a way, for he loved the theater. When he could actually see the characters move, hear them talking, discover the springs of their action and feel their own emotions rising in himself, he unself-consciously laughed or wept and became for a time the very character he saw portrayed. But when he read fiction, when all he had before him was the cold page, it all seemed false, strained, completely unlike the vicissitudes of real life that any man would learn about soon enough. Reading was good, Brigham thought, only if it was useful. Sell your Dickens, he counsels one son, and buy Stephens and Catherwood's *Travels in Central America*, a piece of literary advice not even his most ardent disciple would subscribe to now. Read about the animal, vegetable, and mineral kingdoms, says Brigham to his sons; peruse the lives of good men in all ages; learn of art and science and manufacture: all of these will fit you for future usefulness. But novels, minute descriptions of the heart, of the tender passions, of all that silly business between men and women that began with Adam and has never ended, it is all a butterfly world, my boys. Sell your Jane Austen and buy a set of surveyor's tools, your Thackeray and buy a mule and a plow, your Defoe and Smollett and purchase a medicine kit, a shoemaker's awl, a package of sugar beet seeds, a ram, and a serviceable ewe, anything, anything that is useful.

So we accept that. The unschooled man, the man who has no pretty words must have his small revenges on the clerks. But that same man cannot stay out there, thirty miles from anywhere, saying his ten words and baptizing his hundred converts. The same spirit that drove him into that wilderness will surely drive him back to the heartland, the Kingdom where he will practice the virtues and qualities he wishes to pass on to his sons.

And so those values Brigham lived by began to emerge as themes in his letters to the boys. The first theme that no reader can miss is his constant exhortation to *observe, observe, observe*. On the day when he wrote that first heartsick letter to his daughter after he had heard of the murder of Joseph and Hyrum, after he himself had shed some of that five barrels of tears, he nevertheless, even in his grief, noted that the river was high, the crops were good, and wheat was selling for forty cents a bushel. As the years passed, his interest in these elementary things never waned: he always reported to his sons the price of wheat, the condition of City Creek or the Jordan River, the heat of the sun, the extent of the rains or even the wind, which, one January, blew "as fiercingly as ever I felt it in this valley." One year the grasshoppers ruined the crops in Morgan, Summit, and Wasatch counties but the observant Brigham knew that there was wheat in Davis and Cache. So, with "prudence and economy," two of his watchwords, the Saints would manage; everyone would eat. There would need to be forceful leadership, no time for paperwork or bureaucratic shifts. Grain would have to be moved, farmers mollified and paid something, the fearful reassured. Because he always observed and therefore knew so intimately the state of his kingdom, Brigham could provide.

Nor was it enough to observe crops and climate; rather, the most difficult thing to observe and assess, said Brigham, was man himself. To his son on a mission in England he said what he could continue to say all his life: to combat the world, we must know the ways of the world, and one could know them only by observation, continual alertness, never allowing the slightest thing to escape notice. "Listen attentively," he wrote to his son, "and observe minutely the manners, customs, and remarks of all, for, from the most humble of our fellow creatures, an observing man can learn something that will be useful to him in after life." Such, said Brigham, had been his own "daily and hourly" practice all his life, and he had reaped enormous benefits from it. And when he traveled around the kingdom, while others were talking, he was observing: Are the people industrious? Are they happy? Are they at peace with themselves and one another? Those were the important things for a leader to observe.

Another of Brigham's themes emerges in the letters whenever he sends money to his sons, for inevitably there is a cautionary word about economy, frugality, parsimony. The old New England watchword of "eat it up, wear it out, make it do" was part of the texture of Brigham's thought. Money was the product of work, and the principal work of his time was the gathering of the poor. Every cent "luxuriously expended" was money wasted that might have brought the poor to Zion. He urged his sons to observe the poor carefully, for then they would see how people managed to live on nearly nothing, and the boys might well emulate such prudence and economy. Yet Brigham was never stingy. Always he left a door open for the boys to obtain money; there was always some agent or friend or business associate to whom they could apply whenever "necessity and judgment" dictated. Brigham knew that money had its limitations. The Lord, he said, could work without money, but the devil could not, and anyone bent on acquiring money, an indifferent thing in itself, should always remember that.

Occasionally we get a glimpse of Brigham smarting under the monstrous image of himself that he saw reflected in the world outside his own kingdom. When his son Willard was admitted to West Point, the New York *Herald* inquired editorially if the cadets would "permit the outrage." Only a man in public life can know how he hurts when his enemies strike at his children. So what should Willard do? There was only one thing to do, his father said. Be proud of who he was; live at West Point as he would at home, frugally, prayerfully, chastely (yes, the polygamist demanded chastity from his sons; as a young man he had been chaste; they could be and must be also). Above all Willard must eschew self-righteousness or defensive umbrage. To all his classmates he should be kind, courteous, but firm in his own ways. If Willard's life exhibited his principles, he would soon be "at the head and not at the tail." And surely enough when Brigham received, as all fathers did in those days, a report from the inspector at West Point showing Willard to be first in his class in mathematics and fourth in French, Brigham writes, "We were very much gratified to hear of your success, especially in Mathematics." First place Brigham respected; fourth place he never thought much about one way or the other.

When another son went to the Naval Academy, it seemed to be less of a national outrage, but Brigham nevertheless instructed the boy to be always gentlemanly, courteous, and forbearing; Brigham spoke much to all of his children about courtesy, a trait he loved in anyone. Along with courtesy, he continually asked his children to cultivate honor and integrity. For Brigham, integrity meant that the mouth and the heart were one; and while much nonsense had been spoken about honor, it basically meant that other men trusted you.

Although Brigham was a practical man, he developed a mystique or two, and one of these was the mystique of work. In the Kingdom of God, said Brigham, "an idler shall have no place." And what everyone should work hardest at was self-improvement: he never tired of saying, *improve, improve, improve.* He writes a daughter that she should study continually and that she might also "learn the Pianna." To two of his sons in the East he suggests that instead of coming home for the holidays they might stay where they were and learn to play the piano and the organ. The son who wishes to learn the piano will find good enough teachers where he is; but learning the organ is another matter. Boston is the place for that, and Brigham has already inquired about the best teachers in that city, which was half a world away. He proudly tells his children that now in Zion there is a Mutual Improvement Association in which all the young people can work to improve themselves. From Brigham there flows a stream of constant exhortation to the children to study, to read, to learn an art or a skill. There is little spare time in the world Brigham has known, and so leisure is the most precious thing the children will have if they will use it for self-improvement. Try to learn, he tells one of his sons; try to improve, even though things at the moment are very difficult for you, and then he adds, "I glory in your grit."

The ethic of work was never more fully endorsed than by Brigham in a letter to his West Point son:

> Whoever wastes his life in idleness, either because he need not work in order to live, or because he will not live to work, will be a wretched creature, and at the close of a listless existence will regret the loss of precious gifts and the neglect of great opportunities. Our daily toil, however

humble it may be, is our daily duty, and by doing it well we make it a part of our daily worship.

In the same month he wrote to his son at the Naval Academy:

> You will find that much of the happiness of this life consists in having something worthy to do and in doing it well.... If a man have to drive the plow let him do it well; if only to cut bolts, make good ones; if to blow the bellows, keep the iron hot. It is our attention to our daily duties that makes us men....

And so at last Brigham had found the words he had long been seeking: a man's essential nature is defined by his works, not his words. Let the clerks think about that.

Brigham is sure of one thing all his life: he will never hide from the world; he would rather meet it on its own terms and win. His boys will go to eastern colleges, will travel round the world, will serve missions in far-off places where Zion is only a long memory. When the railroad came and the gentiles said that at last the world would assimilate Brigham, he roared with laughter. God had sent the railroad to make easier that way in the wilderness by which the poor should come to Zion. The telegraph? A marvelous invention for a man with a kingdom. Now conception and execution could be twin-born from the same mind as they never could in the day of horses. A steam engine? It produced even more energy than Brigham himself, and so he felt positively companionable toward it. He would surely like to have one.

And yet one cannot help wondering if Brigham, in the pride of his strength, was not sometimes overconfident. It is not for nothing that so many holy men in all ages and climes have forsaken the world, seeking solitude and isolation. The question arises whether Willard, at West Point, should not perhaps marry an eastern girl who could help further his military career. That is something of a shock for Brigham but he recovers nicely. If it must be so, Willard should marry one of the daughters of General Sherman. If one is forced to jump, he should jump into the king row. And then Feramorz is reading novels and apparently giving insufficient attention to the Bible. Too, a disaffected wife, incited, Brigham says, by greedy lawyers, is suing for alimony and support. Some of his children who are away from home wish to attend the services of other churches. Certainly. Go ahead. Get all the truth you can, but you will never find anything like the Kingdom.

And yet in all this hearty acquiescence, one feels somewhere a note of reserve, a tone of misliking. The world is moving in and each year Brigham has a little less strength to resist it. Less bodily strength perhaps, but no diminution of the will. And then there are the children who must beat the world on its own terms after he is gone, and so he tells them over and over again that they must improve themselves "in the sphere of usefulness"; they must think and write clearly because clarity makes language not more beautiful but more useful; the children must be temperate in pleasures and moderate in expenses, always remembering that there is no excellence without labor, no success in this world without honor and integrity. But the world is proving a little more stubborn than Brigham had thought, the Kingdom a little more difficult of attainment.

The Kingdom. That was the ultimate mystique for this practical man. He never ceased thinking about it; he never stopped working for it. Sometimes he seemed not to remember where God's kingdom began and Brigham's ended. Once when he was bone tired, he had asked a clerk to write a note to his son in England. That note was filled with scribal formularies:

> With much pleasure at the request of your honored father, I embrace a few moments to give you the current items of news of this part of our mountain land. . . .
>
> Promising to endeavor to keep you informed of such items of interest as would be interesting to you, from time to time, as I may be directed, I have the pleasure to subscribe myself. . . .

As his last act of that long day, probably around midnight, Brigham picked up that letter, read those cold formulas and phrases that had come from the mind without consulting the heart, and forgetting his own marginal literacy that made all his scribes necessary, he seized the pen and wrote to the son he loved:

> My Dear Son Joseph
>   It is now late at nigh. The male has arived this evening and I have heard your letter red, and it rejoice my hart to here sush good knews frm you. May the Lord Bles you for ever and ever, is my Prayr for you. . . . You can hardly emagen the joy it gives me to here such good knew from you. My sole leaps for joye. Be faithful my son and the Lord will Bles you and I Bles you. Remember you are my

> oldest son, the arc of the famely, I want you to be faithful that you may [be] worthe of your stashon in my Kingdom.

My Kingdom? Did he mean in my Father's kingdom where there are many mansions, or did he mean in Brigham's kingdom where there was one keystone in the arch, the eldest son? It was late and Brigham was wearier than he realized. Who can know what he meant?

God's kingdom. Such a strange place really, so indicative of the man and his time. A place where everyone works, both men and women, where children continually improve themselves, where every new wonder of technology is harnessed for the poor, where all men strive to be their own best, where above all else men cherish and love their children who alone can make the bright dream come true.

Brigham thinks even more about the children now, for he is troubled with rheumatism; he suffers from fierce stomach pains, and the harassment of the lawyers is more painful than it was. He wearies of seeing his name slain, his children hurt, his intentions misunderstood. Sometimes these days Brigham has the blues. But then he remembers the Kingdom—the homes without tears, a land of peace where the wheat heads out every year under the August sun, where the rains come just before the streams go dry. Honor and integrity, courtesy, alertness, curiosity, striving, striving, wonderment and work and the glory of the Kingdom to give it all meaning. Those are the things, said Brigham to his boys, that you must learn from me. When a man's sons know these things he can die without bitterness; when a man's sons know these things he can sleep peacefully in the valley, lying in the shadow of the Kingdom. When a man says these things to his sons, says them from the heart and the bone and the mind, how can his letters be other than beautiful and strong? And that is what these letters are.

Sleep well, Brother Brigham. You left more sons and daughters than the children of your flesh. They hear you now. They understand.

Introduction

Two things I am very anxious all my sons should be: faithful servants of our Heavenly Father, and useful members in his Kingdom. Integrity to the truth and ability to do good are qualities which I hope will characterize you all.
—BRIGHAM YOUNG, 25 JULY 1871

Amongst the pleasures of my life, at the present time, is the thought that so many of my sons are acquiring experimental and practical knowledge that will fit them for lives of great usefulness, and with this thought, I associate the hope, that by God's mercy, that knowledge will be applied in striving to save the souls of men, and building up the Kingdom of Heaven on the earth.
—BRIGHAM YOUNG, 11 NOVEMBER 1875

Much has been written about Brigham Young. And yet few men have been less understood by their contemporaries than he was. Separated from his countrymen by strange beliefs and a vast distance, he was a subject of intense ridicule and slander during his lifetime. Confident that time would eventually assign him his rightful place in history, Brigham Young studiously ignored the malicious stories that were circulated about him. "I am often made aware," he once wrote Jefferson Davis, "of the utter uselessness, and folly of seeking to vindicate my character from such foul aspersions as are occasionally raised against me; from the simple fact, that . . . when the vile slander is fairly refuted, and truth appears in the most incontestable manner, it is permitted to lie quietly upon the shelf to slumber the sleep of death."[1]

The mountain of false reports made against Brigham Young has been tenaciously quarried and in many cases has served as the main source of information for the biographer. Consequently, the truth about Brigham Young is still largely "upon the shelf," so to speak, because biographers have not sought an understanding of him in the right places.

"The letters of a person, especially of one whose business has been chiefly transacted by letters, form the only full and genuine journal of his life," said Thomas Jefferson. Such is the case with Brigham Young. The voluminous correspondence that comprises a weighty part of the Brigham Young papers in the archives of The Church of Jesus Christ of Latter-day Saints presents a view unsurpassed in its detail of his life. These letters vividly illuminate the character of the man whom Samuel Eliot Morison has described as "among the most successful commonwealth builders of the English-speaking world." A select group of the letters, chosen from among the countless papers of state and ecclesiastical importance, are those he wrote to members of his family. These reveal a dimension of his life that has largely remained hidden from view in the popular studies of him: his role as husband and father. If among Brigham Young's pleasures in the waning years of his life was, as he said, the thought of his children's honorable achievements, then the groundwork for his joy had been laid years before at his own fireside. Few men have ignited the spark of human worth and dignity in their children as effectively as did Brigham Young. Through the numerous letters he wrote to his children, we can see something of the relationships he established with them and get some insight into his family life. And into Brigham Young himself, since personality and character are nowhere better revealed than in the intimate environment of one's family circle.

Brigham Young's family provided much of his happiness in life. "I due think the Lord has blest me with one of the best famelyes that eney man ever had on the earth," he wrote in his own hand, with his own characteristic spelling, on one occasion; and, after returning from missionary service for the Church in England, he noted that his joy was complete when he was able to spend, for the first time in years, an evening by his fireside with his family: "We injoi it and feele to prase the Lord," he wrote in his diary. While traveling back to Winter Quarters from Salt Lake Valley in the fall of 1847, he lamented, "O that I had my famely here." So important was his family to him that regardless of his success and accomplishments in life, Brigham felt that were he to fail in his duty as husband and father, he would "[wake] up in the morning of the First Resurrection to find that he had failed in everything."

Brigham Young's was one of the prominent families of Mormondom—not only because of its size, or because of his position as president of the Church and as governor of Utah Territory, but also because it stood as an example of those principles of industry and service that had long been preached as ideals of Latter-day Saint family life.

Because of numerous burdensome responsibilities of public office, Brigham's personal contact with his family was necessarily limited. After frequent absence from home during the first decade of his Church membership, he was told in a revelation, "it is no more required . . . to leave your family as in times past, for your offering is acceptable to me. . . . I therefore command you to . . . take special care of your family from this time, henceforth." While this statement did not eliminate future absences from his family, it no doubt affected the quality of his association with them, limited though it still must be.

Brigham Young's family was one of the largest in the Church.[2] Sixteen of his wives bore him fifty-seven children, eleven of whom died in infancy or early childhood. Of the forty-six children who grew to maturity, seventeen were sons and twenty-nine daughters. Aside from the awesome responsibilities attendant upon presiding over the Church at a time when detail was not consistently channeled to subordinates and so demanded his attention, Brigham was confronted with the daily care of a household that at its height numbered more than seventy individuals. The logistical problem alone, of feeding and clothing such a number, staggers the imagination, not to speak of providing the education and training that must precede responsible behavior if children are to perpetuate traits of nobility and integrity.

Confronted with chiding and ridicule from friends and enemies alike, who doubted Brigham's ability to even know all of his children, let alone properly care for and instruct them,[3] President Young nevertheless succeeded in providing for their physical, emotional, and spiritual needs in a manner that is both exemplary and profound. He brought a degree of wisdom and understanding to the task of family management that contributed to a positive relationship with his children and remarkably influenced their attitudes and accomplishments in life. Several factors contributed to this, not the least of which was a paternal love and kindness, balanced with firmness and justice. One of Brigham Young's daughters recalled that "home was as beautiful to me as love and happiness could make it." To his children, no other fact of their father's life was so plain a proof of his greatness as "his life at home and the influence which he radiated there." His daughter Clarissa Young Spencer, who fondly remembered her childhood as "one long round of happiness," wrote that her father "had the tenderness of a woman for his family and friends." Susa Young Gates related that although there were the usual squabbles among the children, "we were not a contentious family." Nor did the size of the family preclude a spirit of companionship and esteem between its individual members. Susa concluded that hers "was an ideal father, kind to a fault, tender, thoughtful, just and firm. . . . None of us feared him."

The kindness that characterized Brigham's relationship with his children included a firmness "that neither humiliated the child nor lowered his own self-respect." Discipline was mainly an educational process of example and precept: "It is not by the whip or the rod that we can make obedient children," he stated, "but it is by faith and by prayer, and by setting a good example before them."[4] The few instances of Brigham Young applying the "rod" to his children must be regarded within this framework. If children knew the feelings of their parents when they did good or evil, "it would have a salutary influence upon their lives; but no child can possibly know this, until it becomes a parent. I am compassionate therefore towards children." Governing a home by violence and dictatorship was contrary to Brigham Young's convictions:

> I do not believe in making my authority as a husband or a father known by brute force; but by a superior intelligence—by showing them that I am capable of teaching them. . . . If the Lord has placed me to be head of a family, let me be so in all humility and patience, not as a tyrannical ruler, but as a faithful companion, an indulgent and affectionate father, a thoughtful and unassuming superior; let me be honoured in my station through faithful diligence, and be fully capable, by the aid of God's Spirit, of filling my office in a way to effect the salvation of all who are committed to my charge.

Brigham Young taught that when children are bound to the moral law, "until duty becomes loathsome to them; when they are freed by age from the rigorous training of their parents, they are more fit for companions to devils, than to be the children of such religious parents."

This "indulgent" and "affectionate" father did not lack firmness, however. During the family devotion one evening a noisy young girl "was running about and squealing with laughter." Brigham stopped his prayer, caught the child, spanked her, and laid her sobbing in her mother's waiting arms. He then returned to his chair, where he again knelt and quietly concluded the family prayer.

Brigham Young's adeptness as a child psychologist was demonstrated on one occasion when one of his wives confronted him with a small son who, as soon as he was fed his bread and milk each day, was in the habit of knocking the dish and spoon to the floor. "The next time he knocks the dish from your hand," Brigham counseled, "lean him against the chair, do not say one word to him, [and] go to your work." The mother did so, and the child stood by the chair for a while looking first at his mother and then at the objects on the floor. Presently he got down and crawled to the spoon and dish and placed them upon the table. "He never tried to knock that dish out of her hand again," concluded Brigham. "She might have whipped him and injured him, as a great many others would have done; but if they know what to do, they can correct the child without violence."

Brigham Young's confidence in having taught his sons a correct principle was manifest in an address in 1872 discussing the carelessness of children who not only played in the streets, but even taunted teamsters to run over them. "And sometimes people have to stop their carriages to save the lives of children," Brigham noted, adding, "if one of my boys attempts to obstruct the highway, take your whip and give him a good sound horse-whipping." But, he concluded, "I think of a truth, that a boy of mine never did this, never."

An important institution in the Young household was the evening devotional. "There might be wars and rumors of wars, councils and balls, meetings and dinner-parties," but no matter how busy they were, all family members were expected to be in attendance at home. After prayer, the family would hold council to formulate policy, plan recreational activities, or solve juvenile problems that may have arisen in the family. At these devotionals Brigham Young would often take the opportunity to counsel and instruct his wives and older children. A note dictated by him to his family on April 2, 1866, suggests that schooling them to meet regularly for their daily devotion was not accomplished without repetition:

> I have felt moved upon to write the following, for the perusal of my family, and to which I call their serious attention.
>
> There is no doubt but that my family, one and all, will

acknowledge that my time is as precious to me as theirs is to them. When the time appointed for our family devotion and prayer comes, I am expected to be there; and no public business, no matter how important has been able to influence me to forego the fulfilment of this sacred duty which I owe to you, to myself and to God.

I do not wish to complain of you without a cause; but I have noticed at prayer time that only a portion of my family has been present; some of my wives are absent visiting a sister, a neighbor, a mother or a relative; my children are scattered all over town, attending to this or that; and if at home, one is changing her dress, another her shoes, another getting ready to go to the theater; another has gone to see Mary, and another to see Emily, and I may add, etc., etc., etc.

Now, I have a few words of counsel for my family, which I shall expect them to receive kindly, and obey: namely, when prayer time comes, that they all be at home. If any of them are visiting, that they be at home at half past six o'clock in the evening. I wish my wives and children to be at home at that time in the evening, to be ready to bow before the Lord to make their acknowledgements to Him for His kindness and mercy and long-suffering towards us.

Your strict attendance to my wishes in this respect will give joy to the heart of your Husband and Father.

Church Historian George A. Smith was in Brigham Young's home at prayer time on one occasion. After noting that quite a large number of the President's family were there, he recalled that after a "very fervent prayer," Brigham addressed his family on the subject of his and their positions in the Church. The President told his family that the eyes of the world were upon them and also the eyes of the Saints and that the influence of his teachings was affected by the example of his family.

He said it was necessary for him to observe the word of wisdom, not only for his own sake, but his family should set examples. He wished his wives and daughters always to adopt their own fashions and to set an example and as far as possible to manufacture what they wore. He spoke on the absolute necessity of the saints ceasing to follow the fashions of the world. His first wife, Mary Ann Angell, followed in an interesting address. . . .

Brigham Young's exemplary life of personal integrity was a dominant influence for good in the lives of his children. He was convinced of the necessity of setting "an example before our children that is worthy of their imitation and highest admiration. If we do this, we shall have occasion to rejoice and be exceeding glad, for we shall have influence over them and they will not forsake us." Although the public press painted anything but a virtuous picture of Brigham Young, his family knew the falsity of this image. In setting himself as a reference point to designate the path of virtue and happines, this trumpet gave no uncertain sound. Writing his first letter to his oldest son, Joseph, on the occasion of the boy's entrance into missionary service, Brigham said:

> As you have grown to years of understanding you have had continually the instructions of one who has been appointed to stand at the head of God's kingdom on the earth, the front of the battle; you have seen his energy, observed his deportment both private and public—should not you therefore eventually prove yourself a skillful general?

Another time he advised Joseph to "keep yourself pure before the Lord—your father before you has done it and my constant prayer is that you may. With all my heart I believe you will."

In his association with his family, Brigham was not given to hypocrisy. When he urged his children to be honest, they saw an honest man. For example, while living in Auburn, New York, about 1826, he had contracted a three dollar debt from a local druggist, who, when approached with payment, could not find the note and refused to accept the money, stating that Brigham must have been mistaken about it. Some forty years later and two thousand miles removed from the scene of the incident, having heard somehow that the note had been found, Brigham dispatched his son John W. to Auburn with the charge: "I wish it settled. He [the druggist] may be dead; but his heir or heirs may be living."[5]

Brigham counseled his children that daily toil, however humble it be, "is our daily duty, and by doing it well we make it a part of our daily worship." His children, once again, did not have to look beyond their father for an example. A little over a year before his death

Brigham received a letter from an old friend, George Hickox, whom he had known forty-six years earlier in Mendon, New York. After reporting the death of mutual acquaintances, and recalling how kindly Brigham had been on an occasion when the writer had suffered from "fever and ague," Mr. Hickox reported that a chair built by the Mormon leader in Mendon a half century earlier was being displayed in a forthcoming grand centennial supper in the local Congregational church. "We would be very happy to have you come and occupy it," the writer concluded. President Young replied, expressing his interest in the celebration and amusement at the place his chair would occupy. He continued:

> I have no doubt that many other pieces of furniture and other specimens of my handiwork can be found scattered about your section of the country, for I have believed all my life that, that which was worth doing was worth doing well, and have considered it as much a part of my religion to do honest, reliable work, such as would endure, for those who employed me, as to attend to the services of God's worship on the Sabbath.

A practical philosophy of life lay at the center of Brigham Young's efforts to educate his children. He taught that service to the Lord is more than praying and attending meeting: "We can also serve him in a life of usefulness, honesty and sobriety, remembering that it should be the object of our existence here that when we leave the world it will be a little better for our presence and labors." He further taught that preparation for the "life of usefulness" requires diligence and effort and that "our constant desire, should be to know how to build up the kingdom of God, and of necessity this work calls forth an almost endless variety of talent, skill and labor." He stressed that we cannot excuse ourselves from our duty of building up the kingdom of God, "for all of our time, all of our ability and all of our means belong to Him. It is not the privilege of any person to spend his time in a way that does no good to himself nor to his neighbours." Of the time allotted to man on the earth, Brigham Young was convinced that there was none to waste. "After suitable rest and relaxation there is not a day, hour or minute that we should spend in idleness, but every minute of every day of our lives we should strive to improve our minds and to increase in the faith of the holy Gospel, in charity, patience, and good works, that we may grow in the knowledge of the truth as it is in Jesus

Christ." The more the Latter-day Saint is blessed with knowledge and talent, he believed, the more he is responsible to use his ability for "the spread of righteousness, the subjugation of sin and misery, and the amelioration of the condition of mankind."

Brigham Young taught that a prerequisite for useful service in the kingdom is a sound, practical education. Children should be so taught

> that when our sons are sent into the world as ministers of salvation and as representatives of the kingdom of God in the mountains, they can mingle with the best society and intelligibly and sensibly present the principles of truth to mankind, for all truth is the offspring of heaven and is incorporated in the religion which we have embraced. . . .
>
> We are the guardians of our children; their training and education are committed to our care, and if we do not ourselves pursue a course which will save them from the influence of evil, when we are weighed in the balance we shall be found wanting.

In an age when the father was frequently away from home visiting the Saints, directing the building of settlements, or helping to gather the poor, much of the responsibility for teaching the children in their early years devolved upon their mothers. The formal education of Brigham Young's children began in a small room in the Lion House and later continued at the white schoolhouse built especially for that purpose across the street to the east. Beside the basics of reading and writing, the children were taught "strict probity of conduct."

Brigham Young spared no effort to provide opportunities for the personal development of his children. After elementary education in the local schools, they were given opportunity for further learning and experience in the field of their choice. Having been taught that building the kingdom requires an "endless variety of talent, skill and labor," they were early engaged in a wide range of studies and activities by way of preparation. Collectively, their lives show excellence in many fields of endeavor, including architecture, engineering, railroad construction, art, music, drama, educational administration, teaching, banking, farming, politics, lumber manufacture, law, and literature. They also served in numerous administrative assignments in various organizations of the Church.

Several of Brigham Young's children made important contributions to the Latter-day Saint community and to the nation. His oldest son, Joseph, served many years in the Utah Territorial Legislature; Brigham Jr. was a mission president, a member of the Council of the Twelve, and a counselor in the Church's First Presidency; John was widely known in railroad construction and financial circles and was a counselor to his father in the First Presidency; Willard had a remarkable military career, as an engineer he supervised important river and harbor improvements along the Missouri and Mississippi rivers and in the Northwest, he presided over two colleges, and he was superintendent of Church building; Don Carlos was Church architect for many years and a member of the Utah Legislature; Susa Young Gates, a noted author and editor, played a leading role in state and national women's organizations in addition to raising a large family. While not a complete listing, these examples are indicative of the determination and drive that was characteristic of many of Brigham Young's children. Their accomplishments serve as a monument to a dedicated home life.

Brigham Young's desire for his children was that "they not only walk in the footsteps of their father, but take a course to enjoy life, health, and vigor while they live, and the spirit of intelligence from God, that they may far outstrip their father in long life, and in the good they will perform in their day." And more specifically, "I wish my sons to far exceed me in goodness and virtue." Whatever Brigham's influence may have been upon the lives of his children in their early years, his efforts to direct them continued even after they left home to begin their preparations in life. The letters they received from their father were an important source of direction for them. Many of these letters are a reflection of his belief that Solomon's saying, to spare the rod and spoil the child, ought to be altered to read, "Spare the rod and give good counsel to children and thus draw them to you." Letters written by Brigham to thirteen of his sons as they embarked upon various assignments away from home reveal a unique ability to discern the needs of his children and counsel them in the problems they faced in the different conditions under which they labored.

Eleven of Brigham Young's boys filled missions for the Church. Joseph, Brigham Jr., Oscar, Ernest, Arta De Christa, Lorenzo, and John W. completed proselyting assignments in England; Morris labored in Hawaii and the Eastern States; Heber in England and Switzerland; Don Carlos in the Southern States; and Feramorz in

Mexico. In the letters he wrote to them, their father gave them counsel that is pertinent far beyond its original intent.

"While you are on your present mission," Brigham wrote his son Oscar, "you will lay a foundation for future usefulness in the Kingdom of God."

> If there be any difference in missions probably the first mission that a man takes has more influence on his future than any that he may take in after life. On his first mission he lays the foundation and adopts the principles which are to guide him through his future career, and it has seldom been the case that a young man who has been dilatory and careless while upon his first mission has ever recovered the ground he then lost.

Brigham Young noted that much that is truly valuable in life can be gained in discharging one's calling as a missionary in the Church of Jesus Christ. "There is no position a young man can be placed in that is better adapted to give him a knowledge of God and of His holy spirit than to be sent on a mission." He reminded Joseph A. that education was not all confined to schools, and that while engaged in his proselyting he should

> lose no opportunity of making yourself familiar with all that is useful and likely to benefit you, for to be able to combat with the world we must make ourselves acquainted with the ways of the world. This can only be done by keeping your mind constantly on the alert and when in society never allow anything to escape your notice, listen attentively; and observe minutely the manners, customs, and remarks of all, for, from the most humble of our fellow creatures an observing man can learn something that will be useful to him in after life.

A mission provides an opportunity to obtain knowledge and experience that no book can teach. "Stores of information surround you," Brigham wrote two of his sons in England, "you are in the midst of the world's activities, the discoveries of science and the masterpieces of inventive genius are within your reach and you have many bright opportunities of increasing your range of knowledge and widening your views of man and nature."

After reminding one son that the missionary is called to mingle in society a great deal, Brigham urged him to cultivate his speech and social graces and use every effort to improve his address. "Always exert yourself to be agreeable, and no matter whether poor or rich, treat them with equal courtesy, do not be pompous to the needy, nor condescending to the wealthy." By this, he assured him, "you will gain the love and admiration of those worthy of your esteem, and at comparatively little expense."

Arriving in the large cities of Christendom in their youth—many of them away from home for the first time—Brigham's sons were cautioned to avoid the wickedness of the world with its many allurements.

> Many a young man has fall[en] from a virtuous life through a desire to simply see and become acquainted with the sins of the world. But having once become familiar with the ways of the sinner it has too often proved that the meshes of sin were too strong to allow of its victims escape. Do not on any pretense or excuse allow yourself to be persuaded to visit the dens of iniquity . . . and other traps for the unwary.

To his son Heber, Brigham wrote that a missionary's success depends on his ability to subjugate his passions, appetites, and feelings to the mind and will of God, through self-mastery and determination. "The man who suffers his passions to lead him becomes a slave to them, and such a man will find the work of emancipation an exceedingly difficult one." The father urged his son to "make the doing of God's will and the keeping of His commandments a constant habit with you and it will become perfectly natural and easy for you to walk uprightly before Him." He concluded, "The time of youth and early manhood is the proper time in which to form such habits."

To the young missionary confronted with the added problem of learning a difficult foreign language, Brigham advised diligence, study, courage, and perseverance:

> Never allow your courage to fail you; man's greatest works have been done by men of patience, perseverance and a determined will which would acknowledge no defeat, rather than by those gifted with a natural ability which made success easy but who lacked the tenaciousness of purpose. Then my boy never say fail but work

on in the way you have started and your reward is certain.

Since the main responsibility of the missionary is to take the message of salvation to mankind, he must never neglect an opportunity to enlighten the ignorant, or strengthen the weak. "Raise your voice wherever possible in defence of the truth," Brigham wrote; but, if "when declaring the truth, you are attacked by the wicked, do not condescend to argue with them, much less retaliate." He continued:

> Recrimination proves no truth; it enlightens no man's mind, but it is one of the weapons used by the adversary to produce hatred and malice in the hearts of mankind, and should never be indulged in by a Latter-day Saint. When you may be assailed, heed it not, bear your testimony to the great work the Lord is doing on the earth, proclaim the Truth in meekness, and if they will not listen, leave them to their own folly. We are not called to cavil with the world.

Brigham Young summarized the mission experience by noting, "it is the noblest, happiest life that a man can lead, to be a minister of salvation to the people of the nations."

Two of President Young's sons were appointed to the United States military academies at West Point and Annapolis. Willard Young entered West Point in 1871 when he was nineteen, and Feramorz commenced his training at the Naval Academy in 1874 at age fifteen. While the problems confronted in the military were different from those in the mission field, Brigham's boys in the service also received pertinent and forceful counsel from their father adapted to their needs and circumstances.

Being Mormons and sons of Brigham Young demanded an austerity that was not common in a military environment. "By exhibiting your character and the principles you profess in your daily walk and conversation, and by refraining from every appearance of evil you will not only be admired by the good and the upright, but you will command that respect that even the most unvirtuous are willing to accord to those who truly deserve it." And to the soldier who may have been inclined to slip into anonymity so far as his religion was concerned, Brigham wrote that it was the duty of "every Latter-day Saint, young or old, to serve the Lord. None of us are excused from this duty, as, also, none of us are shut out from the attainment of the blessings of eternal life. Never in all your associations forget that you are a Latter-day Saint."

As Willard launched into rigorous training and study at West Point, he was directed "to treasure up the instruction so abundantly provided there, that in after years you may be prepared to take a place even in the foremost ranks of the great men of the nation." And lest he become over-studious, he was urged to pursue a course of moderation: "A proper regard must be had to physical as well as intellectual exercise, else the intellectual powers become impaired, and therefore, bodily recreation and rest are as necessary as they are beneficial to mental study."

No course of action was urged by Brigham Young upon his sons with more force than that directed to Willard almost immediately after his arrival at the Military Academy. "I understand you cadets are exceedingly popular with the fair sex, and some of them are very, very dangerous when so disposed, just for the sake of having a laugh at their victims; shun such as you would the very gates of hell! They are the enemy's strongest tools, and should be resisted as strongly. Beware of them!"

Another vice confronting the servicemen was idleness. Convinced that happiness consists in having something worthwhile to do and in doing it well, Brigham warned that "whoever wastes his life in idleness, either because he need not work in order to live, or because he will not live to work, will be a wretched creature, and at the close of a listless existence, will regret the loss of precious gifts and the neglect of great opportunities."

An "unmitigated evil" to young men in military service, which Brigham Young felt would impair their mental powers and make them unfit for their daily duties and studies, was the use of tobacco and profane language. "Some young men seem to entertain the idea that to smoke, to chew or to use profane language makes them appear more manly. Never was [there] a greater fallacy." Real manhood, he advised, consists in serving God and keeping his commandments. "The highest type of mankind is shown in such worthies as Enoch, Abraham, Joseph, Nephi, Alma, Joseph Smith, and others. If boys wish to be thought manly let them copy the best men and their virtues, not inferior and vicious men and their follies and vices."

Although several of his children attended the local University of Deseret, three of Brigham Young's sons studied at institutions of higher learning in the East. Don Carlos and Feramorz (after his release from the Naval Academy) studied engineering at the Rensselaer Polytechnic Institute at Troy, New York, and Alfales received a law degree from Michigan University at Ann Arbor. Like his sons in the military service and in the mission field, these students also received their portion from their father's steadying pen.

As he arrived in the little New York university community of Troy to study engineering and architecture, Don Carlos was cautioned that some of his new surroundings would tend to strengthen his faith while others would seek to draw him away.

> As you advance in life you will find every position and occupation surrounded by its peculiar temptations, the great strength and bulwark against all of which is prayer to our Heavenly Father. Cultivate this spirit and you will find that it shall be a wall of fire around you, and your glory in the midst of you. In its practice you will find a safeguard against the wiles of the adversary, and every good resolution will be fortified by it, and every seductive influence will lose its power to annoy you.

Focusing upon the moral lapses that often mar the character of the student away from home, Brigham urged his sons never to abuse the confidence that others had placed in them, "or by folly or criminality break down the character we have built up by a life of industry and honesty. Our character is not entirely our individual property. It belongs partly to our neighbors and we have no right to shake their confidence in us and in mankind generally by acts inconsistent with the good name we have established."

Brigham Young recognized that a contributing element to happiness consisted in the wise selection of associates and friends. He counseled his boys to select companionship among those whose characters were established upon a foundation of truth and honor, whose pursuits were honorable, whose expenses were moderate, and whose lives were temperate.

> Studiously avoid all those whose lives are tinctured with looseness, prodigality, and even among the very best of your associates be sure and only imitate their virtues. Remember that however bright any character may be, however much he may shine mentally or intellectually,

that if he has vices they are blemishes and should not be copied. It would be as foolish, yes more so, to copy a man's moral blemishes because he has the reputation of being a gentleman, a student or a good fellow, as it would be to make an artificial wart upon one's face because some very handsome man had the misfortune to have a natural one on his. We all of us are subject to the influence of others, especially of those for whom we have regard; and from our companions both our character and disposition we'll receive a tincture, as water passing through minerals partakes of their taste and efficacy. How careful then ought we to be to associate only with the upright, the good and the pure.

Finally, to the young student who might be tempted to set his religion aside while obtaining a degree, Brigham wrote:

> The adversary has no craftier snare for the feet of the young of God's people than to persuade them they can be Latter-day Saints and bury the principles of their religion so deep out of sight that when wanted they never can find them. Whilst away from home I hope you will continue your present practice of associating as much as practicable with the Elders and members of the Church.

While the letters of Brigham Young to his sons reveal a deep personal affection for his children, the answers he received from them reveal that they returned the feeling. The numerous letters written by his sons are lavish in sentiments of respect and honor for their father and eagerness to do his bidding. As they began their various assignments away from home, Brigham's sons well knew the size of the shoes they were being asked to fill. They undertook the challenge in the same spirit in which they were sent. After beginning his missionary work in England, Brigham Jr. wrote his father: "I have been afraid that more is expected of me than I can do. They consider the idea that such a father had ought to have a smart son. I can't help it if they are disappointed in their expectations but I will do my best to answer the prayers of my friends." Another time, after being introduced to New York merchants during a trip east, he informed his father, "They take off their hats and make very polite bows [and remark] 'happy to meet you Mr. Young,'" but, acknowledged the younger Brigham, "it is simply the result of your labors, Father, and I give you the credit next to God. I know that you have done the work, and I am reaping the benefit, and I feel that the only way I can repay you is by living as becomes a saint which may God help me to do." Another son, John W., explained his reason for rooming in one of St. Louis's finest hotels when he stopped there in company with other businessmen in 1866: "Personally I feel no desire to make a show, but when the eyes of many are directed towards me and it is said, 'there is a son of Brigham Young,' I feel that to look and act respectably is my duty."

The letters of Brigham's sons leave no doubt that their father's influence upon their lives was lasting and profound. As a missionary in England in 1866, John W. penned these lines: "I seat myself to write to you and it is with great pleasure that I do so because I not only love you as a Father, but respect and honor you as a Prophet of God." Writing from West Point, Willard reflected upon his home life and the guidance of his father as a preparation for his opportunities at the Military Academy.

> I ever feel grateful towards you, my dear father, for the many great kindnesses and benefits you have heaped upon me, and upon all the children, though it is perhaps impossible for me to appreciate their full worth. How thankful we all ought to be (I really think I am) that we have such a loving and indulgent parent, such a wise instructor, and so worthy an example as you.

In 1876, after receiving counsel from Brigham that helped him resolve the question of continuing his miitary career, Willard responded:

> I must say thanks a thousand thanks for your excellent letter. As is always the case it proved interesting beyond comparison. I always have such a 'good' feeling (I cannot better describe it) when I read your words. They seem to do me good' every way, physically, mentally, and morally. The effect of the perusal of this last letter was to make me involuntarily exclaim: Thank God for such a father.
>
> You have satisfied me every way. I shall enjoy myself a great deal better now, I feel sure, for in trying to carry out your advice in the several directions pointed out, I shall be doing just what I need to better satisfy my own sense of duty. I shall serve out the remainder of my time now with a good heart, since I know it to be your wish.

And from England Lorenzo wrote to his father: "Your letters are always repeatedly read, for in them I find spiritual strength, encouraging words, and parental love, which spurs me on to more diligence in executing my duties."

If the congenial image of Brigham Young seen in the pages of his letters to his sons appears to contradict the austere picture that is generally seen of him, it is largely due to two factors:

First was the preponderance of unreliable source material pertaining to Brigham Young. So unfavorable was the popular reaction to Mormonism and its leaders in the nineteenth century that the stream of historical sources dealing with the Latter-day Saints received a taint from which it has never been adequately purified. In 1882, Phil Robinson, a correspondent for the New York *World*, noted that, with the exception of Burton's *City of the Saints*, he was not acquainted with a single gentile work about the Mormons that was not utterly unreliable from its distortion of facts. Yet it is from these works "that the American public has acquired nearly all its ideas about the people of Utah." Since most students of Brigham Young have seen him mainly through the jaundiced eye of a hostile nineteenth century press, their understanding of him has been highly contradictory at best.

A second factor that has obscured the view of Brigham Young has been the difficulty of seeing him from the perspective of his domestic environment. The public view was less obscure; in an effort to correct faulty opinion about his people and himself, Brigham spent much of his time giving interviews. Even as his health failed him in the closing months of his life, he refused to relieve the burden on his time and strength caused by the constant stream of visitors to his office, "all of whom have to be chatted with more or less." He reasoned:

> I am satisfied that such visits are, as a rule, productive of good results. Many a one who comes to Utah filled with all kinds of outrageous ideas with regard to the Mormons in general and Brigham Young in particular, after having visited our City, seen its objects of interest and called at the office, go away with feelings greatly modified, and often afterwards have a kind word for the people of Utah when they hear them assailed, and occasionally will smooth the way of any of our missionaries whom they may chance to

meet. This interviewing, then, though sometimes disagreeable is too valuable a means of correcting false ideas, and removing prejudice to be discontinued whilst by the blessing of the Lord I am able to meet those who call upon me and extend to them courtesies to which, in some cases, they are probably entirely unworthy.

But the attempt was not wholly successful. In the first place, the interviews were too brief to permit more than a fleeting glimpse of the President. Second, many of the visitors who came to his office were looking for other, more intimate things. Their very interest in Brigham Young's family deprived them of a view of it. He noted that almost everyone that came to see him was motivated by an inordinate obsession or depraved curiosity to know how many wives he had. Even some of the Saints were inquisitive on this point. "A great many men and women have an irrepressible curiosity to know how many wives Brigham Young has," he noted in the Tabernacle in 1870. On this occasion he did not disappoint them:

> I am now going to gratify that curiosity by saying, ladies and gentlemen, I have sixteen wives. If I have any more hereafter it will be my good luck and the blessing of God. "How many children have you, President Young?" I have forty-nine living children, and I hope to have a great many more. Now put that down. I impart this information to gratify the curiosity of the curious.

If one senses a note of sarcasm here, it is because many such inquiries about Brigham's domestic life had served only to fuel the engines of ridicule and slander against himself and his family. Consequently, in his contacts with the public one perceives a studied reticence to expose his family to further debasement and contempt. Although willing to extend courtesies, even to the unworthy, in an effort to correct public opinion, Brigham Young hesitated to submit his family to the gaze of the unscrupulous. The volumes that record his meetings with visitors and report his public discourses seldom mention his family. In 1857, as work began on his history, he notified the Church Historian that "he did not wish but little history of his family given." Only by a study of his private writings and correspondence with his family can the researcher adequately discover the sensitive, affectionate nature of Brigham Young that has almost completely escaped biographers.[6]

Every father who reads the letters of Brigham Young to his sons may vicariously experience the satisfaction that he felt in seeing his children grow to maturity and develop themselves as useful citizens and participants in building the kingdom of God. He will note, however, that Brigham's satisfaction was not unearned. Among the paternal influences that had the greatest impact upon the lives of his children were the religious and secular education that he provided for them, the environment of love and understanding in which they were raised, and, above all, the example of his own life.

And every son who reads the letters of Brigham Young will learn that happiness in life rests upon a foundation of responsible behavior and useful service, and that the quality of one's happiness is proportionate to his diligence and preparation. Indeed,

> Our daily toil, however humble it may be, is our daily duty, and by doing it well we make it a part of our daily worship. But whatever be our labor, calling or profession we should hold our skill, knowledge and talents therein, subservient to the accomplishment of the purposes of Jehovah, that our entire lives, day by day, may be made to praise Him, and our individual happiness secured by the consciousness that we are fulfilling the purpose and design of our presence here on the earth.

—DCJ

Notes

[1] Information about Brigham Young and his family is largely derived from the Brigham Young papers in the Church Archives, which contains numerous letters written to and from members of his family. The following published works are also helpful: Susa Young Gates, *The Life Story of Brigham Young* (New York, 1930) and *Brigham Young, Patriot, Pioneer, Prophet* (Salt Lake City, 1929); Clarissa Young Spencer, *One Who Was Valiant* (Caldwell, Idaho, 1940). Brigham Young's sermons are published in *Journal of Discourses* (26 vols., Liverpool, 1854-86).

[2] Heber C. Kimball and Christopher Layton had sixty-five children each; John W. Hess, sixty-three; John D. Lee, sixty; and Brigham Young, fifty-seven.

[3] Non-Mormons in the nineteenth century created the fiction that Brigham Young did not know all his wives and children. See, for example, Albert Richardson, *Beyond the Mississippi* (New York, 1867), p. 355; and Mark Twain, *Roughing It* (New York, 1899), pp. 124-25.

[4] Brigham Young also taught, "Kindness, love and affection are the best rod to use upon the refractory. Solomon is said to have . . . recommended another kind of rod. I have tried both kinds on children. I can pick out scores of men in this congregation who have driven their children from them by using the wooden rod. Where there is severity there is no affection or filial feeling in the hearts of either party; the children would rather be away from father than be with him.

"In some families the children are afraid to see father—they will run and hide as from a tyrant. My children are not afraid of my footfall; except in the case of their having done something wrong they are not afraid to approach me. I could break the wills of my little children, and whip them to this, that, and the other, but this I do not do. Let the child have a mild training until it has judgment and sense to guide it. I differ with Solomon's recorded saying as to spoiling the child by sparing the rod. True, it is written in the New Testament that 'whom the Lord loveth he chasteneth.' It is necessary to try the faith of children as well as of grown people, but there are ways of doing so besides taking a club and knocking them down with it." *Journal of Discourses,* IX (February 9, 1862): 195-96.

[5]The arrival of John W. Young in the small New York town did not go unnoticed in the local newspaper: "A son of Brigham Young, (we didn't learn his number,) was in town this morning, and called at a business house in Genessee St. to settle an account by his numerous progenitor some thirty years ago. Brigham is honest in some things, but rather slow. The debt discharged by him was, we understand, for borrowed money." Unidentified newsclipping accompanying letter of John W. Young to Brigham Young, May 9, 1866.

[6]See also Dean Jessee, "The Writings of Brigham Young," *The Western Historical Quarterly* 4 (July 1973): 273-94.

Editorial Procedure and Acknowledgments

An important part of the Brigham Young papers filed in the archives of The Church of Jesus Christ of Latter-day Saints in Salt Lake City is the books containing the voluminous retained copies of letters he sent during the years of his public administration. Copied by pressing moistened sheets of thin, transparent paper against the face of the original before it was sent—to obtain an offset duplication for filing—these letters, written on a wide variety of subjects and sent to a multitude of individuals, are among the best sources for understanding the life of Brigham Young. Among these writings are the ninety-five letters written by Brigham Young to his sons published in this volume. Although these are not a complete collection of all that President Young wrote to his sons, they are perhaps the best reflection of his domestic relationship with his children. Other letters to his sons dealing exclusively with business matters or detailing local events have not been included here. The letters printed here may all be found in chronological order in those letter books and so need no further documentation.

The letters written to each son, commencing with the oldest and proceeding to the youngest, have been grouped together and arranged chronologically. Circumstances of age, health, and other factors explain the absence of letters to four sons. However, a brief biographical statement on these four sons has been included so that the listing of the seventeen sons who grew to maturity may be complete.

Since Brigham Young relied almost entirely upon secretaries to write for him, (he once stated he had only eleven days of formal schooling), few of his letters written between 1847 and 1877 are in his own hand. It has therefore not seemed necessary to retain punctuation and spelling peculiarities. The four exceptions in this volume where Brigham Young actually wrote a few lines or a postscript with his own hand, as well as quotations from writings of his sons, are published as written, except for minimal punctuation that has been supplied for easier reading.

Preceding the letters written by Brigham Young to each of his sons is a short biographical summary of the boy's life. This is followed by a historical introduction to each letter or series of letters. Blanks, omissions, or illegible words have been noted with an explanation in brackets—[*illegible*], [*torn page*], etc. Missing letters or words in an obvious context have been silently supplied. Conjectural alternatives for missing words are given in brackets. Obvious slips of the pen or strike-throughs have not been retained.

Explanatory notes under the heading of each son are located in a special section at the back of the book. Also, to avoid repetition and to lessen the bulk of notes and cross references, a biographical appendix, identifying persons named in the letters, has been included.

Although diligent effort has been made to collect documents and biographical data pertaining to Brigham Young and his sons, a work of this nature will probably never be complete. Additional information or source material that would have a bearing upon the subject at hand would, therefore, be gratefully received.

Many persons have contributed significantly to the content, accuracy, and readability of this volume. I am especially indebted to the Church Historian, Leonard J. Arrington, and assistant historians Davis Bitton and James B. Allen for their insightful suggestions and direction. I appreciate the painstaking efforts of Maureen Ursenbach and Jill Mulvay, editors in the Church Historical Department. The Church Archivist, Earl Olson; librarian, Don Schmidt; and the staffs of the archives and library have provided important service. Jeff Johnson, manuscript curator, particularly has brought to notice important source materials and information pertaining to Brigham Young's family. Noel Barton of the Genealogical Society has given valuable assistance in genealogical sources. This mention of professional assistance in no way includes blame for any failings that may appear in this volume. Responsibility for any errors in fact or judgment is my own.

Several descendants of Brigham Young have provided information and source material pertaining to Brigham Young's sons: Richard W. Burton, Mrs. Bruce Jenkins, Mrs. Emily Young Knepp, Mrs. Adele McCaman, Mrs. Mary Adele Monson, Mrs. Phillis B. Phillips, Mrs. Naomi Schettler, Dr. Clark Young, Gaylen Snow Young, George Cannon Young, President S. Dilworth Young, and Whitney Young.

The following depositories and institutions have provided additional information and source material: Brigham Young University Library, Provo, Utah; University of Utah Library and Utah State Historical Society, Salt Lake City; Utah State University Library, Logan, Utah; Rensselaer Polytechnic Institute Archives, Troy, New York; and U.S. Naval Academy Archives, Annapolis, Maryland.

The pleasing format and presentation of these letters are the scrupulous work of Keith Montague and the Deseret Book Company.

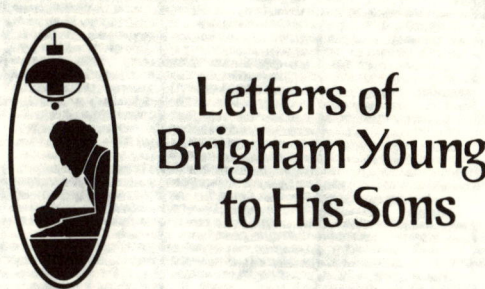

Letters of Brigham Young to His Sons

JOSEPH ANGELL YOUNG

Joseph Angell Young
1834-1875

Joseph Angell Young, the oldest son of President Brigham Young, was among the Mormon missionaries who arrived in Utah from England on October 4, 1856, bringing news of the precarious condition of handcart immigrants on the plains that year. Relief efforts were immediately organized and within hours Joseph A. and twenty-seven other young men, under the leadership of George D. Grant, had started back into the mountains with sixteen wagonloads of food and clothing. Failing to meet the immigrants at Fort Bridger, Joseph and three others were sent ahead with the message that assistance was on the way. When they found the immigrants, the toll of death had already begun to mount. Of the six hundred Saints camped at Red Buttes alone, comprising Martin's handcart company and Hodgett's wagon train, fifty-six had died of exposure and hunger. As the relief effort proceeded, Joseph A. was sent back to the Salt Lake Valley to report progress and the condition of the immigrants. He arrived in Salt Lake City at 4:00 A.M. on November 13 to tell of the tragedy which, but for the effort of the returning European missionaries, would have been even more devastating than it was.

The first son of Brigham Young and Mary Ann Angell, Joseph A. was born on October 14, 1834, in Kirtland, Ohio. At the age of twelve he accompanied his parents to Winter Quarters during the Mormon exodus of 1846. He remained at Winter Quarters with his mother during the winter of 1847-48 and accompanied the family (his father having returned to Winter Quarters in the fall of 1847) to the Salt Lake Valley the next year. During the years 1854-56 Joseph labored as a missionary in England, where he presided over the Bradfordshire

Conference. It was while he was returning from this mission in 1856 that he participated in the rescue operation described above. Although deprived of education early in his life due to the persecution and frequent moves of the Saints, Joseph studied hard in England and familiarized himself with the writings of Bacon, Blackstone, Locke, and Mill. An avid reader, he collected one of the finest private libraries in Utah.

In 1864 Joseph A. was called on a special mission to New York to transact Church business and to take charge of the Church emigration that year. On February 19, prior to his departure, he received a special blessing under the hands of his father and other members of the First Presidency. "We bless you at this time, and set you apart for a mission to the East, to go to the City of New York, or to any other place where it shall be necessary for you to go to attend to business connected with the gathering of the saints. . . . We bless you with that wisdom, knowledge, and understanding and power with God, power with the angels, power with men upon the earth, and power over the elements, and over spiritual agencies, so that you shall accomplish your mission, and the labor you are sent to do. . . . We now say unto you that you shall go in peace, and return in safety with your brethren who are going with you and no power shall have power over you but the power of God and the holy angels who administer to the children of men who are heirs of salvation. You shall travel in peace and in safety whether in wagons, stage coaches, railway cars or in any other kind of conveyance, that traverses the land, the great lakes, or the mighty seas, wherever you are called to go you shall go in safety and shall have power over every evil power that would seek to destroy you, and after you have accomplished a good work you shall return in safety to your family and friends. . . ."[1]

Joseph's mission took him to St. Louis, Chicago, New York City, and across the Atlantic to England. His travel to and from the mission field was not without incident. Five days after leaving Salt Lake City, while crossing Black's Fork of the Green River, the stagecoach in which he was riding broke through the ice in six feet of water, causing a three-hour delay. While returning home later that year he was involved in a severe train wreck four miles east of Syracuse, New York. "The whole train was smashed including the car I was in to within one seat of where I sat, [but] I escaped without a scratch," he reported.[2]

Joseph A. operated a lumber business and was engaged in significant building projects in the Salt Lake Valley. He superintended the building of the Salt Lake Theatre and provided lumber for railroad construction. In 1868, when Brigham Young contracted Mormon labor to build the transcontinental railroad through Utah Territory, Joseph joined with Bishop John Sharp for a grading and tunneling contract through Weber Canyon. In 1869-70 he supervised the construction of the Utah Central Railroad from Ogden to Salt Lake City and was the first superintendent of that road. He was among those sent to Boston to negotiate the settlement of the railroad contract with Union Pacific Railroad officials after that company failed to meet its contract obligations to Mormon builders.

Joseph A. traveled extensively with his father and other Church leaders throughout Utah settlements, regulating Church affairs and visiting the Saints. In April 1872 he was called to preside over the Church in Utah's Sevier district, which covered the area from Gunnison to Panguitch; and he was named president of the first stake organized in Sevier County in 1874. An important accomplishment under his leadership was the opening of a road through Clear Creek Canyon, linking Sevier Valley to the settlements of Millard County and grain markets in southern Utah and southeastern Nevada, an enterprise completed without territorial subsidy. He also organized the United Order in Sevier County, which he described as "one of the best mutual benefit associations in existence."[3] During his lifetime he served the people of five Utah counties—Salt Lake, Tooele, Summit, Sanpete, and Sevier—in nine sessions of the territorial legislature.

Living in the era of plural marriage, Joseph's family consisted of three wives, Mary Ann Ayers, Margaret Whitehead, and Clara Stenhouse, to whom were born nineteen children. One of his sons was a West Point graduate who became Utah's first general, Richard W. Young.

During Brigham Young's later years Joseph assisted in the President's office with his father's correspondence and business affairs. At the time of his sudden death on August 5, 1875, at the age of forty-one, Joseph A. Young was in Manti, Utah, where he had been sent to supervise the construction of the Manti Temple.

Upon hearing of his brother's death, Brigham Young, Jr., wrote in his diary, "Oh, my brother, my brother. In many things he was superior to any man I ever saw. The Lord giveth and the Lord taketh away. . . . He was a great man tho' possesing many weaknesses, but he was humble and full of faith. It seemes like one half of me had been torn away and I deprived of a mighty counsellor. . . . All the people mourned his loss, and I felt to say in the language of David, 'know ye not that a prince has fallen this day in Israel?' "[4]

Letters dated August 31 and September 30, 1854

When the recently released European Mission president, Samuel W. Richards, arrived in Salt Lake City on August 26, 1854, he carried a letter from his successor, Franklin D. Richards, for Brigham Young containing anxiously awaited news about close relatives of the First Presidency laboring as missionaries in England. In June Franklin D. had attended a special Church conference in London, where he had seen George D. Grant, the forty-two-year-old brother of Jedediah M. Grant, twenty-eight-year-old William H. Kimball, son of Heber C. Kimball, and Joseph A. Young, twenty, the oldest son of President Brigham Young. "It would have done yours, Bro. Heber's and Bro. Jedediah's souls good to have heard Joseph, William and George address their brethren in the ministry, on that occasion," reported the mission president. "They spoke gloriously and seemed to stir up the spirits of the brethren from their foundation with life and energy. . . . I feel first rate about them all and I believe you will have occasion to rejoice greatly in their noble careers." With specific reference to Brigham Young's son, Franklin Richards added, "Joseph tells me he is taking particular delight in studying the works of the Church and familiarizing himself with the first principles of the Gospel and feels happy in his field of labour; he left off his tobacco of his own accord while coming through the states."[5]

Joseph A. Young had arrived in England on June 4, 1854, in company with the new mission president, Franklin D. Richards, and five other missionaries, including the kin of his father's two counselors. Called upon to address the Liverpool Saints that first evening in England, Joseph gave his maiden speech, which "extended over a period of ninety consecutive seconds."[6] He spent his first three weeks in Liverpool, after which he was assigned to work in Manchester, where he spent the next five months walking in the streets, preaching in the halls, and observing the scenes his father had witnessed some fifteen years earlier. While in Manchester Joseph received his first letters from his father dated August 31 and September 30, 1854.

Salt Lake City, August 31, 1854

Joseph A. Young
Manchester, England

My dear Son Joseph,

 With no little pleasure I take this opportunity of writing to you before the departure of tomorrow's mail. On the 26th inst. Bro. Sam[ue]l W. Richards arrived in this city in company with Thos. S. Williams bringing a letter from Bro. Franklin [Richards] of 7th July, from which I am happy to learn of your commencement to testify of that work in the midst of which you have been raised, even the kingdom of our God upon the earth, whose kingdom is an everlasting kingdom and whom all dominions shall serve and obey, and which is destined to increase as it has heretofore increased in glory and power henceforth and forever. Joseph, this has been your privilege, to grow as the Church has grown; when it was in its infancy you were dandled on the knees of a tender mother and received the caresses of an affectionate father, and as you have grown to years of understanding you have had continually the instructions of one who has been appointed to stand at the head of God's kingdom on the earth, the front of the battle; you have seen his energy, observed his deportment both private and public. Should not you therefore eventually prove yourself a skillful general, and even now able to wage war successfully with the powers of darkness, superstition, priestcraft, and ignorance, to overcome evil however it may present itself and preserve yourself a pure and holy tabernacle for the residence of the Holy Ghost. And by so doing you will never be led astray. The enemy will never overcome you, but you will be watchful, temperate in all things, and at all times ready to bestow the blessings of the gospel to the children of men. You are away from me now, and among a people who will look more or less to *you* for counsel and advice, to whom *your* words will be as a sweet morsel, as leading on in the path of salvation and to be retained while memory lasts. You then need so to live as ever to hear the soft unerring voice of the Spirit of the Lord [which] will be in you as a well of water springing up to everlasting life, and which *is* a never-failing fountain of intelligence and wisdom.

We also received from Bro. Samuel the first news in regard to the state of our immigration this season, who are much in need of assistance as the church train had lost 120 head of cattle[7] and most of the trains lacking provisions. A large number of teams will start in a few days with many tons of flour to go to the hindmost company some 300 miles out and return leaving none behind.

The weather is fine, and considerably cooler than in the former part of the month, and showers have fallen quite frequently; about 2 AM of the 30th quite heavy thunder with rain. The health of the valleys is generally good. Our Indian relations, although peace has existed through the summer, are at present slightly precarious[8] but our crops being mostly secured, we apprehend no serious difficulty. With the alphabet[9] or characters in which this (annexed) is written, although not perfect, we intend to go ahead and if necessary amend until the system of orthography and writing is revolutionized for the use of our children in Zion.

Sept. 1. The mail arrived last evening; a letter from you was received by myself, one by Mary [Ann Ayers Young], and one by Brigham [Jr.], all very satisfactory. I now wish to say to you, proceed with your studies, and apply your heart diligently to the study of the gospel wherein is true wisdom, so will the Lord bless you continually and you will be enabled to rejoice before Him with exceeding joy and gratitude. Be assured you are always remembered in our aspirations to our Heavenly Father day by day. I now close praying that His choicest blessings may be yours and subscribing myself as ever,

> Your affectionate father,
> Brigham Young.

Salt Lake City, September 30, 1854

Joseph A. Young
Manchester, England

My dear Joseph,

On the 28th we received a letter from you which gratifies me much to learn of your diligence in traveling from place to place and proclaiming the words of life to men. Assuredly industry is one characteristic of the Saints of God on the earth. Whilst the elders are industriously employed in foreign countries promulgating the news of the re-establishment of the kingdom of God on the earth, we are here also busily engaged in building up that kingdom from year to year—indeed it is our study and prayer every day and every night to do faithfully the work required of us and in which we so much rejoice to be engaged. Our youths feel this influence. As they approach to years of understanding the boys are not to be seen loafing about the streets for they hail the opportunity to render themselves available for the general interest of Zion in which, you remember, the Lord has said "an idler shall have no place except he repent."

Your brother Brigham is actively engaged on the island[10] with the cattle, and is well and doing first rate.

We are here in the enjoyment of good weather and that glorious atmosphere that prevails in this high region of country and full of health and spirit with the horn of plenty well filled but not overflowing to the extent to make the bounties of earth, save in good estimation. Wheat is bringing from J. M. Horner & Co. Deseret Store $2 in goods while sugar is selling generally 3 lbs. to the dollar and most other articles have been similarly reduced in price.

Our immigration are arriving [*illegible*]. A company from Texas [arrived] first with Capt. Jolly. Job Smith and Co. [*illegible*] and Capt. J[ames] Brown and company arrived this [mornin]g. The train with goods for public improvements, called the church train, will arrive next week.

Business is pressing and time scarce today, and I must close praying God Almighty to bless you continually and sustain you day by day with his Spirit in the work in which you are so profitably engaged.

Your affectionate father,
Brigham Young

Letter dated December 1, 1854

Joseph A. Young responded to his father's letter of September 30 with gratitude for the expression of approval of his missionary labors in England, and reported that he would shortly be leaving Manchester to begin a new assignment as president of the Bradford Conference. In reflecting upon his first five months of missionary work, Joseph wrote: "When I first came to England, I thought I could have taken charge of the British mission with the greatest ease. I have now, however, not quite such an exalted opinion of myself, for castles in the air will not stand the cold and chilling influences of the sneers of the world; and in fact, the more I learn the less I know." His father's influence in his life was a prominent theme of the letter. "I can now in some degree realize the benefit to be derived from those counsels and teaching you bestowed so liberally upon me, both in private and in public. When I left home I was an ignorant unthinking boy, but I shall try to return a man of God, one whom he will delight to own and bless. I was glad for the line from mother, and will endeavor to follow her advice."[11]

At the request of Brigham Young, Thomas W. Ellerbeck, one of the President's chief clerks, wrote to Joseph A. Young on December 1, 1854, to inform him of current news in Utah. As Brigham Young reviewed the letter late that night, he added a few lines of postscript with his own pen. In this letter the methodical style of the learned scribe stands in sharp contrast to the warm counsel of the affectionate father. This postscript offers one of the rare glimpses of Brigham Young through the intimacy of his own handwriting.

Salt Lake City, December 1, 1854

Joseph A. Young
Manchester, England

Dear brother Joseph,

With much pleasure at the request of your honored father, I embrace a few moments to give you the current items of news of this part of our mountain land. Well your father has sent to St. Louis for a 10 horsepower steam engine for the *Timely Gull*, a boat for the lake, of the building of which you have been informed. This is to be brought out next season. Another item of news is the completion of the walls of an Endowment House erected on the N.W. corner of the Temple Block which will be finished as we have ability to go ahead, for it is much wanted. It is about the size of the Council House, which is now nearly prepared for the assembling of the legislature, who you will remember meet on the second Monday of this month.

Col. [Edward J.] Steptoe and his men, some 200, you know are wintering in the city. He is quite gentlemanly in his deportment, and anxious that his men should conduct themselves with propriety, not making themselves an annoyance to the good citizens of Salt Lake. He wished the mayor, in consequence of their appearing drunk so much in the streets, to assist him in his endeavors to debar them from liquor. Beer drinking and whiskey drinking also having become so frequent and so much more extensive by some of those who would be good brethren, than should exist in our lovely city, the city council repealed every license to sell. And before this it was announced from the stand by Elder [Heber C.] Kimball that all members of the Church who did not return their licenses for making the article during the following week should be cut off. All but one promptly replied with their licenses returned. So we shall have a quieter time with the soldiery than they would love had their palates been consulted.

The mail arrived this evening; we have word that the last mail from here was destroyed by the Indians near Laramie and the carriers killed.[12] Charley Kinkead, along, was left for dead, but was subsequently picked up by some party from the fort, has recovered pretty much.

By a letter from A. S. Siler on Oct 3/54, he requests to be kindly remembered to you; he was then at St. Louis having returned from Georgia.

Bro. [Albert] Carrington is now reading your letter of [blank] to Mary [Ann Ayers Young] here in the office to President, Squire [Daniel H.] Wells, G[eorge] A. Smith, and others in the office. We are all amused and gratified at your description of the difference twixt the Mr. and the Elder Jos. Young.

Promising to endeavor to keep you informed of such items of

interest as would be interesting to you from time to time, as
I may be directed,
   I have the pleasure to subscribe myself,
truly your brother in the covenant,

                              T. W. Ellerbeck

My Dear Son Joseph
   It is now late at nigh. The male has arived this evening and
I have heard your letter red, and it rejoice my hart to here sush
good knews frm you. May the Lord Bles you for ever and ever, is
my Prayr for you. We are jest movin in to our new house.[13] I
suepose Mary and the Chldren will give all the famely knews. You
can hardly emagen the joy it gives me to here such good knew
from you. My sole leaps for joye. Be faithful my son and the
Lord will Bles you and I Bles you. Remember you are my oldest
son, the arc of the famely. I want you to be faithful that you
may [be] worthe of your stashon in my Kingdom. Give my love to
all the Brethern. God Bles you.

                              Brigham Young

Letter dated February 3, 1855

   The appointment of Joseph A. Young to preside over the Bradfordshire Conference of the British Mission on December 1, 1854, placed the welfare of 875 Church members under the care of this twenty-year-old missionary. "They are as affectionate a body of saints as ever lived," Joseph wrote his wife Mary. "Sometimes, after I have preached, I have to shake hands with two or three hundred, and it occasionally makes my arm so lame the next morning that I cannot write." Confronting Church members in England were social conditions that bred extreme poverty. "I see strong, able-bodied men working for ten shillings ($2.42) a week, and they have large families to support out of that; and in addition, it takes some money to support the work. Thus the saints have about as much as they can do; and if they stop a little, the load becomes so heavy that they cannot carry it."[14] "Some of them have not had a full meal at a time for two months; they have just enough to keep them nearly starving to death all the time."[15] Joseph reported that the work of God appeared to be moving ahead quite rapidly in England, but admitted that there were not so many being baptized as in previous years. He attributed this to a change in proselyting method in which the full price of accepting the gospel was explained to new prospects. "Before I baptize anyone, I inquire if they are willing to lay everything upon the altar. The consequence is, that those baptized now are a great deal better, taken enmasse, than has heretofore been the case."[16]

Joseph A. presided in Bradfordshire during the remainder of his mission, which terminated in July 1856. Under his direction 214 persons were added to the fold, of whom 110 emigrated to Zion. Such was the esteem held for Joseph A. Young by the Bradfordshire Saints that they presented him with a silver goblet upon his departure.

The following letter to Joseph is Brigham Young's initial response to his son's appointment at Bradford.

Salt Lake City, February 3, 1855

Joseph A. Young
Manchester, England

Dear Son,

Morning and evening do I call upon the Lord to bless you in your labors. Your course I watch with the eye of an affectionate and loving parent, whose anxiety for your welfare, I hope you will repay with a faithful and energetic performance of the duties assigned to you in the ministry.

Up to this date the most flattering accounts have reached me in regard to your daily walk and the rapidity with which you acquire knowledge. These reports are from those in whom I place the greatest confidence; hence I do not doubt their correctness. I well know that the Lord has given you talents of no ordinary cast and all that it requires is a fixedness of purpose, a reliance in the Most High, together with prayer and humility, to ensure my fondest expectations in regard to you.

I look upon this mission as a sort of probation—a kind of middle period between boyhood and manhood—a time which as you improve or neglect, will make or mar your future career.

Therefore, my son, give heed to the instructions of those who are placed over you to counsel and direct you in the thorny and dangerous paths you now tread, and in no instance let me hear of your having neglected or disobeyed their injunctions.

While you are absent from the Valley, I wish you to lose no opportunity of making yourself familiar with all that is useful and likely to benefit you, for to be able to combat with the world we must make ourselves acquainted with the ways of the world. This can only be done by keeping your mind constantly on the alert and when in society never allow anything to escape your notice. Listen attentively, and observe minutely the manners, customs, and remarks of all, for from the most humble of our fellow creatures an observing man can learn something that will be useful to him in after life. Such has been my course and, from daily and hourly experience of its benefits, I recommend you to pursue the same.

There are many things you can inform your mind upon, the laws of England, her form of government; lose no opportunity in your travels of visiting her manufactures, her works of art, her grand and spacious buildings, and all that is worthy of note, not from a mere idle curiosity but to store your mind with that which will benefit yourself and your brethren in after years.

When in society (for you will be called to mingle in it a great deal) use every endeavor to improve your address, and always exert yourself to be agreeable, and no matter whether poor or rich, treat them with equal courtesy. Do not be pompous to the needy, nor condescending to the wealthy, but show by your manner that you do not respect a man because of his money. By this you will gain the love and admiration of those worthy of your esteem, and at comparatively little expense, for it costs but little labor and attention to be polite and civil to those around you.

I have taken this opportunity to advise and counsel you, as I learn from your letters that you are anxious to improve, therefore I felt that a little well-timed advice would not be thrown away, but would aid and assist you in your endeavors to acquire that knowledge which through the persecutions of the Saints you had not the priviledge of obtaining in your early years.

As you progress in doing good, [and] your desire to make yourself thoroughly acquainted with the principles of our holy religion and all other useful knowledge increases, so will my love and affection increase for you.

The family are all well. Your mother is about the same as when you left. Mary [Ann Ayers Young] and the baby are both doing well, but the more minute particulars Mary and Alice [Young] will write to you about.

The legislature closed their session a short time since and adjourned to meet at Fillmore the next term.

The sugar works are in operation,[17] the building and machinery being complete. Your Uncle Truman [O. Angell] has bestowed a great deal of mental labor on that job and deserves great commendation for the indefatigable perseverance with which he has pursued and searched out the intricacies of the machinery.

An express came from Fillmore reporting that Indian, Walker, is dead. His disease I have not learned.

The difficulty between the Sioux Indians and the troops at Fort Laramie last summer bids fair to stop communication between the valley and the states. For the present our last mail is reported to have been waylaid near Independence Rock and the carriers with one exception killed; therefore it will be best for you to direct your letters by way of California and send a duplicate copy by the regular route across the plains. Let us hear from you often.

Your affectionate father,
Brigham Young

Letter dated February 7, 1855

On February 7, 1855, Heber C. Kimball, first counselor to Brigham Young in the First Presidency of the Church, dictated a letter to one of the scribes in the President's office for his son William, who had accompanied Joseph A. Young to England as a missionary in 1854. To this letter Brigham Young appended the following single page, written in his own hand to his son Joseph. The document is another one of the few examples of Brigham Young's own handwriting during the years of his presidency.

Salt Lake City, February 7, 1855

Joseph A. Young
Bradford, England

    We ware very happy to receive your letter but was sorey to here that you had to goe without drawers and wescoats [waistcoat]. If the peopl due not [help] you so that you can be comfortble you are at liberty to ask Br Franklin [Richards] for a little money to by those nessaries for your comfort. I wish you to be very prudent and lern the worth of money. You are now in a situation to lern poverty and welth. Improve your self so that you will be prepard for more important stations in life. All the gold in Caleforna could not by my good feelings to you and thankfulness to the Lord. You letter gave grate joy and Br Franklin [writes] in high terms of you. I wish you to the Brethern [to] say G. D. G. [George D. Grant], Wm Y[oung], Wm H [Kimball], James F[erguson], James Little and finely all of them, I remember them all in my prayers daly and in our prayer cirkel every Sabath in the afternoon. Your mother wishes me to wright a fue words for hir. Hir helth is about as usual not very well but so she works all day and then till midnight frequently. We feele proud before the Lord when we think what you are duing in the grate cause and Kingdom of our God. Be faithful my son. You went out as a child. We trust you will return a flaming Elder of salvation. Keep your self pure befor the Lord. Your Father before you has don it, and my constant prayer is that you may. With all my hart I beleve you will. May God Bles you forever and ever.

                                      O how glad we will be to see you.
                                        Brigham Young

My Dear Son Joseph

It is now late at night, the mule has arived this evening and I have rec'd your letter, and it rejoice very heart to have such good news from you may the Lord bless you for ever and ever, is my Prayr for you. We are fast growing in to our new house, I suppose Mary and the Children will give all the poverty hureah. You can hardly envagen the joy it gives me to have such good news prove you, my sole leaps for joys, be faithful my Love and the Lord will bless you and I bless you. remember— you are my oldest son the one of the journey, I want you to be faithful that you may worthie of your fathors in my Kingdom

... would ... intending to you from time to time, as I may be directed, ... the pleasure to subscribe myself

Truly your brother in the Covenant,
E. W. Ellerbeck

BRIGHAM YOUNG TO JOSEPH A. YOUNG, DECEMBER 1, 1854

BRIGHAM YOUNG, JR.

Brigham Young, Jr.
1836-1903

Brigham Young, Jr., was one of twins born to Mary Ann Angell and Brigham Young in Kirtland, Ohio, on December 18, 1836. His twin sister, Mary Ann, died in Nauvoo, Illinois, at the age of seven. As a child Brigham Jr. experienced the trying times of the Latter-day Saints in Ohio, Missouri, and Illinois, and accompanied his parents to Winter Quarters during the Mormon exodus from Illinois in 1846. A year later, at the age of twelve, he drove an ox team across the mountains to the Salt Lake Valley. During his early years in Utah he worked on the Salt Lake Temple and supervised work on the transcontinental railroad. An excellent horseman, he assisted in the rescue of snowbound immigrants on the overland trail east of Utah and led a detachment of troops in the Utah War. He later became a director of the Utah Central and Utah Northern railroads, was business manager of the *Deseret News,* a member of the Utah Legislature, president of the East Canyon Coal Company, and a member of the board of directors of Brigham Young Academy. In his life, he was labor boss, business manager, legislator, and diplomat.

Brigham's ascendance to positions of leadership did not come easy. Having been deprived of education and social contact in his early years, he stepped forth reluctantly when leadership responsibilities were first offered him. Especially lacking in the oratorical skills and social graces he felt were expected of a son of the Church president, Brigham Jr. often lamented his lack of ability, and in his early adult years he shied away from public assignments. On one occasion, having been invited to the stand at a meeting in Farmington,

Utah, he arose and ran out of the door. The opportunity that finally prepared him to overcome his social shyness came during his first mission to England in 1862-63. Less than a year after his return, he was called to England again to assist the veteran Daniel H. Wells in the presidency of the European Mission, and in 1865 he succeeded Wells as president of that mission. Most of his subsequent life was devoted to church service.

On February 4, 1864, Brigham Jr. was ordained an apostle and assistant counselor to his father in the Church presidency. Four years later he was appointed to the Quorum of Twelve. A decision in 1900 that seniority in the Quorum of Twelve would be reckoned from the date of appointment to that quorum, and not ordination to the apostleship, ultimately proved to be the factor that kept him from becoming president of the Church.

After returning from Europe in 1867, Brigham assisted his father with Church business in the President's office and frequently traveled with him visiting the settlements of the Saints. After the death of Ezra T. Benson in 1869, he was called to preside over the Mormon settlements in Cache Valley and southern Idaho. While there he was a member of the Logan, Utah, city council, president of the Cache Valley United Order and of the Logan Board of Trade, and commanding officer of the Cache Valley Nauvoo Legion. In 1873 he was named one of seven counselors called by his father to assist in the responsibilities of the First Presidency.

Brigham Jr. was with his father during the President's last illness in August 1877—those days of "extreme anxiety" that preceded his death. "I cannot write of the sufferings of a dear parent, and what language can describe the feelings of my heart? . . . How can we endure this terrible event which seems to be approaching too surely despite the pleadings and tears of a great people?" he wrote.[1] After the death of his father, Brigham Jr. was named one of the administrators of the estate, an assignment that caused him much sorrow when members of his family brought litigation against the Church in a public spectacle before the final settlement.

In 1884 Brigham Jr. traveled into Mexico on a missionary assignment to introduce the Book of Mormon among the remote Yaqui Indians. While there he contracted yellow fever and nearly lost his life.

Having married plurally, Brigham Jr. supported a family of six wives and thirty-one children. As the "polygamy question" received increased attention from the nation's law makers in the 1880s, forcing most of the church leaders out of public life, Brigham Jr. spent much of his time on the "underground," away from his family and friends. During this time he traveled extensively among the Latter-day Saints in outlying settlements and fulfilled a variety of far-reaching church assignments. After the enactment of the Edmunds antipolygamy bill by Congress in 1882, he was called with Charles W. Penrose to Washington, D.C., to assist in the effort to rescind the oppressive legislation against the Latter-day Saints by soliciting support for the admission of Utah to the Union. Among government officials contacted were leading members of Congress and the President of the United States. In 1885 Brigham went to Mexico City where he met President Diaz, and he later visited the governors of seven Mexican states in an effort to obtain permission for Mormons to settle in Mexico. Subsequently, he was instrumental in the purchase of land in northern Mexico that became the gathering place of Mormon colonists. In 1889, with Arizona Church leader Jesse N. Smith, he traveled to New York City, where he assisted in negotiations with the Aztec Cattle Company to secure Mormon land claims in Arizona and New Mexico. When not traveling, Brigham Jr. was "hiding out" in his own home or that of friends as he sought to avoid polygamist-hunting deputies—an exercise he described as the "usual routine of reading and waiting for the Lord." As months of hiding grew into years, depriving Brigham of the society of his family for long periods of time, with telling effect upon his health and his domestic tranquillity, he felt pressure mounting to give himself up. "I have reason to believe," he wrote in his diary at a particularly trying time, "that my worst enemies are one or two of my own family."[2]

One of three members of the Council of Twelve who were still in exile in 1890, Brigham Jr. was called a second time to preside over the European Mission. He remained in Europe until 1893, when he was informed that all indictments against him had been dismissed and that he was free to return home. He arrived in time for the Salt Lake Temple dedication in April.

During the remaining decade of his life Brigham Young, Jr., traveled among the stakes of the Church in his responsibilities as a member of the Quorum of the Twelve. He died in Salt Lake City on April 11, 1903, after several months of illness.

Letter dated June 5, 1862

In the midst of efforts to obtain statehood for Utah in the spring of 1862, senators-elect William H. Hooper and George Q. Cannon were sent to Washington, D.C., to petition the Congress of the United States on that subject. Since Cannon was in England directing the Church's European Mission at the time the assignment was made, Chauncey West, the presiding bishop of Weber County, Utah, was sent to temporarily replace him. When West and Hooper left Salt Lake City for Washington on April 26, 1862, Brigham Young, Jr., then twenty-five years old, went with them to witness the petitioning process and observe conditions in the East, leaving his wives Jane and Catherine in Salt Lake City.

On May 30 President Brigham Young addressed a letter to William Hooper in Washington that contained some advice for his son Brigham: "I want him to be very particular in keeping a minute and correct daily journal of whatever he may see, hear, or do that is of any particular moment; and in case he should forget, I shall be obliged if you occasionally remind him, for I am desirous that he derives all possible benefit from his trip and your oversight and counsels."[3]

Brigham Jr. had arrived in the nation's capital on June 6 after stopping a few days in New York City. Three weeks later he received his first letter from his father.

Salt Lake City, June 5, 1862

Brigham Young, Jr.
Washington City, D.C.

My dear Son,

I was much gratified to learn of your safe arrival in Atchison, [Kansas,] and trust that you also arrived safely in Washington.

Col. R[obert] T. Burton and company returned on the 31st ult.,[4] all well, and having met with neither accidents nor Indians, except a small band of the Denver tribe on their way to Salmon River, that you met on your way down.

At last advices high water at Ham's Fork was detaining the forward companies of the ox train, but grass is now good, and when they cross that stream they will be in condition to make good time, and will probably not be a month later than last year, if so much as that.

City Creek has considerably damaged North Temple Street and the road in the canyon, but the water is now abating a little.

In my letter to Br. [William H.] Hooper, May 30, I requested him to ask you to keep a minute and correct journal of all you might see or hear of interest. I wish you to carefully and regularly attend to this request, for in so doing you will reap many advantages as well as much gratification, and it will be more of a pleasant than irksome duty, if daily attended to.

How would you like to have me forward you an elder's certificate, and take a mission to England, after you have finished your visit to Washington? Please inform me the first time you write.

Should you decline going abroad previous to coming home, I should be pleased to have you, in returning, come by way of Auburn and visit Mr. Worden who lives in Throopsville, three miles north of Auburn, Cayuga County, State of New York. Mr. Worden married James Works' youngest sister, who was also the youngest sister of your sister Elizabeth [Y. Ellsworth]'s mother. His daughter Angeline is living in Auburn and has written me two letters. I wish you to see her, and if she would like to come with you to pay us a visit and return at her pleasure, I would be much pleased to have her do so. If she has not means for so doing, bear her expenses. If you have time to spend a few days in Auburn, Port Byron, and that region, it may be of interest to remind you that I began my mechanical career in Auburn, and helped build the first little market house in that place, when the site of the state's prison was a swamp filled with hemlock and other trees, many of them from three to four feet through, and some of them five and others seven feet through.

Katy [Catherine Spencer Young], Jane [Carrington Young], your children, and all of us are enjoying good health.

We pray for your welfare, and that your trip may prove a benefit and blessing to you.

Your father,
Brigham Young

Letter dated August 6, 1862

President Brigham Young's letter of June 5 proposing a mission to England had a profound effect upon his son, who may not have regarded himself as missionary material. "I cannot describe the feelings of my heart at the sight of that letter, and how it affected me when I came to read it,"[5] Brigham Jr. wrote in his diary. In his letter of acceptance, he said: "You ask me how I would like a elders certificate and go to England on a mission. I shall leave that question with you. If you wish me to go, send the certificate, and I will, God being my helper, accept and fill the mission to the best of my ability. My own feeling on the subject is repugnant to asking to go, but if you send me, I go willingly. I know that it would make a man of me. But here is the point; this is what I should want to say on my return: 'Father you sent me on a mission to England. I have lived humble and pray[er]fully and filled that mission to the best of my knowledge and ability.' Then I'll feel I am a man, but never till that day arrives, can I feel worthy to bear rule in the smallest degree in the Kingdom of God or worthy of being called my Father's son. When I think of the labor you have performed on this earth, in building up the Kingdom of our Lord, and the experience you have had upon missions, I have longed for the time to come when I could realize and understand your feelings, which I shall never be able to do until I've experienced the visisitudes of a traviling elder. . . . P.S. I will endeavour to keep my journal in order."[6]

Planning to accompany George Q. Cannon on his return to England after the adjournment of Congress, Brigham Jr. had leisure time to travel and observe conditions in the East in the midst of the Civil War. After wandering through the streets of Washington, D.C., in weather that was "extremely hot and oppressive" and observing social conditions there, he wrote, "I wish I was a thousand miles from here, or in my mountain home."[7] Adding to his distaste was the grim evidence of the war then raging between the North and South. "Some hundreds of wounded have arrived here to day, from before Richmond minus arms, legs, heads tied up, blood dripping from the hind end of the waggons, as they went through the streets—others shot through the body and puking blood at every step. . . . I would rather be in Utah than anywhere else in the world."[8]

On July 6, 1862, Brigham Jr. visited the long-time friend of the Mormon people, Colonel Thomas L. Kane, at his Philadelphia home, where the Colonel was recovering from a recently inflicted Civil War wound. During the visit, Kane, who was anticipating a momentary advancement to the rank of brigadier general, requested young Brigham to join his staff as aide-de-camp. On July 11 Brigham wrote to his father for counsel. "I do wish that you could say one word of advice to me on that point. I have asked my Father in heaven, and left it with him. If circumstances favor my going to England, right, if with the Col., do, [ditto] . . . but I care nothing about that, unless it will assist me in the building up of the Kingdom of God, which is the desire of my heart no matter how far I may vary from the line."[9]

Hearing nothing further from Colonel Kane or from his father, Brigham Jr. departed for England on July 16, 1862, aboard the steamship *Scotia* in company with George Q. Cannon. They arrived in Liverpool ten days later. The following letter of August 6, 1862, is the initial response of President Young to his son's acceptance of a missionary call.

Salt Lake City, August 6, 1862

Brigham Young, Jr.
42 Islington, Liverpool, England

My dear son Brigham,

Supposing, but not knowing, that you have gone to England with Br. George Q. Cannon, I write you a few lines at a venture, knowing that if you are there you will be glad to receive them, and if you are not, there will be no harm done. If you accompanied Br. George Q. to Liverpool, I am glad of it. And now if I can learn that you are doing good in the vineyard, I shall feel very well satisfied, but spending time and means without any particular benefit to one's self or others, causes me regret.

If you are in England I trust that you will faithfully, humbly, and prayerfully do all the good you can. I wish you to live and fare as the poor elders do. Grub your way along as they do, and thoroughly learn how poor folks live, for you are young and hearty and can endure it, and it will prove of great future benefit to you, and while doing this you have the advantage of having your family all comfortably situated and provided for, relieving you from anxiety on their account.

Make up your mind to stay contentedly for a reasonable length of time, or until you receive advice from me to return home. And while doing all the good you can, strive also to learn and improve yourself all you can at every opportunity and through every laudable available channel, shunning not only evil but every appearance of evil. Upon all these points Br. George Q. will cheerfully give you the aid of his cool judgment and experience, as I have requested him in a letter sent by the same mail which takes this, and which aid I have no doubt you will cheerfully accept and profit by. Your name and personal acquaintance in England will answer in lieu of an elder's certificate, though should you wish it, or any other papers, Br. George Q. has authority to furnish you.

Should there be any interruption between England and America,[10] you and the elders from here had probably better make your way home.

In going to England you have not had to deprive your children as I did you and Joseph and your sisters when I went, for I had to take a part of their scanty bedding and also leave them barefoot and poorly provided for. Catherine [Spencer Young], Jane [Carrington Young], and your children will all be well provided for, so that your mind may be free from anxiety on their account. I see nothing to hinder your going ahead in doing all the good you can, which I hope and really believe you will not fail to do, and I glory in your grit. I do not mention my going to England in the way I had to, with any design to in the least disturb your feelings, but because I cannot help contrasting the way in which I went with the way in which the elders have gone since that date.

Since writing the foregoing your cousin Joseph W. [Young] has telegraphed me that you have gone to England, with which, as before stated, I am well pleased.

The Church trains [11] are all on their way home, and the last train expects to leave Florence [Nebraska] in a day or two, which closes our this year's operations in Florence in time for all to arrive here in good season.

We are all well, and home affairs are in a flourishing condition.

Your father,
Brigham Young

BRIGHAM YOUNG, JR.

Letter dated August 30, 1862

Arriving in Liverpool, England, on July 26, 1862, Brigham Young, Jr., was assigned to labor under William C. Staines in the London Conference. Shortly after arriving there he received his father's letter of August 6. He replied that receipt of the letter had given him new life, and he went on to express his feelings about his new assignment. "I am fairly engaged in working out my Salvation, and I thank God from the bottom of my heart that I have enlisted in this great work. . . . I have been appointed to labor here in this Great Metropolis. My district is Whitechaple, Poplar Barking, [and] Goswell Road. . . . It is pretty hard for me to preach, but I am in a place that I have got it to do and I seek unto the God of Israel for strength, and he has never failed to answer the prayers of his Saints. My mind is made up to stay here until I am *sent* home. . . . When I landed in Liverpool I staid in that City about a week, and then I started for my field of labor, and I am taking it afoot with the rest of the traveling Elders, and I am able to do it with the help of my Father in Heaven. . . . Be kind enough to excuse all mistakes as I have just come in and have been walking some few miles, (which thank God I am able to do) and the joy your letter gave me has made my eyes a little moist, so please forgive me all blunders. Bro. Geo. Q. [Cannon] has furnished me with an Elder's certificate and I feel to bless God day and night for the privilege of earning my Salvation, and of warning others of the evils that are coming upon the earth. Father, I can in part realise what a time you had when you first came to this country. My mission will be a perfect pleasure trip compared with yours, and it is you and others that have brot this about, and you are now (when no longer able to go abroad into the world yourselves) providing for my family and hundreds of others of Elders that are now preaching the principles of the Gospel in every part of the known world. . . . God bless Israel is my prayer day and night. You wish me to do all the good I can, and believe that I will. You are wright. I shall make it my business, and if seeking the Lord all the day long will give me the grit you speak of, then I am striving for it."[12]

Salt Lake City, August 30, 1862

Brigham Young, Jr.
42 Islington, Liverpool, England

My dear son Brigham,

Since my last to you, Aug. 6, yours of July 11th and 18th have come to hand, and I was much gratified in their perusal. I am pleased with your writing, "my whole heart is engaged in building up the Kingdom of God on the earth," and that you so promptly went into the field of labor assigned you instead of tarrying in the Liverpool Office, for that course will prove much the most useful to yourself and all with whom you may come in contact.

So far as you may have opportunity I wish you to improve yourself to the utmost in studying good books and in associating with, and listening to, and profiting by, the conversation and experience of good persons, that when you speak to the people, they may be persuaded that they are not only listening to one having authority, but also to one appreciating and preaching the good, sound, saving doctrines and precepts he teaches. Cease not to lift up your voice in all faithfulness, teaching the people the way of life and salvation, which you know.

As I advised you on the 6th inst., I wish you to carefully observe how poor folks get along, which you will have excellent opportunities for doing, and to be prudent and economical in all your expenditures as much so as consistent and reasonable with your calling and duties, realizing that means unwisely or luxuriously expended had far better be husbanded for gathering the poor. Whenever necessity and your judgment dictate, you are at liberty to apply to Br. George Q. Cannon for such funds or other assistance as you may need, who is authorized to supply your prudent wants.

Ever strive to be humble, faithful and obedient, calling upon the Lord in faith and sincerity, and he will fill you with wisdom and understanding, give you power to influence the honest in heart, guide, bless and protect you, and crown your faithful labors with a success that it has not entered into your heart to conceive possible in your youth and inexperience. Though going forth at an early age to proclaim salvation to mankind, yet you start under many very favorable circumstances, and I doubt not you will seek to and rely upon our God, striving with your might to aid in building up his kingdom and strengthening the same upon the earth, with an eye single to His glory, that he will enable you to overcome, and win many souls to His cause.

Having faithfully labored in the vineyard until about the last of May next, you are at liberty to, and I would be pleased to have you visit the brethren upon the continent and such places of interest that you may wish, in company with some suitable person Br. George Q. may select, of which I have advised him. From about the last of May you can so arrange your visit to the brethren upon the continent as to be back to Liverpool on or before about the first of August, in readiness then to start for home, where you can arrive in about 25 days from the time of starting. This arrangement is of course based upon uninterrupted peaceful relations between England and America. Should troubles or a strong probability thereof arise, they may vary the aforesaid plan of a trip to the continent, and Bro. George Q. is already advised to be ever watchful and ready for a brewing storm, in time for the elders from here, and as many more as come, to make their way safely to these shores.

Day after tomorrow, Sept. 1st, I purpose starting with a small company on a visit to our most southern settlements, expecting to be gone about a month.

Bro. Lewis Bronson arrived on the 29th inst. with a company of some 212 persons, mostly from the states, 74 days from Florence. We expect all the freight and persons of our this year's immigrating operations to be here by and before the 25th of October.

I was pleased to learn from Bro. George Q. that he had placed you at the start to labor with so good and suitable a person as is Bro. W[illiam] C. Staines. Please give him my kind regards, and tell him he is ever remembered in my prayers in behalf of the Israel of our God.

Work on the temple is making good progress, general good health is enjoyed, the people are peaceful and industrious, and our harvests good.

Myself, your mother, your brothers and sisters, Catherine [Spencer Young] and Jane [Carrington Young] and their children, and so on and so forth, are well.

Bro. Heber C. Kimball sends you his best respects, and says, "God bless Brigham Young, Jr.," to which I add the blessings and prayers in your behalf of your father,

Brigham Young

Letter dated October 11, 1862

When first asked to accept a mission call, Brigham Young, Jr., was not informed of the intended duration of his service. The letter from his father of August 30 not only contained that detail, but surprisingly gave the son the opportunity to visit the continent of Europe before his return. Writing to his father in reply, young Brigham said, "I had made up my mind to stay here until you sent for me, be the time short or long, and to do my utmost for the good of the Kingdom, and if I can't preach much I will try and set a good example, and I think that is half the battle. You have given me permission to visit the continent. I thank you from my heart, and will try and improve the opportunity to learn all I can."[13]

In an effort to better acquaint himself with the English culture, Brigham Jr. had visited the London exposition and other sights, collecting numerous books and pamphlets descriptive of the places he visited and the people he met. In comparing the English people with his own countrymen, he wrote that he was happily mistaken in his conception of those among whom he labored: "They are far superior to what I believed them previous to my coming here, just as good men as I wish to meet, and I am ashamed of the feelings I once had with regard to them. I really think that I have brot myself to that point that I do not care what countrymen I meet with, if they are only good Latter-day Saints, I feel like a brother to them and desire to do them good. I can now see the difference between America and England. I have heard more swearing in one day in that land of freedom, than I have since I've been in England. This I suppose is one of the causes that England has been prospered, but they are fast approaching the American system."[14]

Having been advised by his father to "thoroughly learn how poor folks live," Brigham Jr. reported that opportunities for such education were abundant in London, and he described his own daily fare: "In the morning, I have for my breakfast some thin slices of bread and scrape and a glass of warm water with a little chalkey milk and sugar in it. Understand me, I don't mean to complain, but merely telling you the facts in the case. Then for dinner, sometimes I don't have any, but make up for that by walking three or four miles. My supper is pretty much the same as my breakfast. Sometimes a little better, but I don't feel to complain at all for I have all that I want, and I would live this way for months, to save money to send the Saints to the Valley. I shall be as economical as possible and endeavour to be saving. I feel very different from what I used to a few months ago, for I have known what it is to be hungry, and without money, but I never felt better in my life. Thank the Lord."[15]

Salt Lake City, October 11, 1862

Brigham Young, Jr.
42 Islington, Liverpool, England

My dear son Brigham,

You can scarcely realize the gratification I derived from the perusal of your very welcome and excellent letter of August 7th. I was much pleased that you so manfully entered upon the field of active public duties so soon after your arrival in Liverpool, and that you have so strong a desire and determination to walk humbly and prayerfully and do all the good our God may bless you in being instrumental in accomplishing. I am also pleased that you have been privileged to visit the Exhibition and other instructive places you mention, and approve of your plan of buying books descriptive of the noted places you visit, so far as they are to be had, that you may not only learn all you can at the time, but also have the means of refreshing your memory and learning still more when leisure moments permit after your return home.

I fully approbate your course in continuing on to England, being fully satisfied that it will result in far more good to yourself and others than would in your direct return from Washington.

Without doubt there are many poor Saints in that district and in all the manufacturing districts of England, some very destitute, and that you may not be burdensome to anyone who is struggling in poverty[16] I have instructed Bro. George Q. Cannon to furnish you from time to time such funds as your reasonable and economical wants may require. This will relieve your mind of all care on the score of means suitable to your calling, position, and circumstances, and will enable you to give to, rather than receive from, the very poor. Notwithstanding this, it may at times be best, both for yourself and them, for you to accept an invitation from the poor to partake with them their scanty fare. Under this arrangement I presume that you will, as already advised, be prudent in the use of money, realizing that only money answers for immigrating the poor to Florence, and that gathering the poor directly follows their obedience to the gospel, and is obligatory upon us to the extent of our ability in that channel. In this advice about prudence and economy, I do not by any means wish you to heedlessly deprive yourself of the necessaries and comforts of life suitable to the requirements of your position and calling, but to keep a wise watchcare over your expenditures.

On the 1st inst. I started with a few brethren on a tour through the southern settlements and returned on the 25th. In that short time we traveled some 800 miles, visited nearly all the settlements, and held thirty public meetings, in twenty-four of which, I addressed the congregations. The settlers in our Dixie have been very energetic in making improvements, and in raising cotton, &c. Both ourselves and the brethren we saw enjoyed our visit and I trust that it was mutually beneficial.

On the 17th inst. I purpose starting, with a few brethren, on a visit to Cache Valley and the intermediate settlements, and to hold a two days meeting in Ogden City and Logan, and a meeting in North Ogden, Willow Creek, and Brigham City.

As I wrote in my last letter to you, I wish you to make a visit to the continent next season, starting in time to complete your visit and return to Liverpool by about the 1st of August in readiness to start for home. When you make the aforenamed visit I wish Bro. George Q. Cannon to accompany you, if consistent with his other duties at the time; if not, I wish Bro. C[hauncey] W. West to go with you.

Catherine [Spencer Young] and her children are still living where they were when you left, and are all well. Jane [C. Young] and her children remain at the mill where George W. Thatcher and Luna [Y. Thatcher] are living, and are also all well. Catherine and Jane both write to you tolerably often, and I presume give you the family news. Day before yesterday they got two ambrotypes of Brigham [S. Young] and Albert [C. Young] taken together, one for each of them, and the little fellows make a very pretty picture.

In all probability you will be able to entirely omit the use of tobacco while on your mission, if you have not already done so.

In such case I trust you will be wise enough to not resume its use on your return, either while crossing the ocean, passing through the states, nor upon the plains, but permit us to welcome you home with your mouth and breath free from the use and smell of tobacco. It is now going on two years and a half since I have used a particle of tobacco, and I guess a little resolution and faith on your part will also enable you to dispense with its use, in doing which you will ever feel strengthened, prospered, and blest.[17]

If there should be no outbreak between England and the United States, you are at liberty to return at the time before mentioned, or to tarry longer and return with Bro. West, just as you and the brethren may feel and decide at the time, unless I in the intermediate time see it for the best to advise you otherwise.

I am, as already stated, much pleased with your labors thus far and with the spirit of your letters, and feel assured that if you will continue as you have begun, your course and conduct will prove a credit to yourself and your father's house, in honor to your God, and salvation to yourself and others.

The immigrating companies have all arrived in good condition and spirits except three, and the freight train, which are also all coming along in good time. Of the two Church passenger trains still on the road, one camped on the Muddy on the 9th inst., and the other passed this forenoon. The [train] which is in the rear and has over two hundred passengers, camped at Pacific Springs last night, all well, and will probably arrive in a little over two weeks. We have been signally blest in our this season's immigrating operations, having brought in good time and condition all the freight and passengers that were at Florence.

Your mother is enjoying pretty good health, and my health and that of the family is very good.

The weather continues very pleasant, and our crops are abundant.

Please remember me kindly to Bro. [William C.] Staines and give him my good wishes and blessings for his welfare and success in working righteousness. His family are well.

That yourself, Bro. Staines, Bro. Cannon, and all who love and live the truth may be abundantly blest and prospered in doing the will of our God, is ever the prayer of your father,

         Brigham Young

Letter dated January 3, 1863

As the news spread that a son of Brigham Young was laboring as a missionary in England, the Saints were eager to see and hear him; consequently, he was assigned to travel throughout the mission and speak. By January 1863 Brigham Jr. had spoken at conferences in Bedford, Leeds, Carlisle, and London. He had also traveled to Wales and Ireland. But he saw his role as a son of Brigham Young as demanding social graces beyond his ability to meet. "I have been afraid that more is expected of me than I can do. They consider that such a father had ought to have a smart son. I can't help it if they are disapointed in their expectations but I will do my best to answer the prayers of my friends. But I can do nothing without the help of God." Reflecting further upon his seeming ineffectiveness, Brigham said, "I have thought and said many times since I've been here, 'I can't see that I'me doing any particular good here; I don't convert anybody.' But some of the brethren tell me I am doing a good work, but if I don't convert one soul it will make no difference to me; I will do my duty and work just as hard as though I was baptiseing my hundreds."[18]

Probably due to his extensive travels, it was not until February 4, 1863, that Brigham Jr. answered his father's letter of October 11. In this he reflected upon his first half year in England: "I never enjoyed myself better than I have here in England preaching the Gospel of Jesus to the best of my ability. . . . I manage to make some blunders but my intention is good. . . . I am unable to convey to you on paper the thankful feelings that is in my heart for such a father, and for the care that you have shown for me heretofore when I had forsaken the pathe marked out to me by example and would do wickedly, but my repentance with the help of God shall be lasting and with the aid of his spirit will I serve him the remainder of my days. I don't suppose this looks very well on paper. It would be better to talk of something else. I thank you sincerely for the aproval of my plan of buying books connected with the many places I may visit of historical notriety. And I also thank you for the good advice you give me, and that you are satisfied that my mission will result in more good to me and others than my return from Washington. I have made my home among the saints whenever I could, without distressing them. You know they go to more trouble for me to oblige you than they do for some of the elders, therefore I know if I go to some places they will distress themselves for me, so I make them a visit between meals but I have plenty to eat, to wear, sleep and the Lord blesses me with his spirit, and that is all I can ask. Your journey north I have seen in the D. News. How did you manage without me? I don't doubt but that you got along and hardly missed me, yet it is impossible for me to get along without you."[19]

Salt Lake City, January 3, 1863

Brigham Young, Jr.
42 Islington, Liverpool, England

My dear son Brigham,

Your very welcome, interesting and satisfactory letters of Oct. 13 and Nov. 12 came safely to hand and their perusal afforded all of us much gratification. It is a source of great joy to me, and to all your relatives and friends, that you are so faithful, diligent, humble and prayerful in the duties of your calling and field of labor. And whether you personally baptize many or few matters not, as you have justly remarked, for the results of your ministry are under the control of our God, it only devolving upon you that your labors be in all faithfulness to the best of your judgment, ability and opportunities. Besides your diligence in preaching, I am much pleased that you so correctly bear in mind and practice the setting a goodly example in your daily conduct and conversation, for it is a saying as true as it is trite that "example goes further than precept."

I wrote you on the 11th of Oct. that I proposed visiting Cache Valley and the intermediate settlements; I accordingly did so, starting on the 7th and returning on the 25th of Oct. We held two days meetings in Ogden City and Logan, and meetings in Kaysville, North Ogden, North Willow Creek, and Brigham City. In every place the brethren were much pleased at greeting and meeting with us, and we doubt not our visit was mutually beneficial. While I was absent north, Col. [Patrick E.] Connor, commanding the Cal[ifornia] Volunteers, who were ordered to protect the overland mail and telegraph lines in Utah, with 4 or 500 troops, leaving only one or two companies on the line at Ruby, formed a camp on the bench land east of this city and just north of Red Butte Creek. Why they are so safely ensconced where their services are of no benefit is probably a question the colonel and his command cannot answer so correctly as can some of us. But, as heretofore, the plans of those who ordered them where they are will be frustrated, and they also as heretofore, will be filled with wrath and wonder that their efforts against the truth so signally fail. Up to the present Col. Connor and his command have conducted themselves with commendable propriety so far as their intercourse with the citizens is concerned. On Christmas eve the theatre was filled with guests invited to participate in appropriate ceremonies, preparatory to commencing theatrical performances for the season. The proceedings of the evening were instructive and interesting, as you will learn, from the notice thereof in this week's *News*. On the 25th, 27th, and 31st ult. the building was opened to the public, and well-filled houses each night evidence the gratification of the people at so excellent an opportunity for relaxation, improvement and enjoyment. For the present there will be two performances each week, on Wednesday and Saturday nights. Since about the middle of Dec. we have had an occasional snow squall, some cool nights, quite a sprinkling of parties, and some sleigh riding, with about four inches of snow now on the ground, and the clouds promising more. On New Years Day myself and Presidents [Heber C.] Kimball and [Daniel H.] Wells enjoyed a very pleasant family party in the Social Hall and an excellent supper furnished by Bishop [Edward] Hunter and his counselors.

Should you again meet Mr. [Jules] Remy, [20] please give him my thanks for a copy of his *Journey to Great Salt Lake City*, which he was so courteous as to send me, and which came safely to hand. Since its reception, business and a multiplicity of duties have so occupied my time as to preclude my examining it, though I have heard some of the brethren remark that in the main it is quite fair and candid, and calculated to do much good. As to the drill-sergeant you wrote about, Br. [William] Pinnock, if I read the name correctly, I will instruct Br. Cannon to assist him and his family to emigrate next season, having them help themselves all they can.

Secretary [Frank] Fuller informs me that he expects to receive, in the course of a few weeks, the funds to pay off Br. [Robert] Burton's command. For this reason I enclose authority to receive and receipt for your pay,[21] which I wish you to sign and return with your reply to this. I entirely coincide with the idea entertained by Br. Cannon and others of the brethren, that your traveling among the branches and conferences will be a mutual benefit and gratification and production of good, and therefore wish you to do so to the extent Br. George Q. may deem best, until it is time for you to start on your visit to the continent previous to your returning home as already advised. I am so well pleased with your letter that I hope you will write as often as convenient, and by so doing you will at the same time gratify me and benefit yourself. On the 19th ult. Gov. [Stephen S.] Harding read to the Legislative Assembly his message, which they deemed so inappropriate, meddlesome, and abusive that they declined ordering printed the copy he handed to the Secretary of the Council.[22]

My health is very good, as is also the health of the family, your brother Joseph's, and his family, your family, John W.'s, and that of your other relations and the people generally, with the exception of some cases of whooping cough among the children. That you may have a happy new year and as many happy new years as will enable you to complete your probationary labors to the acceptance of Israel's God, is the wish and prayer of,

Your father,
Brigham Young

P.S.

Lest it has not reached you[23] I will make an extract from my letter to you, Oct. 11: "As I wrote in my last letter to you, I wish you to make a visit to the continent next season" (now this season), "starting in time to complete your visit and return to Liverpool by about the first of August in readiness to start for home. When you make the aforenamed visit I wish Br. George Q. Cannon to accompany you, if consistent with his other duties at the time; if not, I wish Br. C[hauncey] W. West to go with you." I will now add to the foregoing extract, that I wish Br. West to accompany you from Liverpool home, if Bro. George Q. thinks at the time that he can consistently permit him to do so. When you leave Liverpool for home I wish you to travel by the speediest modes of conveyance, and when you arrive in New York get Mr. Ben

Holladay to telegraph to St. Joseph, to have seats in the stage ready for you on the day you expect to reach there.

Letter dated March 26, 1863

Upon receiving his father's letter of January 3, Brigham Young, Jr., wrote in his diary, "I thank my God for such a father and pray him in the name of Jesus Christ that I may never more be guilty of doing anything that would grieve him in the least, or cause anything but joy in having me for his son."[24] Within hours he penned a reply. "Honored Father. . . . I really feel the want of language to express the satisfaction and the joy I feel in perusing your letter to find that you are satisfied with the course I have taken in this country, and that my letters breath forth a spirit that is acceptable, and that causes you to rejoice makes me feel like a little child, and can't help singing the praises of our lord for all his goodness to me and my brethren. I have not baptized anyone yet, but I have preached as hard as I can those principles pertaining to our religion that I understand."[25]

On March 25, 1863, Brigham Jr. received a telegram containing the brief message that his father had been arrested.[26] After waiting nearly a month for further word, he expressed his concern in a letter to his father. "I must tell you how I felt some three weeks ago, when I got the news of your arrest. The spirit of the Lord assured me that all was right, but with this assurance in my heart, it was all I could do to keep from asking Bro. Cannon to start me for home. . . . I do not feel easy. We can hear of the doings of Gov. H[arding] and Judges, and I can hardly contain myself. If it was not for deserting my post I would start home tomorrow, but I do not wish to come home until the right time for me. If I did I could not look you in the face. I do not wish to do anything rashly but take things calmly, and consider all points. You can understand how I feel better than I can tell you perhaps, but nevertheless it does me good to tell you that I am alive in Christ and with you to the end." Expecting news from home with each mail delivery, Brigham Jr. waited three days to complete his letter, but after repeated disappointment he concluded his epistle on the 25th with a resolution to abandon his forthcoming trip to the continent and be ready to leave England at a moment's notice. "There is one thing certain. I will not leave Liverpool except it be for [the] U.S. until I hear that things are in a little less critical condition with you there in the valley." He reasoned, "supposing anything should be the matter, that my poor services would be needed by you, and I not where I could get word. . . . I never could forgive myself for leaving when such an event is the least probable."[27]

The long-awaited letter of his father, dated March 26, explained the arrest in sufficient detail as to set his mind at ease, although the son did not receive it for a month after the telegram.

Salt Lake City, March 26, 1863

Brigham Young, Jr.
42 Islington, Liverpool, England

My dear son Brigham,

Your very welcome letters of Feb. 4 and 6 came safely to hand, and, as heretofore, we were all much gratified with their tenor and spirit, and feel assured that you are laboring diligently and with your might in behalf of the great cause in which you are engaged. I cordially approve of your trip to Ireland and visit to different branches in Wales and elsewhere, for, with the spirit you are blest with such visits will prove mutually beneficial.

As probably already advised through Br. [George Q.] Cannon, I wish you to omit purchasing any bolting cloths, for I have made other arrangements.

Gov. [Stephen S.] Harding and Judges [Charles B.] Waite and [Thomas J.] Drake had, by their efforts to stir up strife between Utah and the general government, become so obnoxious to the people that a large and enthusiastic mass meeting convened in the tabernacle early this month, and unanimously adopted resolutions condemnatory of the course of said officers, and a petition to President Lincoln to forthwith remove them and appoint good men in their places. The petition was, in a few hours, signed by some 2500 persons in the city alone, and was handed to Br. H[orace] S. Eldredge to deliver to Br. [John M.] Bernhisel for him to present to the President. Said officials, more or less countenanced and aided [*faded*] Col. [Patrick E.] Connor, continuing their meddlesome and mischievous [*faded*] Judge [John F.] Kinney, upon complaint, issued a writ citing me to appear before him and answer to a charge of bigamy. The writ was served by U.S. Marshal [Isaac L.] Gibbs, to which I promptly responded, and after examination was bound over to appear for trial at the March term in 1864. Since then the hue and cry about testing the operation of the anti-polygamy bill passed by Congress last summer has considerably abated, and Harding, Connor and Co. are at present quite crestfallen and apparently at a loss what to try next. It is probable that their efforts to create trouble will prove futile, and that they and their like will disappear as the grass grows.

Brs. H. S. Eldredge, Feramorz Little, your brother John W. Young and Lewis Hills started for the States in the stage on the 11th inst.

Br. Eldredge goes to New York to transact business and superintend the affairs of our this year's immigration, and your brother John will go with him; Feramorz will stop at Florence and operate there and in the regions round about, assisted by Br. Hills.

We are not yet advised of the probable number of our this year's immigration from abroad, and of course do not know the number that will need assistance across the plains, but presuming it to be unusually large, the brethren are preparing to send 500 four-yoke ox teams to Florence,[28] to leave here about the 25th of April, and to arrive on the frontier about the middle of July. This number we presume will answer the contemplated purposes, as did the numbers sent the two last seasons.

Cotton being high priced in the States, and our facilities for manufacturing it not quite in readiness, arrangements are being made to send by the ox trains a quantity of cotton to the States for sale. This may appear some like "taking coals to Newcastle," but under present circumstances it is thought that it will pay, and at the same time have a beneficial effect in increasing the production to meet home demand as soon as we can get the requisite machinery in operation.

On the 14th inst. in company with Brs. [Heber C.] Kimball and [Daniel H.] Wells, some of the Twelve and a few others, I went to Bountiful to dedicate their recently finished meetinghouse. We held interesting meetings there on the 14th and 15th, and returned home p.m. of the 15th.

As I have already advised Br. Cannon, so I also wish you, as far as you may have opportunity, to counsel the Saints about to emigrate this season, especially those who expect assistance across the plains, to dispense at the start with all useless baggage, for they had better give it away at home than to pay expenses on it to Florence, and then have to leave it through lack of transportation, also to use sacking so far as possible instead of chests, trunks and boxes, in packing such articles as they bring. Also inform them that very many, if not the great majority, of those furnishing teams for their assistance do not use tobacco, tea, nor coffee—all high priced and cash articles—and that cash is very scarce with us, for which reasons it will be a good time while crossing the plains to begin to learn to dispense with the use of said articles, as we do not expect to be able to furnish them only for cases of sickness, or as medicinal stores.

James Cobb and his sister Charlotte started for Boston in the stage on Monday last, 23d inst., and will write to you soon after their arrival in that City.

Lest my Nov. 13 letter to George Q. [Cannon] may not have come to hand, I will here make an extract from it. "In my next letter to Brigham I shall inform him that I wish him to purchase and bring with him one dozen of the best and largest sized *opera* glasses he can find. I do not care so much about the style and finish of their mounting, so it be plain and substantial, as I do about the size and quality of the glasses. I also wish him to have each one furnished with a good well-made leather cover and strap suitable for carrying it when traveling. I also wish him to purchase another dozen in New York City, on his way home, to be, as the dozen first named, of the largest size, best quality, and leather covered and strapped. I would like to have the object glasses of the opera glasses capped, as spy glasses are, if he can get it done."

Katy [Catherine Spencer Young] and Jane [Young] and your children are all well, and the children are growing finely.

My health, your mother's, your brother Joseph's and family, my family's and that of your friends and the people in general is good.

The month thus far has been very pleasant.

Home affairs are peaceful, and bid fair to continue so.

That you may be continually guided, blest, and prospered in

all your desires and labors in behalf of the truth, and return to your home in health and safety, as previously advised, is the prayer of,

                Your father,
                Brigham Young

Letter dated June 3, 1863

Upon receiving his father's letter of March 26, Brigham Young, Jr., replied that had he not been restrained by the Spirit of the Lord, "I would have been with you ere this; but I was assured by that never failing moniter of the servants of the Lord that all would be well."[29] So confident was he that when the President's letter of June 3 arrived at Liverpool containing added assurance to dispel any uneasiness about affairs at home, Brigham Jr. had already departed on his tour of the continent.

Salt Lake City, June 3, 1863

Brigham Young, Jr.
42 Islington, Liverpool, England

My dear son Brigham,

Your very welcome letter of April 22 came to hand on the 25th ult., and you may rest assured that we were all much gratified in again hearing from you, and interested in perusing your account of travels, doings, spirit, and feelings up to that date.

I last wrote to you on the 18th of April, which letter I trust you received about the time yours of the 22nd reached here, and in that letter I informed you that I purposed soon starting on a visit to our southern settlements; accordingly on the 20th of April, in company with Pres. [Heber C.] Kimball, several of the Twelve and others, I started on my visit and returned on the 19th of May, having been absent 29 nights and 30 days. During that time we traveled nearly 850 miles, and held 39 meetings, at which I addressed the congregations 37 times. The brethren in all the settlements we visited greeted us with much gratification and paid strict attention to our counsels and instructions, and in nearly all places there was visible a commendable increase of energy and taste in improvement in buildings, fields, orchards, vineyards, spirits, feelings, &c.

On the 11th ult. I received a right good letter from your brother John W., written in New York City, April 21. He was well, and enjoying himself much amid new sights and scenes, and from all sources I learn that his conduct is very commendable, and that his trip will doubtless be very beneficial, at least to himself. He mentions that he wrote to you, as I had requested him, on his arrival in New York City, and that he expected to soon start for New Hampshire and Boston in company with Br. Horace S. Eldredge.

Gov. [Stephen S.] Harding has been removed, and his clique and plans have all fizzled out. He said the other day, I am told, that he expected to leave Utah in two or three weeks. His departure will probably be soon followed by that of two or more of his more immediate official aiders and abettors, but whether or not, it is certain that the backbone of opposition and strife-stirring slander at home is broken, and there is no apparent prospect of their being able to create any disturbance here at an earlier date than next year at the soonest, so that I think you need have no uneasiness about trouble or affairs at home while on your continental tour, nor within the time previously mentioned for your return home. They are too busy with their own affairs to molest us at present though their feelings are doubtless bitterer and bitterer.

Br. George Q. Cannon's letter containing particulars of W[illiam] G. Mills' trial has not yet come to hand, but the result of that trial caused me no surprise.

The spring just past and thus much of June have been unusually dry and warm, but gardens and fields are luxuriant and promise abundant harvests, strawberries being already plentiful in market, and green peas appearing on many tables. In the meanwhile all the varied in and out-door avocations are being vigorously prosecuted, huge granite blocks being hauled for the temple and cut and laid, and the work on our new tabernacle being vigorously prosecuted.

The trains for Florence are making excellent progress, with prospects that our immigration will not have so long to wait on the Missouri as they did last year, but rather that some of the trains may have to wait a little for arrivals.

Your course, conduct, travels, spirit, feelings, and views, so far as communicated, are highly satisfactory to me, and I have great confidence that you will perform all duties and so shun or overcome all evil and allurements thereto as to perform a mission beneficial to yourself and others, and return to your home with greatly increased faith, profitable experience gained, and none but good works accomplished.

Since writing the foregoing I have received another letter from John W., dated May 17, N.Y. City. He had been to Boston, had visited James and Charlotte [Cobb], and viewed the notable buildings and places of that city. He was in excellent health and spirits, and expected to soon visit Washington in company with Br. T[homas] B. H. Stenhouse.

On your return I would be much pleased to have you visit Col. [Thomas L.] Kane, if reasonably convenient. At any rate you may have opportunity to make a call upon some portion of his family, which, if you can do, will be very agreeable to them, to the Colonel, and to me.

All is well and prosperous at home, with good prospects for abundant harvests.

My health, your mother's, that of my family in general, and of your wives and children, is good.

That all needed blessings may ever attend you upon your continental tour, upon your return home, on or about the time you are already advised of, and thereafter through your probation and to an abundant admission to the celestial kingdom of our God is the prayer of,

Your father,
Brigham Young

Letter dated December 8, 1864

The first mission of Brigham Young, Jr., to England ended with his travels on the continent of Europe in June and July 1863. In summarizing his missionary experience he wrote to his father: "I have enjoyed myself well while on this mission and altho' it has been short I think it will make me look into my own heart, and in a small measure realize the blessings with which I am surrounded. Altho' I do try to do my duty and live as I know you would have me, in placing my whole mind upon the work in which I am engaged, yet I will occasionally wander away to the valley, and I can see you in my minds eye, and I can't help but exclaim in the depths of my heart, that the day I see you again and grasp your hand and those of the brethren will be the happiest of my life, and I look forward to it as the day of the beginning of my existence. I never could apreciate those blessings before and I am afraid I do not sufficiently at the present time, but I know I thank God from my very *soul* that he has given me such a father and altho' I may err in many things, yet my desire will ever be that I may be a source of rejoicing to you and never for a moment give you pain or grieve the spirit of God within me. I know I have your prayers for my welfare with the rest of my brethren who are in missions, and I feel to thank you for the good advice and very kind letters you send me, for those few words from you do me a world of good, and as I have stated before in my letters that as often as you write me (as you have plenty of clerks that could give me the news &c) so often will you confer a blessing upon me, that I am hardly worthy to receive. If I gave the Lord sufficient thanks for all his blessings poured out upon me through you, it would take an eternity and as little as I feel like I could do will be to spend the life he has given me in his praise and to gloryfy his name upon the earth."[30]

Brigham's missionary experience had come at a critical point in his life. "I feel very like I had been in a deep sleep all my life," he wrote in his diary, "and had just waken up. If I live a thousand years, I will never have anything happen to me so opportunely as this mission has."[31] Only after the insight that followed the trial of his faith in England was he able to realize the importance of his religion and the object of his creation. The change in his life caused serious reflection as he looked back at the "horrible gulf" that he had just missed falling into. "I long for the time to come," he wrote his father, "when I can prove to you and mother how much I value your kindness and long suffering towards me. I realize to some extent how wild I've been—and perhaps wicked in many instances—and how patiently ye both have waited for me to change. My constant prayer is that I may never cause you another pang of sorrow, or that you may ever have cause to blush through any act of mine hereafter."[32]

On August 1, 1863, Brigham Young, Jr., left England for America. He arrived in Salt Lake City twenty-six days later. As the stagecoach rolled to a stop in front of the family residence on South Temple Street, his father with all his family was at the gate to meet him. When Brigham Jr. stepped from the coach he was immediately swallowed up in the affectionate greetings of his family. The "gentile" passengers, he recorded, "looked on with surprise no doubt thinking I had many friends." The day of his homecoming ended with this note: "I . . . thank God that I can look my Father and all the Saints in the face and not feel to blush for any action committed on my mission."[33]

Less than a year after Brigham Young, Jr., arrived in Salt Lake City, he was called to return to England with Daniel H. Wells to preside over the European Mission of the Church. The two men, with their wives (Brigham took Catherine), left Salt Lake City on April 30, 1864. After spending some time in the East, they sailed from New York on July 11 and set foot in England on the twenty-fifth.

At the beginning of his first mission, as Brigham Jr. obtained his first real glimpse of the world during his travels in the eastern United States, he was appalled at the moral conditions that existed beyond the cloistered environment in which he had been raised. After several weeks in Washington, D.C., in 1862, he concluded, "the city seems to be one big whore house. I wish I was a thousand miles from here."[34] Later that year, upon observing conditions in England, he noted, "I never had the least conception of the real character of men until within the last three or four months, and I must say that I am completely dumfoundered."[35]

The difference between his own people and those of the world staggered his mind. In London he saw men and women "wallowing in their filth so drunk they could not lay still, cursing and swearing, and poluting themselves by every species of crime that is known. How different from the mountain home that I have so firmly fixed in my minds eye, where, instead of seeing crime, you behold all that makes the Lord delight in the workmanship of his hands. I never could have reallized the gulf that seperates us from the world—not until I had looked down both sides of this mighty chasm, could I thank God truly for the blessings which he has given unto his people."[36] Such were the degraded social conditions that temptation seemed to present itself at every turn. He wrote his father, "Oh, the devil is working hard to destroy the servants of God here and it takes all the faith and prayers that I can muster to keep my thoughts pure before my God. No matter how poor an out I make of it, I am trying to serve God to the best of my ability—and yet I occasionally catch myself wandering from that straight and narrow path. I can feel your prayers for me; they influence my actions. You understand what temptations there are in the world, and how . . . easy it is to fall off and before we know it be sunk in the depths of misery and vice."[37]

While traveling on the continent in 1863, just prior to his return home, Brigham Jr. again wrote of widespread human degradation. "I have thought many times, that if the soldiers, whores, and beggars were taken out of Italy, it would be without inhabitants except those who, like ourselves are merely transient residents."[38] After arriving in Bologna one evening he noted, "I did not like this place at all. They show their vices a little to plain. As soon as we had arr[ived] and fairly got the dust of from us, several ladies dressed in white presented themselves for us to pick from. They waited long and patiently but were disapointed at last. Such things as these make me disgusted with society as it exists at the present time, and long more earnestly for the society of virtuous men and women, which are only to be found as a community in my own loved home."[39]

Brigham Jr. had not been in Milan long—the first city in Italy that really suited him—before he noticed the same corruption that he had seen elsewhere. "I have come to the conclusion," he wrote his father, "that the whole world is turned into one Grand Manufactury of illigitemate children."[40] Now, two years later and traveling to England on his second mission, Brigham noticed that the same pall of corruption hung over New York: "This city is one of the most wicked places I was ever in, and wickedness is on the increase. Nothing but the utter destruction of this people will ever purify the land."[41]

As he donned the cloak of administration over the European Mission with Daniel H. Wells, Brigham faced the problem of human depravity from still another perspective—that of coping with the degraded social environment in which he must direct missionaries of Zion. In an era when moral prerequisites for missionary service were not as tightly drawn as they later became, it was not uncommon for some of the elders to succumb to the temptations around them. A somber theme of Brigham's letters to his father during the years of his mission presidency was the plight of missionaries who had transgressed. Within one year he reported nine cases of serious deviation. In relating a particularly grievous case in which one elder had been guilty of drunkenness, immorality, and assault and battery, which resulted in a two-month prison sentence, Brigham wrote to his father, "I find that the greatest trial the brethren have to meet is to keep their skirts clear of women—that class of people being very plenty, and from the customs of the country they have come to think every man they meet wants to ride them, and about two thirds of the females keep an open shop day and night. If I ever felt sick and tired of the filth and corruption, it is now, and my desire increases daily to gather out the honest, that the Lord may burn up the rotten masses."[42]

The following letter of Brigham Young to Brigham Jr. and Daniel H. Wells was written on December 8, 1864, some three months after they had taken the reigns of the European Mission.

Salt Lake City, December 8, 1864

President Daniel H. Wells and
Brigham Young, Jr.
42 Islington, Liverpool, England

Dear Brethren,

Your welcome favors (Bro. Daniel's [H. Wells] of Oct. 22nd and Brigham Jr's. of Oct. 27th) have been received and perused with much interest, and the business items have been duly noted. Your communications manifest a spirit of improvement which I am pleased to witness, and I hope that you will continue to cultivate this spirit in all your writings and teachings and in the management of your business.

Your continued visits to the conferences, and meeting with the elders and Saints at their various fields and places of residence is time well spent. By such visits the mission will be more likely to be kept in a healthy condition, and the details of affairs throughout the conferences to be more thoroughly known by you. I have been very sorry to hear what you have written to me respecting David Gibson and his operations. Whenever his mysterious disappearance shall be accounted for I am of the opinion you will find that he has been prompted to take such a course by the loss of the Spirit and the shame arising from transgression. It is to be regretted that at this late day, after the Latter-day Saints have had so much instruction upon the plan of salvation, men should fail to perceive that there is nothing that the adversary can offer as a temptation to seduce them from the path of righteousness and truth which they cannot obtain by treading in that path undeviatingly. There is no good thing which is not comprehended in the gospel of Jesus. Every gift and blessing that can enhance the happiness of man, or add in the least to his enjoyment and to the development of his God-like nature, is promised unto man through his obedience to the truth, and he can receive all these things as fast as he prepares himself for them. Strange to say, however, not only are the people in the world blind to this great fact, but men and women, who call themselves Latter-day Saints, and who have been taught the principles of salvation, fail to recognize it, and desert the substantial pleasures which they would enjoy eternally, and go in pursuit of their shadows.

We have had a steady rain, mingled with some snow, now for two days. It is still raining. There is no frost in the ground, and as the rain falls gently, it is [line blurred]. Everything is moving on peaceably in the city and territory. The holding of the convention for the regulation of the price of grain has been attended with excellent effects. Flour and grain have sold at remunerative prices, and the farmers have been able, by the sale of their produce, to furnish their families with many comforts which would have been beyond their reach had there not been a united effort to keep up the prices. This has not been the only advantage. Speculators and others in the adjacent territories have exerted themselves to obtain flour and grain from other quarters, instead of depending wholly upon us, which they would have done had they thought that they could have obtained provisions at the old prices.

The Volunteers on the bench are becoming more insignificant every day. They are becoming tired of their publishing business, and are anxious to sell out the *Vedette* Office.[43] They do not attract the least notice from the citizens, and we all go about our business as though the redoubtable general and his command were not in existence.

A specimen of the silver ore which [Patrick E.] Connor has been digging in the west mountains,[44] and about which there has been so much noise made, was lately showed me. It is nothing but lead, and rather poor quality at that; it contains a much smaller percentage of silver than our Las Vegas lead did.

The line of the proposed canal between Big Canyon Creek[45] and the city is now being surveyed by Bro. Jesse W. Fox. By leveling from the point selected as the most suitable for the canal to cross that creek, we find that the water can be brought to a point in the city nearly as high as the top of Eagle Gate near my Beehive house, which will be sufficiently elevated to answer every desired purpose in navigation or irrigation. The digging will soon be commenced, and it is the intention to push the work through as fast as practicable this winter.

The hard times which the working classes in Lancashire, Warwickshire and other places are suffering, may cause some of the more honest and reflecting portion of the people who have heard the testimony of the servants of the Lord to pay some attention to the truth and to bow in submission to its requirements. We can tell the nations of Babylon that they have only begun to experience, in a small degree, the calamities and judgments which will most assuredly come upon them unless they repent of their sins and turn unto the Lord.

If there are any of the Saints who have means sufficient to carry them across [illegible] this side [illegible] are desirous to come, the better [illegible] to take passage to New York and then take rail from there to Buffalo and cross from there to such points in Canada as will be most feasible and present the best facilities for obtaining employment. If such persons could obtain suitable employment not far from Detroit, on the Canada side, it would be convenient for them to come from there west when they wish to emigrate, but in seeking a place to stop, they will have to be governed by circumstances. I mention New York as the port to which they should ship, because passages can be obtained more readily, and as a general thing at more reasonable rates, than to Canadian ports. If any should choose to come on west into the neighborhood of Wyoming, and seek for employment, there would be no objections. By the time they obtain their outfit, opportunities will very likely offer for them to come on here. But in all this you must be governed by the situation of the country and by circumstances. I indulge in the hope, however, that, before long, the way will be open for our emigration to come by the Colorado River, and that steamship owners will be willing to charter their vessels to carry our people to Aspinwall on the Atlantic side and from Panama on the Pacific side up the coast to the point that will suit us best. The best months for the Saints to cross into Canada will be June, July, and August; they then will have time to prepare for winter.

Ransohoff's store was robbed one night last week of a quantity of clothing. The police have been very diligent in their search after the thieves, and have finally been successful in arresting them, and in finding the greater portion of the goods stolen from Ransohoff, as well as a quantity of coffee and other articles which were stolen some weeks ago from Mr. [Austin] Shipp, the father of Bro. M[ilford] B. Shipp. The property was found on the premises of a so-called saint by the name of Griffin, of Union Fort, and of another by the name of Geo. W. Kent of Session's settlement. Three gentiles have been arrested, who with Griffin and Kent are now undergoing a preliminary examination before Judge [Elias] Smith; they will undoubtedly be committed, as there is no room for doubt as to their guilt.

I should like to continue to receive a monthly cash statement of the business of your office, and that this may be fully reliable, it will be well to see that your books are kept well posted up, and your cash account regularly balanced as often as once a month at least.

It will be well for you to make inquiries as to who would be the best type-founders to make matrices for our Deseret Alphabet, so that you may have an idea where to get fine, well-finished, elegant type made for our books when we need it. Look around, and see where they can be got, and whether they can be got at all or not, and also ascertain whether we will be under the necessity of sending any person over to superintend the business of getting the type up. You have printers there, probably, who can tell what is needed, and who will know when the types are right in every respect for printing.

Both your families have been visited this morning (the 7th) and your wives and children are all well. Brigham's son, Howard, fell from the foundation in his lot, and hurt or sprained his ankle; this confined him to the house for a few days, but he is now able to wear his boot again and go to school with the other children.

Praying the Lord to bless you abundantly in your labors, I remain your brother in the gospel,

Brigham Young

[*Postscript contains drafts on the Liverpool office*]

Letter dated October 18, 1865

As Brigham Young, Jr., entered upon his public ministry in 1862, he had felt ill-equipped with the social graces necessary to meet the challenges that confronted him. "I am not a good speaker, and so I try and make up for it bye visiting the saints in their homes—I exort them to live their religion and try to set them a good example," he wrote in his diary.[46] In explaining the source of his backwardness on one occasion, he said, "My education has been different from that of the young men who are now growing up in the Church. In my youth our parents had sufficient to do amidst the persecutions they were surrounded with, and could not properly attend to the education of their children."[47] Aware of his weaknesses, Brigham did not refuse the responsibilities that faced him, but showed a dogged determination to overcome the "man-fearing spirit" he possessed.

Although he preferred to visit the Saints in their homes rather than speak in their meetings, he willingly complied with the assignment he received shortly after his arrival in England to travel throughout the British Isles to fulfill the desire of Church members to see and hear the son of President Young. "When I stand up to preach, the persperation roles off me, but I put it through and am determined to learn how to warn the people, and how to make myself intiligable, that the truths of the Gospel may come from my mouth in the Simplest and plainest manner possible."[48] After a particularly trying day he confided in his diary, "I can hardly contain my feelings neither can I express them to the people, but I shall continue to call upon the Lord in faith until he will unloosen my tongue."[49] That Brigham Jr. had made some progress in strengthening his confidence before the public was a subject of a letter to his father: "Give my love to Lott Smith and tell him that I am not So afraid to stand up before a congregation as I once was in Farmington where I was called to the Stand and instead of going I ran out of doors. I'me getting broke in a little."[50]

During his second mission to England, Brigham Young, Jr., undertook an intensive study of French, English grammar, and history, with the hope that "by close application" he could compensate for his earlier educational failings. However, his progress report a year later was fraught with discouragement. "I have come to the conclusion that I must be one of those that mature late in life. It seems astho' I am no farther advanced now than I was a year ago. I have discarded the idea of ever becoming a good preacher, and confine myself strictly to the truth, and cheer up the Saints the best I can."[51]

On May 31, 1865, Brigham Jr. left England with his family for a visit to the continent, where the little pride he took in his knowledge of French withered in the face of reality. He veiled his discouragement with the assurance that his study of French had not been entirely useless—it had helped him to better understand his own language. One of his reasons for traveling on the continent at that time seems to have been educational. Writing to his father, he said, "I . . . hope you will approve my course in visiting the Continent. I shall try and improve the time. I find however that I am very slow, and do not learn so fast as some others, but I make every day a day of study, and I hope the time will come when I will have acquired a tolerably good education. It is truly my desire to qualify myself for the duties present and future."[52]

Because of his poor health, the experienced veteran Daniel H. Wells was summoned home from England in August 1865, leaving the administration of the European Mission in the sole charge of the twenty-nine-year-old Brigham Young, Jr. If Brigham's lack of education and oratorical skill had theretofore caused him to shrink from public responsibility, the departure of his talented superior only added to his anxiety. He reflected upon the stark reality of his new assignment in a letter to his father. "When the idea was first suggested of my being left in charge of this mission I felt to shrink, and although I looked upon it as an honor that I scarcely dared to aspire to, yet, I felt my own incapacity; but when I found that Prest. Wells was really going home and would leave me alone, I looked to the Lord for that strength which I knew I must have to honor that station. . . . In these hours of trouble I find a resting place in reflection. I look back into a time when the people of God were driven from their homes, and the enemy, pressing hard in their rear, drove them into an unbroken wilderness, where nought but death stared them in the face. In years gone by I have wondered how you, and those immediately around you, had wisdom to direct matters in such a manner that everything prospered which you set your hand to accomplish. Long since I have ascribed it to the Spirit of God, and I know that he always provides a way for man to accomplish his commands."[53]

The remaining letters transcribed below were written by Brigham Young while his son presided alone over the European Mission.

Salt Lake City, October 18, 1865

President Brigham Young, Jr.
42 Islington, Liverpool, England

Dear Son,
    The last letter which I have received from Bro. [Daniel H.] Wells or yourself was dated August 5th, and was written by you upon your return to England from the continent. Your letters from the continent, describing your travels and the cities and places of note which you visited, have been very interesting to me and the family. My last letter to you was dated Aug. 22nd. Since that was written, I have been almost constantly traveling, and have been compelled to defer writing to you until the present. After writing to you, in company with Bro. Heber [C. Kimball] and several brethren of the Twelve and some other elders we visited Tooele Valley, and met with the people at E.T. City and held a two day meeting with the Saints at Tooele City. On the 4th, September myself and company started on our annual visit to St. George and returned to this city on the 29th of Sep. We had a snow storm at Round Valley and between there and Fillmore. With this exception we had a very agreeable and pleasant journey. In every place which we visited the Saints appeared to feel as well as I ever saw them. They turned out almost in masse to meeting whenever we gave out an appointment, and the Spirit of the Lord rested powerfully upon the elders and the people upon every occasion. The teachings were very practical, and applied to almost every duty and labor connected with life. The people in the southern settlements feel very

cheerful and contented this season; their prospects are brightening, and those who have entertained doubts in the past respecting the practicability of being able to make a living in that region have dismissed their fears and have come to the settled conclusion that, after all, the country is habitable. Probably more than half the breadstuffs the people in that section of the Territory need for the year has been raised in the settlements outside of the rim of the basin. A considerable number of improvements made since our last visit are apparent in St. George. The new settlements of the Muddy and the Beaver Dam streams are reported as being very flourishing and the brethren feel sanguine at their prospects. We are informed that the cotton plant grows finely down there, being especially thrifty in the Muddy. I am intending to move my cotton machinery down to that country so as to be in place to manufacture the next crop of cotton, and have selected a site for the factory at Washington, six miles from St. George.

During our absence on this southern trip we held meetings and preached discourses. We did not go any further than St. George, going straight there and returning straight back. Bros. Franklin D. Richards and A[mos] M. Musser struck off from the company at Chicken Creek on our way down, and visited seven settlements on the Sevier, which contained about 432 families. It is almost a matter of surprise even to us, who have traveled more or less every summer throughout the Territory from the first of our settlement here until the present, how the people have increased and are still increasing and spreading abroad. We have been traveling steadily all this summer which is just past, remaining but a very short time in the city between our trips, yet there are a great number of settlements that we have been unable to visit for the want of time. The time is not far distant when the cry will be heard: "the place is too strait for me: give place to me that I may dwell," and Zion will lengthen her cords and strengthen her stakes and break forth on the right hand and on the left. The increase of the number of our children throughout our Territory is very apparent, and is a matter of pleasure and gratulation to all the Saints. Wherever we have been this summer the children have been paraded by their teachers, and have lined the streets as we have entered the settlements making our hearts throb with joy at witnessing them. The seed of the righteous is becoming numerous in the earth. When the gospel was first revealed in this generation to the Prophet Joseph there were but very few whom the Lord could call who would obey him and take upon them His name. But what a change thirty-five years have wrought! We have raised up a race in these mountains whose highest desire is to serve the Lord, and whose pride is to be called by His name. The friends of the Almighty, they who are desirous of carrying out His will at all hazards, instead of being scattered one or two in a place, and in but a few places, are now numbered by thousands who are collected together in one land, and are a power in the earth that cannot be ignored or passed by, and are daily becoming more numerous. Nothing like this has been seen in the earth for centuries. The Nephites were the last people of whom we have any account who were united in the desire to do the will of God and to acknowledge Him as their head. Since their apostasy, and the withdrawal of the priesthood from mankind, until the time of its restoration again, the Lord has been without a people whom he acknowledged, or who would have been willing to do His will in all things. The bestowal of the priesthood again upon man brings into existence the union which has been so long lost and mourned over, and erects a standard to which every lover of truth and every obedient son and daughter of God throughout all the nations of the earth can rally.

President Daniel H. Wells and wife and child, and Elder Finley C. Free arrived in this city on the morning of Saturday, the 7th instant, enjoying moderately good health, but fatigued from the trip. They came in time to participate in the conference, and they were very warmly welcomed.

Our conference was very numerously attended by the elders and Saints from various parts of the Territory, and was highly enjoyed by all. The conference convened on Friday and continued until Monday evening, and was followed on Tuesday by the meeting of the convention for the regulation of the price of produce, &c. The first three days meetings were held under the bowery, but on Sunday night it rained, and the meetings on Monday had to be held in the tabernacle. It was unanimously resolved at the conference to send five hundred ox teams down in the spring to the frontiers to help up the poor. This will, without doubt, be cheering news to the Saints abroad who are struggling and toiling to emancipate themselves from Babylon. How many of those who will receive help will appreciate the exertions we make to assist them in accomplishing the object for which, at the present time, they so fondly yearn? Many who have been helped through, and who probably would have been compelled to remain in Babylon for years yet to come, had help not been extended to them, come here, and turn away and join themselves to the wicked and abuse the people who have befriended them, and to whom if any regard had been paid to their expressions while they were in the branches where they joined the Church, it might be expected they would be eternally grateful. We have had this to contend with in the past, and we may expect that it will be so in the future while human nature remains so depraved and so subject to sin and sinful influences as it is.

In view of the heavy expenses that will naturally fall upon the Trustee-in-Trust of the Church in sending down so many teams this season to help up the poor, I wish you to be particular in urging upon the people the importance of paying their tithing. Of course, I wish the same policy that has prevailed upon this subject for the past few years to still continue to govern you. Do not make it a matter of fellowship, if men do not pay their tithing. Neither suffer it to be so strenuously urged upon the people as to become oppressive, but let the Saints understand that it is a law of the Lord, and not only a duty but a privilege for them to devote a tithe of their means to the building up of His kingdom on the earth. When they view it in this light instead of it being a task or an onerous burden to pay tithing, it will be a pleasure.

When a man is able, and has something to pay tithing on, and utterly refuses to pay tithing, then they can be cut off from the Church, but when men are poor, they should be leniently dealt with. Persons like the Walker Bros. of this city, who refuse to pay their tithing, we have cut off here, but such cases will scarcely, if ever, occur in your jurisdiction.

I wish you to be prompt and decisive in your counsels to and dealing with the elders, not with harshness or severity, but in a pleasant and kind manner. You know what right is, and you should see that it is maintained.

When the health of any of the elders is likely to fail, continue to take the course which you have done, and move them to places possessing a more congenial climate. In some instances it may be necessary for them to cross the Atlantic to the States; whenever this may be the case it would be well to have them return there.

There have been great expectations indulged in by many who are inimical to us respecting the ingress of a heavy body of troops into the Valley this fall; but, so far, they have been disappointed, and from the best information that can be obtained, their disappointment is not likely to be removed. One thousand men may come in for the purpose of wintering here, but a large portion of them will be composed of men who have served in the rebel ranks, and who enlisted under the Federal flag with the express understanding that they should only be required to fight Indians. It is said that the utmost harmony does not exist among these two classes of troops, the Southern men not being well pleased with the name by which they are sometimes contemptuously called, namely, "galvanized Yanks."

The new tabernacle is being pushed forward and the scaffolding is erected upon which the bents of the roof are to be raised. We hope that by the time for holding our next semi-annual conference it will be sufficiently completed to admit of our assembling in it.

With love to yourself and family, in which Bros. Kimball and Wells and all the brethren join, and praying the Lord to be with you, and to fill you with the revelation and the wisdom which you need for the magnifying of your high calling, and to preserve you in health and peace to return home, I remain

Your affectionate Father,
Brigham Young

P.S. I wish you to purchase three suits of furs namely, a coat, boots, cap and mittens for your Brothers Joseph A. and John W., and Bro. Geo. Q. Cannon. You will know the proper sizes. Bro. Geo. Q. had me a suit of this kind purchased in Copenhagen through Bro. Jesse N. Smith, and there will be the proper place to purchase these suits. They should be carefully packed with camphor and tobacco in oilcloth, and sent across in the charge of careful elders; they can be brought so as to avoid the necessity of paying duty. You can purchase a suit for yourself at the same time, or at any time before you come home, and you should wear fur over your knees, especially in the winter. B.Y.

Letters dated November 17, 1865, and January 22, 1866

One of the most trying responsibilities that had devolved upon the young mission president was the subject of a letter to his father on October 9 wherein Brigham Young, Jr., dwelt at length upon "things which cause me pain and grief," relating cases of fellow laborers who had fallen into transgression. In seeking counsel from his father, Brigham Jr. wrote of his intention to "temper justice with mercy" if there were a determination on the part of the transgressor to mend. President Young responded on November 17, expressing amazement that "men who are called to be teachers . . . should act so utterly at variance with all their knowledge and professions." He urged his son not to be "cast down by the wrong-doing of those who may be called brethren or saints."

Salt Lake City, November 17, 1865

Pres. Brigham Young, Jr.
42 Islington, Liverpool, England

Dear Son,
Since writing to you I have received your favors of Sep. 19 and Oct. 9th, and have been pleased to hear of your welfare and the prosperity of the work under your care. It is grievous to hear of the misconduct and transgressions of the elders, and their deviations from the path of honor, but while men will give heed to the adversary, and not control their dispositions and appetites, such results will be witnessed. It is nevertheless strange that men who receive the holy priesthood, and are called to be teachers of men, should act so utterly at variance with all their knowledge and professions, as your letter informs us has been the case.
We have been much exercised this fall by the detention of

the immigrating Saints on the road, and earnest and thorough exertions have been made to bring them in. We sent out mule and horse teams, many of which went as low down as Red Buttes—about 380 miles east—to meet the last company. No pains or expense has been spared to bring in the people before the snows and rigorous weather of the winter should come upon them. We have been relieved and gladdened by the arrival on Wednesday, the 15th inst., of the last of the women and children from the hindmost (Cap. W[illiam] S.S. Willis's) company; and should the weather keep favorable, the train itself, with which there is none but men now, will probably reach here in a few more days. We were threatened with an early commencement of the winter; but the storms passed off and we have had a most remarkable fall; the weather has been magnificent, and the last company of teams composed of mine, Joseph A.'s, and some few other brethren's which went out to meet the last company, went from here to Rocky Ridge on the Sweetwater in the charge of Capt. Orson Arnold, and returned without experiencing any but the most pleasant and delightful weather. The Lord has heard and answered the prayer of the Saints in behalf of the immigration, and has averted the storms that are usual in the mountains at this season.

You have doubtless seen in the papers which are forwarded to you a description of the three day muster of the militia of this county on the 1st, 2nd and 3rd instant. The men were favored with very fine weather while they were out, and the display was most excellent. There were many strangers present at the review and the universal expression on all hands was that they had never seen a militia muster in which the men marched and performed their evolutions so well, or appeared to so good an advantage. During the entire muster everyone was cheerful, and not an angry word or unpleasant expression was heard from any quarter. How striking the contrast between a muster of Latter-day Saints in the capacity of a militia in this Territory, with the musters usually held elsewhere. For a muster to be held without any person being intoxicated, or the name of the Lord being blasphemed, or without a fight, as our recent muster was, would be something unexampled and unheard of elsewhere. Considerable interest has been felt of late, both on the part of the officers and men throughout the Territory in military matters, and a very commendable diligence has been shown in attending drill and in purchasing arms and uniforms. At the late muster Bro. Robert T. Burton was elected major general of this division to fill the vacancy occasioned by the resignation of Geo. D. Grant. Gen. D[aniel] H. Wells was on the ground every day, and was in command of the troops.

Quiet prevails in and around the city. The military have been making efforts to obtain suitable premises in which to quarter two companies of troops, but up to the present have not secured any. A man by the name of Potter has built a bar-like structure on Thomas Bullock's lot, next to Bro. [Thomas B. H.] Stenhouse's premises, for a theatre. They have played there three nights, but the last two nights the audiences were very small. This institution has been much lauded by the camp sheet, as being peculiarly gentile and as a place of amusement that ought to be supported.

A hall has also been built on the back part of S.J. Lees' lot, as a place of worship for the chaplain of camp and his fellow-worshipers. They call it "Independence Hall," and they think by such devices and schemes as these to overthrow the kingdom of God! They are a miserably low and contemptible crew who are associated together in these schemes. They are really beneath our notice, and with all their fretting and fuming we have never deemed them worthy of any attention, but have permitted them to indulge in their bluster to their heart's content, so long as they have confined themselves to talk. It is with us as it was with a man who had a dreadful termagant for a wife; she would become so violent at times that her abuse would attract the notice of their neighbors, and on one occasion one of them expressed his wonder to the husband at his patient endurance of her conduct. He replied that, as it seemed to amuse her and it did not hurt him, he did not mind it, but he was willing she should enjoy herself.

The new tabernacle is being pushed ahead as fast as practicable, and the main rafters are looming up and making a fine appearance. The present fine weather admits of work being done upon the building, and advantage is being taken of it to push it ahead.

You have every reason to be encouraged and to persevere in the discharge of the duties of your calling. Be not cast down by the wrong doing of those who may be called your brethren or Saints; but strengthen yourself in the Lord your God and He will bear you off triumphantly at all times and under all circumstances. Be faithful in discharging the duties of your calling, and keep your heart so clean and pure that the Lord can write His mind and will upon it, that you may never be in ignorance or be destitute of His word to impart when needed.

Under date of July 24th I wrote to you to take Bro. [William B.] Preston into the office; he can render you efficient aid, I think, and you will probably need both him and Bro. [Nathaniel H.] Felt. You should also procure you a good, trustworthy bookkeeper if one can be found—a man who will carefully keep the books in complete order and be able at any moment to give an account of the entire business of the office.

I wish you to release Brother Heber John Richards so that he can return here early in the spring.

We were much grieved to hear by telegraph that Elder George Sims, who was returning home from a mission to Great Britain, was drowned in the North Platte, at Red Buttes, on the [*blank*] of Octr. while crossing the river on horse back after some cattle. His guileless simplicity and strict integrity had endeared him to all who knew him and the regret at his untimely death was universal.

With love to yourself and Katie [Catherine Spencer Young] in which your mother and all the family join, and praying the Lord to give you every necessary qualification to enable you to magnify your calling and to preserve you in health and purity to return home, I remain your father,

Brigham Young

[*Postscript contains drafts on the Liverpool Office*]

Salt Lake City, January 22, 1866

President Brigham Young, Jr.
42 Islington, Liverpool, England

Dear Son,

Your letters of Nov. 25th and 28 and short note of Dec. 7th, with accompanying enclosure, have come safely to hand, and have been perused with interest and the contents duly noted. The release of the elders who are sick to return home is quite proper; no man should be kept there after he has tried different fields without benefit when his health is failing. I have not been disappointed in the result of C[harles] A. Benson's mission; his conduct at home before leaving on his mission did not inspire any of his acquaintances with any very sanguine hopes as to his future, unless there should be a thorough repentance of his past follies.

Until a few days ago, the winter, from the first of Decr. had been very severe. The sleighing has never before, since our settlement here, been so uninterrupted for the same period as it has been this winter. The snow has been very deep throughout the valley, but it is now thawing and the snow is likely, if the weather continues as at present, to soon disappear. The health of the people has generally been very good during the winter, and peace has prevailed, the bitterness and hatred of those who are opposed to us to the contrary notwithstanding.

We have had plenty of rumors and threats circulated by our enemies, but we have pursued the even tenor of our way without minding them in the least, or allowing them to disturb us. From the beginning of the work our enemies have formed an innumerable number of plans for our overthrow, and they have indulged in great hopes respecting the success which would attend their operation, frequently fixing the time when the complete overthrow of the kingdom of God would be consummated, but in every instance, their schemes have fallen to the ground and they have been covered with shame and confusion. Notwithstanding these repeated failures, the adversary does not appear discouraged. He deludes his servants with the idea that success is sure to attend their efforts, and thus he leads them forward one after another, captives at his will. They are blind to the confusion and overthrow which have befallen those who have preceded them in opposing the work of God, and are full of prognostications about what great things they are about to accomplish. It is a glorious consolation for us to know that God rules, and that he can and does control men and their acts to His own glory and the accomplishment of His purposes.

The territorial legislature has adjourned after an unusually heavy session. Several of the most important bills have not been signed by the governor. It is a great disgrace to a republican government like ours to permit such a condition of things to exist as we have had to submit to for years. A stranger is sent out from a distant part of the Union to our country to govern us who is utterly ignorant of the wants of the territory and the measures which are best adapted to the people. He has the power granted to him to veto every bill that may be passed by the unanimous vote of the legislature through any whim, prejudice, or crotchet that he may have, though such bill may be of the most important character and essentially necessary to the well-being of the people and the country. His judgment is permitted to outweigh the judgment of the Territorial Council and House of Representatives, composed, respectively, of thirteen and twenty-six members, and to undo the patient and well-digested labor of weeks. But we must submit to these things and learn patience therefrom. The time will come, however, when we will be freed from such obstacles and have the opportunity of doing every thing necessary for the welfare and prosperity of Zion without hindrance. As it is at present, though irksome and disagreeable, the progress of the great work is not retarded, neither does it sustain any injury which we can not remedy.

The legislature of the State of Deseret met on Monday, and I delivered my message as governor. The members did not deem it necessary to remain long together, merely long enough to enact that the laws of the territory should be made the laws of the state, and to elect the state officers and to take measures to maintain the state organization intact. We wish to keep the machinery all in gear as it is, so that whenever the time shall come to turn the water on to the wheel, we will have nothing to do but hoist the gate.

We are sending down Bro. Thomas Taylor to act again as the agent of the emigration at New York. He will probably start about the fifth of February. Bro. John T. Caine is also appointed to go to New York to act as clerk in the emigration business; Bro. Wm. C. Staines will also start from here about April for the purpose of also assisting in this business. It will be a very great advantage to the emigration and the agents in New York if you would collect the railroad fares of the Saints at Liverpool, also whatever may be due from them on extra luggage. While at Liverpool, and before they embark, the Saints generally have some money with which to pay for their extra luggage, but after they reach New York, in the best of instances they find a great many uses for all the spare cash they have, and the agents pay for the extra luggage, and are put to considerable loss by not being able to collect the money of the people who own such luggage. They have extra baggage when they embark and have not the means to pay for it; they can lessen it to the weight which is allowed by the railroad company, or by disposing of some articles, raise the amount they need. As soon as Bro. Taylor closes a contract with the railroad companies for the transportation of the emigration and freight, he will advise you what amount you will have to collect for fares, and also what weight of luggage is allowed to each full ticket, and the price per pound of the extra luggage.

In shipping provisions for the Saints on the sea the barrels and other packages have not always been marked so distinctly as to prevent confusion and sometimes difficulty in separating them from the ship's provisions. To prevent this in the future, it would be well to have a stencil plate cut, and every package carefully marked with the plate, and then the agent can have no difficulty in separating them at New York from the ship's packages.

I have appointed your brother John W. on a mission to England, and he will start with the other brethren to the States on or about the 5th of Feb'y. He will make a short visit in the States and then proceed to England. I wish you to put him in the best position to be of use and to obtain experience. I would like him to obtain a knowledge of bookkeeping, of which he has a little understanding at present, but I wish the most of his time to be devoted to the work of the ministry—to travel and preaching and the other duties of the priesthood. When not engaged in this manner I wish his spare time to be used in the office. And I hope you will both be economical in the use of funds, and save all that you can.

I have seen a suit of clothing, which you have sent to your children, and you said in your letter that you could send some more to me if it would suit, but you do not say anything about the price, and I do not know what to say about the matter; I should think, however, that it would be a good way to send garments over, cut out and ready made.

Jane [Carrington Young] has just stepped in and is well, and informs me that all the rest are well. With love to yourself and Katie [Catherine Spencer Young] and all the elders, and praying the Lord to bless and preserve you and enable you to fill your high calling, I remain your father,

Brigham Young

Letter dated February 8, 1866

The news of the appointment of his brother John Willard Young to serve a mission in England was greeted by Brigham Young, Jr., with surprise and gratitude: "I cannot tell how thankfull I feel for the privilege of having John W. with me the coming summer. Your instructions regarding him shall be attended to, and we will be as economical as possible, and above all strive to be worthy the blessings of God, which are so freely bestowed upon us."[54] President Young's letter of February 8 brought further detail of John W.'s call and expected time of arrival in England.

Salt Lake City, February 8, 1866

President Brigham Young, Jr.
42 Islington, Liverpool, England

Dear Son,

Since my last letter was written to you I have received nothing further from you.

Your Bro. John W., Hiram B. Clawson, Wm. Jennings, Thomas Taylor and J[ohn] T. Caine started from my office in the stage last evening at about 8.15 p.m. for the States. As I advised you in my last, John W. is appointed a mission to Europe. He will stop a few days in the States and visit your Uncle Edward who is living in Wisconsin, and a cousin of mine in Cincinnati, and also some of my connections in the state of New York. He will be accompanied on these visits by Bro. Caine, as if any of them should conclude to come out here, I wish him to be acquainted with them and in a position to aid them. John will probably be able to sail from New York about the 10th of March. Bro. Jennings will sail at the same time. Bro. Jennings will attend to some business in New York, and then cross to England on a short visit to his folks and will labor in the ministry as he may have opportunity. Bro. Thomas Taylor and Bro. John T. Caine will attend to the emigration business in New York, the former as agent and the latter as clerk and assistant. You should open correspondence with Bro. Taylor and keep them fully advised of the prospects and movements that they may make their preparations accordingly.

The time for the election of our city officers is next Monday. Active steps have been taken of late to have all our people naturalized, so that they may be fully qualified as voters. This subject has not received that attention in the past that it will doubtless in the future. While we have a subtle and designing foe to contend with we must take every precaution to maintain our position and influence here and the government which the Lord, thus far, has given unto us. Were the Saints to be negligent in availing themselves of their privileges as American citizens, and not go to the polls and vote, our enemies would be delighted, as such neglect would give them such an opportunity as they desire. There is some talk about their nominating a ticket to run in opposition, but they will accomplish nothing, and it is a glorious consolation to know that they never can obtain any success over the church and kingdom of God unless the Saints should be careless and off their guard.

I have sent a draft by John W. to New York for him to collect and have the money applied to cover any deficiency of funds in the Liverpool office arising from the payment, on your part, of the drafts I have drawn on you. I wish you to keep the money in England that may be paid into the office for emigration purposes, that you may be able, therewith, to meet my drafts on you, and instead of sending over the emigration funds to the agent from that side, as is usual, draw on New York for the necessary amount, and let the agent get the money there. John W. will inform you whom the money will be left with at New York and whom you can draw on there. Should the draft which I have sent not be honored, they will advise me in time to enable me to have funds there by the time you will need them.

General health and peace prevails. The weather is much milder than it has been, and the snow is fast disappearing.

Your family and friends are well.

With love to yourself, family and the elders who are laboring with you, and praying the Lord to bless you, I remain

Your father,

Brigham Young

Letter dated February 27, 1866

One of the responsibilities that devolved upon Brigham Young, Jr., as he took the reins of the European Mission was the publication of the Church periodical in England, the *Millennial Star*. He declared his intention to write for and edit the periodical, contrary to the policy of Daniel Wells, who had delegated that responsibility to an assistant. "I am desirous of learning how to do these things, and I can never have a better chance,"[55] Brigham wrote his father. His constant drive to overcome his educational failings was at the root of his determination to edit the *Star* himself. "When I first entered the mission I saw at once that if I wished to make myself useful, I must learn my mother tongue correctly, and with very little exception I have studied grammer pretty faithfully, and more especially for the last two months, but am still dependant on the Sub-editor. How long it will take me to become thoroughly conversant with the English language I know not, but that such a time will arrive I feel confident for I am determined to persevere in my studies."[56] As he eased into the actual writing of the editorials, he informed his father, "I feel discouraged sometimes in writing editorials because they are very tame, but when ever you want someone else to do that labor, just give me a hint, and I will retire. But I feel it to be my duty, and until I learn it is not I shall continue to fill the editorial columns of the Star."[57]

President Young's letter of February 27, 1866, assured the young mission president that his course was "wise and satisfactory."

Salt Lake City, February 27, 1866

President Brigham Young, Jr.
42 Islington, Liverpool, England

Dear Son,

Since my last letter to you, dated the 18th instant, your favor of January 15th has been received, and the business and other items been duly noted.

I am gratified to read of your welfare and progress, and to notice that you are diligent in attending to the duties which devolve upon you and in seeking to obtain the spirit of your calling and position. There is no reason why you should lack in the least degree the necessary spirit, knowledge and revelation which you require to enable you to magnify your priesthood and fill with honor the station assigned to you. It is a highly responsible calling, that which you now occupy, and your mind should be open at all times to receive the teachings and whisperings of the Spirit, that nothing may be neglected in teaching, counseling, reproving or warning the people, or in regulating the various fields and conferences that would forward the progress of truth or increase the love and understanding of it from growing in the hearts of the people.

So far as I can judge from your letters and the *Star,* your course in the management of the affairs of the work and the disposition of the elders is wise and satisfactory. You have our prayers and faith continually exercised in your behalf that you may be blessed in your labors and be preserved from every evil.

There has nothing particularly noteworthy occurred here since I last wrote to you. The weather is becoming milder, and good health generally prevails. The news from the East which we have been receiving these past few days is very interesting and spicy and somewhat exciting. Bro. [William H.] Hooper has informed us in his letters that the feeling at Washington was very intense against us, and there was a deep-seated, sullen determination manifested on all hands to strangle the remaining twin[58] as early as possible. We know what their feelings are as well as they themselves know them. We know that the wicked are uneasy and are plotting continually against the work of God, and the nature of their designs are manifested to us from time to time by the Spirit of God, so that we can be prepared to guard ourselves against their attempts.

Present reports indicate that there are affairs enough of importance to occupy the attention of congressmen at Washington without having any very great amount of spare time to meddle with our business. Our enemies here have been exceedingly jubilant of late in anticipation of the trouble that they have been hoping to bring on us. The train was laid, and as they supposed, it only needed the match to be applied to produce the desired explosion. But they will be disappointed. They will find that when they commence a war with the Almighty and His purposes with a determination to thwart them, they have a power to contend with in the presence of which they are but as vile worms. When they think they have the trap all ready to spring, with the expectation of securing their prey, they will find that the proposed prey is not there.

Measures are being taken at present to organize a company here to supply our northern neighbors in the Territories of Montana and Idaho with flour and other produce at remunerative, yet moderate, prices. It is hoped that if the proposed plan can be fairly carried into operation, it will prevent the unwise competition of our people which has enabled speculators in those Territories to take advantage of them in their dealings. By organization the price can be kept up to something like uniformity, and be a great benefit to our citizens and also to the citizens of the North, as they will not be left to be preyed upon by speculators.

In relation to the chartering of a steamer for the Saints, you had better charter a good sailing vessel or a screw, whichever will answer the best and can be obtained on the best terms.

I am much pleased with the specimen page of the Book of Mormon which you have forwarded. An edition of that size, and in that type, will be very handsome, and I should like marginal notes, if you can obtain them, but if you should have notes arranged, be sure and get as good ones as you can, so that they may be satisfactory.

Your Brother John W. will be with you, I suppose, when you get this. The last word that we heard from the brethren they were at St. Louis, and were well.

With love to yourself and family, John W. and all the elders who are with you, in which the brethren join, and praying the Lord to bless and uphold and preserve you. I remain,

Your father,

Brigham Young

Letter dated May 23, 1866

On April 3, 1866, Brigham Young, Jr., reported the progress of the European Mission under his administration, noting that "inspite of all that I can do, backed as I know that I am by the brethren, baptisms are growing more seldom, and in some instances the people exhibit an apathy that is almost unaccountable." He assured his father that he did not feel discouraged, but in assessing causes for the decline in growth of the mission, he added, "Oh, the corruption that is raging like some terrible epidemic among the people. The primitive innocence so readily found among the rural districts a few years since is fast being replaced by city vices. It seems to me that none are too poor nor too rich to sin—the judge with his perwig [periwig], firey red face and quivering nose, his insufficient legs and gouty toes, rolling homeward in his fine carriage from attending court, exhibits the same markes of disapation that is so indelibly stamped upon the outcast whom he has just sent to the treadmill."[59]

Having been away from home nearly two years, Brigham received the following letter of May 23 from his father with added joy when he read the invitation it contained to return home for a short visit.

Salt Lake City, May 23, 1866

President Brigham Young, Jr.
42 Islington, Liverpool, England

Dear Son,

Your favors of March 27th and April 3rd have been received and the contents duly noted. We have been looking for a letter from you for a few days respecting the chartering of vessels for the Saints, but the mails have been much delayed through bad roads.

Since my last to you, everything has been very peaceable in the city, and we have been enjoying ourselves as well as we do usually. The publication of an ordinance by the city council, giving the marshal authority, upon the warrant of an alderman, to abate illegal liquor saloons, billiard saloons, &c., as nuisances, has created considerable excitement. A petition was signed by about fifteen persons who thought their crafts were in danger from this ordinance, and presented to Colonel [Carrol H.] Potter, commander of the post at Camp Douglas, asking protection from the action of the city council. Col. Potter, accompanied by Captains Grimes and Price, waited upon me on the 8th instant to obtain my promise to the effect that I would prevent the property of gentiles from being destroyed without due process of law. We had considerable conversation, but as I saw there was but little prospect of anything satisfactory being arrived at by such conversation, I requested Col. Potter to communicate his wishes to me in writing, which he promised to do, but which promise he failed to keep, though he did write to me and endeavored to fasten upon me that I had made a pledge to himself and accompanying officers "that the private property of gentile citizens in Salt Lake should not be molested without due course of law." Of course, this was a responsibility that I did not and could not assume; I could not protect the property of gentiles from the thousand and one casualties to which property is subject in this as in all other cities and you would think no person, who entertained the least conception of the duties of citizenship, would make such a request of a private citizen. I had a reply forwarded to him denying the giving of such pledge by me, and reiterating my request to communicate his wishes in writing, and stating that I thought I could answer him satisfactorily. But to this letter no reply was received. There is no doubt that upon consultation with legal friends, shrewder than he, they advised him not to commit himself by communicating to me on paper such requests as he had verbally made of me.

Since receiving this call there has nothing occurred specially worthy of note among the class who felt that they were interfered with by the action of the city council.

The Indians have committed numerous depredations of late,[60] and have killed several persons in Sanpete and Sevier counties, and one man in Utah County. The people in Piute, Sevier, Sanpete, Wasatch and Summit counties, as well as those living south of the rim of the Basin, have been counseled to abandon their small settlements and move together in bodies of not less than one hundred and fifty men in a place, and to build good, substantial forts for themselves and families and safe corrals for their stock which can be easily protected. This has been counsel which has been invariably given in the formation of new settlements, but the pressure to obtain the privilege of scattering into small settlements where a greed for land and stock could be gratified has been heavy and constant.

Fifty of our young men, well-mounted and well-armed, under the command of Colonel Heber P. Kimball, with a company of a similar number from Provo, have gone to Sanpete and Sevier counties to help the people move together and to guard them against any attack that the red men might feel to make upon them. If the counsel which has been given to the people be strictly observed, these Indian troubles will soon cease and they will sue for peace and stop their depredations.

I have had no word direct from John W. since he left home excepting a few lines which he wrote to me on the eve of his departure for Liverpool. I would like him to write me an account of his travels and visits in the States.

Any time that you should wish to send special word to me upon any subject that you may want to get to me quickly you can write to Bro. William H. Miles, New York, and he can telegraph right through to me and not cost anything. Should you send to him to telegraph me, you must study the words that will convey your ideas in the most compact form, say six, eight, or ten words.

If you should like to leave John W. in England and come home on a visit this next winter—say start from there in July or August—and can leave the mission in such a condition that the affairs and business will suffer no injury during your absence, I should have no objections to your coming. This you can do if at any time you should want to come. Bro. Orson [Pratt] could take charge as well as not, and attend to all the business of the mission, writing for the *Star*, &c., if he would only adhere strictly to the counsel which was given in my last letter. It would be more pleasing to John W. to have you stay there until he comes home, and as you have a wife you can stay there pretty well; still, if you should like to slip over for a little while you can do so.

Enclosed I send you two cards containing our new alphabet. I wish to have a fount of long primer type cast in the new alphabet by Messrs. Miller and Richard, Edinburgh. The lowercase letters should be smaller in the face than the body of the type, so that when the capitals are cast the full size of the body, the same proportion may be maintained between the capitals and lowercase letters in the new alphabet that now exists in the old or

Roman that we now use. In the letters which we send you on the card, you will notice that the thick and fine lines are not uniform, that is, the thick strokes are not of uniform thickness, and the thin strokes of a uniform fineness. In making the punches, this irregularity should be avoided, and the coarse and fine strokes be made uniform as they are in the present Roman letters.

Before the fount is cast I wish to receive a specimen of the letters to inspect them and satisfy myself about their form; if they do not suit me, I do not want them. We did order a fount of this new alphabet east in the States, but the work was so miserably done, and the type made such a poor appearance in print that it has done as much as anything else to create a prejudice against the alphabet. We do not want to have such a failure in this fount which I now order, as there was in that. I send this order to you to have it filled by Messrs. Miller and Richard, having understood that they are very responsible and do good work, in the hope that this type will be finished in the best possible style. The letter should be clear, sharp and distinct. You can give them the necessary guaranty that we will take the punches &c., so that they need be under no expense in this experiment that they will not get paid for, if the work is done to suit in a good, workmanlike manner.

Bro. Orson should be a good judge of this work, both of the shape of the letters and of good type.

Your family and John W.'s are well. The children are feeling very fine; they say they used to want to see Pa and Ma very much, but they do not feel that time is so long with them now as it was.

The folks all join me in love to you and family. Give my love to John W. and Brother Orson Pratt and all the elders.

May the Lord bless you and all the faithful is the prayer of your father.

Brigham Young

Letter dated June 15, 1866

Not the least of the challenges facing Brigham Young, Jr., in his administration of the European Mission was supervision of the yearly emigration of Saints from Europe to the United States, a task that required the provisioning and chartering of ships and the organizing of traveling companies. Plans for the emigration necessarily began early in the year so that emigrants might arrive on the frontier of America in time to cross the plains before bad weather. After the departure of Daniel Wells, Brigham handled the emigration of 1866 alone. Much of his time in the early months of that year was taken in emigration matters. "It has been an eventful period in my life," he wrote his father, "and I had but little experience to bring to bear against the multiplicity of business which accumulated on every side, but with the approving smile of our God thus far have I been successful, and I do verily know that it is possible to do whatsoever He may command if we but do it in His name. I have been blessed far above what I could have hoped; men have almost invariably yielded to my terms, and what occasionally loomed up before me like a high mountain, has dwindled to a mere mole hill when I have asked the Lord to open the way."[61]

One difficulty facing the mission leader in the spring of 1866 was the scarcity of ships. The business manager of the British shipping firm Guion and Company informed him in March that "vessels have not for many years been as scarce as they are at present."[62] The scarcity was due to severe storms that had prevailed upon the ocean: within one week 90 vessels were reported wrecked upon the shores of England, and during the first three months of the year 568 vessels were lost at sea. "We hear of shipwrecks every day," wrote Brigham Jr. "Many large vessels have gone down with two or three hundred people on board in mid-ocean, and several of these vessels have been first class steamers supposed to be capable of riding out any gale providing they had plenty of sea room."[63]

After seeing 3,327 Saints safely leave the shores of Great Britain, and an additional 1,100 depart from Denmark, Brigham Jr. summarized his first experience directing Church emigration in a letter to his father: "When first commencing the business of this years emigration, I trembled for the result. . . . I do verily know that it would have been utterly impossible for me to have accomplished the work required at my hands if the Lord had not softened men's hearts and opened the way that vessels were obtained. Many times have mountains loomed up before me, and I had fainted only that I know in whom to put my trust. The clouds which seemed so oppressive, have melted away . . .

and I could smile on what a few moments before seemed insurmountable obstacles. . . ."[64]

Salt Lake City, June 15, 1866

President Brigham Young, Jr.
42 Islington, Liverpool, England

Dear Son,

    Your welcome favor of May 8th containing the intelligence of the sailing of the *John Bright* and the *Caroline*, has been received, and been perused with interest. We have been anxious to hear from you and about affairs in your field, emigration, &c., and the receipt of your letter has relieved the anxiety. It is gratifying to read your description of your efforts to obtain ships, and the signal manner in which you have been blessed in securing suitable vessels upon, what may be considered this year, reasonable terms to carry our people. You are obtaining an experience now that cannot fail to be of great benefit to you. We have remembered you constantly in our prayers asking the Lord to open your way in obtaining ships and to bless you in all your labors. The Lord is kind and merciful and never forsakes nor forgets His children who put their trust in Him.

    Encouraging reports have reached us respecting the progress of the teams which have gone down to bring up the poor, and we hope that, under the blessing of the Lord, all the trains with the Saints will reach this place early in the fall.

    The weather until the last day or two has been remarkably cool and stormy for this latitude. Since the severe storm to which I alluded in my last, we have had considerable rain, and as a consequence the streams are very high; Jordan has never been so high since our settlement here as it is at present. The weather now is fine, and gives promise of being more seasonable than it has been.

    President [Daniel H.] Wells started for San Pete County on Monday, the 11th instant, with a company of twenty-five men; he will push forward as energetically as possible the fortifying of the settlements, that the people may be able to dwell secure from Indian depredations and attacks. On Sunday last, the 10th, the

Indians made a raid on Round Valley, Millard Co., and drove off 150 head of cattle and 5 horses, and killed Father [James] Ivie and another man. They moved eastward with the stock. At the crossing of the Sevier Gen. W[illiam] B. Pace, who was out with a scouting party of 25 men, fell in with them on Monday, the 11th, and a fight ensued. Though the brethren were outnumbered three to one, without counting the Indians who were guarding the stock, they succeeded in inflicting severe loss on the Indians, and, what is worthy of notice, though compelled to fight on the open ground, and part of the time under a heavy cross fire, they lost neither a man nor a horse, one of the brethren only being shot in the leg, but not so seriously as to disable him from active service. The Indians were too numerous for the brethren to recover the stock. Col. Heber P. Kimball's command came up that evening and on the morning of the 12th a command of about 86 men started for Grass Valley—the rendezvous of the Indians. We are expecting intelligence from them every hour. Since Bro. Wells started, upwards of 80 men have started from this city to San Pete Co. The bands of Indians which surround us do not countenance the acts of this predatory band of outlaws. The success of Black Hawk, and the few who were with him, in murder and robbery last season, has enabled him to collect a band of renegade Indians who hope, under his leadership, to gratify their murderous and thievish propensities. They are not a tribe, neither is Black Hawk a recognized chief, but they are banded together for purposes of plunder. It is hoped that their operations will be speedily checked.

Everything is quiet in the city, and good health generally prevails. The prospects for fruit and grain crops continue good. The families of the elders are well so far as known. Accept my love to yourself and folks, and give my love to John W., Bro. Orson [Pratt] and all the other elders in which the brethren here join. Praying the Lord to uphold and prosper you, I remain your father,

Brigham Young

[*Postscript contains drafts on the Liverpool Office*]

Letter dated August 11, 1866

Having been informed that his brother John W. had been called to serve a mission in England and would leave New York about March 10, Brigham Young, Jr., became increasingly watchful for his arrival as April dawned. "My eyes are weak looking for him, and I often think of the old adage 'hope defered maketh the heart sick,' but I manage to comfort myself with the idea that he won't be over a month longer, and that will soon pass. I imagine sometimes that when I see John, I shall to some extent behold wife, children, father, mother, brothers and sisters and the friends whom I have not seen for almost two years, all wrapt up in Johnny."[65]

John W. arrived in England on April 14 and five days later the two brothers left for Denmark on business connected with the Scandinavian emigration. During this trip they also visited Norway, Sweden, Finland, and Russia. While in Denmark they caught a brief glimpse of European royalty when the king of that country and the crown prince of Russia (who was there to wed the king's daughter), arrived in Copenhagen. Brigham described the spectacle for his father: "They seemed very much like other people, and when I saw the King of Denmark stumble on the stairs I thought him rather more clumsy than men generally are. We also saw the crown prince of Russia talking with a lady, and he seemed somewhat embarrassed twirling his hat in a rather undignified stile." He concluded, "It is the mind that makes the man, Royal birth alone never can."[66]

In his letter of August 11 President Young expressed his delight at his sons' opportunity for further travel and education in the nations of Europe.

Salt Lake City, August 11, 1866

President Brigham Young, Jr., and
Elder John W. Young
42 Islington, Liverpool, England

Dear Sons,

As your Brother Oscar, with Elders F[ranklin] D. Richards and N[icholas] Groesbeck, start to England to fill missions on Monday next, the 13th instant, I take the opportunity of writing to you. Your favors of July 4th, written at Christiania, Norway, were received a few days ago, and have been perused with pleasure. Your travels, as you describe them, and your visits to various places of interest must afford you much pleasure, and you should appreciate the opportunities which you now have sufficiently to profit by all that you see and are brought in contact with. Had I the privilege of traveling in the old world, and visiting the various countries and mingling with the different peoples, I should enjoy such opportunities very much. In these respects the young men of our people who go abroad have many advantages over their fathers. When we visited Europe we could not travel very extensively; the want of means prevented our visiting places that did not lay in our path in calling upon the people to repent. Affairs have changed very much since that time.

Since my last (the 30th ult.) Bro. [Daniel H.] Wells has returned from San Pete in good health and spirits. Washakie and upwards of two hundred of his tribe came a few days ago into the city to see me and renew our friendly intercourse. He and his chiefs feel very fine. We fed them well, and they seemed much gratified by their treatment.

We have had uncommonly heavy rains for the past few days which, added to the rain that fell during the previous week, is likely to do considerable damage to hay and grain. The weather has seemed to be more like English weather than that which we usually have here at this season.

Those companies which have started on their return here with the emigrating Saints are, so far as heard from, making good progress on their journey. The first company, Capt. Thos. E. Ricks', passed Sweetwater bridge today. His is the second company. We hear that the last company left New York for the frontiers on the 1st instant, and we are daily expecting to hear of their arrival at Wyoming and their departure on to the Plains.

Our home telegraph poles are set and are ready for the wire which is being brought by the teams. We have ordered 500 miles of wire with insulators, &c. The new telegraph line wire is being stretched from this city to San Francisco, and another line is being put up between here and Montana. A railroad route is to be surveyed from here to the falls of Snake River this fall. The party is now engaged in surveying from the point where they discontinued their labor last year west of this city to Carson Valley. They are pushing the road rapidly from the east and west. It will soon be up to Fort Kearney [Nebraska] and it is the intention at present to have the road finished up to Julesburg by spring, and to have the gap completed that is now open in Iowa. Should this expectation be realized, there will be direct railroad communication between New York and Julesburg.

From the reports which reach us we judge that at our present outfitting point the people in the neighborhood are far from being our friends. The cattle of one of our trains were seized for damages because they were running on the open prairie, but which was claimed by a person to be his grass land. They also attached the telegraph wire that we had there, on a trumped-up claim of indebtedness on the part of myself, Bros. [Heber C.] Kimball, [Newel K.] Whitney and [Parley P.] Pratt, said to have been contracted in Kirtland about thirty years ago. The wire &c., were only released and permitted to come on by the brethren giving bonds. There was no indebtedness of my contracting left unsettled, and none of the other brethren's of which we can get any knowledge. The whole proceeding is a swindle, and designed to vex and annoy and rob us.

We are expecting Capt. [William H.] Hooper and Bro. [Thomas B. H.] Stenhouse home from the States tomorrow. Gen. John E. Smith, the new Assessor of U.S. Internal Revenue for this Territory, is their fellow traveler.

Everything is moving on smoothly and quietly in the city. General health and peace prevail, and all are as busy at work as bees. Your families are all well; Clara [Stenhouse Young] is quite recovered, and is able to be about as usual. Your mother's health is also usually good. Luna [Young Thatcher] was safely delivered of a fine boy on yesterday morning; the mother and child are both doing well. The elders' families, so far as known, are in good health.

I desire to remind you again on the subject of tithing and the emigration fund. The importance of these duties should be kept constantly before the people. A neglect of these will bring condemnation to all who are guilty. We are living in a day, and at a time, when all persons especially who profess to be Latter-day Saints, should stretch forth their hands and exert themselves to roll forth the work of God and to establish His righteousness. The Saints in Zion have shown their faith by their works, and they are witnessing constantly unto the heavens and the earth that they

love the work of God. This year alone the cost of the outfit sent to
the frontiers to bring up the poor Saints is but little, if any, less
than half a million of dollars. This amount is ventured ungrudgingly
and without murmuring. Besides this, there are the other
numerous calls to be responded to. These Indian troubles have
called away hundreds of our young, able-bodied men from their
labor at a time, too, when their services have been most needed.
Altogether these expeditions have been a very serious tax upon
the entire people in spending valuable time and furnishing outfits
which in this country are very expensive. Beside these labors, there
have been poles for five hundred miles of telegraph line got
out and erected, and money furnished in part and the remainder by
myself for the wire, insulators, &c., &c. Then there are roads to
build and keep in repair, water ditches and canals to open, school
houses to erect, and a great variety of other public labors to attend
to, all of which the people of Zion go to with their might to
perform. It is a noticeable fact that the more they do the more
they are able to do—their exertions increase their capacities and
abilities. To keep pace with the people of Zion and to be one with
them the people abroad must make corresponding exertions
according to their ability in their own behalf and the behalf of the
work of God.

Wherever you want Bro. Franklin's [D. Richards] help you
can use him. He, as well as Bro. Orson [Pratt], is accustomed to
emigration and the other business of the mission, and they both can
operate to advantage.

The new tabernacle is being pushed ahead, but the lateness
of the season and the heavy rains have retarded the getting out of
lumber and delayed the work.

We have but few troops here at present, and they are regulars.
[Patrick E.] Connor is out of the service, and is here now as plain
"Pat" engaged in mining business, which, as government pap has
been withdrawn, will very likely, if he pursue it diligently, burst
him up financially. Col. [John E.] Smith still continues friendly. We
have had quite an influx of lawyers into the city of late. Like the
birds of prey they snuff the carcass from afar. Business is poor
where they have been, but they imagine that with the land claims
and other business the enemies of the truth promise them here,
they will reap an abundant harvest. Armies have not been found to

operate well in breaking us up, but it is now hoped that vexatious lawsuits and setting up and enforcing claims for our land may do it.

Your mother and all the family join me in love to you. Presidents [Heber C.] Kimball and [Daniel H.] Wells and Bro. Geo. Q. [Cannon] send their love to you; remember us to Bro. Orson and all the elders.

Praying the Lord to endow you richly with His grace and to make you equal to the performance of every duty,

I remain, your father,

Brigham Young

Letter dated March 28, 1867

In response to his father's invitation on May 23 to return home on a brief visit during the winter of 1866-67, Brigham Young, Jr., left his wife and a newborn son in England and departed for home on September 19. On the eve of his departure he reported on conditions in the mission: "the people will not hear the Gospel."[67] The few who were being baptized, he noted, were mainly from among those who had once been in the Church. He wrote that the mood of the people was ugly—that fear of the hangman was the only thing that restrained them from shedding blood of the missionaries. "The hatred which they bear [toward] the servants of God is quite as deep and bitter as that manifested by the American nation." But, he concluded, "the brethren as a general thing do not feel discouraged, but on the contrary redouble their exertions hoping to see some fruits of their labors, but many of them have been thus far disappointed. Perhaps it may be like bread thrown upon the waters, seen after many days. But it is the opinion of some that the bread has been thrown into the mud and will be seen no more."[68]

While crossing the Atlantic on September 24 Brigham experienced one of the storms that had wreaked such havoc with shipping, some 1500 vessels having been sunk during the first nine months of the year. "The waves are mountains high. The vessel is shipping seas both fore and aft. At 9 p.m. the wheel house tiller and compass were stove to atoms, severely injuring two of the men, washing one of them clear out onto the upper deck. Also our bowsprit was swept away carrying the foretop gallant mast. The Capt[ain] had another tiller which was connected with the rudder, so that we were soon all right again. The sea is breaking over the vessel, and it seems at times as though she would not be able to rise from the watery grave in which she is litterally buried. There were none of the passengers whom I heard express themselves at retiring, that expected ever [to] see another sun. It was all I could do to keep my faith perfect. Nothing but the power of the Lord did save us. The Capt. did not leave the deck for two days. I prayed fervently for deliverance, and the Lord heard my prayers and comforted my heart."

The next day the storm continued: "The gale is fearful this morning, and the vessel looks very like a wreck. The sea looks like mountains and is one sheet of foam. The motion of the vessel is fearful, and we are making very little headway. For two days the saloon was wholly closed, and we were deprived of fresh air. The water was reported two feet deep in the steerage and many of the cabin passengers were washed out of their berths. We continue to ship immense seas. Towards night the storm was much abated. People have found who I am and Mormonism is on the topic. Many men are making enquiries. I have been respectfully treated thus far."[69]

Brigham Jr. arrived in Salt Lake City on October 10. After the harrowing experience at sea, his exuberance upon seeing his home is understandable: "Oh! how glorious the valleys and the mountains surrounding them looked after an absence of nearly three years," he records in his diary. "My father met me with every expression of love and kindness, and the spirit of the Lord manifested unto me that my labors were accepted. What joy to meet again wife and children, father, mother, brothers and sisters, relatives and friends. How shall I sufficiently thank my father and my God for all the blessings which suround me. Oh! Lord give me strength to show my gratitude by a long life of faithful service that I may dwell eternally with Thee is the greatest desire of my heart."[70]

Brigham Young, Jr., spent the winter of 1866-67 in Salt Lake City, during which time he was present in deliberations of the Quorum of Twelve and was named to the exclusive Council of Fifty, an organization that had been created in the days of Joseph Smith as a forerunner of the political kingdom of God. Although his father had given him an option to remain at home or return to England, he chose the latter course of action in order to present his successor in Europe with orderly and well-balanced accounts. He departed from Salt Lake City on February 4, traveling in deep snow that slowed his progress. Even aboard a train powered by two locomotives, he found that progress was measured. As the train plowed its way eastward through snow-drifts, "the concussions were sometimes terrific and then we would become stationary—powerless to retreat or advance, until the road was cleared by shoveling."[71] He finally arrived in New York late in February and after a short trip to Washington, D.C., continued on to England.

President Brigham Young's letter of March 28 was written ten days after Brigham Jr. arrived back in England. The document reveals that in addition to four of Brigham Young's sons—Joseph A., Brigham Jr., John W., and Oscar Brigham—who had labored or were then laboring as missionaries in England, another, Brigham Heber, was about to be sent there.

Salt Lake City, March 28, 1867

President B. Young, Jr.
42 Islington, Liverpool, England

Dear Son,

Your letters of the 18th and 24 written from Chicago, New York, and Washington have all reached me though the two former have been much delayed. We have been much pleased to hear respecting your movements, as with the exception of the telegram you sent on your arrival in New York, we had not heard a word from you yourself, or through Brother [William H.] Hooper. I hope you have had a pleasant trip across the ocean, and that you found your family, John W., and the other elders well.

It is our intention to send a number of elders from here at this spring conference, and as we mean to hurry them over, so that they will probably reach England in time, I would like you and John W. to remain till their arrival and see them distributed. You will then have the most pleasant part of the summer in which to cross the ocean and come home. As soon as they are appointed I shall forward you a list of their names. I expect that your Bro. Heber B. will be one of the co[mpany]. Myself and President [Daniel H.] Wells, and Elders G[eorge] A. Smith and Geo. Q. Cannon have been holding a two day meeting at Grantsville, Tooele

Co. They have a very fine new meetinghouse there in which the people can be comfortably assembled. The meetings were very much enjoyed by all, both speakers and hearers, and much valuable instruction was given; the Spirit leading us to speak particularly upon the subjects of union, and obedience in temporal matters, and sustaining ourselves, and withdrawing support from our enemies, and combining for the purchase of machinery to engage more extensively in home manufacturers.

The weather still continues very cold for the season. We have had considerable snow this last week, and the mountains are covered down below their bases. We had snow and very bad roads going to Grantsville, and in returning we traveled through a snow storm till we reached the confines of the city; being prepared for such a contingency, however, we suffered no special inconvenience.

I have just received a letter from two young relatives of mine, named respectively, Catherine Morton, and Gertrude F. Lewis, their address is P.O. Box 114, Chicago, Ill. They are granddaughters of two of my mother's cousins. They express a desire to come to Utah. Though they are both young, they say they are obliged to depend on their own labors for a living, and are qualified to teach piano music, and one can teach school. Both have had some experience as teachers. I shall write them today and give them the P.O. address at New York where, to the care of Bro. [William H.] Miles, they can write you and John W. and inform you what their address is &c. I shall inform them that if they wish to come to the valley they can do so when you return.

Peace and good health are general here. Your family and John W.'s, and your mother and the folks are enjoying usual health. They all join in sending love to you, John W., Oscar B., Katie [Catherine Spencer Young] and the elders.

It is very cheering to get such news from Oscar, and I hope through perseverance and the favorable circumstances in which he is now placed that he will improve himself and acquire an education, for he will be very useful in the ministry.

You will please attend to what I have written respecting our relatives in Chicago; they are distant relatives, but still I would like to have you treat them as your cousins.

Praying the Lord to bless and preserve you, and to bring you home in safety,

I am your father,
Brigham Young

Letter dated May 21, 1867

Between the time Brigham Young, Jr., returned to England on March 18 and his final departure from the mission on June 29, 1867, he had organized the year's emigration and traveled twice to Paris, France, having been selected by the Utah Legislature to deliver Utah products to the Paris Exposition that year. On both visits to the French capital he went out of his way for a look at European heads of state, which he delighted to describe to his father. In Paris with his brother John W. on May 5, he watched the Emperor Napoleon parade his troops at the Imperial Palace. "He was cheered by the crowd, and the troops followed him with loving eyes, and altho' the French idolize him, yet that cannot keep him from growing old, and it is the opinion of many that he will not live many years longer."[72]

A month later Brigham was at the northern railroad station in Paris when Napoleon met William, the "grisly old King of Prussia," and the crown prince. "The King appeared a hard featured old sinner, and neither did I like the looks of his son. His countenance did not forshaddow a noble mind, but was rather the harbinger of selfishness and contracted ideas."[73] As the two leaders drove away seated side-by-side, he expressed amazement that "these two individuals, who were aching to fight each other six weeks ago, had found a state carriage large enough for them and two others."[74]

The following day Brigham paid twelve francs for a seat to witness the royal review at the Bois de Boulogne. Unbeknown, the price also included the view of an assassination attempt on the lives of the two rulers. After watching a grand charge by some ten thousand cavalry, with helmets and cutlasses glittering in the sun, Brigham saw a "lunatic pole" suddenly take aim and fire at the two emperors. Only quick action by an officer who plunged his horse into the line of fire—embedding the bullet in the animal's head and splattering the royal personages with blood—saved them from serious injury or death. Brigham also noticed the pistol burst in the hand of the would-be assassin, "tearing off two of his fingers."[75]

Upon returning to England, Brigham Young, Jr., terminated his presidency of the European Mission with a valedictory sermon on June 23. Accompanied by his wife and two children, he sailed six days later for America.

The letter of President Young of May 21, 1867, was the last of his correspondence with this son during the latter's British Mission.

Salt Lake City, May 21, 1867

President B. Young, Jr., and John W. Young
42 Islington, Liverpool, England

Dear Sons,

Your favors of March 13 and 28 were received by me on my return from the South whither I had been absent twenty-four days, and have been perused with much pleasure. I write now in hopes that my letter will reach you before you leave Liverpool, as you advise me that you intend to sail on the 29th June. I am depending on your advising me what time you will be at the terminus of the railroad and what you will be likely to need there. My advice is that you buy your own vehicles to ride home in. You probably contemplate stopping in the States to visit your own and Katie's [Catherine Spencer Young] relatives; if so, a telegram from New York may reach me sufficiently early to enable me to have you met at the railroad terminus if it is needed. I calculate there will be a train there for freight between the first and fifteenth of July.

Your brother Heber is about starting from this city on his mission, the train with which he is going down started a day or two ago. He intends to go out with Heber P. Kimball and overtake it. You will probably meet him in New York. I am sure he will be very glad to see you, and you him. Encourage Oscar in his labors; tell him to persevere, seek for wisdom and do right and he will overcome. His family are well. I trust your voyage over will be pleasant to yourselves and Katie and the children, and that you will have a safe and prosperous journey home. Our faith and prayers will be exercised, as they always are, in your behalf.

We have had an exceedingly pleasant trip to Saint George and back. We held thirty-four meetings, at most of which I addressed the people, besides having several councils and attending to considerable other business. The trip was a fatiguing one, though I endured it very well. I suffered on my return with a boil on my ankle, which still troubles me a little.

You have doubtless seen the confession published by Bro. A[masa] M. Lyman. On his return south I was informed that he had conveyed the idea to the people that he had been pinched to make this confession, and that his views were unchanged. His case was investigated as we went south, and it was decided to cut him off from the Quorum of the Twelve Apostles and to take his priesthood from him. His erroneous teachings have been found to be more extensive than was imagined.

We had a fine rain on Saturday night and Sunday last which was very timely as everything was very dry. Scarcely a drop of rain had fallen during our absence from the city. The prospects for fruit and crops are very good, though in the north we hear that the grasshoppers are very numerous, whether they do damage or not, however, will be as the Lord wills.

Times are dull and there is but little demand for flour or grain. The merchants on Whiskey St. can scarcely get enough day by day to pay their rents. The people manifest the strongest disposition we have ever witnessed to carry into effect the counsels which have been given respecting the Word of Wisdom and obedience in temporal as well as spiritual matters. There has been no coercion used, no covenants required. The principle has been set forth and the people seemed prepared to receive and carry it out willingly. Peace and good health prevail throughout the Territory.

Your mother and your families and all the folks are well and all join with me in love to you. Give my love to Oscar, Katie, Bros. Franklin [D. Richards] and Orson [Pratt] (if he has not sailed) and all the elders, in which Presdts. [Heber C.] Kimball and [Daniel H.] Wells and Bro. Geo. Q. [Cannon] join, and praying the Lord to bless and preserve you all and bring you home in safety.

I am your father,
Brigham Young

JOHN WILLARD YOUNG

John Willard Young
1844-1924

On February 11, 1924, John Willard Young, the third son of Brigham and Mary Ann Angell Young, died in an obscure apartment house overlooking Broadway in New York City, where he had supported himself as an elevator operator during the closing years of his life. The obscurity of his final years was not characteristic of his life. Motivated by an intense desire to build up Zion and break down the prejudice that existed against the Latter-day Saints, John W.'s life was an ambitious succession of business enterprises, promotional schemes, and church service that extended from Mexico's Pacific coast to the financial capitals of Europe. Possessed of a suave, flamboyant personality, expensive tastes, and unexcelled drive and determination, John W. admitted that in some instances he had been unwise and overzealous, creating some of the prejudice he had sought to dispel, but he maintained a staunch loyalty to the Latter-day Saints and died asserting that all he did in life was in their interest. "In the character of John W. Young, I find zeal and discretion combined," wrote Thomas L. Kane to Brigham Young after personally meeting the President's son. "His prepossessing appearance and address introduce him favorably to the most prejudiced. I know no one whom you can employ to more advantage for intermediary oral communications. I have given him my own confidence. He loves you."[1]

Born in Nauvoo, Illinois, on October 1, 1844, John W. was four years old when his family arrived in the newly settled Salt Lake Valley. In 1857, at age twelve, he accompanied his father on the expedition to Fort Limhi on the headwaters of the Columbia River. That same year, having organized a juvenile detachment of the Nauvoo Legion, John led his uniformed cohort of fifty peers in review before the Saints congregated in Big Cottonwood Canyon at the 24th of July celebration. He also performed messenger service between Salt Lake City and militia encampments in Echo Canyon during the Utah War. In succeeding years he hauled poles for the transcontinental telegraph line and labored on the construction of the Salt Lake Theatre. In 1862 he enlisted with Robert T. Burton's command, which had been called to protect the overland mail and telegraph lines from Indian depredations. Struggling through deep snow and intense cold, Burton's men faced almost certain annihilation at one point of their campaign when Crow Indians stole all of their horses. John was one of several men who tracked the thieves and recovered the animals.

John Young's introduction to the New York business world, where he was to spend much of the remainder of his life, came in 1863-64 when he assisted Horace Eldredge, William Staines, and his brother Joseph A. Young in the Church immigration business.

Although ordained an apostle by his father on November 22, 1855, at age eleven, John W. was never included as a member of the Quorum of Twelve. At nineteen he was appointed an assistant counselor to the First Presidency. Subsequently, he labored as a missionary in England, was a member of the Salt Lake Stake high council, president of the Salt Lake Stake, and first counselor in the First Presidency. After his father's death in August 1877 he continued as a counselor to the Twelve Apostles until financial difficulties compelled him to resign in October 1891.

A nineteenth century Utah railroad magnate, John W. Young began his railroad building career in 1868 on the transcontinental line through Utah, contracting a portion of the Union Pacific road through Echo Canyon. A year later he was appointed secretary of the newly organized Utah Central, connecting Salt Lake City with the main line at Ogden, Utah, and supervised the track-laying of that road. In following years his railroad enterprises injected economic life into numerous Latter-day Saint communities. His most notable efforts were in connection with the Atlantic and Pacific road in Arizona; the Utah Northern, a narrow gauge line from Ogden, Utah, to Franklin, Idaho; the Salt Lake and Fort Douglas Railway, a belt road connecting the Utah Central and depots in Salt Lake City with the Denver and Rio Grand Western; the Salt Lake and Eastern, linking the mines at Park City with Salt Lake City; the Utah Western, built to haul salt, sand, and passengers between Salt Lake City and the lake twelve miles to the west; and street railways in Salt Lake City and Provo. His most ambitious railroad scheme was a 1500-mile line through northern Mexico, planned to link the Mormon colonies in Chihuahua with Deming, New Mexico, to the north and Guaymas on the Mexican Pacific coast to the southwest. Soon known as the "Mañana Railroad" because of repeated delays of promised payrolls, the North Mexican line failed from lack of finances before any track was laid.

In addition to his railroads, John W. Young was a prime mover in other diverse enterprises including the Deseret Museum and Menagerie in Salt Lake City; a woolen factory at Moencopi, Arizona; two large Arizona cattle companies; the Salt Lake Supply and Forwarding Company; the Salt Lake Rock Company; the Great Western Iron Mining and Manufacturing Company; a two-and-a-half-million-acre land purchase in Mexico; and a pickle factory in Salt Lake City.

During the 1880s John spent much time in the East assisting in efforts of the Church to gain political independence for Utah and freedom from oppressive anti-polygamy legislation. Operating behind the doors of his North American Exchange Company, located across the street from the New York Stock Exchange, and through the pages of his newspaper, the *Saturday Evening Globe,* John wielded an influence with important men in government, finance, and newspapers, which had a definite ameliorating effect upon hostile legislation and sentiment. Significant were his efforts in defeating the Edmunds-Tucker bill and in furthering Utah's bid for statehood in 1887. However, due to his unyielding advocacy of the achievement of Church political goals by a lavish expenditure of Church funds to purchase influence, and his support of the Democrats as the party best able to provide Utah statehood at a time when Church leaders had become disillusioned with that party and were seeking support of the Republicans, his effectiveness in the cause of Zion began to wane. "It is a great pity that he cannot work in harmony with his fellow servants and bring his mind down to be governed by whomsoever may be appointed to take the lead. He is a man capable of doing great good; but of what use are his talents . . . if he will not work in the line which is indicated . . . by him who has the right to dictate?" wrote the First Presidency in 1888.[2]

By the turn of the century, despite nominal success in his business ventures and lobbying activities, John W. Young's course had led to financial ruin, tarnished his dream of building Zion, strained the confidence of his associates, and had a divisive effect upon his family. "The edge of the knife of misfortune is sharp, and cuts to the very core," he noted in recounting the sequence of events that had brought him short of his goal. Struggling to pay a $50,000 debt incurred on his Atlantic and Pacific railroad contract in 1880, he had turned to the development of other railroad and business interests in Utah when he was summoned to Washington, D.C., to assist in the struggle against the anti-polygamy campaign. In 1888, faced with mounting debt from unfinished business interests in the West, and a lavish outlay of money in the political struggle in the East, he prematurely undertook the building of the Salt Lake and Eastern Railway, hoping to check his deteriorating financial condition. Added to this was the purchase of two and a half million acres of land in Mexico in an effort to block the encroachment of outside interests upon Mormon colonists there. To bolster his mushrooming financial plight, he successfully borrowed in excess of one million dollars from European financiers to pay off his accumulated debt in America, including his railroad construction expenses, and was negotiating for an additional sum with which to complete his railways and put them on a paying basis when the failure of the Baring financial house in London in 1890 terminated his contracts for additional money at that time. By 1897, when Utah creditors sued for contract payments, it was too late for any further help from England.

Still seeking to redeem his financial failings in his later years, John W. engaged in maritime enterprises in the United States. In 1908 he wrote the First Presidency soliciting a contract to transport Church members from the defunct Turkish Mission to the United States on a newly established steamship line. Later, he promoted a plan to consolidate ship-building along the eastern seaboard, with a view to standardization of design. His most auspicious promotion was an elaborate 300-million-dollar facility for New York harbor, containing theaters, restaurants, shops, etc., where ocean liners could dock and visitors conveniently enjoy all the comforts of the city.

The misfortune that beset his public career also affected John W.'s domestic life, as four of his five wives left him. "My children will never know in this life what the word father means," wrote one of his wives in a letter of complaint. In 1903 John W. was sorely tried when one of his sons was convicted in a bizarre New York murder case and sentenced for life in Sing Sing prison.

After reviewing the events that led to his financial embarrassments—"I cannot say failure, for I do not acknowledge the significance of that word in my life's work"—John confidently wrote from Paris in 1898: "I have full faith that the Lord will yet reward my labours sufficiently to enable me to pay every debt I honestly owe, and I am thankful to say I owe none, not one, that was contracted otherwise than honestly. . . . My intent has always been to build up the enterprises necessary for the development of Zion,[3] and break down, as far as it lay in my power, the outside prejudice against us, in which in some few instances, I have failed, and may have created it where it did not exist. . . . Whenever I have been successful in raising funds for an enterprise, I have taken them home to Zion and paid them out there. I have never turned from the poor; I have never left a brother or a friend in need when I had the means to relieve them. I never sued a human being in my life, although I have scores of thousands due me at home and abroad; nor have I ever taken a cent of interest from any person for loans or advances. My debts are not accumulations for extravagances of my own, but have been incurred in the manner briefly explained." Convinced that he had "fought a good fight and kept the faith," John W. confidently hoped to "return to Zion with means to settle everywhere, all I owe."[4] He did not live to see that day.

Letter dated June 13, 1863

In March 1863, John W. Young was called on a mission by his father to assist Horace Eldredge, Feramorz Little, and Lewis S. Hills with Church immigration in New York City. Venturing into the fleshpots of the East for the first time, he was given a special blessing by his father and other members of the First Presidency on March 8, just prior to his departure. "Inasmuch as you have desired to go to the Eastern Lands, to see, to learn, to understand, and to assist your brethren in the arduous work of gathering the saints, we seal upon you the blessing of wisdom, understanding, forethought and foresight, to be a wise and safe and efficient counselor to your brethren wherever duty shall call you. Wherever you may go you shall be blessed with wisdom and power to elude the grasp of the enemy, inasmuch as you are humble and faithful before the Lord your God; and great wisdom shall be given unto you, and sound understanding and judgment. Go with your Br. Horace, and be a faithful assistant to him. . . . Pray continually that you may be able to do good on this mission; and inasmuch as you desire with all your heart to do good, and to glorify your Father in heaven, you shall have power over your enemies inwardly and outwardly and no accident shall befall you, . . . and no power of evil shall injure you, inasmuch as you shall be faithful. . . . We pray our Father in heaven to preserve you, and guide your mind while it is young and tender, that you may delight in truth and righteousness, in peace and uprightness, in honesty and equity, delighting to do good to your fellow creatures. Seek to build up the Kingdom of God, to redeem and build up Zion, and to establish it no more to be removed. . . . Let your mind be centered on the things of God, and suffer it not to wander after the things of this world. Seek unto the Lord your God, that you may have the Holy Ghost constantly abiding with you."[5]

Writing ten days later about his trip across the plains, John W. noted that "the hand of the Allmighty has Ben over us. We have ben Blessed beyound almost what we could hope." While en route to his destination, he visited points of interest in Philadelphia and New York, including an Italian opera at the Academy of Music. "It was very nice siting all the evening and not understand[ing] a single woord. However the House is well worth going to see." Marked by poor spelling and little detail (a sharp contrast to letters he wrote a few years later), John's letter to his father concluded with these words: "I don not want to say too much in my letters or Els I will have nothing to tell when I get home. Wall I've ben writing untill I have got to the woord home and there I stick. So I think it is time to wind off this. I don not call it a letter, this batch of scribleing. Father I hope By the time I get home your Sun will Be a better Boy than when he left it. . . . Praying the Lord to Bless you, and all the good, roll on his Kingdom on the Earth. Hope that I may be humble and Be counted worthy of being crowned with all the Sanctifyed is the Prayer of your affectionate Sun and Brother in the Church."[6]

The letter of Brigham Young to John Willard Young, dated June 13, 1863, was received after the latter had arrived in New York City.

JOHN WILLARD YOUNG

Salt Lake City, June 13, 1863

Elder John W. Young
13 Broadway, New York City

My dear son John W,

On the 4th inst. I wrote you at length in reply to yours received up to that date, and on the 3rd I wrote to your brother Brigham, since when your kind and good letter to your mother has come to hand.

I am much gratified that all your letters are written in the enjoyment of such good health and spirits, and evidence that the sight-seeings and temptations of the lower world have not weaned your affections from your religion and home, but seem to have increased and strengthened them, which I doubt not will continue to be the case until we are privileged to welcome you home in health and safety, every way improved by your trip. The courteous treatment you receive from those you meet is also gratifying, for it indicates that our enemies are foiled for the present, and that your conduct and conversation are commendable.

The sojourners on the Bench are few and quiet, and you were quite right in your statement that they would not be able to accomplish anything to our injury.

[Stephen S.] Harding left by stage for the East on the 11th inst., and there were none of any party who thought enough of him to notice his departure. [Patrick E.] Connor is still here, a brigadier without a brigade or the prospect of one, and said to be anxious to get away, with the expectation of soon being gratified by being recalled or ordered to more active service and a wider field. Under these circumstances the mischievous clique, in such full feather not long ago, is entirely broken, and I presume despair of being able to carry out any of their evil plans.

The weather continues unusually dry and warm, and City Creek has not had its usual high-water period, yet gardens and fields look luxuriantly and give a promise of abundant harvests of the rich products of the soil.

Work of varied kinds is so crowding that no common laborers are in the streets seeking employment, which is proof of a healthy feeling and action among the people.

Your brother Joseph A. is busily engaged in overseeing the lumbering business of my mills in Big Cottonwood and City Creek Canyons, and George W. [Thatcher] is looking after matters at the grist mill and its vicinity.

On the temple block the foundations for the pillars for the bents of the new tabernacle, to be 150 by 250 feet outside measure, will soon be laid, and masons are busily occupied upon the pillars. Work is progressing very satisfactorily upon the temple, several teams being busily occupied in hauling the huge granite blocks, which the stone cutters are rapidly shaping, and the masons placing them in the walls.

The parquette of the theatre is being fitted with a sectional floor to extend over it on a level with the stage for the purpose of accommodating large parties, of which one will come off on the 3rd, one on the 16th (Pioneer and Battalion), and one on the 24th of July next.

A few days ago, a band of Indians attacked the California mail stage in Cedar Valley about two miles west of the Jordan River, killed the conductor, Wood Reynolds, the driver, and two horses, cut the mail bags, cushions, and curtains of the coach, and then made off, taking the other two horses with them. I understand that troops have been sent from Camp Douglas to chastise them.

My health, your mother's, that of my family, of Joseph A. and family, of Brigham's family, and of your other relatives, friends, acquaintances, and the people in general is good.

Bro. Thos. W. Ellerbeck's wife died on the 11th inst., and was buried yesterday.

That you may be abundantly blest and rejoice with us in a safe and prosperous return to your home in due time, having accomplished a good work is the prayer of,

Your father,
Brigham Young

P.S. Should Bro. Horace [Eldredge] get through with his business and be returning home before Brigham arrives, you are at liberty to come with him or wait for Brigham as you may choose.

Letter dated February 7, 1866

"With what joy I perused [your letter] no one can appreciate or understand my feelings, except they have experienced the same under similar circumstances," wrote John W. Young from New York in response to a letter from his father on June 4, 1863. "I can go to what few labors I have to do with double the energy now than I could before. If when I get home you can take me by the hand and say that you are satisfyed I shall feel happy." While in the East this youthful son of Brigham Young was in more than usual demand as a speaker. After addressing the Saints a number of times, he wrote his father that his discourse "comes very hard but I can see every time it is easier. Oh, how I think if the young men could only see the opportunities they are throwing away—but it seems they cannot until thrown on their own responsibility, then it is felt keenly I assure you. I know by painful experience."[7]

After returning from his mission to New York in 1863, John W. was sent back again to assist his brother Joseph A. with the immigration the following year. Having been appointed an assistant counselor in the First Presidency by his father prior to his departure, John shows in his letters during the year an awakening to a sense of duty and a desire for improvement and a renewed devotion to the principles of his religion. "I feel it more necessary to live nearer the Lord every day of my life and keep my armor bright that when the final day comes I may not be found wanting," he wrote his father. "You said to me just before leaveing to improve every opportunity to talk and make myself acquainted with the gospel and with the help of the Lord I intend to do so."[8] A few weeks later he continued the theme: "I am not experienced enough in writing to cloth my ideas in [*illegible word*] language as I would like but I am aware the only way to do is to strive to learn continually, seek opportunities to get experience &c., but that will come along in time. I feel the Lord has blessed me with everything I could desire in righ[t]eousness and my desire is, to do his will continually."[9]

The immigration business took Joseph A. and John W. Young to England in 1864, the latter for the first time. While in Europe they traveled to Denmark, Holland, Germany, Switzerland, and France, before returning home. Less than two years later, John W. was back in England, this time as a missionary. His brother Brigham Jr. was president of the European Mission at that time.[10] Before departing on this mission, John W. received instruction from his father on February 7, 1866, to attend to some long-standing business in New York on the way.

Salt Lake City, February 7, 1866

Elder John W. Young

My dear Son,

The following are a few items of business I wish you to attend to.

A man by the name of Richard Steel kept a drug store about forty years ago in Auburn, N.Y. He had my note for three dollars ($3.00), which I wished to take up; but he could not find it, and said that I must be mistaken about it. I offered to pay the amount, but he refused to receive it. Years afterwards, I heard, and do not now recollect how I heard, that he had found that note. I wish it settled. He may be dead, but his heir or heirs may be living.

A note of mine, which was drawn August 28th, 1829, at Bucksville, Cayuga Co., seven miles north of Auburn, for thirty-one dollars and fourteen cents ($31.14), in favor of Aholiah Buck, or bearer, has been presented by Messrs. Holladay and Halsey to me for settlement. My impression is that the note was paid, but was not taken up. If this were so, I would like to find it out. I wish you to ascertain whether Mr. Buck is living, and by whom this note was forwarded here, and to ascertain whether it will be right for me to pay it here, and if I do, whether it will ever get to Mr. Buck, or if he is dead, to his heir or heirs.

The enclosed copy of a letter, which I lately received from Mr. Ezra Sheldon, of Mendon, N.Y., explains itself. The note to which reference is made is dated November 26th, 1829, and was drawn in his favor for ten dollars ($10). I find three dollars ($3) endorsed on the back as having been paid June 15, 1851. I wish you to see Mr. Sheldon and pay this note and interest which will amount to $32.28.

Give my kind regards to all the folks in that country who may know me.

Your father, Brigham Young

P.S. If you pay any of these notes, pay nothing but simple interest on them at the rate of 7 per cent.

           B.Y.

Letter dated February 5, 1867

 On February 7, 1866, in company with Hiram B. Clawson, William Jennings, Thomas Taylor, and John T. Caine, who were going east on Church business, John W. Young left for his mission to England. Four detours en route to New York delayed his departure, however. Feeling duty-bound not to separate from his traveling companions, he stopped first in St. Louis, where the businessmen Clawson, Jennings, and Taylor put up at the finest hotel in the city, the Southern Hotel. In following suit, John W. explained this extravagance to his father: "As it was generally known that I was your son, I felt I could do no less than stop at the finest hotel also, and be as respectable as the rest of them. Personally, I feel no desire to make a show, but when the eyes of many are directed towards me and it is said, 'there is a son of Brigham Young,' I feel that to look and act respectable is my duty."[11] This statement may help explain John W.'s flair for princely attire and fashionable and expensive tastes throughout his life.

 A second detour was made to visit an uncle, Edward Young, whom his father had not seen in thirty years. Arriving at Medina, Wisconsin, with John T. Caine after a snowstorm, John W. hired a man with a sleigh to take them the last few miles to their destination. Confronting his Uncle Edward for the first time, John W. was introduced by Caine as a son of Brigham Young, which "made his eyes hang out considerably"; his wife almost fainted. "If a thunder-bolt had fallen at her feet she could not have looked more surprised." Edward "shook me cordially by the hand," John continued in relating the incident to his father, "but eyed me closely. I returned his look without flinching until he seemed fully satisfied it was a real son and no mistake. By his conversation I concluded that he thought you and your brothers had been seeking more after the 'gold of Ophir,' than after the Lord, and had become very wealthy. For us to find him in a log house cut his pride deeply; he soon rallied from this however, when he found that our answers to the questions he propounded were so frank and open, for they just suited his notions, and we were soon on good terms engaged in an interesting conversation upon Mormonism."

During the visit with his uncle, John W. succeeded in breaking down some of the prejudice that had separated him from the rest of the family. "His wife is a woman of very jealous disposition and I am of the opinion that she is the cause of Edward being separated from the Church; for, as I talked with him and became better acquainted, I found him to be a real Mormon at heart although he did not realize it. The only principles he objected to were those that he did not understand and looked at through the eyes of prejudice; but when I explained them to the best of my ability he seemed fully satisfied. I think he partially realizes the 'wool' has been pulled over his eyes, and that he has been kept from his friends. During the two days we remained with him his wife softened considerably. He acknowledged to me just before we parted that he did not think 'polygamy' so bad after all, for he had had a great deal of difficulty with his wife but now he was bound to have peace. He enlisted in the army for three years during the war, but fortunately for him, he was stationed near New Orleans with those troops that were discharged after ten months service. Soon after his return . . . he lost two of his children, but by the blessing of the Lord his three other children . . . were preserved; it took all of his bounty money to pay the doctors bill, and again he was left with only his hands to depend upon. The day before we left Edward's, he asked us if we would have any objection to him inviting in a few of his friends, and have a social meeting. Of course we were glad of an additional opportunity of bearing our testimony. In the evening there was twelve or fifteen came in to hear what the 'Mormons' could say for themselves. We talked freely and answered all their questions. When we came to part they seemed to do so with great reluctance and I believe many of them viewed the Church of Latter-day Saints very differently from what they had done, for they pressed us to remain a few days and preach in their school house. I feel confident that a good work might be done in their midst."

On March 2, as Edward drove his visitors to Appleton to continue their journey, "he promised . . . if it was possible for him to leave his family so they could live during his absence, he would visit Utah this season. His house and five acres of land that he has cleared, would pay his debts and leave him two or three hundred dollars. I slipped $20 into his pocket and asked him to buy his wife a dress, for

I knew that would do more with her than all the Gospel I could preach. He was very unwilling to take anything, but I knew he needed it and pressed it upon him. We parted the best of friends."[12]

A third stop before his departure for England found John W. with John T. Caine in the nation's capital, where they visited Utah's congressional delegate, William Hooper; President Andrew Johnson; and the popular Civil War hero, Ulysses S. Grant. John reported his impressions of the visit to his father. "My private opinion is that Bro. H[ooper] ought to have some good prayerful man with him who would preach faith into his ear. Bro. H. can do all the wire working, for he perfectly understands the ropes to pull, but he is so very fluctuating in his temperament—either up in the garret or down in the cellar—that it needs some one to apply a little restoration in his desponding moments. The feeling of hatred towards us is intensely strong with the majority of the head men at Washington, but I feel, as I told bro. Hooper; that 'so long as the Saints continue to do as near right as they are doing, I cannot fear.' "[13]

On March 14 John W. Young was introduced by delegate Hooper to President Johnson and General Grant. As they waited to see the President, John observed, "Republicanism was beautifully illustrated, for I could see from diamonds of the millionaire down to the greasy coat of the poor artisan brushing side by side with equal rights to be introduced to the President, and to promenade in the grand saloons." When the third son of Brigham Young was presented to the President, it "excited a great deal of curiosity and caused many a stare."[14] Upon meeting General Grant in his headquarters in Georgetown, John W. found him to be "a perfect stoic, and I think his great forte lies in him knowing just enough to hold his tongue. However, he shook hands very cordially when we took our leave."[15]

John W. Young's final detour before leaving for England came on March 15, when he traveled to western New York to pay the notes designated in his father's letter of February 7. At Clayville he found Richard Steel, who seemed pleased to hear from Brigham Young, and "especially at the prospect of getting a little money." Ezra Sheldon at Lima was also glad to receive some money, but "acted as if he did not care how soon we left after he got it; but I excused it in a 'childish old man,'" John reported. The visit of a son of the illustrious Mormon leader, one of Auburn's former citizens, attracted the notice of the local newspaper: "A son of Brigham Young, (we didn't learn his number,) was in town this morning, and called at a business house in Genesee St. to settle an account by his numerous progenitor some thirty years ago. Brigham is honest—in some things, but rather slow. The debt discharged by him was, we understand, for borrowed money."[16]

In company with William Jennings, John W. Young finally left New York City on April 4 for his mission to England. While crossing the Atlantic they encountered a terrific storm in which three passengers and one steward had their legs broken "in a most shocking manner" by being dashed against the side of the cabin. "I made myself as useful as possible by assisting the surgeon in taking care of the wounded, for most of the passengers were housed and praying for dear life. Fortunately, I had done my praying beforehand. I made myself so handy that even the surgeon himself took me for a surgeon. Bro. Jennings was sick the whole way; but thanks to the Almighty, I was well during the voyage."[17]

John W. Young arrived at the mission headquarters in Liverpool on April 14, where he began his missionary labors under the presidency of his brother Brigham Young, Jr. Twice during the first five months of his mission he traveled to the continent with Brigham Jr., visiting Germany, Denmark, Norway, and Russia.

John W. Young's time in England was spent in traveling, speaking to the Saints, working in the mission office, and assisting with the Church emigration. Assessing the work of proselyting in that land, he noted that "there are but very few who seem to pay the least regard to the admonitions of the Elders." Talking to the people "seems like talking to a wall, or some object that has no ears to hear or heart to understand anything about the Gospel."[18]

On November 29, in the absence of his brother Brigham Jr., who had returned to Utah on a visit to counsel with their father, John W. witnessed the unveiling of an equestrian statue in Wolverhampton by Queen Victoria. After three hours in a biting north wind, when the pealing of bells and the roar of artillery announced the arrival of the Queen, John watched with a critical eye the majestic ceremony that followed. As the town council and some of the borough officials were presented to the Queen, "they passed muster like a lot of frightened sheep; some two or three turned their backs, walked away, which, according to court etiquette, is unpardonable, and some others almost tripped up in endeavoring to retire gracefully. . . . My big opera or field glass done good service that day; for when I looked through that, the Queen, with all her personal defects, stood right before me. My opinion is that Holland does not contribute as much to the healthful appearance of Victoria as some say; but, I think that it is owing to a very wise course on the part of the Queen, for she certainly looks like she had been a true wife and mother."[19]

Shortly before receiving the following letter from his father, and prior to the termination of his mission, John W. reflected upon his missionary experience in England in these words: "I can say that I have enjoyed my mission; and one thing that has added greatly to my joy and peace of mind is, that I am learning to keep cool, and not to get in a hurry, but, do the best that I can, as each successive day with its accompanying events rolls around. The Lord knows the desires of my heart, consequently I feel to trust implicitly in the guidance of His holy spirit. My labours so far, have resulted in great good to myself; for they have learned me that without the assistance of our Heavenly Father, I am a mere cipher, and a very small one too."[20]

Salt Lake City, February 5, 1867

Elder John W. Young
42 Islington, Liverpool, England

Dear Son,

Your brother Brigham started at 8.45 yesterday morning, accompanied by Bro. Geo. D. Watt, on his return to his field of labor in England. We heard from them this morning. They were at Weber last evening and well, though it had been stormy all day. The roads through the mountains are likely to be bad, but further east they are said to be tolerably good. Traveling to the States now is not what it was before the railroad had been pushed so far this way. The time spent in staging is much shortened, lessening the fatigue and the duration of the journey. It is interesting to us out here to see the eagerness with which they are pushing this great work ahead. It will be sure to help us, and be advantageous to the Zion of our God, though the wicked are contemplating terrible things respecting us as soon as they can finish the railroad. The waves of civilization to use their own figure will then surge right up against the walls of barbarism in which we are entrenched and wash them down. We and our religion can then be wiped out and no longer offend the fastidious tastes and senses of the priests and politicians of this enlightened(?) age. We shall see. Had we nothing to depend upon but our own strength and wisdom, then our condition would be pitiable indeed. But can man arrest the diurnal or annual revolution of the earth? Can he say to the sun that it shall not shine, and that its rays shall not illumine and gladden and impart heat unto our planet? Or can he pluck the stars from the firmament? His power is very limited. Disease and death prostrate their victims. They snatch the loved ones from man's arms, and he is powerless to resist or prevent. In a thousand ways is his weakness apparent, and yet he presumed to measure arms with Jehovah, and declared that Zion shall not be built up, the rule and dominion of the Kingdom shall not prevail when God has declared that these things shall all be done.

With Him to sustain us what have we to fear? Men feel strong and capable to accomplish mighty conquests when they have powerful navies and armies at their command, but we have the Lord of Hosts to uphold us, before whom man, with all his boasted pomp and power is as a grasshopper of the field. Improvements will progress, railroads and telegraph lines and cables will be built and stretched; but instead of these things acting as an aid to our enemies, they will increase our facilities and accelerate the progress of the work of the Lord.

The news which we hear from you from time to time respecting your labors and movements is very pleasing. It is a great joy to me to see my sons bearing the holy priesthood and seeking to magnify the same among the nations of the earth. My prayers are constantly offered up in your and your brothers' behalf, that the blessings of the Lord may rest upon you, and you be enabled to do a good work.

We have had very quiet times in the city and Territory this winter. The winter has been open, but we have very bad roads, so much rain and snow having fallen it has made our main roads almost impassable. General good health prevails. Your mother's health and that of Lucy [Canfield Young] and Clara [Jones Young] and the rest of the folks is usually good. Brigham has enjoyed his visit very much, and has been well repaid for the fatigues and trouble of the trip. He will be able to give you many particulars which I cannot write. He will, if he can spare the time, and not miss a good and safe steamer by so doing, make Captain [William H.] Hooper a visit at Washington.

The election for delegate to Congress and for the state representative, &c., came off yesterday. Captain Hooper was our nominee, and a Mr. [William] McGrorty was the nominee of the clique, twenty of whom at their mass meeting voted for him, the brethren present for curiosity giving no vote.

I expect you and Brigham and family will start for home in July or August, as may be convenient. Bro. F[ranklin] D. Richards will be left in charge of the mission; Brigham will give him such instructions as may be needed respecting matters.

Your mother and all the folks join me in love to you. Give my love to Katie [Catherine Spencer Young], Oscar and all the brethren. Praying the Lord to bless you, give you great success, and bring you home safely, I am, your father,

Brigham Young

Letter dated July 31, 1873

John W. Young had been in England with his brother Joseph A. on emigration business in 1864, and had returned as a missionary in 1866-67. In 1873 he crossed the Atlantic for the third time on business connected with the Utah Central and Utah Southern railroads. The following letter of instruction from Brigham Young, dated July 31, 1873, preceded John W.'s departure on this assignment.

At the time of John W.'s departure, the suit for divorce of Brigham Young's seventeenth wife, Ann Eliza Webb Young, had focused the attention of the people of the country upon conditions in Utah and Mormon life in particular. Consequently, when John W. took a room at the fashionable St. Nicholas Hotel in New York, en route to England, he had not been there long before a reporter of the New York *Herald* contacted him for an interview. As the reporter entered John W.'s room, he saw a pleasant-looking, well-built, heavily mustached young man of about thirty reclining in a large armchair, attired in a black velvet jacket faced with light blue silk. John Willard cheerfully welcomed the *Herald* reporter and willingly answered questions regarding the Mormon faith, mode of life, and the suit pending against his father.[21]

Arriving in England on August 28, 1874, John W. Young embarked upon his assignment there with a letter of assurance to his father: "My trust is in the Lord; and my prayers ascend to him continually that I may be permitted to accomplish this business with honor to the Cause, and satisfaction to you."[22]

Salt Lake City, July 31, 1873

John W. Young, Esqr.

My dear Son,

As you are about to start for England to negotiate, sell, or dispose of the Utah Central and Utah Southern Railroad companies bonds belonging to me, I wish to impress upon your mind the necessity of strictly confining yourself to that business, unless you shall be instructed otherwise hereafter.

This is your first visit to England on such business and I hope you will be wise and discreet in the management of it.

Should any influences be employed to direct your attention to business other than the above, pay no regard to them, further than making memoranda for future consideration.

Preserve a steady, calm, and deliberate demeanor and show that you are master of yourself.

Do the business assigned you as promptly as circumstances will permit and return soon as completed.

Elder James T. Little will accompany you for at least a portion of the time, and render you all the assistance in his power.

It will be right for you to make any exchanges to your advantage, of outside stock and bonds in said railroads, provided that such exchanges shall in nowise interfere with your duties as specified.

May you be preserved to return in peace and safety, having accomplished the work assigned to you with success,

Your affectionate father, Brigham Young

Letter dated October 26, 1874

Involvement in business enterprises increasingly demanded

John W.'s time away from home in the financial centers of the East. Having been ordained an apostle in his youth and carefully groomed for leadership, he was appointed a counselor to his father in the First Presidency in 1873, with specific responsibilities in southern Utah and Arizona. However, extended absences threatened to minimize his effectiveness in this calling. Writing to his son in the fall of 1873, Brigham Young had urged, "as the time is fast rolling on, and winter approaching, and affairs at St. George and the south require someone to attend to them, I would like to know definitely when you receive this whether it is your intention to return home immediately so as to take the position assigned to you in the south: if such is not your intention I would like you to say so and we will appoint someone else."[23]

On October 26, 1874, Brigham Young wrote another letter to his son in New York on the same theme.

Salt Lake City, October 26, 1874

John W. Young
New York, New York

My dear Son,
　　Your welcome favor came to hand. I was glad to hear of your good health and hoped you would have completed your business in the East and returned home ere this. You know my feelings on this point. I desire you may complete your business arrangements at an early day so that you will not have to return east again very soon and come here and throw your energies in with ours to move on the great cause. There are too few laborers now in the field and where God has given evidences of his work it is an obligation we owe for the knowledge imparted to blend our energies for the accomplishment of his great work.
　　I am pleased to have you visit Ferry [Feramorz] and to hear of the good counsel which you give to all with whom you meet, and trust you take a course to enjoy the spirit of the Lord altho I think you might have much more of that good spirit if you would follow out my counsel in relation to your mission in the South.
　　From your letter I presume you are getting along pretty well with your business. I would like very much if you would manage it so as to clear my bonds and give them to Bro. John Sharp

to bring home. You will see him, no doubt, although he does not expect to remain away from here very long.

I hope to go south before long and would like to loan or buy some of your furniture and beds which you have in the South, unless you expect to be there to use them yourself. Please write and let me know as early as convenient. Direct outside envelope to A[lexander] F. McDonald, St. George, Washington County, etc.

If you see Gen. [Thomas L.] Kane and family present my compliments and say that I often think of the pleasant hours that I have passed in their society, and the interesting conversations which I had with the General during our southern tour. I hope to meet them again at no very distant day and pray the blessings of Almighty God may attend them through the journey of life.

Your mother's health is pretty good generally and she wishes to be remembered to her dear son John. Alice [Young Clawson] is still stopping with her, but expects to leave for the South with her boys in about a week. She seems determined to make the South her home for she really believes that the boys will have a much better opportunity to learn the principles of their religion far from the turmoils and temptations of this much demoralized city.

Mrs. Eleanor Pratt died very suddenly last evening of apoplexy, sick but a few hours.

Your wife Libbie and friends started east yesterday so I understand. Lutie [Thatcher] remains with the children who are looking well, so I hear.

B. Young, Jr., sends his love. So do all the family. Luna [Young Thatcher] and her family are pretty well now but some of her children have been very sick with scarletina.

The courts are not doing much, neither the grand juries at Beaver nor in this city. They try hard enough but it is hard kicking against the pricks. The Lord has overruled most admirably, and the Saints are pushing forward the good cause. The temple is looming up fine and we may expect the rock work to be pushed another season as it has never been. Our increased facility for laying rock and the prospect of working into the United Order bid fair to complete both temples at an early day. Some three hundred men from the northern counties have volunteered to go to

St. George for the winter which will expedite matters in that region of country.

I believe that all is right with a majority of the Saints, and God will bring us safely through if we are faithful.

God bless you and preserve you in the truth is the prayer of

Your affectionate father,

Brigham Young

Letter dated August 7, 1875

Within nine months in 1874-75 a brother and a sister of John W. Young passed away. Alice Young Clawson, the wife of Hiram B. Clawson, died on November 2, 1874, at thirty-five years of age, and Joseph A. Young, John W.'s oldest brother, died suddenly on August 5, 1875, at forty-one. News of his brother's passing was the subject of the letter of Brigham Young to John W. on August 7, 1875.

Salt Lake City, August 7, 1875

Elder John W. Young

My dear Son,

As Dr. [Joseph M.] Benedict purposes starting for Long Island tomorrow, and has kindly proferred to take a letter to you, expecting to call upon you, I hasten to write a few lines.

One week ago yesterday, July 30, your brother Joseph A. left this city with me and others for Provo, apparently usually well, but complaining some of a disagreeable feeling from the ether he had recently taken when having a tooth pulled. Previous to his late visit here he had been traveling and preaching very laboriously for some two weeks in the district over which he presided, over-laboring in the extremely dusty and hot weather. A week ago today and tomorrow, July 31st and Aug. 1st, he attended a two-day meeting with us in Provo, still feeling a little unwell from the ether and over-fatigue. On the 4th, he reached Manti, having had an attack of congestive chills while passing through Salt Creek Canyon. On the 5th he ate breakfast with apparent good appetite, also dinner, and in the afternoon drove in a buggy with his son and B[righam] T. Young's wife to the site we selected on my late visit to Sanpete for a temple near Manti. Soon after returning from his short ride his health failed rapidly, and at 8.45 p.m. he ceased breathing.

Your mother was on a visit at your brother Brigham Jr.'s when she heard the melancholy news, which she received with much of the spirit of resignation. Your mother, Brigham Jr., and his wife Elizabeth [Fenton Young] came here on last evening's train. Your brother Joseph A's. wife, Clara [Stenhouse Young] and her children are expected here tonight, and the funeral will be observed at the White House tomorrow at 10 a.m.

Bishop Wm. Miller died at Provo last night, and Bro. Alfonzo Green, of American Fork, and Bro. Amos Fielding of this city, the night before, although the health of the people is generally good, the mortality in this city for July not being 45 per cent of same time last year.

My family are generally well. My wife Emmeline [Free Young] was buried three weeks tomorrow, and a short time previous to her death, your brother Joseph A. remarked to her that he should soon follow her.

Your telegram of today was received at 9.30 this morning cheering us with word that your health is improving.

Ever praying for your true welfare, I remain,

Your affectionate father,
Brigham Young

Letter dated August 30, 1875

"Sorrow is our heritage in this life," wrote John W. Young upon receiving news of his brother's untimely death. "How does poor Mother bear the sad loss? Her faith I know, therefore do not feel as though it would prove more than she can live through, but two (*dear Alice*) out of five, in eight short months, must wring a mother's heart. You, dear father, have other sons, and many to comfort you, but poor Mother so wrapt up in her children. Thank the Lord my brother Joseph died with the Gospel harness on his back. To die so is to give exaltation to the man, honor to God and a living joy to those who mourn and half the grief is taken away—we know he has gone to a far Better world. May we all meet there. . . . Please give my love to dear

Mother and accept dear Father that portion which belongs to a Prophet of God and a dear father combined. . . ."[24]

John W. Young's religious background was a strong motivating factor in his life. Not only did he regard his numerous business enterprises as contributive to the building of the kingdom of God, but as his circle of friends and associates among influential men increased, he often found opportunity to inform them on matters of his religion. While engaged in railroad business in the East in 1875, John W. met a prominent attorney, a Mr. Olmstead, as he traveled from New Haven, Connecticut, to New York, with whom he discussed the subject of Mormonism. Before the two men parted, Olmstead "asked for some of our works and remarked that a great many people wanted to know what we believed. I read to him from the *Compendium* which I had with me and preached to him all the way. He invited me cordially to see him, and often." On another occasion, John W. met H. K. Beecher, a brother of Henry Ward Beecher, who was so impressed with John W.'s beliefs that he proferred the use of his new church, "a very fine building," for the Mormon missionaries.[25] After observing him at close range for many months, a secretary noted of John W. Young that "he preaches the gospel to all friends and in his letters he often expresses his living faith in God and inspires even strangers, and it seems very strange to see such a business man spending so much of his time remembering his Heavenly Father."[26]

During his labors in the East in 1875, John W. Young's health became impaired, and his condition was aggravated by the pressure of fatiguing work, resulting in surgery and much suffering. Apprised of his son's ill health, Brigham Young wrote the following letter on August 30.

Salt Lake City, August 30, 1875

Elder John W. Young
Philadelphia, Pennsylvania

My dear Son,
I was exceedingly glad to hear from you through your letter of the 21st inst. Though extremely pained to learn that you had suffered so much, my great hope is that the operations that have been performed upon you will exercise no permanent injury

upon your constitution. I could wish that you would take more care of yourself. When you are in good health do not overwork; be regular in your meals, and more carefully observe the general laws of health.

Bro. William W. Riter will hand you this and pay you a short visit. I do not wish you to keep him with you however much I should like you to have his company, were it possible for him to stay. But the railroad to Coalville requires his presence. Besides, his health will not admit of a prolonged absence from home.

President George A. Smith was until a few days ago rapidly improving, but I regret to say has suffered a relapse. He gets but little rest; he cannot sleep more than three or four hours out of the twenty-four.

I received a telegram from your brother Brigham this afternoon from which I learn that his health is at present not very good. Elder Geo. Q. Cannon is about to visit Cache Valley and Brigham intends to meet him at Mendon on Thursday afternoon.

Joseph A.'s family are doing nicely. Brothers [Albert K.] Thurber and [William H.] Seegmiller and his son Brigham T. have been appointed administrators to his estate. Mary [Ann Ayers Young] and Clara [Stenhouse Young] will go south, may possibly live together at Richfield, whilst Margaret [Whitehead Young] will remain in this city.

I shall not write you a long letter this evening, but leave it to Bro. Riter to detail to you the principal items of current news, but will add that I am thankful to be able to say I am in the enjoyment of excellent health, calm and buoyant in spirit, and as ever, rejoicing in the gifts and blessings of our Heavenly Father. Your mother's health is good, so is that of the family very generally. Peace be with you, and may you be abundantly blessed of the Lord in all your labors is the prayer of

Your affectionate father,
Brigham Young

Letter of December 17, 1875

Expecting John W. home before the holidays, Brigham Young expressed disappointment when his son failed to arrive by December

JOHN WILLARD YOUNG

17. A copy of the President's letter, written on that day as dictated to a scribe, appears in a Brigham Young letter-press book in the Church Archives. Missing, however, are a few penciled lines, written upside down in Brigham Young's own hand, crowded around the salutation of the original letter, which is filed at the Brigham Young University library. The holograph, which is added below as a postscript, shows the intense concern of Brigham Young for the return of his son.

Salt Lake City, December 17, 1875

Elder John W. Young
New York, New York

My dear Son,

 I received your letter of Nov. 22d in due course, but did not answer it, as I had been expecting to see you home. I thought you would have come with Bro. [William C.] Staines, and if not with him, would have been with us at the holidays. But as you have not come, I now write you this, with the hope that on its receipt, you will settle up your business, as such is my wish, and come home and stay with me and help me, as I have much to do, in which I should like you to assist me. I read your letter to your mother and was pleased to hear from you, and the reason of my writing this is that I there learned you could not come until along in January. Your mother was delighted to hear from you; she is in good health as am I also, with the exception of a very slight touch of rheumatism. The family are mostly well though the present is not a very favorable time for health. A thick white frost has covered the city as with a fog for several days past, and coughs and colds are becoming abundant. I am thinking of going to Provo by special car tomorrow morning and shall probably stay until Wednesday. On my return I have an appointment to meet the priesthood of Davis Co. on the Friday of that week.

 We have excellent news from the missionaries throughout the country, baptisms are not unfrequent and much preaching is being done. The brethren generally realize that the Lord is working with them and for them, and opening up their way marvelously. We think of yet sending out other elders to open up fresh places this winter.

The new ZCMI building is now completely covered in and the elegant iron front in place. You will be surprised to note the difference in Main St. when you return, the improvement manifest in the erection of the massive new Co-op building, and the imposing structure on the Deseret Bank corner, whilst the late fires have made ugly gaps in the Mathieson block and at the First National Bank building, which will not be filled up for some time yet.

Judge [J. Alexander] White, accompanied by his son and Col. Betts, leaves for California in a few days. He does not expect to return before the opening of the January term of the Supreme Court of the Territory. *I want you here.*

With much love, I remain,

Your affectionate father,

Brigham Young

O Jonna I pr[a]y for you and yours continuly. If you nue [knew] how I want to see you, you would come. My dear Jonna, I due hope you will see as we see thing[s]. I send your dear Br Brigham and Br Stanes to prevale on you to come home and stay with us. M[a]y God Bles my d[e]ar Boy. B.Y.

Letter dated January 11, 1876

Neither his father's caution against overwork nor his own severe illness in 1875 served to change John W. Young's work habits. "In your surmises of my over working," he explained to his father, "you were quite right for it has seemed impossible to get along without using every moment, and I feel the need of rest and quiet for a month or two, but my business prospects are not in a condition to warrant me in taking one day."[27]

When Brigham Young, Jr., arrived in New York City to visit John W. in December 1875, he saw the tenacity with which his younger brother pursued his work and the telling effect it was having upon him. The two brothers met at a hotel in Bridgeport, Connecticut, about eight-thirty on the evening of December 29: "It was a joyful and sorrowful meeting," noted Brigham Jr. "We thought and talked of our dear brother Joseph, our parents, home, the Kingdom. . . . John still troubled with piles, his wounds are not healed. John says he will do everything in his power to get released so as to go home. But there is no one to lift the obligation of the UWRR [Utah Western Railroad], only he. I mourn to see my dear brother with not a moment to call his own." Five days later he added, "I have passed a miserable day seeing John harrassed by duns. My head is like to split with the noise and worry of Broadway and Wall streets. Money could not hire me to endure the torture which my poor brother suffers every day. I know it must be terrible on his mind. . . ."[28]

In a brief respite, on December 31, 1875, four sons of Brigham Young met in John W.'s room in the Metropolitan Hotel in New York City to usher in the New Year together. Besides John W. and Brigham Jr., Willard had joined them from West Point and Don Carlos from Rensselaer Polytechnic. After a pleasant reunion, the four, along with George Q. Cannon and William C. Staines, attended Booth's Theater.

The opening paragraph of the letter of Brigham Young to his sons Brigham Jr. and John W., dated January 11, 1876, refers to letters written by Brigham Jr. after he had met John W. in the East. Although copies of the letters have not been found, the contents may well be imagined from Brigham Jr.'s comments noted above.

Salt Lake City, January 11, 1876

Brigham Young, Jr., and
John W. Young
New York, New York

My dear sons Brigham and John W.,

It was with no ordinary feelings of emotion that I perused the contents of Brigham's letters of Dec. 29, and Jan. 1 and 4. To me they were a sad commentary on the condition of John W.'s affairs, and I more than ever fear that if he does not soon manage to throw off some of the harrassing cares and embarrassments that now beset him, his life will be the forfeit of his persistency. But cannot this be done? Cannot he transfer his business into someone else's hands, so that they will carry the burden instead of him, and he be relieved from the annoyances and worry that are incidental to his present responsibilities? If he could do so I should be more than pleased, and have him come home and rest, and build up his body, and then, when he became strong enough, to work with all his heart with the rest of us in building up the kingdom of God. I sincerely hope you will come home together and that before long.

My health is excellent, your mother's is now good; she was a little unwell last week and did not leave the house for several days. The weather was exunpropitious. The family generally are in good health.

The Legislature met yesterday afternoon at 2 o'clock. All the members present were sworn in with the "Iron Clad" by Sec. [George S.] Black, except Mr. [Erastus S.] Foote, the "ring" representative from Tooele Co., whose seat is contested by Bro. Geo. Atkin. Elder Lorenzo Snow was elected president of the council, and Orson Pratt, speaker of the house. The governor informed the committee appointed to wait on him that he would communicate with the assembly at two this afternoon.

The Supreme Court of the Territory met yesterday. It is probable that the term will be a short one as there are at present only nine cases on the calendar, eight of which are from this district. It is possible that one or two others may be added before the term closes. Bro. [George] Reynolds' case will most probably go over to June.

Yesterday morning father James Allred of Spring City, San Pete, Co., died at the ripe old age of 92. I well remember how hearty and well the old gentleman and Sis. A. seemed when I saw them last summer when I was in San Pete.

Many of the members of the Legislature have called in to see me; they all appear in splendid health and excellent spirits, and bring very encouraging reports from their various localities.

As Bp. [John] Sharp starts east tomorrow morning on business connected with the Union Pacific Railroad and other matters, I thought it would be a favorable opportunity to let you know I had received your letters. Since writing the above I have received John W.'s note of the 5th inst. I am very glad to hear he is better in health and I am much pleased at the expression of his feelings contained therein. I hope you will both write to me often and let me know how things are. May the Lord bless you all; may His preserving and guiding spirit be continually with you and may you soon again be with me in the home of the Saints,

> Your affectionate father,
> Brigham Young

Letter dated March 29, 1876

Arriving in Salt Lake City from New York on February 14, 1876, John W. Young was home for one month before the relentless demands of his railroad affairs called him east again. On March 14, the day before John W.'s departure, his father blessed him that if he were faithful, he would have power to free himself from his railroad bondage, for he wanted him to return to Utah. The President added that he desired to make John his first counselor in the First Presidency if he would walk up to his duties. As he bid his father goodbye the next day, John W. expressed a determination to terminate his business affairs and begin to labor for Zion.[29]

In his first letter to his father after arriving in New York, John wrote, "I can truly say dear Father I am really pained at being back here again and most truly and humbly desire and pray that the Lord may open the way for my speedy return."[30] His father's reply is dated eight days later.

Salt Lake City, March 29, 1876

Elder John W. Young
134 Grand St., New York

My dear Son,

Your telegrams from Omaha and Elmira and your letter from New York [were] duly received and much satisfaction received from their perusal. I am glad the fatigues of the lengthened journey had no ill effects upon your system. My own health has been improving ever since you left, and now that we are treated with a spell of moderately fine weather, I am enjoying myself excellently. Your mother's health is good and so is that of the family generally.

Things here are quiet and still; we have no very marked opposition to contend with just at present. Judge [Philip H.] Emerson still continues to find excuses for putting off the hearing of the arguments in the Ann Eliza case. I presume he wants to stand from under the responsibility of giving an opinion thereon, and thinks that a little judicious delay on his part will stave it off until Judge Coughlan comes, who, by the bye, it is rumored, does not exactly know if he will accept the nomination or not, as he is earning more in his present position than he would as chief justice of Utah.

It would please me very much if you would let me take little Johnny and take care of him, and see that he is well done by. I had only seen him once since you left until today, when I went down to the house and saw him. The next day after you went away he went out and did not return at the time he was told to. And since that time his mistress has not let him come out, except last Sunday when his grandma sent little Walter for him and she ventured to let him come up.

ZCMI is busy removing its stock of goods to the new building where we intend opening next Saturday, April 1st. It is quite a work to transport so heavy a stock so short a distance even as between the old store and the new and it keeps a number of hands and several teams constantly employed. The stock of goods is in excellent condition and the institution is on a far firmer footing today than it has been for many months past.

Your Uncle Lorenzo [Dow Young] has resigned the bishopric in the 18th Ward. He found his health would not permit him to attend to the active duties of his office, so preferred to give way in favor of a younger man. Elder John Nicholson will probably be his successor, with two of the younger brethren as his counselors.

I am glad to hear that you had a pleasant visit from Spencer [Clawson] and Nabbie [Young Clawson]. Whenever you see them give my best respects to them, as also to Willard, to Rudger Clawson and to any other of the brethren or our friends whom you may meet.

I hope that you will be successful in settling up your business so that you can return home.

If you will let me have Johnny telegraph immediately. Just

use these two words. "Take Johnny!" That will be all sufficient, I will pay it.

Your mother joins me in love and prayers in your behalf.

Your affectionate father,

Brigham Young

Letter dated November 23, 1876

Brigham Young's repeated plea to his son John W. to settle his business affairs in the East and return and dedicate himself more fully to the building up of the kingdom of God struck a responsive note in the mind of his son. Writing on April 2, 1876, shortly after his return to New York, John W. took occasion to pour out the deep feelings of his soul, not only on the subject of his business affairs, but also his feelings toward his father.

"It is with more than ordinary interest and affection that this letter is penned for your perusal. My confidence, esteem, and love, can be three times estimated; first by the undying and unbounded confidence I have in your mission as a Prophet of God bearing the Holy Priesthood; second, by the duty I owe to an able, faithful leader of a Great People; third, by the warmest affection that burns within my heart for a beloved father. In writing this letter there is but one object, that, to assure you the *Gospel burns within* my bosom. In my prolonged absence from home there has been no private motive of mine save as the business in which I am engaged compels me. So completely has my mind been on Utah, her interests, and our people, that I suppose I have never realized my absence as my friends at home do. Where one conversation has been upon business, many have been upon Religion, and it may not be that the Lord condemns me for my labor.

"My protracted illness of last summer, although severe, was productive of good: it gave me time to think, to contemplate, to see my work, to contrast an occupation for lucre, with that for Eternal Lives, and Glory in God's Kingdom.

"The death of my dearly beloved brother and sister, Joseph A. and Alice, sank deeply, and I said, by the Lord's help, when I die, I will die too with full harness on, and not tear and wear my strength and life to shreds promoting any private enterprise. By thus speaking of my labors East, I do not wish to convey the idea that money has been my object, for the Lord knows it has not, but to build up the Country occupied by the Saints, and learn the commercial and material standing of the world and show them ours, and this, that I might be more useful at home.

"The light in which it presents itself is this: where is the place for a servant of the Lord to do the greatest work. The answer comes, at home, in Zion! My mind is fixed dear Father, and just as soon as I can complete my labors here, and discharge my duty to others honorably, command me then henceforth, and with God's help I will obey.... Hereafter it will be my delight to pass all the time alloted in your society and under the counsel and control of your great experience.... Sincerely praying God to give you health and happiness, and power to lead the people and defeat our enemies, and with love to all the Brethren I am, your affectionate son, John W. Young."[31]

By October 1876 John W. had so arranged his railroad affairs in the East that he was able to return to Utah and accept the appointment as his father's first counselor in the presidency of the Church, to which position he was sustained in general conference six days after his return.

Writing to his father in St. George, Utah, a month after his call, John W. assured him, "The responsibility of the position which you have called me to is ever before me and I am, with the help of the Lord, bound to honor and magnify it, and let the follies of this world go, and occupy my time with the Things of the Kingdom; all I want is to get out honorably."[32]

The following letter of Brigham Young, written about two months after John W. Young's appointment to the presidency, shows that the son was already engaged in the responsibilities of his new calling.

St. George, Utah, November 23, 1876

John W. Young
Salt Lake City, Utah

My dear Son,

I have received some few telegrams from you, and I believe all are answered.

This morning you asked if I would sell Bro. John Parry some thirty acres of land south of the city, near Shirtliff's place. I would rather not do so at present. The land I would rather keep than sell short of fifty dollars an acre. The Co-op stock that you mentioned in your telegram as part pay is good for to keep, but not to sell. I would not give more than thirty five cents on the dollar for it. And I am opposed to the brethren [selling] so cheap. I control some three hundred and fifty thousand dollars worth of this stock. This is as much as I ought to carry. The people that own the stock ought to keep it. The institution is for the benefit of the people, and they do reap the reward whether they know it or not, though not in the shape of dividends but in keeping down the price of goods. I did not say as much to you in my telegram about the railroad as I wish to. As to the Pacific R.R. company buying my stock and bonds, they are not disposed to do any such thing unless they can make a speculation of it. I do not care about their buying it. If they would bring our coal for a reasonable price we would rather they should do so. We would be willing to furnish our own cars, and if they will *not* do this I think the people had better build a road to the coal fields. If we build a railroad I want to do it openly and on the square, not in secret.

I do really wish you was not obliged to go east again this winter, but could spend a little time here in St. George with me.

I am glad to hear you are doing all you can to encourage the brethren where you are. If Bro. Edward's wife is not able to go to the farm over Jordan this winter, he can go and take care of the things through the winter and come home at night.

I have answered a letter from Bro. [Daniel H.] Wells about Grantsville. You and Bro. Wells had better go over there and ordain a bishop; Edward Hunter, I think, should be the man; he lives there.

I am thankful that I have you to help me. Brigham is here but his health is not very good; his head troubles him some, but is doing what he can. He has just returned from a short tour south with Bro. [Erastus] Snow and others to hunt out a road to a large field of pinion pine and cedars.

How is your mother's health? And Libbie and the children, and all the rest of the folks?

How does Bro. [Joseph H.] Ridges prosper in getting up the work in the new house?

How is the Co-op doing, are things prospering there? If it comes right, get some one to buy back the Hooper carriage and your carriage. If not handy, no matter, there are plenty of carriages in the world and they are making more.

I said to you in one of my telegrams: If you are obliged to go east take no one with you and bring no one back, and stay as little time there as possible. Learn to save your dimes, that you may have dollars, and your dollars that you may have hundreds and thousands, so that you can do business and not be distressed or worried at any time.

I wish you could be with me the most of the time, and you could were it not for your railroad business, but you must get along with it and it will give you a valuable experience.

I wish Joseph F. Smith could look into the temple in this place before he goes to England. I think it would do him good. And I think it would do you good to do so. If Joseph F. could come down and make a flying visit before he leaves I would very much like it.

If you were at leisure so you could take him in a light buggy you could put him through in quick time.

The temple is now almost entirely completed. The upper room needs a few days more labor; then it will be finished.

Give my best respects to Bro. Wells and the brethren and to all my wives and children.

I pray for you constantly and for all the Saints. God bless you.

Brigham Young

BRIGHAM HEBER YOUNG

Brigham Heber Young
1845-1928

Brigham Heber Young, the son of Brigham and Lucy Ann Decker Young, was born June 18, 1845, at Nauvoo, Illinois, amid preparations for the Latter-day Saint departure from that city. Having survived the rigors of crossing the plains, the small child arrived with his mother in the Salt Lake Valley in the fall of 1848. Growing up in the new settlement, Heber assisted in odd jobs at home and was educated in the family school. He excelled in mathematics and expressed interest in engineering but did not pursue higher education in that field.

There is evidence that Heber was one of at least four of Brigham Young's sons ordained apostles by their father, although he was never numbered with the General Authorities or named to the Council of Twelve.[1] During his teen-age years he traveled extensively with his father and brothers Joseph A., Brigham Jr., and John W., visiting the settlements of the Saints. At seventeen he drove an ox team to the Missouri River to assist with the Church emigration. In the summer of 1865 he was employed by the Union Pacific Railroad under Samuel B. Reed on survey work between South Pass and Humboldt Wells. A few days after returning home, Heber and seven other young men were sent east with provisions as part of a relief force to assist the Willis emigrant company, which had been delayed on the plains by a stampede of their cattle and heavy snow. The relief column found the emigrants in a destitute condition at the Sweetwater River. "The morning we met the company they had eaten nearly the last of their provisions and were much pleased to see us with fresh supplies," Heber noted.[2] In 1866 he was again employed with the railroad survey along the

Humboldt River to the California border.

At the general conference of the Church in Salt Lake City in April 1867 Heber was one of fifty missionaries called. A month later he was en route to Europe, where he served a year in England and two years in Switzerland. Five months after his return to Salt Lake City, he married Vilate Ruth Clayton, a daughter of William Clayton, on November 24, 1870. To them were born three daughters.

After receiving a special blessing from their father, Heber and his brother Arta De Christa traveled to Soda Springs, Idaho, with their families in the spring of 1872; there they opened a branch of Zion's Cooperative Mercantile Institution. Not accustomed to the climate of Idaho, which he described as a "godforsaken isolated snow prison," Heber remained less than a year in Soda Springs. Subsequently, he moved to Logan, Utah, and finally in the fall of 1873 back to Salt Lake City, where he spent the remainder of his life. In the settlement of his father's estate Heber received $18,000, which provided a basis for his support in following years. Upon moving to Salt Lake City he was employed by the Deseret Woolen Mills and E. J. Swaner and Company, a watchmaking and jewelry firm; and, beginning in 1889, he engaged in the insurance and real estate business, where he became president of the Young and Fowler Company.

Heber Young died June 3, 1928, in Salt Lake City at eighty-two years of age.

Letter dated September 30, 1867

Having been called as a missionary at the general conference in April 1867, Heber Young and some twenty others started east for the railroad terminus with John Sharp's wagon train on May 10. The missionaries had just headed up Emigration Canyon when the wagon containing Heber's possessions tipped over and rolled into the creek. The accident forced him to return to the city and delayed his departure another two weeks. "Many and strange were the thoughts that crowded my breast as I left the home of my friends, my companions of youth, and all that was dear to me on earth. As the City grew small in the distance, and I was to take, for some years, my last look upon the valley I loved so well, clouds of trouble seemed to be lowering around me. I was young, I was inexperienced and my only solace, was trust in a gracious God,"³ the twenty-one-year-old missionary wrote in his diary.

As they traveled to the railroad terminus at Julesberg through inclement weather, Heber noted, "We had a good trip and were signally blessed and protected by the unseen hand of providence, for while we were allowed to pass, not only uninjured, but really uninterrupted, many a poor unfortunate soul, whose bones now lie mouldering on the desolate plain fell a victim to the remorseless savage. Many mail stations were still burning, which had been destroyed by the Red Man, as we passed along. Destruction of mail matter and pools of human blood where had been committed the most formidable massacres, were still the unwelcome sight to those who ventured along that dreary road."⁴

At Julesberg Heber saw his first railroad train. The missionaries continued east by rail to New York City, and after "a dire voyage of thirteen days," they arrived in Liverpool, England. After being greeted by the mission president, "who promised us work for the future two or three years," Heber went shopping and bought a "neat clerical suit, which felt as uncomfortable as it seemed to me to be misplaced." The following day, Sunday, he gave his maiden speech, "which was as short as it was meaningless. I thought I would drop through my collar into my boots, but by one overwhelming effort I managed to survive and believed I should yet live for many years."⁵

Assigned to work in the London Conference, Heber Young left Liverpool on July 28 for his field of labor. About three months after his arrival in London, he received the following letter from his father, the contents of which so motivated him that he had the epistle published in the British Mission periodical, the *Latter-day Saints' Millennial Star*.

Salt Lake City, September 30, 1867

Elder Heber Young
42 Islington, Liverpool, England

Dear Son,

Your letter of [*blank*] was received and perused with pleasure. I am glad to learn that you feel so well in your ministry, and I trust that this feeling will increase within you so long as you remain on your mission. I hope you will write to me often and keep me informed of your progress and labors. You have now entered upon a new sphere of action; the responsibilities and cares of manhood, and especially those which pertain to the priesthood, are resting upon you, and much more is expected from you now than ever before. There is this consolation which God has given to His servants—that as their day their strength shall be, and He will bestow His grace upon them so that they may be equal to every responsibility and emergency. You are now in a position to find Him a present help in time of need, and He will be to you all that you can desire if you only seek to Him with faith and diligence.

There is no position a young man can be placed in that is better adapted to give him a knowledge of God and of His holy Spirit than to be sent on a mission. If you are humble and prayerful He will reveal Himself to you with a power which you have never heretofore known, and you will have greater joy in your labors and in your existence than you have ever before been capable of comprehending. We pray for you constantly, and we feel assured that our prayers will be heard in your behalf. It will give us great pleasure to hear of your success and of your magnifying your priesthood and fulfilling this mission which has been assigned you honorably before God and your brethren, that when you return you may come pure and unspotted. To this end I pray you to remember your high calling. You are young and inexperienced in the ways of the wicked world, therefore as Paul wrote to Timothy, so write I to you, "Flee also youthful lusts." Bring your passions and appetites and all your feelings into complete subjection to the mind and will of God. If you are determined to maintain the mastery you can do so by the Lord's help. The man who suffers his passions to lead him becomes a slave to them, and such a man will find the work of emancipation an exceedingly difficult one. Make the doing of God's will and the keeping of His commandments a constant habit with you and it will become perfectly natural and easy for you to walk uprightly before Him. The time of youth and early manhood is the proper time in which to form such habits.

You know the truth sufficiently to be capable of teaching it. Let your example show it forth more strongly, even, than your words, that others seeing your good works may be constrained to acknowledge that they are better than theirs and may, perchance, be influenced to go and do likewise.

Your mother and the children and all the family are well. Alice [Young Clawson] buried her youngest child yesterday, and one of Vilate [Young Decker]'s is buried today. The present is rather an unhealthy season and we have had a good many deaths among the children, but it is hoped that the cool weather will correct this and make the elements more healthy. The grasshoppers or locusts that we have had have probably helped to poison the atmosphere and produce sickness, and the high waters may have had a tendency in the same direction.

Everything is peaceable in the Territory. We have never been more free from annoyance on the part of our enemies than at the present time, and the Saints are rejoicing in their religion and are increasing in the works of righteousness.

In company with a number of the Twelve and other elders I left this city on the 2nd instant on a visit to Bear Lake Valley. We returned on the 17th, having traveled three hundred miles and held twenty-five meetings while we were absent. It was one of the most agreeable trips I ever made, though in returning from Bear Lake we had a two-day snowstorm. We noticed great improvements in the settlements and in the circumstances of the people. Much valuable instruction was given to the people during our sojourn amongst them.

Our new tabernacle, though not quite finished in every respect, is yet so forward that we expect to hold our fall conference in it, commencing next Sunday. It has been pushed forward during the latter part of the summer with great diligence, and the workmen have manifested great zeal in their labors. It is a magnificent place and will answer the purpose for which it was constructed, admirably.

Brigham Jr., John W., and Katie [Catherine Spencer Young] and the children with a number of other returned missionaries have reached here in good health and spirits. We had discourses from several of them yesterday in the Bowery, all expressing their delight at reaching home. The company of immigrating Saints will probably be in within two weeks. Six four-mule teams, besides many individuals who have friends in the company, have gone out to meet and assist them.

Give my love to all the elders who are with you, and

accept the same to yourself, in which your mother and the family and Presidents [Heber C.] Kimball and [Daniel H.] Wells join, and praying the Lord to be with you, and to bless you with the power and wisdom necessary to magnify your calling, and to fill your mission with honor, and to preserve you and to bring you home in peace and safety, I remain,

> Your father,
> Brigham Young

Letters dated September 3, 1868, to February 16, 1870

After laboring nearly a year as a "traveling elder" in the London Conference of the British Mission, Heber Young was transferred to Switzerland, where he continued his missionary work for another two years. In company with Willard B. Richards, he left London on July 6 and reported to Karl G. Maeser in Switzerland two days later. "We are now in the beautiful country of Switzerland, where we can enjoy the pure mountain air, which brother W. B. Richards and myself highly appreciate, after being cooped up in smoky London for the past 12 months. . . . One thing I think worthy of note," he continued, "is that farming can be carried on, wheat can stand out in the open field without being protected by stone walls, and still permitted to grow and not be subject to prowling 'critters' which are so great a pest in our own country."[6]

Accepting the challenge of a foreign language, Heber made rapid progress with the new tongue. After attending his first conference, shortly after arriving in Switzerland, he confessed that because he was not able to speak German he was unable to give much instruction. However, within a few months Karl G. Maeser wrote Brigham Young that "beyond my expectation, I found your son Heber so much advanced in German that he preached here on Sunday Nov. 29 in my presence a fine German discourse without using a single English word to the edification and understanding of a large congregation."[7]

In August 1869 a meeting of the Saints in Fuerstenau, Germany, was interrupted by two Methodist preachers who ridiculed the Mormons, Utah, and Brigham Young, whereupon Heber arose and, in the most fitting terms he could muster, informed the gentlemen that he was a son of Brigham Young and that he had been raised in Utah and was well versed in Mormon habits and customs. He corrected the statements of the clergymen and testified to the integrity of his father and the Latter-day Saints in general, and after talking with the visitors for some time, "found more toleration than I had dared to hope for." He concluded, "I think their visit will aid to slacken the bands of bigotry and prejudice which have existed to so great a degree in the past."[8]

Desirous to retain his knowledge of the German language, Heber wrote his father before leaving Switzerland for some money with which to purchase a good German dictionary and some German publications, "as I do not wish, as soon as I reach home, to forget the little I have learned, and for which I have so assiduously studied."[9]

During his stay in the Swiss-German Mission, Heber Young successively presided over the East Swiss Conference and was secretary of the mission, president of the Zurich District, and first counselor to President Maeser in the mission presidency, before his release in June 1870. The following letters of Brigham Young dated September 3 and October 22, 1868, and February 16, 1870, were written to Heber Young during his stay in the Swiss-German Mission.

Salt Lake City, September 3, 1868

Elder Heber Young
Swiss, Italian and German Mission

My dear Son,

Your letters of the [*blank*] insts. are received and it was very satisfactory to me to hear that your health was good and that you enjoy your mission and like your new field of labor; it is a source of great benefit to the elders to travel in different countries and preach the gospel; they become acquainted with the various habits and customs of the nations, and learning other languages gives them a more perfect knowledge of their own.

It is good to hear that the spirit of inquiry is increasing among the people in that region and that some are embracing the truth, for the time is near when judgments will overtake the wicked and they will have cause to mourn for the manner in which they have treated the message God has sent His servants to declare unto the nations. Since last I wrote you, Israel has endured the loss of one of her chieftains, President Heber C. Kimball, who passed away on the 22nd of June after an illness of ten days. We feel his loss and his memory is held dear among all the faithful Saints at home and, I trust, abroad. Capt. Wm. H. Hooper arrived lately from Washington. He has had quite a contest with [William] McGrorty, who made an absurd attempt to rob our delegate of his seat, but the effort proved as unsuccessful as it was illegal.

The railroad is progressing rapidly. A great portion of the work on my contract is completed and considerable interest is manifested in the matter. It is not yet known on which side of the lake the line will run, but it is probable we shall soon hear the snorting of the iron horse through our valleys giving us the facilities, commercial and otherwise, which invariably accompany such a speedy mode of transit.

Your brothers Joseph A., Brigham Jun., and John W. are actively engaged in the work as my agents. The grasshoppers have done some damage to our crops; in Morgan, Summit, and Wasatch counties they have taken pretty much all the grain, but in Davis and Cache the brethren have sown such a quantity that I think with prudence and economy we shall have sufficient to last us till another harvest.

Bro. Albert Carrington left on the 17th ult. for Liverpool to take the presidency of the European Mission.

Some of the trains loaded with immigrants have arrived, others are expected shortly; the Saints look well and appear to appreciate being gathered home. It is a great privilege to those coming from other countries now, to be able to perform so much of their journey by rail, leaving but about 350 miles to travel with teams. The journey is far less tedious besides the advantages gained in the saving of time.

Your mother is well and also the children. Ernest is my main man on the forest farm.

I started on the 17th ult. accompanied by Bros. John Taylor, Wilford Woodruff, Geo. A. Smith, Geo. Q. Cannon, Joseph F. Smith, A[mos] M. Musser and others on a trip to Cache Valley. We held meetings in the principal settlements and preached to the people on their various duties, urging upon them to keep their covenants sacred, take care of their grain, and live uprightly before the Lord; we returned on the 25th in good health having held fifteen meetings and traveled 176 miles.

The brethren join me in kind love to you. I trust you will continue to enjoy the spirit of your mission, and labor for the spread of the gospel with that energy which shall rid your garments of the blood of the nations to which you are sent.

Be faithful to your religion. Remember your covenants. Eschew all impure thoughts and feelings and live humbly and prayerfully before the Lord, and that you may be greatly blessed and prospered in the ministry and return unspotted from the world, is the sincere and earnest prayer of

Your father,
Brigham Young

P.S. I received both your letters referred to, but I handed them to your mother to read, and they have got misplaced.

Salt Lake City, October 22, 1868

Elder Heber Young
Zurich, Switzerland

My dear Son,

The perusal of your letters always affords me great pleasure, manifesting as they do, by the spirit in which they are written, that you realize the importance and sacredness of your calling as an elder in Israel sent to bear the glad tidings of the gospel of salvation to the nations who sit in darkness and unbelief. If there is anything that gives joy to the hearts of the fathers in this kingdom it is the knowledge that their sons seize the holy principles for which they have so long labored in the name of Jesus, and that their children are preparing themselves by faith and good works to bear off the kingdom triumphant and accomplish the work their fathers have commenced. Be prayerful to the Lord continually and humble in His hands; trust in Him for His holy Spirit and in every circumstance remember how great is the responsibility placed upon you to set an example amongst Saints and strangers worthy to be copied by all men, that the cause of God may be honored in your life, and His name glorified by your good deeds.

I wrote to you on the 3rd of last month. I hope my letter has reached you safely before this. Yesterday I read your letter to your mother of the [blank] Sept. I was pleased to hear you were well and enjoying your mission.

Myself, your mother, and your brothers and sisters are well. Exactly at twelve o'clock last night Fanny [Y. Thatcher] had a fine girl; mother and daughter are both doing well. Ernest is now on the road having gone to meet the last of the immigration, those who were detained at New York through sickness. They will be here the day after tomorrow. They compose the last company I anticipate we shall have to send out to meet, as before another immigration season comes around we have every reason to believe the railroad will be running through these valleys.

Joseph A., Brigham Jun., and John W. are busily engaged on my grading contract. Joseph A. is associated with Bro. John Sharp in a large contract in Weber Canyon. They have some very heavy work to do, including two tunnels. John W. has a contract also. His is a heavy piece of work in Echo, while Brigham is engaged in superintending the whole of the work as my representative.

The brethren have now got used to the labor and can work to much greater advantage than when they first started. A great portion of the earth work is now finished, but there is a large fill at the head of Echo which we are now crowding with all our might. The tracklayers are advancing with giant strides. Already they have passed Brian, 18 miles this side of Green River, and they intend to make a temporary track round the tunnels and heavy work that may not be finished in time. Dr. [Thomas C.] Durrant, the vice-president of the road, was here a few weeks ago. He talks of getting the road through to this valley in sixty days. He has not yet learned what it is to crowd tunnel through our canyons in mid-winter.

Hyrum, Arta, and several of the other boys are attending the classes at the Commercial Department of the University of Deseret under the care of Elder David O. Calder; they are there practically taught in the various branches of a business education by actual business transactions, which familiarizes them with the practice as well as the theory of commerce.

Caroline [Young] and Zina [Young] have been married within the last few weeks, Zina to Bro. Thomas Williams and Caroline to Mark Croxall. At our last conference the vacancy caused in the quorum of the First Presidency by the departure to another sphere of usefulness of Bro. H. C. Kimball, was filled by the appointment of Elder Geo. A. Smith, Brigham Jun. being called to be a member of the Quorum of the Twelve to fill the vacancy caused by Elder Smith's removal. About one hundred and sixty elders were also then called to strengthen the mission on the Muddy, the majority being residents of this city, but quite a number also from American Fork, Pleasant Grove, Farmington, and other settlements. They are most of them men of weight in the places in which they have lived, and I expect to see the southern mission greatly benefited.

Remember me most kindly to Elders [Karl G.] Maeser, [Octave] Ursenbach, [Willard B.] Richards and the other elders associated with you in the Swiss and German Missions, and to the Saints.

May God our Heavenly Father continue to bless you and give you the wisdom of His Spirit, and power to do much good that you may return home when the time comes full of joy and gladness, is the prayer of

> Your affectionate father,
> Brigham Young

P.S. You need not marvel to see some of the boys with you next summer. I rather think I shall send James Little. I wrote to Bro. Maeser yesterday; he will no doubt show you his letter. From it you will be able to learn the steps we are taking to build up Zion in our deal and trading.

Salt Lake City, February 16, 1870

Elder Heber Young
Sihlhalle, Aussersihl, Zurich

My dear Son,

Your welcome letter of Jan. 11 has been received and read

not only by myself, but by some of the brethren who frequent the office, by your mother, and others of the family and we are extremely well pleased to hear from you and of your continued good health and prosperity in your field of labor.

For my part, I had supposed that a letter was long since due from you, but upon inquiry I have ascertained that your last, having been taken into the house for the folks to read, was not returned to the office and hence was not answered.

It is truly gratifying to hear of the spread of truth in Switzerland and of the faithfulness and zeal as displayed by the elders—native and foreign. May God bless them with joy and peace in their labors and crown them with success. We are constantly receiving communications from the elders laboring in the States, but how different is their testimony with regard to the work of God there. There is a coldness in the minds of the people, a total indifference to the gospel and its glorious truths and the whole sum of their inquiries [is] how and where can we make the most money. Of course there are a few exceptions, but what a condition of things does this indicate! Every species of wickedness is on the increase, and so rapidly, that it is difficult to conceive otherwise than that the people are fast ripening for destruction. And why is this? The gospel door was opened on this land, prophets and apostles have traversed it preaching the divine message, temples have been erected upon it where the sacred ordinances of the priesthood have been administered, but these ordinances have been held in derision, the truth has been rejected, prophets and apostles have been slain for the testimony of Jesus, and now the people have become hardened in iniquity and are led captive to the will of that evil power they prefer to serve. Yesterday I read in a N.Y. paper of the discovery of a secret organization there, where perjurers could be hired to give evidence on any subject, at so much an oath.

The times are interesting and probably there never was any more opposition manifested to the kingdom of God than there is now. Foes without and foes within, apostates and outsiders, and among the former class are some who have hitherto professed the strongest fidelity to the kingdom of God. We have, verily, the world, the flesh, and the devil to contend with. All are against us, but those among us who have understanding and in whom the light of Christ dwells feel as unruffled as the bosom of the ocean when heaven is smiling and the winds are at perfect rest, or, to speak more popularly, they feel that God and one good man are a vast majority. No less than five bills are now before Congress, having in view the disintegration of Utah and, in short, to deprive us of every vestige of constitutional liberty and reduce us to a condition of moral and political serfdom but, as the proverb says, "man proposes, but God disposes."

The Godbe Planchette Church,[10] of which you have doubtless heard, is not making the progress its founders and advocates anticipated, but it is picking up a class who have already apostatized and who, like a drowning man, are ready to catch even at a straw. Their doctrines are as antagonistic to God and his righteousness as hell is opposed to heaven. They ignore the efficacy of the atonement, and they practically repudiate celestial marriage on the plea that the principle may do in the heavens, but they are not pure enough for it on the earth. On the 10th inst. we had a mass meeting in this city of a somewhat peculiar character. It appears that a few nights previous to that, the Godbe clique held a caucus, and got up an opposition ticket for city officers. Accordingly, they placarded the city with bills, the object of which was as set forth, "for the nomination of a people's free and independent ticket for mayor, aldermen, councilors &c. to be voted for on Monday the 14th inst." This bill was headed "Come one, come all!" and was subscribed "many voters." The consequence of such a general invitation was not what was expected by those who issued it, for at an early hour "Walker's Original Store" was crowded with *our* citizens, who, in an orderly, systematic manner, elected chairman, secretary, reporter &c., after which the chair announced that nominations were in order, and the legitimate ticket was put and sustained with extraordinary unanimity. The president or chairman of the meeting was Col. J. C. Little, (not Eli B. Kelsey, as had been intended) and the Planchetteites felt rather crest-fallen at the unexpected turn things had taken. But the invitation was to all the citizens, consequently, there was a large attendance. On Monday (14th) the election of city officers was held. The opposition votes were 297, the legitimate ticket,

2004. About 25 women voted, on the occasion. You must know that woman suffrage is a law now in this territory! Last week it passed both houses and on Saturday was signed by the governor.

I expect to start with a small company for Dixie and probably across the Colorado. In the latter event we may be gone perhaps a couple of months.

The Utah Central Railroad is a success. Trains are running regularly and the business bids fair to be very prosperous. The cost of constructing and furnishing the road will reach about one and a quarter million dollars, not a dollar of which is owing to anyone outside of the Church. It will seem a novelty to you that we have a railroad of our own running into this city, but so it is, and we hear the steam whistle in the office with great plainness as the iron horse comes snorting on to the Babbitt block. The fare to Ogden is $2.00 at present, but it will be reduced for the benefit of our citizens in way of excursion trains and return tickets to about half that rate.

My health, I am happy to state, is at present good, and has been as a general thing, through the winter, though I suffered a little with the mumps. Your mother is well and so are all the folks. Fanny [Young Thatcher] is visiting at the Beehive House. She is afflicted some with her eyes. Bro. [George W.] Thatcher has moved all his family to Logan.

Remember me affectionately to all the faithful brethren and an especial manner to Bro. Maeser. We pray for you continually that you may be blessed in all your labors for the welfare of Israel.

Your affectionate father,
Brigham Young

OSCAR BRIGHAM YOUNG

Photo Credit: Utah State Historical Society

Oscar Brigham Young
1846-1910

The only son of Brigham Young and Harriet Elizabeth Cook Young, Oscar Brigham was born in the Nathaniel Ashby home in Nauvoo, Illinois, on February 10, 1846, five days before his father left Nauvoo to lead the Mormon exodus to the west. Harriet and her small son joined Brigham Young in Winter Quarters later that year, and they continued on to Salt Lake Valley in September 1848. Before the completion of the Lion House in the mid-1850s, Oscar lived with his mother in a one-room log house on a hill north of the city. His mother was known to Indians in the area as Brigham Young's brave squaw from an incident in which she had courageously driven a thieving Indian from her home and chased him over the sagebrush-covered hills, beating him with a broom. Oscar's frequent contact with Indian children rewarded him with a fair knowledge of their customs and language.

Oscar attended school in the Lion House, where his mother, who had been educated in a private school in Pennsylvania, taught Brigham Young's children. He also studied at the family school east of the Eagle Gate and later at the University of Deseret. Although he loved to read and draw, his fondness for the outdoors eclipsed his desire for education—a fact he later regretted. One incident during his school years that reinforced his dislike for formal education occurred when he was placed on a stool with a dunce cap before the class on one occasion, after having been caught drawing instead of working an arithmetic assignment.

At sixteen Oscar assisted with the Church emigration, driving an ox team to the Missouri River and back. His marriage in 1865 to Paralee Russell, by whom he had one child, terminated in a divorce a few years later. Prior to this he left his wife and child to serve as a missionary to England for nine months in 1866-67. While living with his mother at Leeds, Washington County, Utah, in his early twenties, Oscar learned the blacksmith trade and established the only blacksmith shop in town. Later he worked at his trade in Salt Lake City in a shop on North Temple Street, servicing teams and tools for the workmen on the Salt Lake Temple. Severely injured in an accident that resulted in occasional mental disorder, Oscar nevertheless led a normal, active life as a blacksmith, farmer, rancher, railroad worker, and manager of the Deseret Woolen Mill.

In October 1875 Oscar married Annie M. Roseberry, a daughter of Swedish converts to the Church. They became the parents of eleven children, including three sets of twins born within three and a half years.

While living in Salt Lake Valley, Oscar resided first near the mouth of Parley's Canyon and later on an eighty-acre farm in Sugar House. In 1890 the family moved to Provo, where the children attended the Brigham Young Academy, and Oscar served as a member of the Board of Trustees until shortly before his death from a paralytic stroke on August 4, 1910.

Letter dated March 16, 1867

Leaving his wife and a three-month-old daughter, Oscar B. Young boarded a stagecoach in Salt Lake City on August 13, 1866, to begin his mission to England. Crossing the Atlantic on the steamer *City of Paris* in the record time of ten days, on September 11 he arrived in Liverpool, where he was greeted by his brothers Brigham Jr. and John W., who had preceded him as missionaries to England, the former as president of the European Mission. Except for a visit to the Paris Exposition with his brothers in the spring of 1867, Oscar spent the nine months he was in England laboring in the London Conference.

Two months before the termination of his mission, Oscar received the following letter from his father, dated March 16, 1867. Oscar's response some six weeks later is the only example of his rough but sensitive prose in the Church Archives. The document gives some insight to his personal feelings and character: "I have resived the lettear that you seante me. [Oh] the joye that it gave me to resived a lettear from my Father.... I have visetied the Paris Exhibition and it was ... a veary nise time. Brigham and John W. neaver was more kinde to a brother than they ware to me.... If God gives me poweare I will returne a beatere man than any one in the City of Greate Salt Lake thought when I leafte ... but thare is meany things in which I wish to inprove. The expearince that I have gained is good. Thare is a good meny of the Elders that will returne some of which are going to make greate men in this kindom they are them which have lived the relinen [religion] of Jesus Christ the Survents of the moste High. The Brothen teale me that I muste not preach to you. They say that you know all that I can teale you and a greadel more but then it is borne in me.... The injoymente of pleasure in this greate worke is to me one of the greates blesings that I can injoye.... The way that this Cuntrey a greeas with me is beatere than I could like. The saints are veary kinde to me. The Bretheren give me good counsele.... The time that I have been in London the saints have showen the veary beaste of fealings the way that you have showen the fealings of a veary kinde Fathear.... Please Remeambeare me to all the Bretheren that wourke for the Bilding up of the Kindom of God, to J. A. Young, the Famley, to mothear, all my Brothers and Sistears, the Prayears of A Kinde Brothere is raised for them eveary night. The Bleasings and Pawear of God be with you is the Prayear of your Kinde and A Effectnet Son in the Gospel and the New and Eveary Lasten Covenant the Powere of God unto selveation and your Son. Oscar B. Young. P.S. this Country a greeas well with me. OBY."[1]

Salt Lake City, March 16, 1867

Elder Oscar B. Young
42 Islington, Liverpool, England

Dear Son,

Two letters have been received from you, in both of which I was pleased to see the good feelings and desires expressed by you respecting your mission. It gratifies me to see my sons manifest a desire to magnify the holy priesthood, for I know if they are faithful in the callings of that priesthood, their power and influence

on the earth will increase and they will have the favor of God and
His people. You are called in your youth to go forth and bear the
message of life and salvation to the nations of the earth, and this is
the most honorable and glorious calling that our Heavenly Father
can bestow upon His children in this life. Since you left home you
have no doubt seen considerable of the glory of this world. London
is one of the greatest cities in Christendom; the wealth of ages has
accumulated there, and human dignity receives the greatest honor
that can be bestowed. But there is no king or queen, or potentate
of any kind, whose honor can be compared to that which God
bestows upon men when He gives to them the holy priesthood.
Their glory fades away; it lasts only while life endures, but the
holy priesthood when received and magnified by man is an eternal
honor, which increases as years roll by, until, by faithfulness, man
is brought back into the presence of his Maker, and is crowned with
glory, immortality and eternal lives. By faithfully keeping the
commandments of God and living humbly and faithfully before
Him so as to partake of His power, while you are on your present
mission, you will lay a foundation for future usefulness in the
kingdom of God. If there be any difference in missions probably the
first mission that a man takes has more influence on his future than
any that he may take in after life. On his first mission he lays the
foundation and adopts the principles which are to guide him
through his future career, and it has seldom been the case that a
young man who has been dilatory and careless while upon his first
mission has ever recovered the ground he then lost or obtained the
confidence of his brethren to the extent that he would have
enjoyed had he been more faithful. You now have opportunities of
gaining experience in, and a knowledge of, your religion that you
could not have obtained and to live so near to the Lord that you
will have his holy Spirit to rest upon you to enable you to teach the
people. This experience, if properly appreciated by you, will be of
great benefit to you through your future life. When you are in the
presence of elders who are older and more experienced than
yourself, listen to their counsels and teachings, and try and profit
by your intercourse with them. By watching their course among
the people and listening to their teachings you will obtain a better
idea of what is required of you, and when you go forth and have to
act as counselor and guide to the people, you will be better

prepared to assume that responsibility. I am desirous of seeing my sons honor the holy priesthood, and be faithful and reliable servants of God. Nothing connected with them would give me greater pleasure than this, for I know if they take this course everything else will be added to them. You and your brothers have my prayers for your continued preservation from every evil and for your safe return in peace and purity to your home.

Your mother's health is much better than it has been, and the family generally enjoy good health. Paralee [R. Young] and child are well. Paralee appears very steady.

We have had very peaceable times in the city this winter, and but little or no drinking. Money is very scarce and times dull. The strangers here have but little money to spend in drink; the result is that Dr. [Jeter] Clinton has but little to do. The few soldiers who are here are scarcely noticed, and were it not for the presence, occasionally, of an officer or soldier in uniform on our streets, we would not know that there was a camp in our vicinity. The regulars who are here are much more peaceable than the volunteers we had here a year or two ago.

The winter has been rather mild, but we have had considerable rain and snow. We are having colder weather now than we have had previously during the winter. There is a prospect of high water. The banks of the River Jordan are now full, and there is a probability that all the streams will be filled to their utmost capacity.

The telegraph wire is in successful operation from Logan to Saint George, and there is a branch line extending from Nephi to Manti in San Pete. All the offices are occupied by our boys as operators and this reports very well. This institution is a great benefit to the people and the Territory.

With love, in which your mother joins, to you [*illegible*] and to Brigham and John W., and to all the elders and Saints who may be with you, and praying the Lord to fill you with His holy Spirit, to give you wisdom and power to discharge the duties of your mission faithfully and acceptably before Him, and to bring you home in safety, I remain,

                        Your father,
                        Brigham Young

HYRUM SMITH YOUNG

Hyrum Smith Young
1851-1925

Hyrum S. Young, son of Brigham and Emmeline Free Young, was born on January 2, 1851, four years after the arrival of the pioneers in Salt Lake Valley. Educated at the family school and at the University of Deseret, Hyrum became well known in Utah banking circles. In 1872 he married Georgiana Fox, the daughter of the pioneer surveyor Jesse W. Fox, to whom were born ten children. For several years Hyrum was paymaster and treasurer of the Utah Central Railroad. In 1882 he went to Ogden, Utah, where he assisted in organizing the First National Bank. Seven years later, in 1889, he returned to Salt Lake City as cashier of the Deseret National Bank, which position he held until his death thirty-six years later. He died at his home in Salt Lake City on February 28, 1925. Hyrum lived sufficiently near to his father that mail correspondence between the two seems to have been unnecessary; at least if any letters were written, none remain.

ERNEST IRVING YOUNG

Ernest Irving Young
1851-1879

Ernest Irving Young, the second son of Lucy Ann Decker and Brigham Young, was born April 30, 1851, in the newly established town of Salt Lake City. Ernest received his education in his father's private school, located first in the Lion House and later in the white schoolhouse east of the Eagle Gate. On November 19, 1871, he married Sybella White Johnson, to whom were born five children. He was called to the Salt Lake Stake high council in October 1873 and eight months later, in May 1874, his name was read in general conference to serve as a missionary in England.

After returning from his mission in June 1876, Ernest was employed in his father's office, and he worked for a short time at ZCMI. A letter addressed to his father in St. George, Utah, on December 27, 1876, containing a request for a farm, is the last known communication of Ernest to Brigham Young. "Since I returned from England I have been thinking, I would like to follow farming, and earn my livelihood in that manner should it meet with your approval. I am tired of depending on other people for work, and if I can get a farm, I feel assured I can, at least, make a living, and that is all I have done by working for other people. Heber and myself are of the same mind on this subject, and we thought if it met your mind (for us to so make a start) we would ask you to give us the Mill Farm. We believe we have brain and muscle enough to make a success of such a business. We hope you will think so too, and grant our request." He closed the letter with a Christmas greeting and best wishes to his father. "Christmas passed off very quietly, and all seemed to have enjoyed themselves, and have had generally a good time. The Mattinee at the

Theatre seemed to be the Center of Attraction, and hundreds of children went to witness the performance of 'Cinderalla' and the young folks enjoyed it hugely. I am very sorry to hear of your being sick. I hope and pray this will find you enjoying as good health and spirits as I do, for I am well and happy as the day is long. With fondest love from all at home to yourself, and all with you, wishing you and all a Merry Christmas and a Happy New Year, I remain your son, Ernest I. Young."[1]

Little is known of Ernest's activities after this. Following the death of Brigham Young, Ernest was one of the seven litigant heirs in the suit against the administrators of his father's estate.[2]

After retiring and complaining of a severe headache, Ernest I. Young died suddenly the night of October 8, 1879. He was twenty-eight years of age.

Letter dated February 4, 1875

At the general conference of the Church held May 9, 1874, Ernest I. Young, twenty-three-year-old member of the Salt Lake Stake high council, was called, with others, by vote of the conference to serve as a missionary in England. Traveling with a cousin, Brigham T. Young, Ernest arrived in Liverpool on June 14, 1874, and was immediately appointed chief clerk of the mission.

From St. George, Utah, where he had gone to supervise construction of the temple, Brigham Young addressed the following letter to his son Ernest on February 4, 1875.

St. George, Utah, February 4, 1875

Elder Ernest I. Young
Liverpool, England

My dear Son Ernest,

Your welcome letter of January 3d was duly received by last mail and was read with much satisfaction. I am glad that your health is so good in the English climate, and trust that you may continue to enjoy the blessing of health and vigor to minister in usefulness wherever the Lord may direct you to labor.

I am much gratified, my son, that you are able to write: "I feel good continually, and feel that I am blessed beyond expectation." It is your privilege to feel thus as a laborer in the vineyard of the Lord; for the powers of the heavens are on your side, while you seek to walk in the path of your duty in trying to promote the interests of Zion, True, you must be tested in the great school of mortal experience. There are, as you properly state, "many temptations, seen and unseen, to lead one astray, the tempter being always ready to take advantage where he can." This is the common lot of man, but especially of the young and inexperienced. There is no exception. It was written of our Savior, that he "was in all points tempted like as we are." But our duty is pointed out by him in the words, "watch and pray that ye enter not into temptation."

It should ever be borne in mind that sin does not consist of simply being tempted to do, to say, or to think wrong, but that the sin is in yielding to the temptation.

One strong safeguard against doing evil is to cultivate good thoughts, and when evil ones are presented, to *promptly* and manfully reject them, to dismiss them from the mind at once. This habit, together with never knowingly or heedlessly putting yourself in the way of temptation, will greatly aid in proving to you the truth of the scripture which saith, "Resist the devil and he will flee from you." And further, this course will assist in cultivating that high moral and religious tone which is indispensable to those who would wield the power of the holy priesthood.

My son, I am pleased to read your expressed determination to pursue a course which shall be acceptable to our Heavenly Father. May God aid you in all your efforts to this desirable end. This determination is right, at home or abroad, at all times, and in every place.

You, and all the brethren with you, and all the Saints in every land, have my constant prayers that the righteousness of God may increase on the earth.

I am thankful to our Father that my health is reasonably good. I have deemed it prudent to refrain from speaking much in public this winter. Last Sabbath and the Sabbath before, I addressed the Saints in the St. George Tabernacle.

I and Brother George A. Smith leave this city on the 10th inst. for Salt Lake City, if all is well. We expect to stay and attend the April General Conference at Salt Lake City, and then return to St. George.

We are vigorously pushing forward the building of the St. George Temple; it is progressing finely. A goodly number of volunteers from the North are assisting, and a good spirit prevails.

Just as soon as the roofing is on, and it is safe inside, we shall begin that great and all important work on baptizing for the dead, and attend to other ordinances of the gospel, as the building can be got ready.

Remember me kindly to Brother Joseph F. [Smith] and to the other brethren with you.

May the God of Israel ever bless and empower you, my son, for every good word and work, is the fervent prayer and desire of

Your father,

Brigham Young

Letter dated August 24, 1875

In addition to his assignment in the mission headquarters at Liverpool, Ernest traveled and spoke extensively in the various conferences of the British Mission. As he visited London for the first time in March 1875 with L. John Nuttall, an associate on the staff of the *Millennial Star*, Ernest viewed the metropolis as the most impressive sight he had ever seen. "It makes me wonder where all the people come from, and where they are all going, and how they live. Judging from the appearance of some of them, I should say, they don't live, but get along in a way not much to be envied."[3]

Writing in March 1875, Ernest expressed gratitude for the good counsel he had received in his father's letter of February 4, and added, "I will endeavor to put it into practice." He spoke of the contentment of mind that his missionary experience had brought him, and described the nature of the proselyting work in England. "It is a hard matter to get the people to turn out and visit our meetings for the Clergy are doing all they can to prevent those who would attend. The minds of the people are prejudiced to a considerable extent, and it requires constant labour with them to allay this prejudice, and when once allayed—sometimes they will stop to reason with you and ascertain what we do believe in—then they conclude that the Latter-day Saints teach sound doctrine, and they will often obey the Gospel. These cases are few and far between, still there is some few. I hope that God will open the hearts of the people that they may receive the truth. For I believe there are many honest in heart in these lands, and would embrace the Gospel if they could only be reached through the right channel, but this channel is hard to find, and unless God will show unto the Elders the way, and lead those souls to the place where they can hear the sound of the everlasting Gospel, I dont know in what manner they can be reached."[4]

On May 29, 1875, Ernest's brother Arta De Christa arrived in England as a missionary and was assigned to the Nottingham Conference. Although separated from each other in their missionary work, the two sons of Brigham Young were co-recipients of the following letter from their father dated August 24, 1875, which brought news of the death of their brother Joseph A.

Salt Lake City, August 24, 1875

Elders Ernest and Arta D. Young
England

My dear Sons Ernest and Arta,

I have taken the occasion of the departure of Elder Albert Carrington for Liverpool to take charge of the churches in Europe, to write you a few lines, to express the happiness I feel at the favorable reports that have reached me of your health, progress, and general welfare, as well as at the feelings and desires expressed in the letters I have at different times received from you. I shall be greatly pleased to hear that Ernest is seeking to overcome his diffidence with regard to public speaking, and that he, trusting in the strength of the Lord and the assistance of the Holy Spirit, is aiding his brethren in proclaiming the truths of the gospel to the nations who wait in the darkness of unbelief.

You were no doubt very much surprised and deeply grieved at learning of the death of your brother Joseph A. which occurred very suddenly at Manti, San Pete Co. on the 5th of this month at 8.40 p.m. Joseph had been paying a visit to this city, and left with myself and other brethren on 30th July to attend a two-days' meeting at Provo, from whence he started at my request for Manti to make some drawings of, and to superintend the erection of, the temple at that place. Whilst on his way up the canyon from Nephi he was suddenly seized with cramp or inflammation of the bowels. The next day, however, though sick, he visited the spot selected for the building of the temple and from thence drove to the house of Bro. Geo. Peacock, where the same evening his spirit took its departure from our midst. His remains were at once brought to the city and he was interred in my family burial ground on the Sunday morning following.

I have had much comfort and satisfaction in the last days of Joseph's mortal sojourn upon the earth. He had labored with great zeal, diligence, and wisdom in establishing the United Order in the midst of the Saints in Sevier Co. by whom he was highly respected as a president and greatly beloved as a brother. His labors in establishing the order of Zion amongst the Saints under his watchcare were greatly blessed of the Lord, and are made manifest in the harmony and union existing among the people, and the affection they bear for him who was their leader and guide in this work of regeneration and advancement to celestial lives.

Last week I had a very pleasant visit amongst the Saints in Cache Valley. Your brother, Brigham Jun., returned to the city with us, stayed a few days and returned to Logan yesterday. He is laboring assiduously and doing much good in instructing the people in the principles of the United Order whilst the feeling amongst the Saints is improving, with an increase in the comprehension of the laws of the gospel of the kingdom. In Salt Lake City a few of the brethren have united with the intention of devoting the whole of their surplus property, that is, all they do not require to support their families with economy, to the building up of the kingdom of God as directed by a board of directors which they have chosen. In other words, to consider first the kingdom of God, to give their hearts to him, and their lives with all they possess to his service. In fact, to hold themselves subject in all things to the voice God has placed upon the earth, to put into active practice that which as Latter-day Saints they have always professed to believe.

President Geo. A. Smith's health is now rapidly improving and we earnestly hope that the improvement may be permanent.

Regarding my own health I am pleased to be able to say that it is good, and my feelings are as calm and buoyant as ever. Notwithstanding the desperate and almost frantic attempts of the power of evil to do us harm, those who are living their religion realize that no power can hurt those whom God has in his watchcare.

The health of your mother and the family is good and they join me in love to yourselves. Remember me most kindly to the brethren from Zion, and the elders and Saints amongst whom you labor.

May God bless you abundantly in all your labors, strengthen you to accomplish all his righteous will concerning you, and bring you home safe to us when your work abroad is accomplished is the heartfelt prayer of

> Your father,
> Brigham Young

Letter dated December 13, 1875

Ernest Young was released from his mission in June 1876, after two years in England. Two months before his release he traveled among the Saints on the continent and in Scandinavia with his brother Arta and the mission president, Albert Carrington. The following letter of Brigham Young sent to his sons Ernest and Arta was written six months before Ernest left England for home.

Salt Lake City, December 13, 1875

Elders Ernest and Arta D. Young
England

My dear Sons,

Since my last letter to you I have heard from you several times, either directly from yourselves, or indirectly through Bro. Carrington and other elders. I am pleased to be able to tell you that all that I have heard has been grateful to my feelings and fills me with the hope that I shall continue to receive cheering news of your welfare, your labors, and your progress until you are honorably released to return to your friends and families in the valleys of Israel.

I have no doubt but that you appreciate the privileges you possess as ministers of salvation to the nations who sit in the shadow of the darkness of unbelief and of ignorance of the ways of the Lord. You have also had opened to you an inviting entrance to the living world of human thought and action. You are surrounded by influences from which you can learn lessons that will be of increasing influence in after years, and by comparing things as you meet them today with what they will be when the truth holds the sway, you will create within you a becoming respect for the dignity and honor of our sacred religion, and of the responsibilities of your holy calling. There is no position a man can occupy in this world, be he young or old, rich or poor, wise or simple, wherein he can learn so much of that which is truly valuable and worthy of acceptation as that of an elder in the Church of Jesus Christ in the active discharge of his calling. The present is the day of your opportunities, to mold your characters, to strengthen your faith, to develop your powers of mind and thought, and to acquire knowledge of men and manners that no books can teach or theoretical instruction impart. Stores of information surround you; you are in the midst of the world's activities. The discoveries of science and the masterpieces of inventive genius are within your reach and you have many bright opportunities of increasing your range of knowledge and widening your views of man and nature.

My health has been exceedingly good of late, though I had quite a severe attack of rheumatism in the stomach on Saturday last, but I am thankful to say it left me after a severe struggle of probably sixteen hours. Today I am in real good health with the exception of a very slight touch of rheumatism in my lower extremities. Your mother, brothers, and sisters are all well, as are also your immediate families. Richard W. [Young] goes down to Manti tomorrow to take charge of the high school at that place. Mahonri and Lorenzo are at the Co-op, Hyrum on the railroad. I often hear from Willard, Alfales, Don Carlos, and Feramorz; they are all doing admirably. Willard speaks of his duties as light, instructive, and interesting, giving him considerable time to study, which he assures me shall be used to the best advantage. Alfales appears to be very successful in his studies and is laboring energetically to make himself proficient in the profession he has chosen. Feramorz became a little discouraged a short time ago, but he is now gaining on his studies and has acquired fresh courage to master the difficulties that occasionally confront him.

I feel as contented, peaceful, and unconcerned as a human being can possibly do. Our enemies are active, but their labor is lost, that is, so far as their desires are concerned.

The grand jury at Beaver—all outsiders with one exception—has presented a stinging arraignment against the condition of things in the U.S. Marshal's Office, which plainly charges wholesale speculation and organized stealing on the part of [George R.] Maxwell, or whoever acts for him. They state that thousands of dollars entered as paid out to witnesses, jurors, &c., on the marshal's books have never been received by the parties named and that the vouchers therefore have been forged. This will doubtless give use to a very pretty little quarrel in that happy family known as the "ring."

Your mother and the family generally join me in warmest love and heartfelt prayers for your welfare, happiness and salvation.

Hoping you will write to me often, I remain,

      Your affectionate father,
      Brigham Young

WILLARD YOUNG

Willard Young
1852-1936

Willard Young was the first native-born Utahn and first Mormon to enroll at the United States Military Academy at West Point, New York. "Joven," as he was known to his classmates, was born in Salt Lake City, Utah, on April 30, 1852, the only son of Brigham and Clarissa Ogden Chase Young. While enrolled under Karl G. Maeser in his father's private school, Willard and one of his brothers, in typical teen-age fashion, thought they knew about as much as they could learn from school, and went to their father one day and asked if they could not leave school. "Brother Maeser," they reasoned, "couldn't teach us very much." "Well, if that's your attitude," replied Brigham Young, "I see no reason why you should not leave school and go to work. I will let you go to work—but with the understanding that you cannot go to school until such time as you are willing to stay put." Whereupon, Willard and his brother were permitted to work nine months and attend school three months in the winter.[1]

Willard's preparation for the Military Academy consisted of driving a supply wagon between Salt Lake City and the Missouri River by the age of fourteen and later, attending classes at the University of Deseret, where he was studying at the time of his appointment. He entered the academy in July 1871, at a time when national sentiment against his father, and the Mormon people generally, was very unfavorable. Prominent national news sources and some of his fellow classmates resented the tincture of "polygamy" that Willard's enrollment placed upon the Military Academy. However, at the time of his graduation in 1875 he was highly respected among his associates, and he graduated among the top students of his class with a commission in the Corps of Engineers. His classmates at West Point included a son of the Civil War general Ulysses S. Grant; Tasker H. Bliss, chief of staff of the Army during World War I; and Robert P. Wainwright, father of the World War II general Jonathan M. Wainwright. Following his graduation Willard served two years with the engineer battalion at Willet's Point (later Fort Totten), New York. While there he saw special service in Baltimore and Philadelphia, when federal troops were called to quell violence that had erupted in the wake of railroad strikes in the East in the summer of 1877. Later that year he was appointed to the Wheeler geographical survey west of the hundredth meridian, which undertook, among other things, a careful scientific study of the Great Salt Lake, defining its shoreline, measuring volume of inflow, evaporation, and other factors necessary to determine the volume of that body of water.

Willard returned to the Military Academy in 1879 as an assistant professor of civil and military engineering for four years. He proudly numbered among his students George W. Goethals, the builder of the Panama Canal. The congressman who made possible Willard's professional career in 1871 also provided him with a wife on August 1, 1882, when he married Hattie Hooper, daughter of Utah's former congressional delegate, William H. Hooper. They became the parents of six children. Between 1883 and 1887 Willard supervised the construction of the Cascade locks, forty miles west of Portland on the Columbia River in Oregon, the completion of which permitted navigation along 230 miles of that river. After this he directed harbor improvements at Portland and construction work on the Mississippi River at Memphis, Tennessee. In February 1891 he responded to a call by President Wilford Woodruff to resign his commission in the army and accept the presidency of the Young University in Salt Lake City. In 1894 he was appointed Salt Lake City engineer, and he later became state engineer of Utah.

Willard returned to military life in 1896 as head of the Utah National Guard with the rank of brigadier general, a post he resigned in 1898 to accept a commission as colonel in the regular army. He organized and commanded the Second Regiment of the U.S. Volunteer Engineers during the Spanish American campaign in Cuba. After the Cuban War he was named superintendent and later president of the

National Contracting Company, a New York engineering firm engaged in several large building projects, which included a drainage system for New Orleans, electric power construction at Niagara Falls, excavations for the Boston subway, a sewer system for Boston, and an electrical power dam at Glen Falls, New York.

A devoted Church member, Willard served as president of the Latter-day Saints University in Salt Lake City from 1906 to 1915. He was assistant to the president of the Logan Temple, where he was serving when he applied to General Black for active service with the U.S. Army engineers in World War I. General Black refused the request because of Willard Young's age, but he asked him to become U.S. agent in charge of the army's Kansas City Engineer District, thereby relieving one or more officers for active duty. He accepted. Stationed at Kansas City, Willard supervised improvements along the Missouri, Osage, Gasconade, Kansas, and Republican rivers until his release in July 1919.

Upon returning to Salt Lake City, Willard was placed in charge of all LDS Church construction, remaining in that capacity until his death in Salt Lake City on July 25, 1936, at the age of eighty-four. At that time he was the oldest living son of Brigham Young.

Letter dated May 19, 1871

In May 1871 word was received in Utah that a vacancy existed at the United States Military Academy at West Point, New York, and that Utah's delegate to Congress, William H. Hooper, would name a candidate to fill the opening. When John R. Park, president of Deseret University in Salt Lake City, was asked if he had any students sufficiently advanced for consideration, he named, among others, Willard Young, the nineteen-year-old son of President Brigham Young, who was regarded as the "best scholar and strongest boy at the University."[2] After expressing a desire to enter West Point, Willard was told by his father, "I will let you go but will send you as a missionary,"[3] whereupon the young man's name was presented for approval at a general priesthood meeting, and he was set apart for his mission under the hands of the First Presidency: "We set you apart to this mission and we seal this Priesthood upon you, even the Priesthood of the Most High, with the blessings pertaining thereunto, that you may go and fulfill this high and holy calling and gain this useful knowledge, and through the light of truth, make it subservient for the building up of the Kingdom of God."[4]

Willard's name appeared on the missionary lists of the Church for the next twenty years. Four days prior to his departure from Salt Lake City he received the following letter from his father.

Salt Lake City, May 19, 1871

Mr. Willard Young
Salt Lake City

My dear Son,

As you are about to leave home for a season and those with whom you have been in the habit of associating for years, many of whom are near and dear to you, a few words of advice may not prove unseasonable.

In entering the academy at West Point you are taking a step which may prove to you of incalculable advantage. You are thereby enjoying a privilege which falls to the lot of comparatively few. You will do well to treasure up the instruction so abundantly provided there, that in after years you may be prepared to take a place even in the foremost ranks of the great men of the nation. Experience will teach you that the greatest success does not attend the over-studious, and a proper regard must be had to physical as well as intellectual exercise, else the intellectual powers become impaired; and therefore, bodily recreation and rest are as necessary as they are beneficial to mental study.

Every facility will be afforded you at home by your friends in the furtherance of your studies, and I have no doubt that a straightforward, manly, upright course on your part will give you favor with and ensure you valuable aid from your fellow students.

Bear in mind, above all, the God whom we serve. Let your prayers day and night ascend to him for light and intelligence, and let your daily walk and conversation be such, that when you shall have returned home you can look back to the time passed at West Point and see no stain upon your character. You will doubtless have your trials and temptations, but if you will live near the Lord, you will hear the still, small voice whisper to you even in the moment of danger. Attend strictly to your own business, be kind and courteous to all, be sober and temperate in all your habits, shun the society of the unvirtuous and the intemperate, and should any person ask you to drink intoxicating liquor of any kind, except in sickness, never accept it. Select your own company rather than have others select yours.

If at any time you feel overtaxed or homesick, seek relaxation in the society of our elders in New York, or in other places where they may be traveling, that is, when the rules of the institution or special license permit you leave of absence.

Write to me frequently and any assistance you need that I can furnish will be provided. May God bless you and preserve you from every snare and give you His holy Spirit to light your path before you, and help qualify you for usefulness in His kingdom.

Your affectionate father,
Brigham Young

Letter dated June 17, 1871

On May 23, 1871, Willard Young left Salt Lake City for West Point, accompanied by his oldest brother, Joseph A., who was well accustomed to travel on the Great Plains, having served as a missionary in England and having assisted with emigration and railroad matters between Salt Lake City and Boston.

In an era dedicated to the eradication of those "twin relics of barbarism," slavery and polygamy, the coincidental admission of the first Negro and also of one of Brigham Young's sons to the West Point Military Academy in 1871 did not go unnoticed by those who monitored the nation's conscience. As observers across the country anxiously watched this "outrage," the Chicago *Evening Post* reported that the colored appointee passed his entrance examination with higher marks than a large number of the white applicants, and that Brigham Young's son "came out from the ordeal unscathed." The paper added, "It is time that West Point began to be considered something better than an asylum for dandies."[5]

After passing the entrance requirements, Willard was admitted as a cadet on July 1, 1873, the first native Mormon to be so honored. In a letter to his father on June 3 he wrote of his successful completion of the entrance tests and enclosed a certificate of acceptance to be signed by his father and returned to the War Department. "Since leaving home I have seen much that is new, and to me very interesting, and have enjoyed myself immensely. Joseph A. seemed to very well employ the time in showing me all there is of importance to be seen." Reporting on his initial impressions of the academy, he continued: "The older students of the school here ask many impertinent questions, and in many cases act very ungentlemanly toward the new Cadets. This, it seems, cannot be helped, as the students of any class are obliged to obey the commands of those of a higher class." However, he concluded, "West Point is a most delightful place: and the members of the Academic Board, so far as I have seen, are perfect gentlemen."[6]

Salt Lake City, June 17, 1871

Mr. Willard Young
West Point, New York

My dear Son,

Yours of the 3rd inst. with your certificate of acceptance enclosed for my signature [was] duly received.

We were all well pleased to hear from you, and to know that you passed a successful examination. This news was considered of sufficient importance to be flashed across the wires with the general telegraphic dispatches.

I signed the certificate and forwarded it yesterday (16) to the Department. I have instructed Bro. [George Q.] Cannon[7] to send you regularly a copy of the *Deseret News* which will keep you posted in general news. Anything else you require from time to time, let us know and we will endeavour to supply you.

It appears from some of the eastern papers, they are rather exercised over your admission among the cadets and one correspondent writing from this city to the N.Y. *Herald* wants to know, "Will the boys permit the outrage?" It is easy to guess the source whence this emanated, some member of the notorious ring[8] here who leave no stone unturned to create friction between us and the Government. You are aware how signally they have failed and this malicious though very paltry effort only serves to show them up as they are.

Since I wrote to you on the 19th May nothing out of the ordinary course has transpired here. I will mention, however, a very agreeable circumstance which transpired on the 1st of June—that being the 70th anniversary of my birthday—a surprise was prepared for me which, though it has been in preparation several days, was kept entirely from me. I stepped into dinner as usual, suspecting nothing, and was greeted by a concourse of children in the lobby, neatly dressed and each bearing a bouquet. I was ushered into the parlour where to my astonishment I was met by not less than 80 persons assembled to congratulate me on the occasion. We all proceeded to the dining room and 87 persons sat down to table. An address prepared by Sister Eliza R. Snow was then read to me, which embodied in a beautiful composition the affectionate sentiments of my family and immediate relatives and friends. While it was being read, many were moved to tears, and altogether it was a really pleasant time which will not easily be forgotten by those who were present.

Work progresses finely on the U.S.R.R.[9] The iron is laid for miles and the grading continues steadily along.

We are having a novelty in the shape of a Methodist camp meeting[10] located on the Orson Spencer lot just across the street north of Henry Lawrence's house. Meeting is held in an extraordinarily large tent said to accommodate 3000 persons. I am not aware they have made any converts as yet, though a large number of our people attend nightly. We have advised all to attend, young and old. I have only been present at one meeting. The affair is very dry. Mr. Boole who preached on that occasion put me in mind of an old, dried-up wooden pump, laboring and creaking in a dry well, working very hard but producing no water. I understand their services will close tomorrow.

Though you are absent from us and far from home and your dearest friends, be assured we are not unmindful of you. Our prayers are constantly exercised in your behalf that you may be kept free from the contaminating influences that will doubtless surround you. Let me again advise you that you cannot be too careful to shun the temptations of the day. We are not afraid of you, but you are in a more conspicuous position, probably, than you realize. The eyes of many are upon you to see what is likely to be your future. You will meet with those of your companions who will try every means to induce you to deviate from the path of virtue; but with a firm front, you can easily parry every such effort and still be kind and courteous. And rest assured that this course will win for you far greater respect, even from the unvirtuous, than that which would follow, were you to fall in with the dissolute habits of the day.

Above all things, seek closely to the Lord. Pray for His holy Spirit to guide your steps and to deliver you from every snare.

Write to us often, and at length; your letters will be looked for with pleasure.

You will be pleased to learn my health is good, and that all the family are well.

May peace be and abide with you, and the blessings of heaven constantly surround you.

I was just about to mail this when your letter to the folks was handed me to read which I did with great interest. When you write I would like to learn in detail the routine of your daily life, and what your studies will consist of. Whether your friends are allowed to visit you, and if so, are they restricted to certain times? Indeed, a brief description of the entire rules of the academy would be quite interesting to us, and might furnish an interesting article for the *News*.

Your letter to me of the 11th I have just this moment received. Thank you for writing me, and should you meet Gen. [Rufus] Ingalls again soon, present my compliments to him.

Your affectionate father,
Brigham Young

June 20.

P.S. I am particularly desirous to know the regulations about visitors because, if allowed, I shall request all our elders visiting in your neighbourhood to call upon you. Bishop Sharp sends his respects and will be with you to see you while he is east, which will be shortly.

Letter dated July 25, 1871

Away from home in a strange environment for the first time, where he was confronted with a hostile press and subjected to the usual trials of a plebe at the Military Academy, Willard Young was not without friends. Members of his family and friends who were engaged in Church business in New York or studying and traveling in the East frequently visited him. In addition, friends of his father went out of their way to meet the son of Brigham Young. Shortly after arriving at his new quarters on the Hudson, Willard was contacted by General Rufus Ingalls and ex-Governor Johnson of California, both of whom wished to be kindly remembered to their friend Brigham Young and expressed their willingness to do anything in their power to aid and comfort his son. On June 18 Joseph A., who had been in New York on business, paid Willard a surprise visit. As he departed he presented his brother with a "fine gold watch."

In a letter to his father on June 11, Willard wrote that although West Point was a "most delightful place," his appreciation would no doubt increase when he had more to engage his mind. "The academic duties do not commence until about the first of September; and as our military exercises are conducted by the older cadets, I have not yet become acquainted with the preceptors of the Academy."[11] A few days later he noted that "conformity to military rule seems to agree with me, my health being excellent. I think I will find many friends as you promised me before leaving home I would do if I conducted myself in a straight-forward, upright manner. The cadets, unless having conscientious scruples, are required to attend church each Sunday morning, the service being that of the Protestant Episcopals. Do you wish me to attend? If not, please let me know. I desire your faith and your best wishes, which no doubt I have, to enable me to master the work before me, that I may be fitted for future usefulness."[12] Brigham Young replied on July 25.

Salt Lake City, July 25, 1871

Mr. Willard Young
West Point, New York

My dear Son,
    When your last letter to me reached this city, I had started

for Soda Springs [Idaho], accompanied by a small party of brethren and sisters from this city. We started on the 26th June and returned on the 24th July, staying at Ogden City to celebrate the pioneer anniversary and got home in the evening.

A synopsis of your letter was telegraphed to me at Franklin [Idaho], which I was pleased to receive. I wrote to you on the 17th June, which I suppose you have received. On the 16th I signed and forwarded your acceptance to the department. In case my letter failed to reach you, I will briefly repeat the substance of a portion of it. Bro. [George Q.] Cannon has been instructed to mail the *Deseret News* to you regularly. And anything you may require from time to time, such as books, or anything else, let us know and we will endeavour to supply you. We would like to learn in detail the routine of your daily life, what your duties and exercises consist of, what the regulations are about visitors, whether ladies have access to the cadets and under what restrictions, if any. This last is a matter I am quite concerned to know about, as I understand you cadets are exceedingly popular with the fair sex. And some of them are very, very dangerous when so disposed, just for the sake of having a laugh at their victims. Shun such as you would the very gates of hell! They are the enemy's strongest tools, and should be resisted as strongly. Beware of them!

I think that such a description of the rules and routine of the academy as I have mentioned would form an interesting article for the *Deseret News*, and would be read with great interest, not only by your relatives and friends, but by our citizens at large.

Since your letter, Bro. Dusenbury wrote to me concerning your progress, and with verbal reports from John W. and Bishop [John] Sharp we hear considerable about you. The bishop tells me you are kept so busy that you have barely time to attend to your correspondence. All who have written to or spoken with me are well satisfied with your course so far, and the bishop assures me whatever may have been the feelings of the cadets towards you at the first you are now looked upon by them as "a pretty good fellow." I will go still further with this and say that we hope yet to see you a pattern for all of them. By exhibiting your character and the principles you profess in your daily walk and conversation, and by refraining from every appearance of evil, you will not only be admired by the good and the upright, but you will command that respect that even the most unvirtuous are willing to accord to those who truly deserve it. There is no question but you can do a great deal of good among your fellow students and we hope to see you accomplish it. No matter what the world at large believe, or say about the Latter-day Saints, if we do our duty, and live for it, we will be found, among the children of men, at the head, and not at the tail.

With regard to your attending Protestant Episcopal service, I have no objections whatever. On the contrary, I would like to have you attend, and see what they can teach you about God and Godliness more than you have already been taught. When the Methodist big tent was here I advised old and young to attend their meetings for that very reason, but I was well satisfied it would not take our people long to learn what Methodists could teach them more than they had already been taught.

Our celebration at Ogden was a spirited affair, as was also the celebration of the 4th in this city.[13] You have doubtless heard and read a great deal about the latter, but the facts are that the brethren had one of the best, if not the very best, ever had in the mountains. As to what some term the backing down of the Lieut. Gen[eral], the only backing down was done by the self-styled "acting governor and commander-in-chief of the Nauvoo Militia," for, according to his own statement, he had orders to *suppress* the procession if the militia marched in it, and on the 3rd inst. he voluntarily assured Gens. [Philip Regis] De Trobriand and [Henry A.] Morrow that he would make no arrests on the 4th. With this concession Gens. De Trobriand and Morrow, with U.S. Marshall [M.T.] Patrick and Attorney [Charles H.] Hempstead, waited upon Prest. [Daniel H.] Wells, and upon the urgent solicitation of De Trobriand, it was finally decided, after consulting with our committee, that the militia would not carry arms while in the procession.

My health is good and I feel first rate with the exception of being a little tired, which is rapidly wearing off.

I will write you again as soon as I hear from you. May God preserve you from every evil, and bestow upon you every requisite blessing.

                            Your affectionate father,
                            Brigham Young

Letter dated January 26, 1872

After some six months in the East, Willard reported to his father on December 9. "Thinking that perhaps a few words from me would prove interesting to you, remembering that when I left home you told me to write often, I improve the present opportunity. I am happy to tell you that your promises to me when I left are being fulfilled. I am succeeding quite well with my studies, and I never enjoyed more the spirit of our religion." With reference to the adverse comment that his entrance to the academy had brought forth from among his classmates, Willard added, "I have heard several of the young men here, who, no doubt, six months ago were 'death on the Mormons,' say that the U.S. officials were entirely wrong."[14]

Having received the November progress report from the academy which showed Willard Young near the top of his class, Brigham was surprised to notice that the number of demerits charged against his son was considerably higher than the average. In his letter of January 26, 1872, he requested an explanation.

Salt Lake City, January 26, 1872

Mr. Willard Young
West Point, N.Y.

My dear Son,

On my return from the south I was much pleased to receive and read your letter of Dec. 9th. We returned from our trip to southern Utah on the 26th Dec. not only in time for my trial on the day fixed by the court, but soon enough to enter court one week before that time to answer to a charge of murder,[15] the writ for which had not then been served, and to ask for bail. The judge refused to take it although Mr. [George C.] Bates, the U.S. district attorney, strongly urged him to, and it was expected some regard would have been paid to the fact of my voluntary appearance in court. But the judge saw proper to refuse, and stated that as there was no U.S. jail in the Territory, and as it was at the option of the military officer commanding the post to receive or refuse prisoners, and as he understood the defendant was the owner of several houses, he said he would consign him to the custody of the U.S. marshal in any one of those houses he might select. The result of this decision is that I am held a prisoner in my own house, although, partly from the kindness and good sense of the deputy marshal, Capt. Evans, and partly from his instructions, the burden imposed upon me is not very hard to bear, while at the same time Judge [James B.] McKean has added another laurel to his judicial crown which he wears with most unenviable notoriety. All jury cases have been postponed until the March term pending the settlement of the question whether or not the U.S. will pay the expenses of those prosecutions.

The 9th of Jan. had been fixed by the inexorable judge as the day for my trial although my attorneys had asked for a continuance until the March term, and our return to this city from St. George was necessarily made in very severe weather with snow, rain, and mud in superabundance in the most inclement season of the year. It soon transpired, however, that it was not my appearance that was wanted but my *dis*-appearance and, failing in that respect, the court, at the instance of the prosecuting attorney, without any further application on my part, granted a continuance until the 2nd Monday in March.

My health is much improved and had I been left alone in the south until March it would, doubtless, have improved still more. However, I am thankful everything is as well as it is, and so far as I am personally concerned, as well as what pertains to our affairs in general, I have no doubt of their final success and the entire discomfiture of our malicious enemies.

Capt. [William H.] Hooper, after spending the holidays here, returned to Washington on the 15th full of hope, and filled with a firm determination to battle for our rights as American citizens. Mr. [George C.] Bates, district attorney, started 2 days earlier. As he is going to Washington it is supposed a part of his business will be to raise funds to carry on the trials, and in a short time, doubtless, we will learn the result.

For my part I do not believe Congress will so far countenance these unhallowed persecutions as to appropriate one cent towards continuing them, and, if I am not mistaken, the reign of the McKeanites is drawing to an inglorious termination.

We have had a remarkably mild winter, although a great deal of rain and some snow has fallen; but for the last few days, the frost has been more severe, and today the wind is blowing as fiercely cold as I ever felt it in this valley.

I suppose the folks keep you posted with regard to family matters, and I will merely remark, we are all pretty well. My health has much improved by my trip south, and my spirits are light and buoyant, for which I feel very thankful.

I find from the inspector's report for November that your record shows you to be in Sec. No. 1 in mathematics, and No. 4 in French. We were much gratified to hear of your success, especially in mathematics. This report shows the total demerits since the commencement of the academic half-year at 18, and I observe while the average number on the reports is 4, the one for Sept. shows 8, and as this is so much above the average, I would be pleased to ascertain the reason, or whether there is any mistake in the report.

Your offer to furnish any desired information concerning West Point, I accept, and will always be happy to hear of your progress as often as you can find opportunity. Your success and welfare is the best information the institution can furnish for your friends here. Still, if it were not for the press of your studies, there is much interesting detail concerning the affairs and management of the academy that would doubtless form an article for our newspapers, and be read by the people with considerable relish. But I have no desire either to overtax you or seek to infringe upon your allotted studies.

May your heart be comforted, and the light of the good spirit abide with you continually to direct your steps and inspire you in all your pursuits. We pray for you continually and it is our earnest desire that you may be preserved from every evil.

Your affectionate father,
Brigham Young

P.S. As you will naturally feel anxious to know to what extent I am deprived of liberty, I assure you anyone would find it difficult to know there is any guard here at all. The marshal sits in my office or goes outside to walk, or ride, or go to the theatre, or elsewhere, but never follows me, nor asks any questions, nor knows where I go. If I go out to ride I ask him to accompany me—if I feel like it. If not, he stays in the office; he eats in the east house in company with Bro. [David] McKenzie, takes breakfast at 8, dinner at 1, and supper at 6. He sleeps in the little room between the offices in the rear of the telegraph office, but never goes into any other room than the one he eats in. From this you will readily perceive the whole thing is a farce, and we have many a joke about it.

B.Y.

Letter dated August 14, 1872

Receiving a bundle of mail from home after the "long blockade" of the winter's snow, Willard read his father's letter of January 26 "with more than ordinary pleasure." He wrote, "your kind assurance that I ever have your faith and prayers will indeed incite me to greater efforts. My constant desire is to satisfy your wishes, my dear father, and to honor the people whom I represent. Having you and the folks at home to pray for me, I trust I may live so as to merit that favor of our Heavenly Father which alone can enable me to succeed."

In explanation of excessive demerits on his November progress report from the academy, Willard gave a lengthy reply to his father's inquiry. "As you perhaps do not know what these demerits are, I will mention a few of the many ways in which they accumulate. If, by chance, we happen to be a few seconds late at any of the formations during the day, we are reported; if at inspection of quarters the washbowl is not inverted, the towel not neatly folded, shoes or articles in clothespress not neatly arranged; or, if the room is not properly swept and dusted, we are reported. If at drill or parade we do not understand the command distinctly, and execute or commence to execute the wrong movement, we are reported. If, by mistake, we send clothing to the laundry with an incorrect list, sending perhaps one handkerchief more than thereon marked, or perhaps a collar or a pair of gloves not marked with name, we are reported; at any of the inspections under arms, if our trimmings are not adjusted just so, if our belts, gloves, or collars are soiled, if there is any dust or dirt about our guns, or if our shoes are not blacked, we are reported, and so on in almost hundreds of ways we may get reports, and each report gives a certain number of demerits, ranging from 1 to 5, according to its grade. You see from this, that what are recorded against us as demerits, are not so bad as the word *demerit* would ordinarily imply. It is true that if a person has a good excuse to offer, and will present such excuse in writing through the proper channel, in many instances the report will be removed; yet it seems almost impossible to go without getting some demerits. I will relate a little circumstance that happened a short time since, so that you may not wonder if the number of my demerits appears large. The facts are, I had written a permit to go skating, which I got signed by the proper officer; when the named time arrived, I went to look for the Officer of the Day in order to report my departure, (all of which is necessary). I found out that he was in the Academic Building, which, by the way, is off cadet limits, except during recitation hours, and seeing another cadet who had been to report his departure on permit, coming from there I thought I would go and report my departure also, thinking then that it would be all right. When I found the Officer of the Day, however, he told me I had no business in there at that hour, and so reported me for entering Academic building without authority. I wrote an explanation for the offense, stating the facts; still the report was recorded against me giving me four (4) demerits."[16]

As spring dawned upon the Hudson, drills and parades resumed, bringing relief to the monotonous daily routine of the winter months. In a letter to his father on April 7, Willard described the change that had transformed nature in the East: "The Hudson which has been blocked by ice nearly all winter, is again open. Almost countless boats plow the river; large steam tugs, with their long trains of loaded flat boats, sometimes thirty or forty of them in one load, are passing and repassing incessantly. Schooners can be seen at anytime, their large white sails adding much to the beauty of the scene; and occasionally a fine passenger steamer is seen furrowing the waters. Looking up this river a distance of ten miles, Newburg, a city of about 25,000 inhabitants can be seen. On either side of the river are high and rugged cliffs, frowning, as it were, upon the waters; a small island, apparently in the middle of the stream, rises out of the water about four miles distant. Altogether it is far the nicest scene I ever saw, and I believe is acknowledged to be perhaps the finest in the United States for real beauty."[17]

The termination of his first year at the Military Academy was awaited with joyful anticipation by Willard Young. It marked the end of his plebedom, "and we will be received as a class among the other classes." In recalling the circumstances of his appointment, he wrote his father on May 12, "It will be one year next Wednesday since you first asked me, 'Willie, how would you like to go to West Point?'

Though beyond my dreams or hopes, I was ready to do whatever you counselled, and would have responded as quickly if it had been to go to Australia or the Cannibal Islands." He concluded his letter with this sentiment: "It is my constant prayer that what I learn here may serve in aiding me to do God's will and to build up his Kingdom here on the earth. And I think I shall never be sorry that I passed through West Point and received its education."[18]

As his first year at the academy came to a close, Willard greeted the removal of the cadets from their barracks into camp for two months of "practical military instruction" as a welcome relief. "Our time is pretty well occupied, but after nine months steady and close application to our books, we accept with pleasure the *physical* exercises."[19]

Salt Lake City, August 14, 1872

Mr. Willard Young
West Point, New York

My dear Son,

I have nothing special to bring to your notice, still I thought a few lines might not prove uninteresting. We were well pleased to hear from Bro. [William C.] Staines of an agreeable visit he had with you, and his report of your progress. I trust your present exercises will prove an enjoyable relief from your close indoor studies.

Peace continues to prevail among the Saints notwithstanding the assiduous efforts of our enemies to disturb it.

Last Friday myself and a small company took a ride over the Utah Southern Railroad a distance of about 23 miles to examine the work through the point of the mountain. The cuts and fills are very heavy. The large fill is about 700 ft. in length with an average depth of about 175 feet. The work is progressing quite rapidly, and it is thought the locomotive will be through within three weeks. Had we not been disappointed with our iron, we would have crowded this work and had it completed long ere this. It appears now, however, as if the iron were coming and we will push on without delay.

We are having remarkably good crops this season and labor is in great demand not only in the agricultural interest but in mining and railroading. Besides the Utah Southern, two other roads—The American Fork Canyon Railroad and the Utah Northern Railroad —are being built here. The former is the property of English capitalists having large mining interests in American Fork. The latter is going ahead with vigor; its connection is made with the Central Pacific Railroad at a point 17 miles west of Ogden, and it is built and carrying passengers and freight some 27 miles from that point towards Cache Valley. It is considered a great success. Both those railroads are narrow gauge, or 3 foot track.

The S.L. City Street Car Railroad is another recent improvement and is very well patronized by our people. The two last-named enterprises are John W. Young's.

Last Monday (3rd inst.) was election day. Elder George Q. Cannon was elected Delegate to Congress, Bro. [William H.] Hooper having requested a release from his labors, which have been very arduous to a person of his temperament.

[George R.] Maxwell is the opposition candidate. The official returns are not all in, but, of course, Bro. Cannon is elected by an overwhelming majority.

Many improvements are being made in this city, and you will observe great changes when you make us a visit, an event which I am sure you will hail with delight as will all your friends here to welcome you.

We are now using gas in the theatre, which is a great improvement. The house when lighted to its full capacity is dazzling. We use the maxim gas manufactured from gasoline, and we hope it may prove a success.

A company has been chartered in this city to manufacture gas from wood and coal, and their machinery and materials for manufacturing are now on the way.

The city authorities intend erecting water works shortly and for this purpose have secured the services of an efficient engineer.

Buildings for stores, hotels, tenements, &c., are springing up all around us. The Fennings building used by ZCMI, with the additions now being made, will show a frontage to Main St. of 107 feet extending back 190 ft. The Walker House built by Walker Bros. for a hotel on the site where John Kay's house formerly stood is a handsome 4-story building of brick having all the modern improvements for the accommodation of guests, which will doubtless bring many more visitors to our city.

My health continues excellent for which I feel very thankful. We remember you constantly with the very best feelings and wishes, and we pray that you may be preserved from every snare and permitted to return home, having accomplished a good work in preparing yourself for a life of usefulness.

Your affectionate father,
Brigham Young

Letter dated April 14, 1873

One of the highlights of Willard Young's military career occurred toward the end of his second year at West Point when it was announced by the War Department that the corps of cadets would participate in the presidential inauguration ceremony of Ulysses S. Grant in Washington, D. C., on March 4, 1873. "We are all delighted at the thought here, and will look forward to the time with great eagerness," Willard wrote his father. "I am doubly pleased for, in addition to being a nice out and a relief from study, it will afford an opportunity of seeing Washington and other great cities. It will be a gratification, also, to be a witness of so great a day's proceedings. It is believed that the cadets will be invited to attend the grand 'Inauguration Ball,' or, if not, that a ball will be gotten up specially for them. Now all the boys are very fond of dancing, and I among the rest, as you doubtless know, so we regard this as one of the 'big things' of the occasion."[20]

Willard concluded the announcement of his trip to Washington with the assurance that he had not surrendered to the vices of military life. "It may be gratifying to you to know that as yet, I have given myself up to none of the temptations which surround me. Perhaps I should not say temptations, for thanks to the good training of my parents, swearing, using tobacco, drinking whiskey, and other kindred vices to which I have alluded, never were a temptation to me. In myself I can perceive no change, but am the same grateful and loving son as when I left home."

Three months elapsed before Willard again wrote to his father —a silence that he attributed to his lack of talent as a letter writer, "and so I take but little interest in trying." Nonetheless he held his family in sacred remembrance. "I ever feel grateful towards you, my dear father, for the many great kindnesses and benefits you have heaped upon me, and upon all the children, though it is perhaps impossible for me to appreciate their full worth. How thankful we all ought to be (I really think I am) that we have such a loving and indulgent parent, such a wise instructor, and so worthy an example as you. Every time I look at your picture, which I always keep handy, I seem to be running over with love and gratitude. I daily pray that you may be allowed to remain with us, and that you may have God's Spirit to abide with you in continuing the good work in which you are now busied."[21]

As Willard approached the completion of his second year at the Military Academy, he wrote his father that with the permission of their parents or guardians, the cadets were allowed a furlough of two months between their sophomore and junior years. "It is customary for all the members of the 'furlough class' to take advantage of this privilege, which is regarded as the great event of the course. I am anxious to make the most of it by visiting home and friends, but must first get your consent. I will not ask this, however, till you understand the circumstances in which I am or will be placed. I shall have sufficient money to get me an outfit and to procure my passage home, but I shall be compelled to encumber your hands with my keeping there, and shall have to draw on your pockets to get me back. I shall contentedly abide by whatever you think best, and I now leave it for you to decide what I shall do." And lest the added economic burden upon his father's pocketbook should give cause to hesitate, Willard added, "should I get a furlough at all, it would cost nearly as much to remain in this country as it would to go home; I infinitely prefer the latter. If you think I ought to come home, please write out and sign an application . . . and send it to me. . . . With much love, I am your ever grateful son."[22] Brigham Young replied on April 14.

Salt Lake City, April 14, 1873

Mr. Willard Young
West Point, New York

My dear Son,

Your interesting letter of the 5th inst. was gladly received. We are always pleased to hear from you, and look forward with pleasure to the time—now rapidly approaching—when we can receive you in person, shake each other's hands, hear each other's voices, and interchange our feelings in a way that cannot be done in writing.

With this you will find a request for your furlough written in the form suggested.

My health is excellent, for which I feel very thankful, and also the health of the family.

I attended every meeting of our late conference and spoke very frequently and without any sensible injury to myself.

Everything is moving along in a prosperous and satisfactory manner, and I do not know a time that the Saints ever had greater reason to be thankful to our Heavenly Father or more need to be humble and faithful than at the present. All the machinations of our enemies, every time, serve but to advance the kingdom, while each effort they make they seem to become weaker.

Our commercial enterprises, such as the Mercantile Institution, Deseret National Bank, railroads &c., besides mining interests in which outsiders are immediately interested all through the Territory, have a powerful effect in heading off those who would introduce strife and discord in our midst, as it is so much to the interest of capitalists wherever we deal to have business undisturbed here.

The missionaries for Arizona are starting out from the various settlements and gathering at Winsor Castle, where they will be organized and sent forward to make settlements among the Moquis Indians, and in time become acquainted with the Apaches, Pimas, Navajos and other Indians; for we believe that if we are prudent and diligent in the conduct of this mission, we can make a favorable impression among them, in accordance with Prest. [Ulysses S.] Grant's peace policy, and induce them to abandon their thieving, murderous habits.

We have favorable reports from some of those Indians. They are anxious to have us come among them. They say they don't want us to provide for them, but they are extremely anxious that we teach them how to labor and provide for themselves. If we have the blessing and approbation of our Heavenly Father, which I think we will have, and the brethren will do right, a good work will be accomplished.

I would like very much, my health permitting, to go and help the brethren found a city somewhere on the Colorado River on the line of the projected Southern Pacific Railroad. Hitherto my immense business has rendered it difficult for me to leave home, but I have so arranged matters now that I will be left more at liberty, which is a great and satisfactory relief to me.

Spring is rather backward here; we have quite cold weather for the time of year.

We are looking for John W. home in a day or two, as he left Philadelphia on the evening of the 11th. Brigham Jr. is with me, assisting me in my private business for a short time; he desires to be affectionately remembered to you. Geo. A. Smith, Daniel H. Wells, George Q. Cannon, Lorenzo Snow, Albert Carrington, Brigham and John W. have been added to my counselors.

Geo. A. Smith succeeds me as T[rustee]-in-Trust and he has twelve assistants, whose names are on the next page.

Accept my warmest feelings of affection and rest assured that you have my constant prayer for your well-being and every success in the prosecution of your studies.

> Your affectionate father,
> Brigham Young

P.S. This letter was not mailed last night, and it is now the night of the 16th. I went up to our granite quarry today with a party of brethren, and we had a very pleasant visit. We go to "Sandy," a station on the U.S.R.R. opposite Little Cottonwood Canyon, and then by a narrow gauge road, now building, up to the mines in Little Cottonwood. By this means we are enabled to put the granite blocks right on the cars and haul them by rail on to the Temple Block.

John W. has not got in; a storm on the U.P. delayed the train; we look for him tonight.

The names of the asst. trustees elected at conference are John Sharp, Joseph F. Smith, Joseph W. Young, Moses Thatcher, A[mos] M. Musser, E[lijah] F. Sheets, John Van Cott, John L. Smith, J[ames] P. Freeze, Thomas Taylor, F[rederick] A. Mitchell, and

Le Grand Young.

B. Y. (by DMcK) [David McKenzie]

Letter dated August 11, 1874

As the time for his furlough approached, Willard received the anxiously awaited letter from his father containing the necessary document ("to me very dear") for procuring his two-month leave. However, the anticipation of a visit home, after a two-year absence, had a stagnating effect upon his studies. "I have not been doing so well in my studies as I could have wished, but still am progressing fairly. Furlough I think runs in my head a little too much for my own good, but it is the case with all of us. Two years from home in a place which cannot be left and with the knowledge of this fact constantly present is a thing well calculated to make the first privilege fully appreciated. This absence does more for me at least, for it makes me appreciate some of the privileges and blessings enjoyed by those around you."[23]

As Cadet Young, dressed in his uniform and showing the composure of two years' military discipline, stepped off the train at the Ogden rail terminal on the afternoon of July 1, 1873, he was warmly greeted by his aging father and a concourse of relatives and friends who had journeyed the thirty-five miles to meet him. "Utah will welcome and honor him today," reported the local newspaper, "because he has done honor to himself and them as their representative." Two weeks later eastern papers reported Willard's promotion to the rank of sergeant.

Willard's return to the academy did not warrant a letter from him until November, when he finally wrote to his father: "I trust that my long silence has not led you to believe that I am forgetful of you. I assure you such is not the case, for I think of you daily; indeed I am assured that I never can think of you too much. I esteem it the greatest possible honor to call you father, and the greatest privilege to be directed by your counsel. I am ever conscious of your goodness and kindness, for which I shall never cease to be grateful. I see in every new development the wisdom of your advice."[24]

Brigham Young's letter of August 11, 1874, notified Willard that his fifteen-year-old brother, Feramorz, would soon add the name of Young to the U.S. Naval Academy.

Salt Lake City, August 11, 1874

Willard Young
West Point, New York

My dear son Willard,

    Your letters dated June 5th and July 2d were received in due time.

    It is gratifying to know you hold so good a standing in your class as that which, in your last, you inform me.

    I suppose that now you are regaling yourself in camp life and recruiting your energies for another term of hard study.

    Through Aunt Zina I suppose you have before this learned the lamentably sudden death of Brother Thos. Williams. It was so entirely unexpected that it filled every heart with sorrow.

    Things move along slowly. The Order is being taken up gradually by the people and as it becomes more and more understood will be appreciated accordingly. It requires some time for the great majority of the people to grasp the many points of advantage to them that are embraced by it, but it is advancing.

    Fera has received his papers as candidate for admission to the Naval Academy; I have hopes that he will pass creditably. Bro. [John R.] Park takes a great deal of interest in him, examining him every day, and endeavoring to post him on all necessary points, and he is studying very hard indeed.

    If government will release you after you have graduated, it will please me very much to have you here with me.

    I am highly gratified at the good spirit which is manifested in your letters, and trust you will continually have the spirit of the Lord to lead and guide you right.

    I presume the "ring's" effort at the election on the 3d was the best they could do, but it was insignificancy itself; they unfurled their colors and showed to all how "liberal" minded they could and would be, did they hold the reins of power.

    I am blest with very good health, as also is the family,
Peace be with you and God bless you.

                        Your father,
                        Brigham Young

Letter dated February 6, 1875

The following letter of Brigham Young, dated February 6, 1875, was written from St. George, Utah, where the President had gone to spend the winter and supervise the construction of the temple. Although Willard's letter of January 23, which preceded this response, has not been found, it is evident from the context of his father's reply that Willard was writing at the mid-point of his final year at the Military Academy and that he had sought counsel from his father regarding the relative merits of the different branches of military service available to him and the effect his choice may have on his forthcoming career. The question was not resolved at this time, nor was it resolved three months later on the eve of Willard's graduation.

St. George, Utah, February 6, 1875

Cadet Willard Young
West Point, New York

My dear son Willard,

Your welcome favor of January 23d came to hand by last mail, and was perused with much pleasure.

I congratulate you on the proficiency you report, and most heartily encourage you to strive by every lawful endeavor to realize the hope, which you express, to increase its standard before next June.

I am pleased with the good and cheerful spirit in which you write, and trust that your course, not only now, but ever, may be such as to cause you to preserve yourself in honor and in every good word and work, that you may stand justified before the Lord and all the righteous.

Willard, I have not decided fully, as yet, in relation to your future course; but when I am in Salt Lake City I will try to inform myself as to the best for you, and will then give you my judgment on the matter. At present I prefer the Engineer Corps. I appreciate, and shall keep in view, the several points of advantage and disadvantage presented in your letter relative to the different arms of the service.

I feel thankful in stating that my general health is good. I have deemed it prudent, because of the condition of my speaking organs, to refrain from much public speaking this winter; but the last two Sabbaths I have addressed the Saints in the St. George Tabernacle at considerable length.

I have watched the progress of the temple in this city with much interest the past winter. The weather has been beautiful and the work has been continued almost without interruption. About two hundred and fifty men are engaged on the walls and in quarrying and cutting rock. Under the concentration of this labor, and that of teams, teamsters, and lime burners, the building is growing at the rate of about two and a half feet per week. The walls are fifty-six feet above the grade at the present time, and eighty out of the ninety-three arches in the building have been completed.

I leave here for Salt Lake City on the 10th inst., if all is well, and shall arrive there about the 20th. Bro. George A. Smith will accompany me. I expect to return here in April.

And now, my son, may the blessing, protection and guidance of the Almighty be ever with you, which is the desire and prayer of

Your affectionate father,
Brigham Young

Letter dated June 4, 1875

Academically, Willard Young stood far above the average in his class at West Point. However, as the day of his graduation drew nigh, his chances of achieving top honors in his class seemed to be slipping away. "I am very sorry to have to tell you," he wrote his father on May 22, "that I have *not* done so well as I hoped nor confidently expected to do the last few months, and I am afraid it will result in my failing considerably in standing." Since a cadet's standing in his graduating class determined the branch of service he entered upon graduation—commencing with the engineers for those of the highest standing, and ending with the infantry, for those with the lowest—Willard analyzed his prospects: "Up to January I stood 'two,' and had a fair prospect of graduating there; now, however, I fear I cannot come out above five. This will, perhaps, exclude me from the Engineers, so I must think of what will be my next choice. Your wishes will determine me. I will of course apply for the Engineers, if I succeed in getting the recommendation of the Academic Board for that branch of the service. If not, I wish to know if it shall be Artillery, Infantry, or Cavalry, each of these branches being open to me. The Artillery is considered next to the Engineers, but the part of the country where a person wishes to be stationed must be taken into consideration. Four of the Artil. regiments are stationed along the Atlantic coast, from Maine to Florida; the fifth in California. There are more vacancies in some than in others, and therefore, a better opening in some than in others, as the rank would be correspondingly higher. The Infantry, usually the last choice, is scattered throughout the southern and western territories. The Cavalry, mostly in New Mexico, Texas, and the south west, decidedly the worst places to be stationed at. If I enter the Artillery, which is now my choice (the Engineers of course excepted) I will have to go through another year's study at Fortress Monroe, provided I remain in the service more than a couple of years. I hardly know whether to regard this as an advantage or not, as the instruction is only that which an *officer* would need in actual service. I think I would prefer to spend a year at Columbia College on the study of engineering, mining and civil, as offering the most advantages to me if I am not to remain in the army any considerable length of time. This, however, is merely prospective, as my term of service will be regulated by the time it is thought proper for me to remain. Unless you advise me otherwise, I will apply for an Artil. Reg. stationed east, perhaps the 2nd, stationed at or near Baltimore, this offering the most vacancies and being near Ferry [Feramorz]."

As Willard anticipated his visit home after graduation, regardless of what his future would be after that, he closed his final letter to his father from the Military Academy with these lines: "I will procure me a uniform to take home, that the folks may see their young 'Lieutenant,' and besides, I will have to procure myself an outfit of clothing &c. This will take all the money I have been able to save from our cadet pay, and I will have to call on you for money to take me home. I am not ashamed to ask you for it, for you know how I am situated, yet I would much prefer not to do so if I could help it. I cannot help thinking how much you have done for me and all the children, and how little we have repaid you for all your kindness. I feel I can never repay the great debt I owe you. . . . Your loving son."[25]

Brigham Young's response came on June 4, just before Willard graduated from the academy.

Salt Lake City, June 4, 1875

Elder Willard Young
West Point, New York

My dear son Willard,

Your very welcome letter of the 22nd ult. came safely to hand on the 31st, and its perusal gave me much gratification.

We rejoice with you at the near prospect of again extending to you a most cordial welcome to, and enjoying your society in, your "mountain home."

As to your class standing, we have no fears but what it will result very satisfactorily to me, to yourself, and to all your relations and friends.

With you, we hope the academic board will see proper to recommend you to the Corps of Engineers, but should that expectation fail, I quite agree with you that so far as I comprehend the matter, the next best position, all things considered, is in the artillery, and they would, I presume, give you your choice as to regiment in that arm of the service.

As to Fortress Monroe and Columbia College, it may be in season to conclude which of the two bids fair to be most advantageous in case you do not succeed in joining the Engineer Corps. But, if it is necessary for you to have my opinion before you leave for home, I think going to Columbia College much preferable of the two.

As to money matters, I trust you have been reasonably economical, as that is wisest, so I will cheerfully see that you are furnished means for returning home, for which you are hereby given my permission to check on the Deseret National Bank in this city for such amount as you may need.

Pres. George A. Smith has had a very severe attack of illness, but his health at present seems to be improving. My health is very good, and the folks are all usually well. I purpose going to Logan on the 5th inst., and expect to return next week.

Utah affairs are very quiet, excellent prospects for good crops of all kinds, and our local enemies rather chop-fallen and going slow. God bless you,

> Your affectionate father,
> Brigham Young

Letter dated November 11, 1875

When Willard Young was graduated from West Point on June 16, 1875, he was the 2,553rd cadet to receive a commission since the academy opened in 1802. In his class of forty-three, Willard stood fifth in engineering, fifteenth in law, eighth in geology and mineralogy, sixth in ordnance and gunnery, and second in discipline. He was fourth in over-all standing. His record brought him the highest distinction conferred upon a cadet—an appointment to the Corps of Engineers. Those whose moral sensitivities were disturbed when the son of the polygamous Mormon leader had entered the academy in 1871 were equally disturbed when he graduated in 1875 with academic honors, in the face of a popular conception that the minds of children of plural families were inferior to those of monogamic parentage.[26]

Following his graduation and a three-month visit with his family in Utah, Willard reported for duty with the engineer battalion at Willet's Point, New York, on October 1, 1875. En route he stopped at Ann Arbor, Michigan, and Troy, New York, where he visited his brothers Alfales and Don Carlos, who were studying in the East.

Upon arriving at Willet's Point, Willard found the post "a nice one" and very conveniently located, a dozen miles from New York City. After one month he evaluated his new assignment for his father. "The duties, as a general thing, are instructive, and therefore pleasant. The greatest fault to be found with them is, that they are too few, but this is a fault that can be more easily overlooked than almost any other. I find I shall have a splendid opportunity to read the coming winter and expect to profit some by it. The post library, though not large, contains not a few books whose perusal will repay the time thus spent. I have also with me almost a complete set of Church works and can inform myself by becoming more familiar with them. I consider myself very lucky in getting into the Engineer Corps, as it is every way better than the line. I have even heard my companions say, and they are men who have been in the service some time, that they would not exchange a position as a 2d Lieutenant in this corps, for that of Captain in the Artillery, which is considered next to this. This is saying a good deal, where men covet rank as they do in the army. This is doubly true for me as I only want the experience and do not expect to remain long in the service."[27]

Brigham Young answered his son on November 11.

Salt Lake City, November 11, 1875

Elder Willard Young
Willet's Point, New York

My dear Son,
   Your very welcome communication of the 3rd inst. has come duly to hand, cheering us with its glad news of your health, progress, and prospects, for all of which we feel very pleased and thankful.
   Whilst listening to the perusal of your letter, I was gratified to learn that your quarters are so comfortable and your duties so instructive. I admire your determination to use your leisure hours in studying, especially of our holy religion. I am desirous that you should also give especial attention to engineering, chemistry, minerology, and geology. If there are works on these sciences in the library of your post, I think it would be wise of you to use them to the best advantage, and read up on these branches. Amongst the pleasure of my life at the present time is the thought that so many of my sons are acquiring experimental and practical knowledge that will fit them for lives of great usefulness. And with this thought I associate the hope that by God's mercy that knowledge will be applied in striving to save the souls of men, and building up the kingdom of heaven on the earth. This knowledge and this work will prove your happiness, for every human being will find that his happiness very greatly depends upon the work he does, and the doing of it well. Whoever wastes his life in idleness, either because he need not work in order to live, or because he will not live to work, will be a wretched creature, and

at the close of a listless existence, will regret the loss of precious gifts and the neglect of great opportunities. Our daily toil, however humble it may be, is our daily duty, and by doing it well we make it a part of our daily worship. But, whatever be our labor, calling, or profession, we should hold our skill, knowledge, and talents therein, subservient to the accomplishment of the purposes of Jehovah, that our entire lives, day by day, may be made to praise Him, and our individual happiness secured by the consciousness that we are fulfilling the purpose and design of our presence here on the earth.

My health is slowly improving, yet I must continue to take great care of myself. I am still a prisoner,[28] but do not think I shall long require the watch care of the United States marshal. Possibly you may hear by telegram in the newspapers before this reaches you that some movement has been made for my release. The continued ill health of Chief Justice [J. Alexander] White (who, by the way, is improving) has prevented the matter being brought before him, and it would be worse than useless to present it in any shape before Judge [Jacob S.] Boreman. So far as the action of the authorities at Washington is concerned, I anticipate we shall have to wait some little time before we hear from them.

The missionaries called at the late conference have all left, with a very few exceptions, for their fields of labor. They carry with them the faith of the priesthood and people, that they will be the instruments in the hands of the Lord of doing much good in bringing many of the honest in heart to a knowledge of the principles of eternal salvation. The elders for Australia sailed from San Francisco yesterday, and I learn by telegram from Elder D[aniel] W. Jones that his party would probably reach Sonora about the 15th of this month. Undoubtedly some of the elders will visit you whilst on their travels. Elders James A. and Feramorz Little and Jesse W. Fox Jr. will labor a part of their time in New York City. The family are all well.

You will find it a great advantage through life if you, in connection with your studies, acquire the faculty of imparting the knowledge you possess to others. All true science, which is the true knowledge of God and God's works, is incorporated in the great plan of the redemption and salvation of the human family, and all the rest of the world. And to be enabled to enlighten others with regard to the dealings or the works of our Creator is greatly to be desired by all who seek the welfare of mankind.

May God bless you, may His peace abide with you, and His power sustain you continually, is the prayer of

> Your affectionate father,
> Brigham Young

Letters of February 17, 1876, to April 26, 1876

"I am always very much gratified on receiving a letter from you, for I can always rely on having good instruction and advice imparted," wrote Willard upon receipt of his father's letter of November 11. "It seems that my desires and determination to prepare myself for doing a good work are strengthened by reading your good words. I need a continual stirring up to keep my mind on the great work that is before me, and before all of us, who are interested in the upbuilding of God's Kingdom here on the earth. The influence of my associations and associates is only too strongly felt, and I realize that I am continually being affected by it. Instead of the single thought of serving God, by which my whole conduct, thoughts, words, and deeds, *should* be governed, I find myself, though never entirely losing sight of this great truth, entering more or less into the worldly feelings and thoughts of my comrades. But, on the other hand, I am brought by my position, which allows me to comprehend the doings and motives of the outside world, to compare the light and knowledge which a fulness of the Gospel affords, with the groveling ignorance, manifested by the world at large, in all that pertains to future welfare and glory; and this comparison gives me greater joy in, and a better appreciation of the privileges and blessings of the Gospel. I hope I may live faithful to my covenants, and so conduct myself as to please you. If I do, my desire to prove a useful instrument in the upbuilding of the kingdom will be realized."[29]

Willard's tenure of service at Willet's Point lasted from October 1, 1875, to September 3, 1877, during which time he corresponded regularly with his father. Willard's response to three letters written by his father in the early months of 1876 has not been found.

WILLARD YOUNG

Salt Lake City, February 17, 1876

Elder Willard Young
Willet's Point, New York

My dear Son,

    Your very interesting and very welcome letter dated Jan. 6th 1875, but which I presume should be Feb. 6th, 1876, came duly to hand, and I was cheered to hear of your continued good health and prosperity. I concur in your idea that it would be advantageous and desirable for you to occupy quarters where you will be free from the annoyances and interruptions incidental to the presence of others in your room: "talking, smoking, playing cards &c." I am desirous that you should use the golden time now upon your hands to the very best advantage. It may be that you will never have such another opportunity amidst the care and bustle of after life as you now possess. Two things I am very anxious all my sons should be, faithful [*illegible*] members in His kingdom.
Integrity to the truth and ability to do good are qualities which I hope will characterize you all. And I will acknowledge that I have much happiness in the thought of how well my boys are doing at the present time. I shall not enter into any details with regard to family news as Nabbie [Young Clawson] will no doubt be only too pleased to tell you about her marriage and reception, also of Morris's fatherhood, and of the arrival home of Brigham Jun. and John W.

    I expect to start for the South very shortly and it is most probable Brigham Jun. and Bro. Wells will accompany me. And whilst there they will possibly visit our new settlements, whilst other brethren will, as soon as spring opens, start on an exploring expedition to learn the advantages of the country between the termini of the various railroads that run into southern Colorado and our settlements in Arizona. Already the railroad lines are rapidly pushing towards that section of country, and I have the idea that there are many desirable valleys for the homes of Latter-day Saints within a radius of 100 miles of the point where Utah, Colorado, New Mexico and Arizona meet. It is quite possible that we shall have this season's immigration settle in this new country and thus extend the borders of Zion and strengthen her stakes.

We have had quite a change in our municipal officers. The election took place on last Monday and as was of course fully expected, resulted in a complete victory for the People's Ticket. Bro. Feramorz Little is now mayor and quite a number of fresh faces adorn the council chamber.

It must be very encouraging and pleasing to you in your thoughts of home, to realize the present activity in the works and feelings of the Saints whilst the progress of the work of God is made manifest in so many quarters. From every point we receive encouraging news from our missionaries out in the field and baptisms are not infrequent. The elders appointed for Australia have arrived and have entered heartily upon their duties and have divided themselves amongst the various colonies. The call for settlers to Arizona has been nobly responded to and most of the families are now far on their way. When we think of the vast amount of preaching our elders are doing far and wide out in the world, the spirit of reformation amongst gathered Israel, the work of the Father commenced amongst the degraded children of Lehi, and the spreading out and strengthening of the settlements of the Saints, we cannot come to any other conclusion than "Zion is growing," nor refrain from praising our God for his manifest and repeated preservation of his people from the evils the enemies of righteousness seek to bring upon them.

My health is good and I am enjoying life, though I shall be glad to rest for a time when I reach St. George as business has been crowding me considerably of late, whilst the legislature has been sitting and we have been getting off the Arizona emigrants.

Are you likely to have a furlough this next summer, or is there any probability of your being stationed anywhere in these mountains?

With love and continued prayers that every blessing may be yours that you can righteously desire.

>
> I remain,
> Your affectionate father,
> Brigham Young

WILLARD YOUNG

Salt Lake City, March 28, 1876

Elder Willard Young
Willet's Point, New York

My dear Son,

    Your welcome and interesting communication of 18th inst. reached me a few days ago. The same mail brought me a letter from Alfales, and I was gratified with the good news of your health and prosperity which both contained. I have just written to Bro. Carrington asking him, if consistent with the welfare of the mission, to release Ernest, so that he can visit Ferry at Annapolis on the closing days of the term the 18th of June and accompany him home, as Ferry is going to pay us a short visit and is anxious to have his brother's company on the homeward trip. I presume you will have the opportunity to see them in New York on 22nd June or thereabouts.

    It would very much please me to have you give especial attention to the study of chemistry, more particularly of those branches which can be applied to the business of daily life, so that you can be sufficiently proficient therein that your knowledge will be of advantage to yourself and an aid to the progress of the kingdom of God.

    The family are all well, of which fact they, no doubt, kept you well informed. The boys at home are mostly at the same duties and business as when I last wrote. Morris has gone south with Bro. M[ilton] H. Hardy in the interest of the Young Men's Associations. I am thinking of having Mahonri go to my woolen factory and learn the business with a view to his eventually taking charge there if he likes the trade. Heber is working at the Co-op. I expect he will do so permanently. Nelson Empey anticipates going down south with me after conference, as he feels his health failing and he thinks an out would do him good.

    ZCMI is now moving into its new building, and a busy scene it presents. It requires quite a force of men and teams to move their extensive stock. We shall open in the new building on Saturday 1st prox. On Friday evening myself and the brethren of the Quorum of the Twelve will go down to the building and dedicate it.

Our new marshal has arrived; from the descriptions of the brethren I should imagine him to be a quiet, everyday person, a kind of third-rate politician. Our new chief justice, Mr. Coughlan, is not yet with us. Some of the members of the ring claim him as their particular friend. When in Congress he never showed any friendship for Utah, and very little can be expected from him. If he will but do right, judge righteously and administer the law with justice and equity, is all we ask.

My health is good. Give my love and best respects to the children and to the brethren as you may from time to time see them, and with continued prayers for your welfare, happiness and prosperity,

I remain, your affectionate father,
Brigham Young

Salt Lake City, April 26, 1876

Elder Willard Young
Willet's Point, New York

My dear Son,

Your good letter with its varied items of news of the family and information regarding your progress and prospects reached me yesterday. I am well pleased to hear that you are now in a better position to continue your studies and researches, with regard to which things you know my mind, whilst I have the fullest confidence that you will do your utmost to carry out my wishes, which are all for your benefit, happiness and well-being.

Whenever you see John W., Don Carlos, Nabbie [Young Clawson] or any of the rest of the folks give them my best love.

I had a very fine letter from Arta D. a few days ago; it breathes an excellent spirit. He is now I presume with Bro. [Albert] Carrington, Ernest, and one or two others making a tour of the churches in continental Europe, which should, and I have no doubt will be, a pleasant and profitable experience for both the boys. Lorenzo D. will accompany us to St. George (for which place we start, all being well, on Monday next) before he goes on his mission to Europe, where possibly he will labor first in Great Britain, afterwards in Germany.

I should have mentioned just above that Brigham Jun., who is one of our party for the South, is already on the road. He will preach to the Saints in the settlements on the way until the rest of the party overtake him. Bro. [Daniel H.] Wells, Brigham Jun., and a few trusty brethren will not go direct with me to St. George but will continue their journey to the new settlements in Arizona, when, after visiting and counseling the new settlers, they will join me in our Dixie. So far as we have yet learned the new settlements are prospering. They are located not far from each other and near the point where [the] Wingate and Prescott mail route crosses the river, sometimes called the Sunset Crossing.

We have very cheering news from two of the party who went with Bro. [Daniel W.] Jones—Bros. [Ammon M.] Tenney and [Robert H.] Smith—but who by his direction returned from El Paso up the valley of the Rio Grande Del Norte and who have been preaching to the Pueblo Indians until the mobocratic spirit of the greasers, Spaniards, and others made it desirable that they should change their field of labor for a short time, or until the storm has blown over. Their words, however, had been received with much faith by the Indians. Leaving the valley of the Rio Grande they traveled westward until they reached a point nearly on the Arizona line. Here they tarried and preached to the Zuni Indians who dwell near the headwaters of one of the tributaries of the Little Colorado. They had baptized thirteen of this tribe when last heard from and Bro. Tenney writes that a thousand more were ready for baptism and would enter the waters when the weather had become a little warmer.

My health has been for some days past, and still is, good, and with care I hope to be able to reach St. George without any great inconvenience or injury to my constitution. I shall enjoy a rest in the southern country, if I am permitted to have one, but I anticipate the duties of the temple, the visits of the Lamanites, the necessities of the new settlements, and other responsibilities will pretty fully occupy my time and attention.

With many prayers, and much love,

I remain, your affectionate father,
Brigham Young

Letter of October 19, 1876

Looking back upon his first year at Willet's Point, which he had anticipated as a year of intensive study and preparation, Willard was less than enthusiastic at the prospects for the future. His worst enemy, one that seemed to be eating away at his incentive and "sense of duty," was an oppressive idleness, nurtured by some of his associates —career men, to whom life at West Point had become an ultimate goal rather than the means to an end. "I know my time here cannot be so productive of good as it would elsewhere," he wrote his father. "Did I intend remaining in the Army all my life, I might think differently, and would, perhaps, think better of my present advantages. The greatest mistake is made in sending young officers here as soon as they leave West Point and *keeping* them here. They are worked out and need rest, it is true, but in coming here, they have too good an opportunity, for it leads to laziness. A year here is sufficient; if then they should be sent out where they would have some responsibility, until habits of life were formed, I know the results would be better. A young officer sent from here last summer, to join the Wheeler Expedition, has just written me from Nevada, that he has learned more of the world and of life in the short time he has been there, than he would have done 'in sixteen years at Willets Point.' "[30]

When William T. Sherman, commander-in-chief of the U.S. Army, visited Brigham Young in Salt Lake City in October 1876, they discussed Willard's military future. In Brigham Young's letter of October 19 he reviewed these details and offered some carefully worded advice to his son.

Salt Lake City, October 19, 1876

Elder Willard Young
Willet's Point, New York

My dear Son,
Knowing that a few lines from your father would not be unacceptable, I avail myself of this, possibly the last opportunity I may have before going south to spend the winter and attend to the dedication of portions of the temple at St. George.
When in this city a week or so ago, the Secretary of War and

Gen. [William T.] Sherman called upon me. I had a very pleasant chat with the general, during which your name was mentioned. I was rather in favor of your going into active service with some one of the U.S. surveys now being prosecuted by the government in the West. But the general assured me that you would be taking a course of study in torpedoes and other branches of military engineering which would be of the greatest use to you, and he thought it would be the very best thing for you to stay for the present at Willet's Point, and as soon as it would be to your advantage he would take great pleasure in assisting you to a good position such as you would desire.

I have lately deeded to a board of trustees, for the purpose of erecting an academy thereon, the block (20x20 rods) immediately north of the Naisbitt place where Thomas Jennings now resides, and shall probably yet further endow the academy which will be known as the "Young Academy of Salt Lake." It will be open to the children of the Latter-day Saints only. In it the Bible, the Book of Mormon, the Doctrine and Covenants, and other works of the Church will be the standard textbooks, and the preceptors will be especially enjoined to instill into the minds of our youth a faith in the religion of their fathers. We have enough and to spare, at present in these mountains, of schools where young infidels are made because the teachers are so tender-footed that they dare not mention the principles of the gospel to their pupils, but have no hesitancy in introducing into the classroom the theories of Huxley, of Darwin, or of Miall and the false political economy which contends against co-operation and the United Order. This course I am resolutely and uncompromisingly opposed to, and I hope to see the day when the doctrines of the gospel will be taught in all our schools, when the revelation of the Lord will be our texts, and our books will be written and manufactured by ourselves and in our own midst. As a beginning in this direction I have endowed the Brigham Young Academy at Provo and [am] now seeking to do the same thing in this city. Believing that my own boys will best accomplish and have regard to my wishes, I have appointed a board of seven trustees, of whom five are my sons, viz., Brigham Jun., John W., Ernest I., Hyrum S., and yourself. The other two members of the board are brothers D[avid] O. Calder and Geo. Reynolds. The deed will require your signature as one of the trustees which I think can be deferred until your return. If this pleases you, and you are willing to act as one of the trustees, so inform us in your next letters so that we can place your name in the deed and have it duly recorded.

It was my intention to have started for St. George on Monday next, but the enemies of the kingdom of God who are always seeking to harrass me, law or no law, are striving to have me committed to prison for contempt of court in not paying the alimony in the Ann Eliza case. The matter will most probably be heard next Tuesday, when, if the judge is corrupt and bitter enough to decide against me, I shall go to prison, without my mind very much changed, if I have to remain there all the rest of my days, for I certainly shall not pay the plaintiff or her lawyers one cent. But in this, as in all other things, I rely upon the protecting hand of our Father in heaven. I shall be guided by His Spirit and He will bring out all things right.[31]

My health has been good of late and still remains so, as well as that of the family generally. I have lately heard from Alfales, Fera, and Lorenzo D., all of whom were well. The last named had reached England safely when I last heard from him, but had not then been assigned to his field of labor by Bro. Carrington. Arta D. still remains, laboring in the Liverpool Office.

Direct your letters to Salt Lake City and they can then be forwarded to St. George by express.

Since writing the above I have received your letter of 12th inst. and have taken great interest in its contents. I should like you to visit as often as possible, if it could be every Sunday, the Saints at Williamsburg and talk to them and feel therein that you have, at any rate, a small preaching mission to perform. Nor do I think it would be detrimental to you, if in wisdom, you chatted with your comrades with regard to the principles of the gospel and loaned to them the works of the Church. In this way the dullness of the everyday routine of your life will be released by efforts to do good, the monotony of your studies will be broken, and the time will pass much more rapidly. Considerable of the four years of your service has already passed, and if you serve out your time the United States will have no further claim on you, without you volunteer, and I would much rather you remained in time of peace than when trouble might come. Looking at the matter as I do now,

I would prefer you to remain in the service with the understanding that on the first favorable opportunity, advantage be taken of Gen. Sherman's offer and you be transferred to some active engineering or topographical expectation, and in the meantime that you prepare yourself by study and by faith to enter the missionary field and to be a profitable laborer in the Master's vineyard after the four years have expired.

With regard to your reflections about getting married and choosing from amongst the daughters of the East, you must be aware of the risk that you run if you take unto yourself a wife who does not believe the gospel, and whom you have no idea will make a good Mormon, one who probably would oppose you in faith and feeling all the days of your life and teach your children to despise the religion of their father. Perhaps in other things she might be as good as many of our western girls, the course of some of whom I cannot commend. Gen. Sherman has some daughters who might not say *no* to you, were your inclinations to run in that direction. But I have never taken a wife since I received the gospel from amongst any but the people of God. Neither, as yet, have any of my sons.[32] Nor am I anxious that they should do so. Still further, I have no objections at all to your coming home and taking a wife whenever it pleases you. You have my entire sanction in so doing, and if you wished to take her back and have her stay with you wherever you are stationed, it would be entirely agreeable to my feelings for you to do so.

With many prayers for your happiness, welfare, comfort, and salvation.

I remain, your affectionate father,
Brigham Young

Letter dated May 23, 1877

Few letters written by Brigham Young to his children came at a more opportune time, or had a more profound effect, than that of October 19, 1876, to Willard. In the face of discouragement Willard had lamented the rudderless course he seemed to be steering at Willet's Point. His father's letter of the 19th gave him an entirely new outlook: "I must say thanks a thousand thanks for your excellent letter. As is always the case it proved interesting beyond comparison. I always have such a 'good' feeling (I cannot better describe it) when I read your words. They seem to do me good every way, physically, mentally, and morally. The effect of the perusal of this last letter was to make me involuntarily exclaim: Thank God for such a father. You have satisfied me every way. I shall enjoy myself a great deal better now, I feel sure, for in trying to carry out your advice in the several directions pointed out, I shall be doing just what I need to better satisfy my own sense of duty. I shall serve out the remainder of my time now with a good heart, since I know it to be your wish."[33]

Aware that his father had endowed a Church academy at Provo, Utah, and learning of plans to do the same in Salt Lake City, Willard responded to the request that he join with four of his brothers as a trustee of the proposed school. "Your idea of the 'Young Academy of Salt Lake' is a very pleasing one to me. The education of our youth is a thing in which no pains should be spared. How many times have I had occasion to regret the want of proper instructions amongst even the few playmates of my school days at home. Amongst them there are not a few who take a kind of pride in rejecting the religion of their parents, and believing themselves infidels. In these cases, it was not, perhaps, the instructions they got that misled them, so much as the *want* of proper instructions. Home is the great school where the young should have instilled into them the principles of truth; yet how much could be done by the successful inauguration of an academy such as you project. It is a very high compliment, indeed, you pay me, and one which I appreciate, in numbering me amongst the trustees of such an institution. I give a most hearty consent to have my name appear on the deed as such, and promise to lend myself to the faithful carrying out of your wishes, so far as lies in my power."[34]

Brigham Young's caution against choosing a wife from among those "who do not believe the Gospel" brought a firm reaction from his son. "Thus far, I have always felt just as you do about the subject of outsiders, and, luckily, have had no inducement to change my mind, thus far; as, amongst our own girls, my experience leads me to believe, I can suit myself just as well as elsewhere. Whenever speaking of the subject, mother has always said, 'Whatever you do, get a good Mormon for a wife,' and I have grown to regard it as a duty to make this the first essential requisite. Even to those who told me, on my leaving home, that they expected me to marry some eastern girl, I always replied, such would not be the case. I have been at home so little of late, that I do not know the girls sufficiently well to properly appreciate all their good qualities; nor have I yet found one to claim my especial affection. For this reason, and more especially as my position and duties, with the uncertainty of my movements, getting quarters &c. would hardly warrant such a step, I think it best to decline (for the present) with thanks, your kind permission for me to 'come home and get a companion.' I have no fear that I shall find somebody to suit me (and whom I will suit) as soon as I see my way clear."[35]

In December 1876, having learned that his aging father had been very ill, and hoping that a few lines might prove some comfort, Willard addressed a letter to him on Christmas day: "I know the deep interest you feel for your children's welfare, and of course it is natural we should feel some sympathy for you in return. For myself I have always felt grateful for having been blest with a father, who always inspired me with perfect confidence, who always felt so jealous a care for my wellbeing, and who always set so worthy an example for me to follow. . . .

"Since leaving home I have felt a desire to worthily represent you and our people. Wherein I have failed it has been my own fault, I know. I am told, how truly I know not, that I have succeeded in inspiring at least some few at home with confidence in me, and I hope it is so. If I can be the means of doing good in establishing God's Kingdom on the Earth, and can succeed in doing all that is expected of me, I shall feel happy indeed. . . .

"One thing I very much lack, that would prove of greatest service to me in life—it is the gift or faculty of communicating my thoughts and ideas to others. You have noticed this, and have advised me to acquire it by practice. I have not succeeded very well as yet. Your instructions for me to talk to the Saints at our Williamsburg meetings, whenever opportunity offers, I feel, is calculated to give me confidence in myself, and the experience I need. Thus far I have not been called upon, except to dismiss the meeting, since receiving your letter; before that, it was thought wisdom not to call upon me. I do not know how I will do when I am called upon. That indiscribable feeling which nearly all new beginners have, tells me I certainly do need experience. As with every thing else it is necessary, I suppose, to *learn* to preach. . . ."

Willard wrote further that his duties at Willet's Point "are still very light, so that I have plenty of time on my hands to study, or read, or waste—and I am afraid I do waste a great deal too much of it." He closed his letter with a report of his visit on Thanksgiving Day to his brothers Don Carlos and Feramorz, who were studying at the Rensselaer Polytechnic Institute in Troy, New York, at the time.[36]

Salt Lake City, May 23, 1877

Elder Willard Young
Willet's Point, New York

My dear Son,

    My time since my departure from St. George has been so fully occupied that not until now have I been able to reply to your welcome letter of April 29th. Of the circumstances that attended our return journey to Salt Lake City, and the work we performed on the way, you have no doubt been advised by members of the family, so I shall not here enter into details. Since my return the duties of my calling have kept me actively engaged. What with the councils of the priesthood, the meetings of the city council and of the board of directors of ZCMI, of the Deseret Bank, of the Street Railroad Co., &c. &c., I find my time most completely engaged. But I am happy to say that my health is excellent, and my feelings as calm and pleasant as at any period of my life. I look back with great satisfaction at my labors during the past six months and feel much joy therein, and the assurance that the Lord has accepted our offering of the House built to His name adds to my happiness and inspires me to fresh efforts. Since my return home I have spoken frequently and at considerable length, and I have but to a very slight degree felt any inconvenience therefrom to my stomach or speaking organs. Already we have held local conferences at Salt Lake and Logan cities, and shall during the next two weeks do the same at Ogden and Brigham cities. In our visits to the different parts of these valleys we shall more fully organize the priesthood and organize stakes of Zion with a president, high council &c. &c. wherever desirable. This will be the work of the First Presidency and Twelve during the present summer, and by the time every portion of this mountain region in which the Saints dwell is organized, we shall probably find that we have about twenty-one stakes of Zion. To visit these stakes, hold local conferences once in about every three months to strengthen, direct, and lead the Saints in the paths of holiness will be the work of the Twelve Apostles with the assistance of the First Presidency as far as they can. You may inquire, why organize so many stakes of Zion? We will answer, to more completely carry out the purposes of Jehovah, to give greater compactness to the labors of the priesthood, to unite the Saints, to care for the scattering sheep of Israel in these mountains who acknowledge no particular fold, to be in a position to understand the standing of every one calling himself a Latter-day Saint, and to consolidate the interests, feelings, and lives of the members of the Church. These are some of the reasons why we now more fully than heretofore organize the holy priesthood after the pattern given us of our Father in heaven.

As you may suppose, these labors, combined with the energy now shown by the Saints in raising temples to the name of the Most High, have aroused the ire of the evil one and incensed the anger of his agents here on the earth. The fountain of lies has apparently burst forth with tenfold vigor to overwhelm the people of God. But our trust is in Him who controlleth all things and turneth the people as the rivers are turned. Already there seems to have arisen a conviction with many that the slanderous reports spread about us are not to be relied on, and that some sinister motive prompts their dissemination. The troubles in the South having been plastered over for a little while, those who live on the misery of their fellow men find their occupation gone in that direction, and are very willing to help on a contractors war against Utah, which the ring in this city is only too anxious to inaugurate. We have, however, today the same assurance as of old that the Lord will make the wrath of men to praise Him, and the rest of it He will restrain.

Of the family I may say all are well with the exception of Brigham Jun., whose health, ever since we left St. George, has been very poor. He was so enfeebled that we had to leave him at Parowan, in the care of Bro. [George Q.] Cannon, who remained to nurse him, and by very slow stages they reached this city, and after a few days' rest he continued his journey with me to his home at Logan, where he now is slowly, but we hope, surely improving. John W. is with me attending to the duties of his calling; Don Carlos and Fera will not return home during the present vacation but will devote their unemployed time to the study of music. Mahonri and Oscar are still at the woolen mills. Heber is more immediately helping me round the premises. Ernest and Alonzo are at ZCMI. Morris will shortly start on his mission to the States. Alfales is home again, having completed his law course, whilst we expect Arta D. home with Bro. [Albert] Carrington in a very few weeks. Lorenzo will remain in England another year. Walter Beatie will soon start on his mission, and may possibly call on you on his way.

Praying the Lord to bless you, my dear son, with every needed blessing and good He has to bestow on His faithful children,

>
> I remain,
> Your affectionate father,
> Brigham Young

Letter of July 28, 1877

In answer to his father's letter of May 23, Willard wrote, "I am, as you know, always interested in what you have to say of the progress of the Latter-day work, and in the way of encouragement and advice. If I do not keep all your counsels it is through weakness on my part, and not for lack of faith in your ability and right to direct me."[37]

Since Willard's pay during the summer of 1877 was dependent upon an allocation of funds from Congress that was not forthcoming until fall, and he was not desirous of taking a loss by selling his pay accounts prematurely at a discount, he closed his letter of June 4 with a request to borrow $500. His letter arrived in Salt Lake City just as his father was leaving for southern Utah. When the President heard that the U.S. Government couldn't pay his son, he jokingly remarked to his secretary, George Reynolds, that Willard had better tell the commanding officer at the post that he would resign and save the expense of keeping him. Brigham Young then advised Reynolds to answer Willard's letter. Not sensing in the written reply the jest with which his father spoke, Willard carefully weighed the counsel that he discontinue his military career: "I need not tell you I am ready to do just what you wish me to do in the matter.... To resign ... would be to abandon a very good position, a profession, in fact, for which I have been specially educated. It is not simply leaving the army, but the very best position in the army—the Engineer Corps. I have salary sufficient to keep me comfortably, besides pleasant, congenial work, and a social position and consideration that I can hardly expect to enjoy in civil life.... I feel desirous of taking that course which will allow me to do the most good, and it certainly seems to me now that I will do this by going home. I cannot deny that much might be done in my present position, especially in making friends, and removing prejudice, and goodness knows there is plenty of it that ought to be removed. It is certainly wonderful that even amongst intelligent and cultivated people so much ignorance, I might almost say bigotry, exists in regard to our people and their professions. In spite of this, however, a better field seems open to me at home. I find my greatest argument, perhaps, is my own feelings, for it is certainly pleasing to think of being associated with people whose sympathies are with yours, and whose object and aim in life are yours. I cannot outgrow the love of home and home associations, and especially if I am to be continually reminded that there *is* no sympathy for me in the world, and I am so reminded very frequently. My associations and intercourse here sadly lack that feeling of confidence, of congeniality, and love, that is so marked at home. I almost feel a barrier that is hard to describe, a kind of ostracism in my associations here, that is entirely wanting at home. It is true I have a great many acquaintances here, whom I call friends, but they are not friends in whom I could trust, as I could those who are numbered with the Latter-day Saints. I cannot deny that I am anxious to get home as soon as possible. I am willing, though, to do just what you think is for the best. If you think it wisdom for me to serve the four years out, and then resign, as was your wish, all right. I had fully made up my mind to do this, before Bro. Reynolds wrote. His letter, I think, will be my best excuse, if excuse is necessary for again referring to this subject."[38]

Three days after Willard wrote these lines, the battalion of engineers at Willet's Point, along with other federal troops from the forts in New York harbor, was called to restore order in the wake of railroad strikes that had erupted in the East in the summer of 1877. Willard's unit was sent first to Baltimore, Maryland. Their orders were to relieve the Sixth Regiment of Maryland militia, which was confined in the Baltimore armory, where the men had taken refuge after having been stoned and fired upon by a mob, and in turn had fired upon rioters, killing several. When the federal troops arrived in Baltimore, the situation was volatile. "The mob followed us on our way to the armory, and a few stones were thrown at us, one of our men being knocked down. The command was halted, and this was enough; for, thinking we were going to shoot, they very soon cleared out. We arrived at the armory without further incident." From Baltimore, Willard's unit was transferred to Philadelphia. "How long we will remain here I do not know. Much of the trouble is over, and our presence will not be necessary much longer, I think. Unless some new outbreak occurs, I shall expect to be back at Willet's Point within a week."[39]

Neither an invitation to Willard earlier in the year to join his father at the dedication of the St. George Temple, nor talk of his resignation from the army, materialized in a trip home for Willard Young prior to August 29, 1877. Consequently, he did not see his father again, for on that date the President died. The following letter dated, July 28, 1877, was the last written by Brigham Young to his son Willard.

Salt Lake City, July 28, 1877

Elder Willard Young
Willet's Point, New York

My dear Son,

Your letter of the 18th inst. was somewhat delayed in its transit, owing, I presume, to the troubles with the railroad strikes; but it was none the less welcome on its arrival.

My reason for saying what I did to Bro. [George] Reynolds was that I thought if I had to support you, I might as well have the benefit of your talents. But if the government intends to pay you, after taking all things into consideration, I would rather you do not resign until the four years are up. We shall see what Congress will do when it meets, and until then will not make any move in the matter. But if Congress refuses to make the necessary appropriation, I shall be much inclined to say to you: tender your resignation. In the meantime, learn all you can of that which will be the most useful to you, whether you resign now or complete the term of your four years' service. If circumstances should transpire that you should think it best to tender your resignation, I do not wish you to do anything until you have communicated with Genl. Sherman, laid the facts before him, and asked his counsel in the matter.

On the 16th inst. I wrote to Carlos and Fera (I have since received Carlos's favor of 19th) and therein told them to let you see what I had written. Since that date little has occurred of exciting interest in our midst. It has been said, "happy are the people who have no history." History, as usually written, is principally filled with the wars, the troubles, and misfortunes of mankind, and so perhaps it is well that nothing of special moment has occurred within our borders during the last few days, as it tacitly proclaims that peace, quietude, and the blessings of God prevail. However, it is the Lord alone that we have to thank for this pleasant condition of matters in these valleys.

The enemies of virtue and righteousness are striving earnestly to have it different. They have lately trumped up charges against Bros. R[obert] T. Burton and Dr. [Jeter] Clinton for murder, on account of their being present at the time of the suppression of the Morrisite[40] outbreak by the order and direction of the chief justice of this territory.

We also learn that 23 indictments were found last night by the grand jury. Of course we have not yet learned the names of the unfortunate objects of so much undesired attention. The charge against Dr. Clinton is understood to be that whilst professional attending Jno. [John] Banks, after he was wounded, the Dr. poisoned him. With such outrageous charges as these they seek to aggravate us to some word or act out of which they could make capital to our disadvantage.

We had a very happy time on the Twenty-fourth. Several thousand Sunday School children gathered in the large tabernacle, which had been newly decorated, and very sweetly sang a number of new pieces—the productions of our local composers. I talked for some time to the children, giving them a slight synopsis of our history and the reasons why they were here. Large celebrations were also held in Ogden, Logan, and other places.

All is well with myself and the family. Brigham Jr. is now in the city paying a visit. He is much better.

Brigham and Jno. W. join me in love to yourself, Don Carlos, and Fera.

God bless and preserve you and peace be with you,

Your affectionate father,
Brigham Young

MAHONRI MORIANCUMER YOUNG

Mahonri Moriancumer Young
1852-1884

Mahonri Moriancumer Young, the only son of Margaret M. Alley and Brigham Young, was born in Salt Lake City, December 19, 1852. Named after a Book of Mormon personality, "Hon" Young was an avid sportsman who enjoyed the outdoors and was a master of rod and gun. Educated in Salt Lake City, Mahonri worked for a time at ZCMI, and prior to his father's death, he was appointed manager of the Deseret Woolen Mill at the mouth of Parley's Canyon in Salt Lake Valley. The mill was later deeded to him as part of the settlement of his father's estate. A letter written by Mahonri to his father from the mill on December 16, 1876, reveals a thorough understanding of the wool business by its twenty-four-year-old manager. It also gives this brief glimpse of his personality: "When I go into town, I do so with a horse and buggy. Said horse has to be tended to; I have to do it. I am able to do it, but not disposed to, if I can get out of it. You have two men in the barn who have ample time to put out or hitch up my horse when I want it done, I don't care to smell like a horse when I go to the Co-op or any other place to attend to your business. If I was a stranger attending to this business, my horse could be tended to, but because I am *one of the President's boys* I can tend to him myself. Other men who have charge of other parts of your business have only to go to the barn and ask for the horse and buggy. It is got out at once. Why can I not be respected as much as they? . . . Ever praying for your health and welfare and that of the saints, I am your loving son."[1]

Having suffered from inflammatory rheumatism since he was

seven, Mahonri never left the state of Utah, which no doubt explains the absence of correspondence from his father. On October 22, 1876, he was sealed to Agnes Mackintosh in the Salt Lake Temple, and they were the parents of three sons, one of whom was the world-famous sculptor Mahonri Mackintosh Young. In addition to managing the Deseret Woolen Mill with woefully insufficient capital, Mahonri did some farming. He was a member of the Salt Lake Yacht Club. His death resulting from his rheumatic condition occurred in Salt Lake City on April 20, 1884, at age thirty-two.

ALFALES YOUNG

Alfales Young
1853-1920

The only child of Brigham and Eliza Burgess Young, Alfales Young was born in Salt Lake City on October 3, 1853. He was educated at the family school, and in his early teens he drove a team with his younger half-brother, Don Carlos, hauling construction materials for the Salt Lake Tabernacle and public works. By the late 1860s he was living with his mother in Provo, Utah. When Brigham Young gave his sons an opportunity to study in the East, Alfales enrolled at the University of Michigan, from which he was graduated in 1877 with a degree in law. In the midst of trying legal difficulties in 1876 brought on by unscrupulous efforts to harass him, Brigham Young wrote to Alfales, "it would be very pleasing to us if at the present time you had finished your course of studies and had been admitted to the bar, for you could materially help me in the numerous vexatious suits that are being brought against me to rob me of my property." Upon returning to Utah, Alfales was admitted to the Utah bar in the Third Judicial District. In 1878 he was one of the litigant heirs in the settlement of his father's estate. However, his practice of law in years that followed was minimal, as he devoted most of his remaining life to editorial work with three Utah newspapers—the Salt Lake *Democrat*, the Salt Lake *Herald*, and the *Deseret News*. "Some of the strongest editors in the West are found in Salt Lake City," noted the Omaha *Herald* in 1885; "among them are . . . Alfales Young of the *Democrat*, who . . . is one of the brightest and most promising young journalists in this part of the country."[1]

An avid reader, Alfales had an extensive private library and, in addition to the general knowledge of his profession, was well versed in botany and ornithology. A nephew, Mahonri Young (the talented Utah sculptor), having spent many boyhood days in his uncle's home, attributed much of his own learning and refinement to the influence he received there. Mahonri noted that Alfales's interests were more centered in literature than in law and recalled that though his uncle and aunt never corrected him in the use of language, "I was always in the presence of English intelligently and grammatically used."[2]

On April 16, 1884, Alfales married twenty-two-year-old Ada Cottle, a talented Episcopalian schoolteacher who was teaching at St. Marks School in Salt Lake City. To this union were born four sons. After twenty years' service as telegraph editor of the *Deseret News*, where he was known among his colleagues for his diligence and punctuality, Alfales Young died in Salt Lake City on March 31, 1920, at sixty-six years of age.

Letters dated September 2, 1875, to December 29, 1876

Alfales Young was one of four sons of Brigham Young to seek professional training at institutions of higher learning in the eastern United States. He entered law school at Michigan University in 1875 and was a member of the eighteenth graduating class in 1877.

The university archives contain no information on his activities while enrolled there, nor does Alfales appear in the class picture. Only two letters written by him to members of his family during his school years at Ann Arbor are extant in the Church archives. One congratulates his brother John W. in his appointment as counselor in the First Presidency of the Church. "I pray that you may have the wisdom you may need and that you may receive the full and entire confidence of the people."[3] The other expresses gratitude for a biography of his father that had been sent to him (probably Tullidge's *Life of Brigham Young*), a reading of which had ignited his sense of devotion and a response that is illustrative of his prose: "It is a well writen work as far as I can judge. I think it also an opportune work, as too many of our people were forgetting the 'wrongs of Mossouri.' As I read it, I cannot but think of the hardships and wandering of our people. Although I hope and pray we may never again have to leave our homes, yet, if we must, I hope that none will be found who are not willing to rase every home to the ground, and cut down every tree. I think we should more frequently sing that hymn of Bro. Penrose:

> 'Up, awake, ye defenders of Zion!
> The foe's at the door of your homes;
> Let each heart be the heart of a lion,
> Unyielding and proud as he roams.
> Remember the wrongs of Missouri;
> Forget not the fate of Nauvoo!
> When the God-hating foe is before ye,
> Stand firm and be faithful and true.'

"I think the most interesting time I ever had was when I went to Soda Springs five years ago this fall, and as we were going through Echo, Brigham Jr. showed me all the points of interest in the kanyan, and told me of the early troubles on Bear River with the mountaineers. I should much like to take the trip again with him. All is well with me. I had letters from Willard and Carlos a day or so since and they are well. Remember me to the folks in St. George and to all friends. Praying for your health and welfare. I remain, your loving son."[4]

The twelve letters of Brigham Young that follow were written to Alfales between September 2, 1875, and December 29, 1876, while he was studying at Michigan University.

Salt Lake City, September 2, 1875

Elder Alfales Young
Ann Arbor, Michigan

My dear Son,

Your letters to me have been a source of much satisfaction and many happy reflections. It affords me great joy to know that you are realizing some of the powers of the gospel and the knowledge of its truth. Give your heart to God and your life to his service and this testimony will continually increase with you and will never grow dim, and your strength will increase with your increasing years until you will have passed away, and your faith in the Lord and in His work will be undivided.

The death of Pres. Geo. A. Smith has cast a gloom over the entire community. It is true we were well aware that if he did not soon take a change for the better he must before long leave us.

It was not, however, expected that when he did depart he would do so with so little warning. During the night he had been very restless, got up and back down several times, and shortly before his death walked out into another room and sat down in a common parlor chair. Whilst there at 8:40 o'clock in the morning, he drew two long breaths, stretched back a little, and all was over. Heartfelt, indeed, have been the prayers that he might be restored to health, and earnest have been the hopes for a continuance of his long and devoted sojourn upon the earth; but it has pleased the Lord to take him from us and he has gone with as good a record, I believe, as any man who ever lived upon this earth—God's footstool. According to his wish he will be buried in a large, plain coffin, and his funeral will be inexpensive. The services will take place on Sunday morning at 10 o'clock. You will find all the details of Bro. Smith's death in the columns of the *Deseret News*.

The family, I am happy to say, are all well. Your mother has been paying a visit in this city; she appeared to be in very fine health. She returned home yesterday. I have much confidence in the course you will pursue; still let me impress upon you to be faithful in your duties and prayers, diligent in your studies, and prudent in your life and expenditure.

Bp. [John] Sharp will hand you this. Your brother Don Carlos and the bishop's son, William, are accompanying him as far as Troy, N.Y., where they are about to enter upon a course of studies at the academy at that place.

May God bless you in all your life and His peace rest continually upon you is the heartfelt prayer of

Your affectionate father,
Brigham Young

Salt Lake City, September 21, 1875

Elder Alfales Young
Ann Arbor, Michigan

My dear Son,

Since my last to you, your favor of 11th inst. has come to hand, and it is needless for me to add, was perused with much pleasure. I note with interest every expression in which you manifest your faith and confidence in the revelations of God's purposes in these our days.

Nothing gives me greater joy than to realize that my sons are taking hold of the principles of eternal truth and applying them to their lives. The strength of Zion is in the virtue of her sons and daughters. Her foundations are laid in the practical observance by her children of the principles of faith, humility, truth, justice, mercy, and love. Each of us, my son, must cultivate these principles in our lives to make the whole bloom with the power and knowledge of God. No people ever prospered as the chosen ones of heaven who left to their high priests and elders the whole duty of serving the Lord. But God is making of us a nation of kings and priests; and none of us are of so little importance that we are excused from keeping the commandments of heaven, or are excluded from the blessings of eternal lives. In all your associations, never be afraid to acknowledge your faith; never be ashamed to do what is right, nor to resist temptation when it is presented before you. So shall the blessing of heaven rest upon you, and so shall you be prospered in all your avocations.

I have very little in the way of news to tell you. Gov. [George W.] Emery has appointed Judge [Jacob S.] Boreman to the 3rd Judicial District, and court will open in a few days. We learn by telegraph that Judge [J. Alexander] White of Alabama has been appointed by President [Ulysses S.] Grant [as] chief justice for Utah. Since Judge [Philip H.] Emerson's return home the ring have, through their organ, covered him with the vilest abuse. He appears to be the especial object of their vituperation just at present.

The family are enjoying good health. My own is excellent, with the exception of occasional attacks of rheumatics. Your mother is here, looking and feeling exceedingly well. Willard left on Monday for his station in the State of New York and I suppose has paid you a passing visit. Mahonri is still at the Co-op. I have lately heard from Ferry [Feramorz]. He had just returned from his cruise, and was settling himself down with renewed vigor to his course of studies. Through Bro. [William C.] Staines I learn of Don Carlos's safe arrival at Troy. Lorenzo is studying hard here to make himself efficient in his studies. Of Joseph A.'s sons, Brigham T. has chosen surveying as a business, whilst Richard W. is preparing to conquer both the theoretical and practical parts of the duties of an architect.

We propose to call a number of missionaries at conference for the Eastern and Southern States and for Canada. Some of them may possibly be from the circle of your acquaintance, and will probably call on you as they pass along.

I want my sons to realize and would be glad if all the world could understand that no matter whether a man is a lawyer, a doctor, a mechanic, or indeed, be he engaged in any occupation whatever, that thorough honesty and integrity will always lead to success, influence, and respect. If a young man wishes to prosper in his profession, this is the only sure road to progress. On the other hand, if he allows himself to be led from the direct path of honesty, either through the desire to make money fast, or, as appears to be the idea with some members of the legal profession, that in the advocacy of a cause or the defense of a client everything is proper that the law does not condemn, if he permits this feeling to guide him he will be looked upon with jealousy and distrust by those who are acquainted with his course, not to say anything about the sinfulness of being dishonest. There is no doubt but that Benjamin Franklin's motto is a true one that "honesty is the best policy." I wish to impress this truth firmly on your mind and on the minds of our other brethren who are studying law, as no other profession seems more open to this evil than theirs, that you will not forget it through all the intercourse and associations of your lives.

May the peace of heaven rest upon you, and the wisdom of God's Spirit guide your life is the constant prayer of

Your affectionate father,
Brigham Young

Salt Lake City, April [October] 6, 1875[5]

Elder Alfales Young
Ann Arbor, Michigan

My dear Son Alfales,

Your letter to your mother reached her safely and a copy has been sent to me. I am happy to find from its contents that you are methodical and earnest in your studies. By order and perseverance combined with a reliance on the Lord you are bound to progress in your studies and make a useful man in the midst of God's people. Do not ever forget, in the whole course of your life, the advice I gave you in my last communication.

I regret to learn that Brother A. B[ruce] Taylor does not understand better than to be too full of argument. I am pleased with the sound judgment you manifest when you give expression to the truth that it is by living your religion and not contending about it that you expect to gain influence with those with whom you associate. Let your example be such that none can righteously or truthfully find fault with it. Take your brother Willard, for instance. He has said but little about his religion. Certainly he was always ready, as he should be, to answer any questions with regard to his faith and his brethren, but his great strength and the source of his influence has been that he has lived his religion in his every-day walk and conduct. No young man ever went out from Utah who carries a better influence, or is more respected, than is Willard. I would not have you shirk the subject of your religion or appear in any way ashamed of its principles. But do not discuss or argue these topics, for no good can arise therefrom, and if Bro. Bruce Taylor insists on taking such a course—if he will not desist after you have kindly talked with him about it—and still continues to make himself disagreeable and foolish, I would tell him that he cannot room with me any more, and have him go somewhere else. There is another thing which I desire you to remember, I do not wish you to lend Bro. Taylor any of your money. If you do, you must do so on your own convenience, as I do not feel like sustaining him. His father does not know anything about his source of supplies and my opinion is that he intends to try to beat his way and fall back upon your purse when he fails elsewhere.

We have had a pleasant little excitement this week in the visit of Pres. [Ulysses S.] Grant and party to our city and territory. The ring attempted to corral him but signally failed, and he very impartially bestowed his attentions on all persons and parties alike, at which they, fancying themselves his especial pets, feel very much chagrined. The party—the ladies especially—expressed themselves very much delighted with their visit to the home of the

Latter-day Saints. I send you a copy of the *Herald* with the account of his visit.[6]

Conference commenced this morning. It promises to be a very interesting one and is largely attended by the Saints from the outside settlements.

The weather is lovely, warm and pleasant, which adds very much to the pleasure of our meeting.

Bro. Wells and his party will be in this evening.

I understand Judge [Philip H.] Emerson gives a splendid account of you which is very gratifying. Please tender my warm regards to Mrs. Emerson for her kindness to you.

Your mother is well and feeling well, and is very much pleased at the good news she hears of you.

Regarding a watch, I presume you can purchase one as cheaply there as you can here. Were I you, if I purchased I would buy a cheap silver watch which will do for the present until you need a first-rate one. I cannot send you one for I have none excepting what I carry.

With much love, and praying the Lord to bless you in all your labors and studies,

I remain, as ever,
Your affectionate father,
Brigham Young

Salt Lake City, October 20, 1875

Elder Alfales Young
Ann Arbor, Michigan

My dear Son,

I have been very much gratified with the receipt of several letters of late from Willard, Don Carlos, Ferry, and yourself, through which I learn that you are all nobly exerting yourselves to do your duty and to put your time and talents out to usury, that the results may be made manifest in your after life.

The day before yesterday Ann Eliza's lawyers moved in the Third Judicial District Court for an order to compel me to show cause why I should not be adjudged guilty of contempt of court in not paying the alimony *pendente lite,* ordered by Judge [James B.] McKean. Judge [Jacob S.] Boreman granted the order, the papers were served by Deputy Marshal [A. K.] Smith, I accepted service, and the hearing of the motion is set for Saturday morning next at 10 o'clock. We hope to be able to put off the hearing of the matter until Judge [J. Alexander] White arrives, as it is understood that the governor has only assigned Boreman temporarily to the Third District.

Our conference was a very delightful one. Much good instruction was given, and the Spirit of the Lord was copiously poured out upon the speakers. You have, no doubt, read the details of what was done during the session in the columns of the *Deseret News.*

Quite a number of improvements are going on in the city. Bro. [Thomas W.] Ellerbeck is working away with his accustomed vim superintending the waterworks and the laying of the pipes. He has developed a quite unexpected genius for mechanism, and the work done under his charge is highly satisfactory. The new bank building on Capt. Hooper's corner has a very fine appearance, and is rapidly nearing completion. The long continued spell of dry weather this fall has been very acceptable to our builders and enabled them to push ahead vigorously with their contracts. The farmers, however, just at present would be thankful for a little rain to enable them to get at their fall plowing.

Your mother is in good health and it is probable, if I am not in the penitentiary, that I shall pay a visit to Provo ere long. I have deeded my property at that place on which the university building stands to a board of trustees, composed of Bishops [Abraham O.] Smoot, [Leonard E.] Harrington and others, for the purpose of endowing a college, to be called Brigham Young's Academy of Provo. I have had this in contemplation some time, and I hope to see an academy established there that shall do honor to our territory, and at which the children of the Latter-day Saints can receive a good education unmixed with the pernicious, atheistic influences that are to be found in so many of the higher schools of the country.

Since writing the above yours of the 16th inst. has reached me, and been perused with pleasure.

May God bless, preserve and prosper you in all things is the heartfelt prayer of

                    Your affectionate father,

                    Brigham Young

Salt Lake City, November 18, 1875

Elder Alfales Young
Ann Arbor, Michigan

My dear Son,

    I know that you will be more than pleased to hear that I am once more free. This morning His Honor, Chief Justice [J. Alexander] White, discharged the prisoner. As you are aware, my attorneys brought the matter of my imprisonment before the chief justice on a writ of *habeas corpus*. Yesterday was spent in the pleadings of the opposing counsel. The judge confined the gentlemen to the consideration of two points, viz: did or did not the order for alimony lapse through no action being taken in the matter during the same term of court as the decision of Judge [David B.] Lowe was given, and was not the order of Judge Lowe's a final order and if so, how could it be reconsidered by the same court? The judge this morning decided that the order of Judge Lowe was final, that the court could correct its error during the same term as that in which the error was committed, but no action having been taken during that term it could not be reconsidered at another term. If either of the parties were not satisfied with Judge Lowe's decision of May 10th, their proper course would have been to have taken an appeal to the Superior Court. Therefore my commitment by Judge [Jacob S.] Boreman was illegal and the order must be vacated and the prisoner discharged. By this peculiar side issue that, so far as I can learn, had never been considered by my attorneys, I am once more delivered from my persecutors. I shall now be able to take the fresh air, that is, as soon as the storm which at present prevails here is over. And I hope by the blessing of the Lord to soon be in the enjoyment of thorough good health.

    A most extraordinary verdict was rendered by a jury in this city last night, more than half of which was composed of persons claiming to be Latter-day Saints. In the case of Kate Flint vs. Jeter Clinton *et. al.* (in reality the city council) the jury returned a verdict in favor of the plaintiff, assessing the damages at $7000.00. A motion for a new trial or an appeal, I suppose, will now be in order.

Since my last letter to you I have received two of your ever welcome communications. I am especially pleased to note the remarks in your last, with regard to the habits of those students with whom you are the most intimate. The old saying is no doubt a true one that "a man is known by the company he keeps," as is also the statement made by Paul the apostle that evil communications corrupt good manners. None of us are so strong in well doing that we can afford to associate with the depraved, keep company with the dissolute, and pick out our friends from amongst those who love sin and delight in iniquity. It is a mockery to pray to God to "leave us not in temptation," and then seek the companionship of the tempter. However strong in the Lord men may feel, it is always the wisest policy to drive as far as possible from the precipices of sin, and in handling coal, to remember that that which will not burn may probably blacken. By choosing your companions from those of correct morals and temperate habits you manifest your comprehension of these truths, and altogether I must acknowledge I am very much pleased with the course you are taking.

The family are well, the weather is stormy, and business generally is brisk. Your mother has been in town for the past few days and joins me in love to you and in prayers for your welfare.

Your affectionate father,
Brigham Young

Salt Lake City, January 7, 1876

Elder Alfales Young
Ann Arbor, Michigan

My dear Son Alfales:

I received another of your cheering letters this week and was no less pleased to hear from you than on previous occasions. I am gratified to learn that you are still progressing, and are in good health. With regard to your rooms, however anxious I may be that you should be economical, I would not have you be in the least inconsiderate or ungenerous to those who may have trusted you, or treated you with kindness. There is one duty we all owe to ourselves and to our fellowmen, it is to never abuse the confidence others may place in us, or by our folly or criminality break down the character we have built up by a life of industry and honesty. Our character is not entirely our individual property; it belongs partly to our neighbors and we have no right to shake their confidence in us and in mankind generally by acts inconsistent with the good name we have established. I am pleased that you acted so promptly, honorably, and kindly in your deal with your landlady.

My health and that of your mother is good, so is that of the family generally, though at the present time there is considerable sickness in the city, especially among children. I, however, learned a pleasing fact from the report of our sexton, that during the past five years the ratio of the mortality of the children in this city has been gradually and continuously decreasing. The present is a very mild winter in this valley and possibly may be less conducive to good health than if we had more bright, frosty weather.

We have had quite a reformation in our parties this season. In accordance with my advice those who control them have gone back to the good old style that obtained in the early settlement of the territory, of commencing early in the afternoon and of eschewing all round dances, which always savor to me of the unvirtuous, amongst whom they took their rise. I was invited by the ladies, it being leap year, to attend a party conducted on these principles at the 14th Ward school house on the 3rd inst. The party opened at 2, and closed at 10 o'clock. I can assure, we all enjoyed ourselves. A spirit of peace, good feeling and fellowship was there which all felt, but some did not comprehend the cause, that it was because they were acting in obedience to the word of the Lord through his duly appointed servant, that blessings follow obedience in the business and pleasures of life as well as in the direct service of the Lord's house. This is a fact that many do not realize, but it is none the less true. There is nothing, no matter how small, that Latter-day Saints should set their hands to do that they cannot ask the blessing of the Lord upon or wherein they would be unwilling to obey his word.

Your brothers are all well and in the same positions as when I last wrote. Brigham Jun. is now in New York with John W.; they may possibly return together.

The new bank building is now occupied by the Deseret National Bank, and the stores immediately north, by Dr. Taggart, and Daynes & Son. The building is a fine ornament to our city, and with regard to our new co-op building [ZCMI], there is no finer front in the city of New York than it is.

May God, the Eternal Father, continue to bless and preserve you is the prayer with much love of

>Your affectionate father,
>Brigham Young

Salt Lake City, February 15, 1876

Elder Alfales Young
Ann Arbor, Michigan

My dear Son,

The receipt of your letters is a continual source of pleasure to me, especially as all breathe the desire to acquire useful knowledge and to do right. I have sometimes wondered if you ever received a letter I had written by Bro. [George] Reynolds making inquiries of a certain idiotic human being which in its habits and appearance very much resembled a bear, and which was confined in a poor house in Michigan. As you have never mentioned the receipt of the letter, nor in any way referred to the matter, I have come to the conclusion that most probably it miscarried. Your brothers are all doing well. Morris had a daughter born to him on the evening of the 13th, and he is proportionately elated. He is taking a great interest in the establishment of Young Men's Improvement Societies throughout the territory, and with Bro. M[ilton] H. Hardy and others has visited quite a number of settlements. I received the usual monthly report from Annapolis yesterday. From it I find that Ferry is catching up in his standing in his class. Out of the six studies reported, in five he stands in the upper half of the class. I had a most excellent letter from Arta D. a few days ago. He is full of life, energy, and good feeling, and is laboring assiduously in his calling as a missionary. He still sometimes feels the effects of his last game of baseball at St. George, especially when he has had to take one of those long walks incidental to the life of a traveling elder in the old country.

Whilst Brigham Jun. was east he visited Willard, Don Carlos, and Ferry, and brings me good news from all three of them. The two latter are striving manfully to master their studies, whilst Willard has a very pleasant gentleman's life, but with plenty of time and many opportunities for improvement.

It is my intention, all being well, to leave for St. George about [illegible] this month. Your mother [illegible], Bro. Wells and some others of the brethren will be of the party.

I was very happy in greeting John W. home last night in good health. It is so long since I saw him, since which time his health has been so precarious that I have had many anxious thoughts on his account. [Illegible] will be but the precursor of his permanent and speedy return to his home in the midst of his friends.

Nabbie [Young] was married today to Bro. Spencer Clawson. I performed the ceremony. The young couple will start east shortly, as Spencer's duties at ZCMI will require him to visit the eastern markets to make the usual spring purchases.

We held our election for city officers yesterday. The People's ticket polled, on an average, 2860 votes. The so-called Liberals, about 640. All passed off very quietly, nothing like so large a number voted as at the last election.

I will instruct Bro. [James] Jack before I leave for St. George to let you have some money when you apply for it. So when you are really in need of funds write to him and he will remit as you desire.

My health is excellent. I find plenty to occupy my attention, but the missionaries to Arizona having started, the city election being over, and the legislative sessions being drawn to a close, I shall feel glad of a rest in our Dixie. Though there I anticipate starting work in the temple so soon as it is sufficiently finished to admit of it.

With much love and constant prayers for your happiness and welfare.

I remain, your affectionate father,

Brigham Young

ALFALES YOUNG

Salt Lake City, March 24, 1876

Elder Alfales Young
P.O. Box 1025
Ann Arbor, Michigan

My dear Son:

Your welcome favor of 18th inst. reached me yesterday. I need not tell you I was pleased to receive it as you well know that I am always glad to hear of your welfare and progress. Tomorrow I am going down to Provo and I shall be happy to tell your mother that I have had good news from you so lately.

Spencer [Clawson] and Nabbie [Young Clawson] have written back that they had a very enjoyable visit with you in Chicago, and tell us that you have very much improved. So after that, you must not say that though your credit is good, your looks don't amount to much. You have no idea what the girls say about you when they think you are out of hearing.

We have had one of the stormiest seasons during the last few weeks that I ever recollect in Utah. The bottoms have gone completely out of the roads and travel outside of the railroads has almost entirely ceased. It is reported that there was a slight earthquake in San Pete Co. yesterday. So soon after conference as the weather and the roads permit, I intend to start for the south. I shall be accompanied part of the way by Bros. [Daniel H.] Wells and Brigham Jun., who will proceed directly to our new settlements in Arizona, whilst I shall most probably go straight on to St. George. Your mother is going along with us as also [Harriet] Amelia [Folsom Young] and Lucy B[igelow Young]. Susie [Young Dunford] and her husband are going to live at St. George.

Today Bro. [James] Jack sent you a hundred dollars, which I hope you will receive safe. Please advise me when it reaches you so that I may know that you got it. Probably next week he will send you another hundred; I send you one hundred dollars at a time because I do not think you need all at once and I can send you that amount by post office order.

All the family are well. The boys are just in the same business as when you last heard from me. I had a letter from Willard yesterday, which, in its sentiments and expressions of feeling, entirely coincides with your own.

We are busy moving into the new co-op building, but are still continuing the business at the old stand. It is quite a work to transfer so many goods. We hope to open in the new premises on Saturday, April 1st, in time for conference, though owing to the terrible state of the roads I fear our meetings will not be as large as usual, without there is an almost immediate change for the better in the weather. Very high waters are looked for this spring owing to the vast accumulation of snow in the mountains.

With love and constant prayers, I remain,

Your affectionate father,
Brigham Young

Salt Lake City, August 17, 1876

Elder Alfales Young
Ann Arbor, Michigan

My dear Son,

Your interesting letter from Willet's Point reached me a few days ago. The varied items of news it contained rendered its perusal a very pleasant task. By the time this reaches you, I presume you have quietly settled down to the routine of your studies with fresh energy and renewed zeal. It would be very pleasing to us if at the present time you had finished your course of studies and had been admitted to the bar, for you could materially help me in the numerous vexatious suits that are being brought against me to rob me of my property. The present bench appears to be not only willing but anxious to give my possessions away to anyone who has the effrontery to ask for them. If I met three highway robbers who demanded my money or my life I should know what to do, but these, worse than highway men, despoil me under the pretense of the law, which they and all the world knows, who know anything about the matter, does not give them the shadow of an excuse for acting as they do. I have a short time ago been served with papers in another case, "Charlotte Arthur vs. Brigham Young," in which Mrs. Arthur, who once belonged to your Uncle John, sues me for the north half of the lot immediately south of the theatre, because at one time I found her a home thereon. For a long time none of these pettifoggers would take her case, but the word having reached here that she had received a legacy in England, a remarkable change came over their feelings and they quickly became eager for the fray. I am told that Ann Eliza's father intends to sue me for the property where she once lived but which is now occupied by Nelson Empey. Such is the path they hope to force me to walk in.

Bro. Joseph Shaw, who has been in my employ so long, died shortly before six last evening. One of the causes that doubtless hastened his departure from us was the rough usage he received from Deputy Marshal [Arthur] Pratt at the time [George R.] Maxwell was helped off the porch by Bro. James Cushing for using profane language, for which acts they are both now under indictment, the present grand jury having raked the matter up and found true bills against them, after it was thought the whole matter had dropped. Bro. Shaw is at any rate now beyond their power.

I anticipate taking a trip to Provo next Friday evening and staying there over Sunday, and towards the end of next week hope to go to Logan to spend a few days with Brigham Jun. My health now is good though I have been suffering until quite lately with rheumatic pains in my feet which kept me considerably in my room. Now I am almost entirely free from trouble in that direction and my bodily health is otherwise good. The health of your mother is also excellent. Don Carlos and Fera are at home enjoying a very pleasant visit. They expect to return to their respective studies in about three weeks. Lorenzo D. expects to start on his mission to Europe next week. He will accompany Bro. [William C.] Staines east, the latter being on his way to resume his duties at New York as our emigration agent.

I believe that I have mentioned in former letters that we had a large force of men working upon the temple here who have been sent by the various quorums of the priesthood and sustained by them during their labors. They have been doing a good work and we have now commenced to again lay the rock, and hope to finish five courses before we stop. For the first time in the history of building temples to the Lord, so far as I am acquainted, we are now laying the rock by the help of the steam engine, and the speed and ease with which it does its work is very encouraging. Our news from the St. George Temple is also very pleasing. The work is being pushed ahead there with much energy and success.

May God bless you abundantly in all your studies and labors and enable you to do much good in the path of life you have chosen.

Your affectionate father,
Brigham Young

Salt Lake City, September 25, 1876

Elder Alfales Young
Ann Arbor, Michigan

My dear Son,

I have lately received four of your interesting letters, the last one dated Sept. 16, in which you give an account of Fera's visit to you. I am happy to hear of your good health and general welfare, and though I may not always answer your communications immediately, they are none the less appreciated.

With this, I send you the first half of a note signed by Mr. John J. Heeley of East Saginaw, Michigan. On receipt of a letter from you informing me that you have received it, I will forward you the second half. Mr. Heeley is a lawyer by profession and married a niece of Bro. Folsom's. Last winter he came to this country for the benefit of his health, and during the greater portion of the time has been my guest. His disease is consumption, which is rapidly carrying him to the grave, and as it was evident he was not improving we all thought it best that he should return home. Having been disappointed in some remittances, he was out of funds at the time of his departure, and I lent him the money for which this note is given. When it comes due you can write to him a friendly letter and let him know that you have the note, and will await his convenience. If he is able to write he will answer and probably open up a correspondence with you. Should he die you must take such steps as are necessary under the laws of Michigan to secure payment from the estate. If you receive the money you are at liberty to use it when your needs require it.

Nothing more has been done in the Ann Eliza case since the

marshal returned the execution into court unsatisfied. The attorneys for the plaintiff did talk of getting out an attachment for my person, but as they have done nothing I presume that they have discovered that in law, an attachment will not lie when an execution will, until every cent's worth of property is levied on and sold. The court has given them the redress they sought for and it has done them no good. Now they will have to wait until another month's alimony is due before they can take any new shot. At least it appears so to us.

I noticed a marked improvement in the plainness of your handwriting. I am very glad to see it, and hope you will continue to take pains to improve. No one will think you any less a good lawyer because you are a plain writer, but rather seeing the clearness of your handwriting will judge therefrom that you are clear in your thoughts and perceptions, two great requisites for a successful lawyer.

My health has been but moderate during the past week but I am feeling excellently now. Your mother's health is good. She paid us a visit in Salt Lake City last week, and I expect to take a trip to Provo in a few days.

May God abundantly bless you in all your studies and in all your life is the prayer of

Your affectionate father,
Brigham Young

Salt Lake City, October 26, 1876

Elder Alfales Young
Ann Arbor, Michigan

My dear Son,

Your letter of 21st inst. reached me this morning. I was gratified to learn that you were in good health. My own health is moderately good; possibly the excitement of the past few days, the press of business and the fatigues consequent on the preparations for our coming journey south, have altogether been a little too much for me. But except the feeling of fatigue during the day time, and restlessness at night, I do not know that I have much to complain of regarding my health.

I hear from the rest of my boys occasionally. Fera does not seem to increase in love for a sailor's life. In fact he would prefer to resign if he could do so honorably and without reproach. Brigham Jun. will accompany me to St. George. Mahonri, who has now charge of the Deseret Woolen Mills, Oscar being with him, took himself a wife on Sunday last. The favored young lady is a daughter of Bro. Dan[iel] Mackintosh who many years ago was chief clerk in my office. I presume I need say no more on this point; it is quite possible you are acquainted with her and have been fully posted by your mother.

Yesterday morning there was some little excitement in town. The ten days had expired which the court had given me to pay the alimony *pendente lite*, and it had not been paid. So far as appearances went it seemed as though the judge had no other course left but to commit me to prison. The faith of the elders, however, was strong that the Lord would provide some means of escape, and so it proved. At ten o'clock I went into court. The courtroom was densely crowded, mostly by our brethren. My attorneys endeavored to carry the case up on appeal. The judge said it was too late to adopt that course, and refused to hear any argument. He then made a very remarkable ruling, discharging me, but ordered that my horses, carriages, &c., formerly levied upon, be now sequestrated, that Doc. A. K. Smith be appointed a special commissioner of the court, without bonds, to seize and sell the property and pay over the amount ordered and costs. But it is claimed that the court has no power under such circumstances to sequestrate property, or appoint a special commissioner for such a purpose, and the legal fight will now take another shape. If I do nothing else I shall [*illegible*] the moment it is sold; in fact, I do not think they will find [anyone] foolish enough to purchase it under the circumstances. It is asked, by what authority the district judge appoints an officer without bonds to act in the place of the marshal or sheriff and sell property to satisfy an interlocutory order, and how an execution can be issued before a formal judgment?

These are questions that, as yet, have not received a satisfactory answer, and to my mind never will. And like many other things connected with this interminable alimony outrage, this order is altogether without sense, reason, justice or law. But then, some of our judges always act as though the Mormons have no rights which they are bound to respect.

It was my intention to have started south on Monday last, but these legal complications have caused me to delay my departure until next Monday. It is possible that in the meantime the testimony on the direct issue of divorce will be taken before the commissioner as, I am told by Le Grand [Young] that the present judge is anxious to get the case off the docket. Your mother has been visiting us for several days past. She appears to keep her health, strength and spirits remarkably, and to be feeling exceedingly well.

May God the Eternal Father have you in His watchcare, preserve you in all places from evil, and constantly guide your feet in the paths of wisdom and of peace, is the prayer of

Your affectionate father,
Brigham Young

St. George, Utah, December 29, 1876

Elder Alfales Young
Ann Arbor, Michigan

My dear Son,

Your letter of the 16th inst. duly received and contents noted.

I am pleased to learn that you are in good health, and feel well in spirit.

In reference to John W., I should like you both to have had the pleasure of meeting when he was on his way east. He arrived in Salt Lake City on last Thursday night. I received a greeting telegram from him yesterday.

You have correctly learned that Fera has resigned his position in the Naval Academy. In doing this, it is by the sanction of the principal of the academy, Rear Admiral [Christopher R. P.] Rodgers, and in a manner to maintain his honor without the least particle of impeachment. Testimonials from the principal are highly complimentary to Fera and as you may be sure are gratifying to me. The cause of Fera resigning was that the further prosecution of his studies at the Naval Academy was to more particularly qualify him for naval service and consequently was of less value to him in his relations to our people in their present inland position. I appreciate your kind brotherly feeling in desiring that he should join you and study at Ann Arbor, and am pleased that you have an eye to economy as manifested by your stating that his expenses would be less in your school than elsewhere, but he has already applied for, and received, my sanction to join Don Carlos in his studies at Troy.

In response to your application for funds I have telegraphed to Bro. James Jack. If you shall not have heard from him by the time you receive this, you can communicate with him on the subject.

In relation to the political situation to which you refer, it is indeed a crisis. The nation has attained its centennial, and there is too much reason for the statement that it has attained its zenith in political power, influence, and glory. But a few years ago it would have been a strange, even a startling event for a state to have two governors and two legislatures. Yet today we find this to be so in South Carolina, with a possible contingency of its being repeated in Louisiana and perhaps in Florida. The blood of prophets, apostles and righteous men and women has been spilled upon the ground in this, our country, and when county, state, and federal officers turn a deaf ear to the cry of the oppressed and will not be swayed by the spirit of the heaven-inspired constitution of the land, it is not hard to believe that *mene mene tekel upharsin* is written upon the wall.

The weather here is and has been so far this winter very beautiful and the health of the people good.

My health has been very good except an attack of my old complaint in my feet but I am thankful in stating this is much better.

The Lord being willing we will make a preliminary dedication of the temple here on Monday the first day of the New Year.

May blessings, peace and a long life of usefulness be vouchsafed to you.

       Brigham Young

BRIGHAM MORRIS YOUNG

Brigham Morris Young
1854-1931

On November 6, 1875, Brigham Young called his twenty-one-year-old son Brigham Morris to his room in the Lion House and appointed him and two others to continue the work of organizing "improvement associations" among the young men of the Church in the absence of Junius Wells, who had previously held that responsibility but had been called on a mission. "I want this work to continue and grow and not die out," the President told his son, adding, "I am going to appoint John Henry Smith, Milton H. Hardy, and you to take up and continue this labor. I want you boys to go and travel through this Territory in every settlement and organize these associations."[1] Within a year Morris Young and Milton Hardy had visited more than a hundred settlements and organized ninety-one Young Men's Improvement Associations. Their labors marked the effectual beginning of the YMMIA in the Church.

Born on January 18, 1854, Brigham Morris Young was the thirty-fifth child of Brigham Young and the only child of Margaret Pierce Young. The youth was educated at his father's private school east of the Eagle Gate and at the University of Deseret. Out of deference to his mother's wish that he remain at home, Morris did not continue his education or training at institutions of higher learning outside of Utah, although his father had provided his sons with the opportunity to do so, and some of them were so engaged. During his teen-age years Morris drove a horse-drawn streetcar in Salt Lake City between Wasatch Springs and the Utah Central Railroad depot on First South Street. After this, he devoted practically all of his life to Church service, as a missionary and employee in the Salt Lake Temple.

Morris completed his first of three missions during 1873-74 in Hawaii. On March 29, 1875, three months after his return, he married Celestia Armedia Snow, a daughter of Lorenzo Snow. Writing two days before the wedding, the bride's parents explained to Brigham Young that circumstances would not permit them to attend the ceremony. "I hope you will excuse us," Lorenzo urged, and added, "As Armedia is almost a stranger to you allow us to say what our modesty would withhold if we were present, viz., Armedia has always been a good, obedient, industrious and affectionate daughter, and has had as good an education as our schools could afford, and we hope and trust that she will prove a true 'help meet' to her husband and that this union may prove a happy one which has our sanction and blessing."[2] That these sentiments were realized is evident from the ten children that blessed this union and the notice of a golden wedding commemoration held in the Lion House on March 28, 1925, in honor of Morris and Celestia Young.

While traveling through Utah in the interest of the Mutual Improvement Associations in 1876, Morris was called on another proselyting mission for the Church, this time to the Central and Eastern states. Leaving his wife in Brigham City, he labored successively in Nebraska, Iowa, Illinois, Pennsylvania, and Washington, D.C. In company with his cousin Eli Pierce, on August 30, 1877, Morris had stopped for dinner in Mosquito Creek, Nebraska, when he received news of the death of his father. "I had just got some chicken and potatoes on my plate, when Sister Powers arrived in a buggy with the sad news of my dear Father's death. I was very much surprised and seem[ed] as though I could not relize it. I felt very bad and could not eat any dinner." He and his companion then walked seven miles to Council Bluffs, where he telegraphed his brother John W. asking "if it would be expedient for Eli and I to return home." The answer came the following day. Morris and his three brothers, Don Carlos, Willard, and Feramorz, who were engaged in education, military, and missionary assignments in the East, were advised to remain and continue their labors. Although the news of his father's death brought him deep sorrow, Morris noted, "still I realize it is all right, and say, not my will but thine be done Oh, God."[3]

Traveling through Illinois as he continued on his mission, Morris stopped in Nauvoo where he located his father's old home ("the house looks prity delapidated"), took a drink of water from the temple well, and visited Emma Smith, who at seventy-three appeared to be "failing very fast." In New York a few weeks later he had a joyous reunion with his brothers Feramorz and Don Carlos, who were studying at the Rensselaer Polytechnic Institute in Troy. As Morris took leave from his brothers, Don Carlos assisted him by paying his fare to New York City. After continuing his missionary labors in Pennsylvania and Washington, D.C., Morris returned home in the summer of 1878.

Five years later, in April 1883, Morris was called on a second mission to Hawaii, accompanied by his wife and two children. While there he labored on the island of Kauai and assisted in building a new meetinghouse at Laie, the dedication of which was attended by the Hawaiian king, David Kalakauna, in October 1883.

After returning from Hawaii in October 1884, Morris started a confectionery in Brigham City; in 1890 he moved to Logan, where he labored at odd jobs while a daughter attended Brigham Young College. Having received an aggregate of $18,000 in property, stocks, and bonds as his share of his father's estate in 1878, Morris had hoped by careful management to multiply these assets for the support of his family and "the building up of the Kingdom of God." However, the economic depression of the early 1890s reduced his property and left him on the brink of poverty. Upon the completion of the Salt Lake Temple in 1893, he was offered full-time work in the temple by Lorenzo Snow at a salary of $60 a month, a position that he held for the remaining thirty-eight years of his life.

Morris was well known as an entertainer and humorist and was often called to perform at stake and ward social functions, where he frequently posed as "Madam Pattirini," a great female opera singer. An extant invitation lists B. M. Young as manager of "a Grand Character and Dress Ball" held in the large room of the Brigham City Woolen Factory in 1889. On one occasion Morris and a friend, dressed in colorful costumes, called at the office of his father-in-law, President Lorenzo Snow, and as one spoke "Chinese" and the other "interpreted," introduced themselves to the secretary, George F. Gibbs, as visiting Chinese dignitaries. After being ushered into the Church leader's office and conversing for some time, the two visitors disclosed their real identity to a very surprised President. Not wishing to be alone in the joke, President Snow sent the "foreign emissaries" to call upon his counselor, Joseph F. Smith.

At the age of seventy-seven, Brigham Morris Young died in a Salt Lake City hospital on February 23, 1931, a week following an emergency operation for a ruptured appendix.

Letter dated July 24, 1873

Having been called to labor in the Hawaiian Mission (then known as the Sandwich Islands), Brigham Morris Young left Salt Lake City on May 20, 1873, and arrived at his destination on June 3. Whatever the Pioneer Day celebration may have been that year on July 24, Brigham Young spent part of the day writing the following letter to his son at Laie, Oahu.

Salt Lake City, July 24, 1873

Brigham Morris Young
Laie, Oahu, Sandwich Islands

My dear Son,
    Your very welcome letter to me of the 6th inst., also one to your mother which I read, both with great pleasure, reached here on the 22nd inst.
    Bro. Geo. P. Nebeker got in the day following. He delivered a letter to your mother which you sent, and informed us that the parcels you wrote about were with Bro. [William] King and would not be in before the 25th. Bro. King was traveling with a freight train.
    We were all exceedingly well pleased with the spirit of your letters.
    Your mother is in good health and spirits and the folks feel first rate. Willard is making a good visit and is enjoying it hugely.
    My health is good for which I feel very thankful. My business keeps me constantly and actively engaged, and I am pleased to be able to attend to it. On the 22nd I attended a railroad mass meeting at Lehi, for we are expecting iron soon to run to Provo and wish the Utah Co. folks to help build the road. Tomorrow morning I start for Tooele to attend 2 days meeting there. Those 2 days meetings are held quite frequently since conference and I have attended a number of them, and they are calculated to do considerable good.

Samuel P. Richards called lately and reported himself on hand to go to the Islands when required. We told him to get ready, and it is probable he may join you before long, and perhaps others of the young brethren who may feel disposed to go.

Your labors to acquire the native language will doubtless be a task at first but diligence and perseverance will give you the victory. You have everything to encourage you, for heaven and good men are on your side, and you know the saying, "heaven and one good man is a large majority." You have just started out and your future is in a great measure depending upon your course now. Be diligent and prayerful. It is your privilege to know for yourself God lives and that He is doing a work in these last days and we are His honored ministers. Live for this knowledge and you will receive it. Remember your prayers and be fervent in spirit. Shun the very appearance of evil, and in all your intercourse with [others] preserve an upright decorum and in preaching to the people or conversing in private be cool, and keep command of yourself. Don't get flurried; trust in God and words will come to you, and you will know just what to say. Your calling is to be a teacher to the world. There is no honor or dignity in the power of man to bestow that can begin to compare with this in importance or greatness. It is a high and a holy calling and if you honor it, you will enjoy constant peace and win the respect of all good men wherever your lot is cast, and that is the path we hope and pray you will always walk in.

Give my best respects to Prest. [Frederick A. H. F.] Mitchell and family, Sis. [Mildred E.] Randall, Bro. [Richard J.] Taylor and all the brethren. Write often when you have the time, and remember we will watch your course, and that you have our faith and prayers, that you may be enabled to do a good work and return with clean hands and a pure heart.

Your affectionate father,
Brigham Young

Letter dated October 23, 1873

The cultural shock produced by a confrontation with strange customs and language in Hawaii had a definite impact upon Morris

Young. Speaking at his first conference in the Hawaiian Mission in October 1873, four months after his arrival there, he had not learned enough of the language to communicate without a translator. Writing to his son later that month, Brigham Young gave Morris advice to meet the problem of strange customs and a strange tongue.

Salt Lake City, October 23, 1873

Elder B. Morris Young
Honolulu, Hawaiian Islands

My dear Son,

    As some of the missionaries are about starting for the islands, I embrace the opportunity of writing you a few lines which one of the brethren will bear to you. You will all doubtless be very glad to see the new arrivals. Your very interesting letter of Sept. 5 was read with great pleasure, as it indicates that you have taken right hold of your mission, and that is what we are anxious you should do, as therein is your peace and happiness and welfare, and we pray that your mind may continue to be led in that channel.

    Traveling among the natives and mingling with their society is a better way to acquire the language than attending school. Besides, you learn the manners and customs of the people and become personally acquainted with them. The immoral habits of many of the natives will doubtless impress you very unfavorably, still you must bear in mind that their practices are apt to be as they are traditionated, just as the rest of mankind are in theirs, and we have to deal with people as they are, and by giving them the gospel and showing them a good example, strive to make them better.

    Bro. [Richard J.] Taylor's health appeared very much reduced when he returned home, and his shipwreck gave him quite a shake in addition to his former sickness. We are glad that he returned when he did, and we hope that he will soon recover his wonted health and strength.

    Another conference has passed and the Saints had an excellent time. The work is onward, growing, increasing, and expanding, notwithstanding the malice and hatred of our enemies who appear to be using every means in their power to destroy it. But they meet with very little success indeed, and Zion grows stronger year by year, while in the governments of the earth there is an increasing distrust more and more manifest as their corruptions are brought to the surface and exposed. The hand of our Heavenly Father is outstretched and He guides and directs everything according to His good pleasure and He will give His Saints the victory when they are prepared to receive and wear it.

We are sending quite a number of missionaries to England this season, the most of whom started on the 20th inst. Bro. [Albert] Carrington is released to return home and Joseph F. Smith will take his place after the adjournment of the legislature. Business has been rather dull here for some time past, although our improvements continue. By the end of this month or early in the next we expect to have the southern railroad running to Provo. The northern road is rapidly approaching Franklin, and they are connecting that road direct to Ogden. Our street railroad is nearly completed to the bath house, and is running to the east bench on 1st South St. The temple is progressing finely, as we are now getting rock from the quarry, the entire distance, by rail, and a large force is engaged quarrying, cutting, and setting the rock. The theatre has been nicely refitted since you left, and looks very much improved. Bros. [Hiram B.] Clawson, [John T.] Caine, and [Thomas] Williams are managing it.

On the 11th inst. I started to attend two days meeting at Provo with Bro. George A. [Smith] and some of the Twelve, and we remained over to dedicate the new County Court House there on the 14th inst. During our visit I contracted rather a severe cold which brought on a chill followed by fever from which I have been confined to my room for several days. I feel thankful to say I am recovering, however, and hope to be around again soon. If all is well I hope to be able to start south soon, and I have always found my health improved in southern Utah during the winter.

Remember, I do not wish you to lack for clothing or any other necessary. If there is anything you need, consult with Bro. [Frederick] Mitchell, and he will either arrange it, or you can draw on me for such things as you shall require.

The health of the family is generally good. The brethren will give you general local news.

I am happy to be able to say my health is so far restored that I am able to be around again much as usual, although the weather at present is rather cold and unfavorable for outdoor business and travel.

Let us hear from you frequently, and bear in mind that we are watching your course and are deeply interested in your success, for you are now laying a foundation that will determine your career.

May peace be with you, and the spirit and power of your mission continually abide with you is the prayer of

Your affectionate father,
Brigham Young

P.S. Remember me kindly to Bro. Mitchell and family, and Sister [Mildred E.] Randall, and all the brethren on the mission. Enclosed you will find twenty-five dollars which I send to relieve you of any immediate want.

B. Y.

Letter dated September 7, 1874

One of the difficulties confronting Morris Young upon his arrival in Hawaii was the problem of learning the language. At least four letters of his father contained counsel and encouragement on the topic, which reveals the presence of the problem; but in the absence of Morris's own correspondence from Hawaii, the full extent of his plight is not known. After a year on the islands Morris received a letter from his father on May 5, 1874, advising him, "if you cannot with reasonable ease and facility learn the language of the S.I. [Sandwich Island] natives, you are at liberty to consult with Bro. [Frederick A. F.] Mitchell, and regulate the length of your mission on the Islands as you and he may deem wise." That Morris never completely mastered the language is noted in the remarks opposite his name in the list of Hawaiian missionaries in the manuscript history of the mission. This should not be interpreted to mean, however, that he did not develop some facility with the language. Letters received by him containing Hawaiian phrases, and his father's words of congratulation in the following letter, dated September 7, 1874, suggest that Morris had some success with the language.

BRIGHAM MORRIS YOUNG

Salt Lake City, September 7, 1874

Elder Morris Young
Hawaiian Islands

Dear Morris,
    Your kind letters of June 11th and Aug. 6th were received about a month from date and it is with much pleasure that I learn of your success in instructing the natives in the principles of the gospel. Your difficulty in learning the language will disappear, I hope, by the study which I know full well you will give it. Never allow your courage to fail you; man's greatest works have been done by men of patience, perseverance, and a determined *will* which would acknowledge no defeat, rather than by those gifted with a natural ability which made success easy but who lacked the tenaciousness of purpose. Then, my boy, never say fail, but work on in the way you have started and your reward is certain.
    The United Order is moving along nicely and wherever the people have entered into it, [it] has given entire satisfaction. In St. George and many other places it is in practical running order and the harvest is being got in under the direction of the board; all accounts from there show the advantage of united labor. The sawmills and almost all the great interests are in the Order and all work well.
    The crops are very large at St. George, especially the fruit crop. The work on the temple at St. George progresses very well indeed and men are being found to go down and work through the coming winter.
    The harvest is bountiful all over Utah and is nearly gathered in.
    Fera started with Bro. [William C.] Staines about the 6th of last month for New York where he will be for about two weeks before going over to Annapolis to enter the Naval Academy.
    I have every hope that he will pass the examination creditably; he has studied very hard and Bro. [John R.] Park informs me that he is very well prepared, and has great confidence in him. It will undoubtedly seem strange to him to be, for the first time he ever left home, placed among entire strangers with not a

familiar face to look to or a tried friend to whom to turn for advice in the hour of need, but it will make a man of him; it will develop his latent powers, and teach him to put his trust in our Father in heaven.

Times are dull and business is pretty slow but our co-op trade I think is recovering slowly, but gradually. It is an "ill wind that blows nobody good" and by this scarcity of money we hope to starve some of these adventurers out; the devil cannot work without money, whereas the Lord can. We lived here about twenty years without hardly a dollar circulating among us, and we not only lived but improved and grew rich.

Very much obliged for the epistle enclosed in your last. Bro. Alma Smith has put it in English for me.

By Bro. Alma Smith I send you some fifty ($50.00) dollars in gold which you can dispose of for clothes and other necessities.

Either form of bestowing the Holy Ghost is correct, but I use the form "receive ye the Holy Ghost."

Your mother's health is as good as usual, I believe, as is all the folks. My health continues good.

Peace be with you.

Your loving father,
Brigham Young

Letter dated October 6, 1874

Brigham Morris Young was appointed counselor to President Frederick Mitchell of the Hawaiian Mission in December 1873 and spent most of his time working on the islands of Oahu and Hawaii. Prior to his departure for home in December 1874, he received this final letter from his father. The document is important because it contains a short postscript in Brigham Young's own hand, one of the last extant examples of the President's handwriting. The brief request suggests that in his later years Brigham was still eager to learn and that his interests were varied and detailed.

BRIGHAM MORRIS YOUNG

Salt Lake City, October 6, 1874

Elder Morris Young
Hawaiian Islands

My dear Son Morris,

It is some considerable time since I wrote you last, but the delay was not occasioned through my forgetting you but through neglect.

It is the first day of our semiannual October conference and there are large numbers of the country people in to attend the meetings. I was there this morning which is about the first time I have been out to attend any meeting or look after any business for nearly three weeks; my health has been very bad for that length of time, but is now improving and with care in not taking cold I think I will be around as usual in a few days.

Your mother's health is good, as is that of all the folks.

Fera passed his examination at the Naval Academy, Annapolis, on the 24th Sept.

You left here a year ago last spring and you have been gone nearly a year and a half which is a good long mission in a strange land with a language to learn; so, I would like for you to come home with Bro. [Frederick] Mitchell.

It will please your mother and me very much to have you here again.

Get everything settled up in first-class order before you leave.

By this mail I have written to Bro. Mitchell telling him I wanted you to come home along with him and also to Bro. [Alma L.] Smith asking for your release.

I hope that your health is good and wish you a pleasant and safe journey home.

God bless you.

                        Your affectionate father,
                        Brigham Young

P.S. Bring me all the specemens you can from the water and the Iland.

                        B.Y.

ARTA DE CHRISTA YOUNG

Arta De Christa Young
1855-1916

Named for a "handsome Indian" his mother had seen in a dream, Arta De Christa Young was born in Salt Lake City on April 16, 1855. He was the third son of Brigham Young and Lucy Ann Decker. Educated in the family school and the University of Deseret, Arta became a proficient accountant and bookkeeper. He spent two years in England, from 1875-77, as a missionary, laboring part of the time in the mission office where he kept the books.

After returning to Utah he was engaged in farming, and later assisted his brother Heber with the ZCMI Co-op store in Soda Springs, Idaho, for a short time. Anxious to excel in business, Arta did not, however, accept the offer of his father, who had agreed to finance further education and preparation of his sons in the East. Arta thereby may have planted the seeds of financial failure: he had a strong desire to excel as a businessman but did not have the training and wisdom to successfully manage his affairs. He sold valuable Salt Lake City property to invest in Utah and Idaho mining ventures and was engaged in a horse-raising enterprise, all of which terminated in financial loss. Finally settling in Ogden, Utah, he was an accountant and bookkeeper for the Bear River Irrigation and Water Works and the Ogden Water Works Company for many years. He married Susan Snow, a daughter of Erastus Snow; to them were born five children. Arta De Christa died in Ogden after a long illness on April 7, 1916.

Letter dated April 24, 1876

At the April conference in 1875, Arta De Christa Young was

called to serve as a missionary to England. En route he visited his brothers Willard and Feramorz at the military and naval academies. "I found Willard enjoying good health and looking anxiously for his examination to come to a close, so that he can visit the folks in Salt Lake. Fera is looking remarkably well and I think he will come out all right. One of the officers told me that he was doing very well and would come out all O.K."[1]

Arta was welcomed to England on May 29 by his brother Ernest, who had already been there a year. After a few days with his brother in Liverpool, Arta was assigned to his place of labor in Nottingham, arriving on June 6. That evening he gave his first speech to the local Saints. "I bore my testimony, but it did not take me as long as George Francis Train gave Grant to tell all he knew, but just about half the time. I am in hopes before I am released from this mission to be able to get up and express what I feel, and I believe that God will help me, if I am humble and seek his Spirit."[2]

During his first year in England Arta traveled extensively, proselyting in the shires of Nottingham, Leicester, Derby, and Stafford. He wrote to his father in October 1875 that he and his companion had baptized sixteen persons and hoped to add many more before spring. Explaining his method of proselyting, he continued: "I am doing all I can to forward the work and I can truly say that I have been highly blessed of the Lord in my labors. Sometimes brother Bryan and I go on a preaching tour together, and sometimes I go alone. I find it much pleasanter when I have someone to travel with, for then a person don't get so lonesome. But I find one thing when I go alone. It is better for me, because the responsibility then rests entirely upon me and I can't shirk one bit. I have been out alone since the 7th and have held meetings in Langley, Eastwood, Pinxton, Sutton and would have held one in Somercotes, but owing to circumstances I did not. I have been greatly blessed in all my labors thus far and have lacked for nothing. The Saints treat me very kindly wherever I go, and altho' the fare that I have to put up with sometimes is not what I have been used to, yet I receive it with a thankful heart and bless those who provide it.... Outdoor preaching is about over and we will now have to preach in the houses. I am kind of glad of it for one thing and sorry for another, glad that we don't have to stand on the streets anymore but can have houses to preach in, and sorry that we will have so few strangers to talk to. As for myself I would much sooner talk to strangers than I would to the Saints, but it is seldom you can get a stranger into the house."[3]

In April 1876 Arta and Ernest Young accompanied the mission president, Albert Carrington, and others on a visit to branches of the Church in Scandinavia and the continent, returning to England on June 5.

The following letter of Brigham Young, dated April 24, 1876, was waiting for Arta when he returned to England.

Salt Lake City, April 24, 1876

Elder Arta D. Young
England

My dear Son,

    I was much gratified with the perusal of your frank, affectionate, and good-spirited letter, which reached me a few days ago. I have no doubt but that your trip amongst the continental missions will do you a great amount of benefit as you can learn many valuable lessons from travel and contact with mankind that you can never reach through books. This experience should also strengthen your testimony of the great work God is performing in this generation amongst the children of men, and enable you all the more wisely to teach the principles of eternal life and to give timely counsel and advice to the Saints amongst whom you labor.

    Before leaving the subject of your letter I want to give just one word of caution with regard to your style of composition. I notice you are inclined to use unnecessary repetitions in your statements which neither give strength nor beauty to your sentences. For instance you say "gradually, every day" when referring to the strengthening of your leg, either of which conveys your idea correctly and with sufficient plainness and force. Too great minuteness often weakens rather than strengthens a writer's style.

    There are some kinds of experience which a person having passed through once in this life, never desires a repetition. Of this kind was the explosion of the powder magazines on Arsenal Hill on 5th inst. The terrific reports following each other in rapid succession, the trembling of the ground, the crashing of windows and doors, the volleys of rocks and boulders falling all around, the frightened teams rushing in all directions, went to make up a tableau and excite feelings that it would be difficult for anyone to realize or sense who was not present to witness it for himself. No one can calculate the damage done, as nearly every house in the city received more or less injury. I am a sufferer to a considerable extent. The Empire Hill, being so near, was injured very extensively. To show you the force of the concussion of the air at that time I may mention that some pieces of glass forced out of a shattered window were hurled a considerable distance through the mill and imbedded a half an inch deep in the solid red pine joists. The mill house nearby will have to be pulled down, it is so shattered and shaken. In the Gardo House a great many windows are broken.[4]

Your brother Lorenzo D. has been called on a mission to Europe, but before starting he will accompany me to St. George, for which place we propose to start, all being well, on 1st May. Brigham Jun. started this morning and will preach at the settlements along the road until my party overtakes him.

We had the Emperor of Brazil here yesterday. He would accept of no attentions from the city council, but preferred to travel in every respect as a private gentleman, paying his own bills, and going where he pleased, and doing what he chose. He left by the regular afternoon train on his way westward.

The family are all well, and the boys are occupied much the same as when I last wrote to you. Mahonri is now engaged at the Deseret Mills as I want him to learn the manufacture of wool in all its branches so that he can eventually take charge of some of my factory business. The letters I receive from Willard and the rest of your brothers who are away from Utah are uniformly good. There is not one of them but is doing his utmost to improve himself in the sphere of usefulness which he has chosen. The reflection is very gratifying to me that every one of my sons is doing so well.

Praying the Lord to comfort and bless you,

I remain, your affectionate father,
Brigham Young

ARTA DE CHRISTA YOUNG

Letters dated July 17, 1876, and February 15, 1877

Upon the release of Ernest Young, who had been mission secretary, to return home in June 1876, Arta De Christa was appointed to take his place, a responsibility he held during the remainder of his mission. In addition to his clerical assignment, he often traveled with the mission president, visiting branches of the Church throughout England. On May 30, 1877, two years and a day after his arrival in England, he started his journey home, in company with President Albert Carrington.

The two letters of Brigham Young that follow were received by Arta while he was engaged as mission secretary during the last year of his mission.

Salt Lake City, July 17, 1876

Elder Arta D. Young
Liverpool, England

My dear Son,

Your letter written immediately after your return to Liverpool from the continent reached me a few days ago. I am pleased that you have taken hold of your new duties with so much zeal and willingness and hope the experience that you will gain in the Liverpool Office will be of lasting benefit to you. I earnestly hope that while you diligently attend to your labors therein you will also not forget your calling as a preacher of righteousness, and that whenever opportunity presents itself, or you can make the opportunity, you will raise your voice in the streets and in the halls of the towns and cities of England in advocacy of the principles of eternal truth. You did so well last year whilst laboring in the Nottingham Conference in outdoor and other preaching that I hope you will not slacken your labors in this direction whilst in Liverpool. There is another thing that I wish to impress on your memory. It is to be very careful that you choose your associates from among those who love to keep God's commands. You are young and the ways of the world may have many allurements. Many a young man has fall[en] from a virtuous life through a desire to simply see and become acquainted with the sins of the world. But having once become familiar with the ways of the sinner it has too often proved that the meshes of sin were too strong to allow of its victim's escape. Do not on any pretense or excuse allow yourself to be persuaded to visit the dens of iniquity—gambling houses, drinking places, and other traps for the unwary—which so greatly abound in Liverpool. I hope also that you will avoid all those habits so prevalent in Christian countries such as smoking, chewing, &c, which the Lord has declared, and our experience has proved, is not good for men to indulge in. You are now building up your character and the foundation which you lay whilst on this, your first mission, will have much to do with the superstructure raised in after years. I have much confidence that you will take a wise and exemplary course, and you ever have my faith with constant prayers to our Heavenly Father in your behalf. Brigham W. Carrington, from his lengthy experience in Europe, should be a great help and a strength to you in fulfilling the purposes of your mission. If you find him such, and his influence salutary, I shall be pleased to learn that you are mutual friends. But if his course is one that you know I should not approve of, if he visits disreputable places, if he keeps bad company, if he drinks strong drink, or if he leads a life that the principles and preaching of the gospel do not warrant, I do not wish you to associate with him in any way, nor go where he goes, nor choose your companions from his circle of acquaintances. Treat him with kindness, present to him a good example, but do not permit him to lead you one step from the path of right and duty.

I shall not attempt to give you the general news, as I have written at considerable length to Bro. [Albert] Carrington regarding our trip to St. George and other matters of interest, and you will doubtless have an opportunity of perusing it.

Ernest, Carlos, and Ferry are now at home, all in good health and in splendid spirits. Carlos and Ferry will return after their vacations, respectively to Troy and Annapolis, to resume their studies, at which both of them are making commendable progress. Lorenzo D. is now in Sanpete, and will start on his mission as soon after his return from there as he can find some friend who is going eastward who will accompany him. The other boys are variously engaged in the same occupations as when I last wrote to you. Your mother and the family are well, whilst my general health is also good, but I have been suffering considerably from rheumatism in my feet since my return home.

May the blessing of heaven rest abundantly upon you is the prayer of

>Your affectionate father,
>Brigham Young

St. George, Utah, February 15, 1877

Arta D. Young
Liverpool, England

My dear Son,

Your acceptable letter of Jan. 19th has been duly received and its contents carefully noted. This is the first letter we have received from you since yours dated November 13th. I take pleasure in receiving letters from my absent children and more particularly from those who are out in the missionary field as bearers of the message of life and salvation. I am very anxious that my children deport themselves as becometh members of the Church and Kingdom of God. The responsibility resting upon us is very great, called upon as we are to assist in bringing about that happy state of things when the will of our Father shall be done on earth as it is in heaven. The duty to keep the commandments of God rests upon us as upon no other people upon the face of the earth. The sure word of divine instruction by revelation from the heavens has been imparted to us and there is no refuge, no safety, nor power, nor glory of celestial life for us, but in keeping those commandments which have been given to us. To obtain the full benefit of that infinite atonement made by our Lord and Savior is within our reach—is ours—fully and completely, but only so, on condition of our faithfulness in observing our covenants and obligations to keep the divine commandments given to us. My dear son, I realize you are young in years, but this has been the tenor of the instruction of your life. And in this you have been greatly blessed of the Lord, over and above those to whom you are called to administer on your present mission, born, as they are, outside of the covenant and surrounded by the darkening mists of sectarian traditions and unbelief. You, in common with the thousands of the sons of Zion, are born heir to the holy priesthood, having the inherent right to administer in the things of God, than which there is no higher calling on earth or in heaven. These privileges and powers are great, and surely should stimulate the noblest effort within us to rise up with humility, and in trust in God, but with unswerving firmness, to bear our respective part in the great work. Personal habits, in opposition to the spirit and tenor of the instructions you have received, must be persistently striven against until overcome. Smoking, and everything of the kind, you should not indulge in a particle. Your age, experience, position, and responsibility demand an abandonment of such practices.

We are very thankful for the information relative to the general conditions of affairs in the British Mission, monetary and otherwise.

In the matter of the Book of Mormon, we are having prepared the text for a new edition, but if Brother Orson Pratt has not about got this ready, we shall have some printed from the stereotype plates now in Salt Lake City and will forward some to the Liverpool office.

It is represented that Bro. Francois Pahud, who has been presiding elder of the Geneva Branch for a number of years, is a worthy man, and now quite in years, and is very desirous to come to Utah. If this is as represented, we would like to have him sent the ensuing season. His address is à Apples, Canton de Vaud, Switzerland. This matter you will of course submit to Bro. [Albert] Carrington, to whom, and those of his family with him, and Bro. [Henry W.] Naisbitt, you will present my kindest regards. Peace and God's blessing be with you—is the desire of your affectionate father,

                Brigham Young

JOSEPH DON CARLOS YOUNG

Joseph Don Carlos Young
1855-1938

Joseph Don Carlos Young, the second son of Brigham and Emily Dow Partridge Young, was born May 6, 1855, in the "white house" east of the Eagle Gate on Brigham Street (South Temple). At an early age Don Carlos was enrolled at the family school; however, his chair was frequently empty as he preferred accompanying the men who drove teams for his father to the rigors of mental exertion—even with such talented instructors as Dr. Isaacson, Dr. Maeser, Romania B. Pratt, Sister Hoagland, and Sister Randall. Having heard that Carlos was truant in his school attendance, Brigham Young took him to the barn one day and told Brother Sewell to hitch up the blind mules. Then placing Carlos on the seat he said, "Now, my son, if you really want to go to work instead of going to school, I'll give you this opportunity, and Brother Hamilton G. Park will tell you what to do." For the next year Carlos worked as a family teamster, transporting produce from the farm, hauling ice from the Jordan River, "moving families from one home to another," and bringing wood from the canyons. Within a year he was given the best team in the barn, and at the age of twelve, he drove a four-horse team from Salt Lake City to Logan and back with a load of wheat. With his brother Alfales he hauled lumber, lime, and adobe for the construction of the Salt Lake Tabernacle and other buildings in the city. It was not long, however, before he became "thoroughly tired" of his work and was only too anxious to return to school.

While attending school Carlos accepted his first paying job driving the delivery wagon for ZCMI, a task he fell heir to when his friend Stanley Clawson was discharged for leaving a wagon containing a forty-gallon barrel of molasses in the barnyard overnight, only to find the next morning that someone had pulled the spigot and two inches of molasses covered the barnyard. In succeeding years Carlos worked in the ZCMI crockery department, where he sold stoves in addition to the usual wares, and the drugstore, where his expertise at the fountain ranged from making everything from syrup to whiskey. Finally, he was entrusted with the books at the cash desk.

After attending the Deseret University in Salt Lake City, Don Carlos enrolled at the Rensselaer Polytechnic Institute at Troy, New York, in 1875. While there he was a member of the Pi Eta Scientific Society and one of the editors of the school yearbook, *The Transit.* He also played football and baseball and sang tenor in the Glee Club. He graduated in 1879 with a degree in engineering, but his main interest in life was architecture. While in the East he also studied music under the renowned organist Dudley Buck.

Returning to Utah, Carlos contributed significantly to Mormon architecture. As architect of the Salt Lake Temple during the final years of its construction, he redesigned the towers, which were originally planned of wood, covered with tin; he also designed the temple interior, the annex, and heating plant. Don Carlos was sustained in general conferences as Church architect from 1889 to 1893. He continued to direct the Church's building program for fifty years. Among the monuments to his architectural skill are the Church Administration Building at 47 East South Temple Street in Salt Lake City, the race track and coliseum at the Utah State Fairgrounds, the base of the Brigham Young monument, the Eagle Gate that spanned State Street from 1891 to 1963, the Mormon Tabernacle at Paris, Idaho, the original Brigham Young University building facing University Avenue in Provo, Utah, and such former landmarks as the Presiding Bishop's Building, Templeton Building, Barrett Hall, and LDS University buildings.

While serving the first of two terms in the Utah Legislature in 1886, Don Carlos received a little notoriety when he became offended by a local newspaper report referring to him as "the booby of the House." Confronting the reporter who had written the disparaging line, Carlos's blunt demand for a public apology met with an equally blunt refusal; sharp words followed, and the reporter left the scene with a bloody nose. The next day Carlos's method of redress cost him $17.50 in the local court.[1]

Supporting a family of two wives and fifteen children, Don Carlos was called on a mission to the Southern States in 1895, where he presided over the Middle Tennessee Conference with headquarters in Nashville. While there he participated in the renewal of missionary work in Hickman County, where two Mormon missionaries had been killed at Kane Creek by a mob twelve years earlier. During his mission he traveled extensively without purse or scrip. On one occasion while passing out tracts near Holmansville, Tennessee, he and his companion found a bundle of hickory branches attached to a gate post with a note saying, "This is for you Mormons that come around here." Another time, after stopping at a house where they were met by a vicious dog, the missionaries were greeted by a lady who told them she was surprised to see them enter that place, as most strangers turned away. "We told her who we were and she said she thought some power was with us. I said we sometimes had to meet more things than dogs." While preaching in a schoolhouse one evening to what started as a "good sized congregation," the missionaries were disappointed as the evening wore on and the people "all went off and left us, except two young men."[2]

After his mission Don Carlos moved to Provo, Utah, where he taught mathematics at the Brigham Young Academy for a year. He later was appointed to the board of trustees of that institution, and also the Utah State Hospital in Provo. Returning to Salt Lake City in 1900, he continued his profession as architect with the Church and established the firm Young and Son.

Don Carlos Young died in Salt Lake City on October 19, 1938, after a long illness. At the time of his death he was the last survivor of Brigham Young's twenty-six sons.

Letter dated October 21, 1875

In 1873 Brigham Young gave six of his sons permission to study at the University of Michigan at Ann Arbor, but after hearing a sermon by his counselor George A. Smith, who suggested that it was unwise to send young Latter-day Saints away to attend school, President Young added two conditions to his original offer: (1) they must spend two years at the University of Deseret, and (2) the knowledge gained in the East must be used for the upbuilding of Zion.

Having complied with the first requirement, twenty-year-old Don Carlos Young, with his friend William Sharp, left Salt Lake City to begin his schooling in the East in September 1875. In company with John Sharp, William's father, who was traveling to a railroad directors' meeting in Boston, the young men went with the elder Sharp as far as Troy, New York, where they parted to begin their studies at one of America's most prestigious engineering schools, the Rensselaer Polytechnic Institute.

At RPI the westerners received a rather cool reception from Mr. Drowne, director of the institute, who apparently felt that two Mormons would not add appreciably to the credentials of the school. As they went about their preschool orientation, Carlos and William were approached by prospective classmates who, not knowing the origin of the strangers, explained elaborate plans for hazing "a couple of Mormons and a negro" that they heard would be enrolling at RPI, and they urged the newcomers to join them. Carlos and William were delighted with the idea and invited their new acquaintances to their room, where the men of Troy soon discovered the Mormon background of their confidants and all had a good laugh.

Brigham Young's letter of October 21, 1875, was the first received by Don Carlos from his father after he began his studies at RPI.

Salt Lake City, October 21, 1875

Elder Don Carlos Young
Troy, New York

My dear Son,

You will doubtless within a day or two see Bro. James Sharp who is on his way to England to fill the mission to which he was called at the last conference, and who intends giving you a flying visit as he passes. Nevertheless, I apprehend a few lines from home will be acceptable, though you will get from him a general understanding of what is transpiring in the midst of your friends.

From your own letters and those of Bro. William Sharp I gather that though you have to study very diligently and continuously, yet you are very comfortably situated, and have excellent instructors. With these advantages I doubt not but that you will make rapid progress in your studies. Today is the day of your opportunities to acquire useful knowledge, and I am sensible that you are aware of the fact and will do your duty. Solomon of old wrote to his son, "with all thy getting get understanding," to which I will add, and associate with thy understanding faith in the Lord, dependence on His power, trust in His goodness, and reliance on His assistance in time of need. And in your daily life, conduct, and conversation always remember that you are a Latter-day Saint, each one of whom should set an example such that the whole world might follow and be benefited thereby.

The day before yesterday, Ann Eliza's lawyers moved in the Third Judicial District Court for an order to compel me to show why I should not be adjudged guilty of contempt of court in not paying the alimony *pendente lite,* ordered by Judge [James B.] McKean. Judge [Jacob S.] Boreman granted the order, the papers were served by Deputy Marshal [A. K.] Smith, I accepted service. and the hearing of the motion is set for Saturday morning next at 10 o'clock. We hope to be able to put off the hearing of the matter until Judge [J. Alexander] White arrives, as it is understood that the governor has only assigned Boreman temporarily to the Third District.[3]

Our conference was a very delightful one, much good instruction was given, and the Spirit of the Lord was copiously poured out upon the speakers. You have, no doubt, read the details of what was done during the session in the columns of the *Deseret News.*

Quite a number of improvements are going on in the city. Bro. [Thomas W.] Ellerbeck is working away with his accustomed vim superintending the waterworks and the laying of the pipes. He has developed a quite unexpected genius for mechanism, and the work done under his charge is highly satisfactory. The new bank building on Capt. Hooper's corner has a very fine appearance, and is rapidly nearing completion. The long continued spell of dry weather this fall has been very acceptable to our builders and enabled them to push ahead vigorously with their contracts; the farmers, however, just at present would be thankful for a little rain to enable them to get at their fall plowing.

Your mother is well and so are your brothers and sisters. My own health is excellent, though I have occasional touches of rheumatism.

May God bless you and His peace rest upon you is the prayer of

>Your affectionate father,
>Brigham Young

Letters dated February 16, 1876, to October 27, 1876

In later years, as Brigham Young saw his sons engage in an ever-widening circle of activity and preparation for their life's work, he not infrequently counseled them on topics of importance to their spiritual welfare and conduct and rehearsed their whereabouts and accomplishments, as he did in the following three letters to Don Carlos written in 1876.

Salt Lake City, February 16, 1876

Elder Don Carlos Young
Troy, New York

My dear Son,

It has been very gratifying to me to hear from various sources, including your own letters, and the reports of Bishop [John] Sharp and Bro. Little of your very satisfactory progress at the academy and also of the comfortable manner in which you are fixed at your lodgings. From the other boys out in the world the news is equally satisfactory; their faithfulness and diligence in their studies is very commendable, and their health and spirits are good. Arta D. is laboring diligently in England preaching the gospel and has much pleasure and satisfaction in his labors. Sometimes his leg troubles him, where he hurt it at St. George, especially after he has had to take one of those long walks which so often occur in the travels of a missionary elder in England. I have just received a letter from Bro. [Albert] Carrington, dated Jan. 27, in which he says, "it affords me much pleasure to state that your good sons Ernest I., and Arta D. continue blest with excellent health and spirits, and are very efficient in their several duties seeming to delight in performing them in the best manner possible."

Yesterday your sister Nabbie was married, Bro. Spencer Clawson being the happy bridegroom. In the evening there was quite a brilliant assemblage of the friends of the young couple who gathered at the Beehive House to wish them much joy. This morning they left for New York, where Spencer's duties call him. I hope they will call on you, as I know a visit from them will be appreciated. By the way, I must not forget to tell you that Morris is now a father. He had a daughter born to him on the evening of 13th inst. Brigham Jun. and John W. are with me now and are both in good health. It is probable that Brigham Jun. will accompany me to St. George, for which place I shall most probably start about the end of next week. Bro. [Daniel H.] Wells will probably go with us and so will others of the brethren. When I reach our Dixie I shall, if the temple be ready, commence to officiate in the ordinances of the house of the Lord therein. It is possible that Bros. Wells and Brigham Jun. will visit the settlements we are forming in Arizona before they return north, whilst Bishop Abram Hatch and other brethren will, as soon as spring comes, start on an exploring expedition to learn the advantages of the country between the termini of the various railroads that run into southern Colorado and our settlements in Arizona. Already the railroad lines are rapidly pushing towards that section of country, and I have the idea that there are many desirable valleys for the homes of Latter-day Saints within a radius of 100 miles of the point where Utah, Colorado, New Mexico, and Arizona meet. It is quite possible that we shall have this season's immigration settled in this new country and thus extend the borders of Zion and strengthen her stakes.

We have had quite a change in our municipal officers. The election took place on last Monday and as was, of course, fully expected resulted in a complete victory for the People's ticket. Bro. Feramorz Little is now mayor and quite a number of fresh faces adorn the council chamber.

Your mother, myself, and the rest of the family are in excellent health and we are always pleased to hear from you. In conclusion, let me exhort you to live your religion, to be fervent in prayer, and to always remember the weight and excellency of your calling.

With constant prayers that you may be blessed of God and aided, guided, and inspired by His holy Spirit,

                        I remain, your affectionate father,
                        Brigham Young

Salt Lake City, April 17, 1876

Elder Don Carlos Young
Troy, New York

My dear Son,

I was much interested in the perusal of your last letter, and was glad to hear therefrom that you are giving such strict attention to your studies and to the acquirement of those branches of practical knowledge which should be of so much benefit to you in after life. You are now surrounded by new circumstances, new scenes, and new faces, and with surroundings to which you are entirely unaccustomed, some of which will tend to strengthen your faith in the gospel of the Son of God, whilst others will seek to draw you away from the principles of righteousness. As you advance in life you will find every position and occupation surrounded by its peculiar temptations, the great strength and bulwark against all of which is prayer to our Heavenly Father. Cultivate this spirit and you will find that it shall be a wall of fire around you and your glory in the midst of you. In its practice you will find a safeguard against the wiles of the adversary, and every good resolution will be fortified by it, and every seductive influence will lose its power to annoy you. In the principles of our holy religion you have a strength in the wisdom and power of the Spirit of God which no revivalist can supply, or no uninspired preacher afford. Mrs. Van Cott's way of bringing erring youths to the penitent's seat may be a very original and very effectual one, but I apprehend the God whom we worship requires no such aids to the proclamation of His laws. A religion based upon a conversion brought about by such means would probably last as long as Mrs. Van Cott was around, and but very little longer. As far as her morals go, perhaps her teachings are excellent and worthy of all acceptation, but as to the priesthood of God and the gospel of the kingdom she knows nothing of it.

JOSEPH DON CARLOS YOUNG

Our annual conference convened on the 6th inst. and continued in session until the afternoon of the 9th. The weather was inclement and the tabernacle cold. This brought a severe cold upon me which prevented my being present at the meetings of the last two days. I am, however, pleased to be able to say that my health is now tolerably good, and improving every day.

ZCMI was opened for business on 1st inst. and since that date the institution has been doing a largely increased business. The building is a success in every way, has all the light and ventilation that could be desired, is so compact and convenient that we expect to be able to do the same work with 25 percent less employees, and has many other advantages for the rapid and efficient conduct of business. The scene within is grand and unique, as in certain portions of the house a general view can be had of all three floors with their varied classes of merchandise.

All being well, myself and party will start for the South a week from today. It will, however, depend much upon the weather and the roads as the latter still remain very bad, much snow having fallen within the past few days in Sanpete and contiguous valleys. This spring in these mountains is unprecedentedly late, and the farmer and the horticulturist have as yet scarcely been able to commence their labors on the soil.

The family are all well. Your brother Lorenzo has been called on a mission to Europe.

Notify Bro. [James] Jack when you want any money, and he will send you what you need from time to time.

May God bless you, my son, and preserve you from every evil, and add unto you every needed gift and blessing through life is the prayer of

Your affectionate father,
Brigham Young

Salt Lake City, October 27, 1876

Elder Don Carlos Young
Troy, New York

My dear Son,

Your welcome favor reached me a few days ago. In reply to

one of its paragraphs I enclose you [blank] New York Exchange, payable to your order for $200 currency, which Bishop [John] Sharp informs me will be just as good to you as the greenbacks, as you can get it cashed at par without the slightest difficulty in Troy. Please acknowledge the receipt.

From what you tell me regarding Fera and the information you have gleaned from a former student of the Naval Academy now with you, as also from his own statements, I am inclined to think I shall permit him to resign if he can do so honorably and without reproach. I should have been glad had he in the first place chosen some other school than the Naval Academy to which his tastes seem entirely unsuited. Your brother Brigham Jun. will accompany me to St. George for which place, all being well, we shall start on Monday morning next. I had arranged to start last Monday, but the peculiar condition of the Ann Eliza persecution caused me to remain a few days longer in town.

On Sunday last I solemnized the marriage of Mahonri, who has now charge of my Deseret Woolen Mills, and Miss Aggie Mackintosh, daughter of the late Daniel Mackintosh and sister to Emma's husband.

This interminable alimony outrage shows some slight tokens of drawing to a close, as the case has come up today on the direct issue of divorce before the U.S. commissioner. I presume were I to tell you all the ins and outs of the case it would not greatly interest you, suffice it to say that on Wednesday everybody except those of our elders who had faith in the over-ruling providences of the Almighty, expected that I should be sent to prison by Judge [Michael] Schaeffer, but affairs took a most unexpected turn, and he allowed me to depart without arrest, but sequestrated the property formerly levied upon, and placed it in the hands of Doc. A. K. Smith, the deputy U.S. marshal, without bonds for him to sell as the officer of the court. Thus I was again delivered from the power of the wicked, and it is an easy thing to fight them by writs of replevin to regain the property. If any man on the earth has cause to trust in the arm of Jehovah it is surely myself, for His protecting care is over me all the time. It is admitted by those who knew anything about the matter that there never was a case with so many surprises, turns, and twists as in this one, known as Young vs. Young.

Affairs generally are quiet, business moderate, money scarce, and the people healthy. Unfortunately this last statement does not apply to Ogden, where the smallpox has been, and still is, prevailing. The authorities assert they are doing their utmost to control the disease and prevent it spreading. We hope it is so. My own health is good, as is that of the rest of the family, with the exception of Phebe (Walter Beatie's wife), who was prematurely confined a few days ago.

With love to yourself, and the kindest remembrance to Bro. William Sharp, and with constant prayers for your peace, preservation and salvation,

I remain,

Your affectionate father,

Brigham Young

My Dear Brother,

How are you? I would be very glad indeed to see and visit with you. God bless you.

Ever your affectionate Bro.,

Jno. W. Young

Letter dated May 11, 1877

In Brigham Young's letter to Don Carlos of October 27, it became apparent that the President would permit Carlos's brother Feramorz, who had been attending the United States Naval Academy at Annapolis, to resign in favor of a more practical education elsewhere, if Fera could do so honorably. Upon reading this, Carlos urged his brother to join him at RPI. On December 20, 1876, Carlos wrote his father that Fera had just arrived in Troy and that the two brothers, along with William Sharp, were rooming together. "I think Fera will be able to enter our class in full standing the coming Session, which begins the first of February. Professor Adams—our present Director—has given him a great deal of encouragement and assistance, and thinks he will get along all right. He says he would like to get as many western students here as possible, for he thinks that this school gives them just the kind of a practical education they will need in the western country."[4]

The remaining letters of Brigham Young were addressed jointly to Don Carlos and Feramorz at Troy, New York. As the 1877 school year drew to a close, Brigham counseled his sons on the use of their time during the summer recess.

Salt Lake City, May 11, 1877

Don Carlos and Feramorz L. Young
Troy, New York

My dear Sons,

It has been my intention for some time past to write you regarding the employment of your time during your vacation, but circumstances have occurred which have rendered it difficult to do so until now.

I deem it desirable, and for your best interests, that both of you should spend your time, if you so desire, in learning the theory and practice of music, instead of spending the holidays at home. If Carlos wishes to study the organ I think it would probably be best for him to go to Boston and place himself under one of the leading organists of that city. I learn that the following named gentlemen, residents of Boston, are leaders in the art: Dudley Buck, Washington Morgan, [Julius] Eichberg, and besides there is the Boston Conservatory, under either of whom it would be desirable for him to study. The Boston Conservatory of Music is highly recommended by those who have studied there, and Bro. [George] Careless recommends it.

If Fera simply desires to learn to play the piano I presume that there would be no necessity of his accompanying Carlos to Boston to do so, as he could doubtless find many competent teachers in Troy who could give him all the necessary instructions upon that instrument.

I am thankful to tell you that my health remains excellent. I am in the best of spirits striving all the time to the utmost to bless the people called Latter-day Saints. I am thankful too that God has blessed me exceedingly in my labors, and that I have much joy therein. In fact, I may say that I never felt more satisfied with my labors and duties, than those which occupied my attention during the six months I was in St. George. Brigham Jr. has been very sick of late. He was so unwell that on our return from St. George we had to leave him at Parowan with Bro. [George Q.] Cannon, and by slow stages was brought to the city. He has now slightly recovered. Your brother John W. has also been sick since his return; he also is vastly improved, in fact, is almost entirely well.

With regard to the rest of your brothers and sisters, they are all well. Mahonri and Oscar are working at my woolen mill; they are manifesting a great deal of energy in conducting its affairs, and are producing some excellent quality of cloth. Ernest is now engaged in my office; Heber is also working [illegible]. Morris has been called to take a mission [illegible] States; he will probably start not before fall. Alfales has returned home feeling and looking exceedingly well. I believe he has given his study great attention, and returns having made good use of his time. He has already been admitted to the bar of the 3rd Judicial District of this territory. I lately received a letter from Lorenzo; he writes a very good encouraging letter, and enjoys good health.

We intend to hold a two-day conference on Saturday and Sunday next, and on Wednesday next I, my counselors, and the Twelve will go to Logan to select and dedicate the land for the temple to be built there, and on the following Saturday and Sunday we hold meetings at the same place. Brigham Jr. will accompany us. The work of excavation of the Manti Temple has been commenced, and is being busily prosecuted.

Bishop [Edwin D.] Woolley's son Joseph, who was a blacksmith, died on the 9th instant and was buried today.

If you spend your vacation in the way that I have intimated, it will be the best for you, but be sure do not study so closely as to injure your health.

                         Brigham Young

Letters dated June 28, 1877, and July 16, 1877

Having been urged to remain in the East and utilize their time in learning the "theory and practice of music," rather than return home during the summer vacation of 1877, in June Don Carlos and Feramorz Young went to Brooklyn, where Dudley Buck, the noted

Boston organist, was spending a few weeks of the summer and had consented to tutor one of the Mormon president's sons. "He informs me," wrote Carlos to his father, "that he will be very glad to learn me all he can in that time, but he thinks it absolutely necessary for me to first take a number of lessons on the piano. He says people make a great mistake by trying to learn the organ before they can master the piano. Another great objection is the difficulty of procuring an organ to practice upon. His pupils are all professors and have their own organ to play upon. Mr. Buck gave me some very good advice, and says he will give me several lessons on the piano and if I get along well he will be able to give me a very good start on the organ. It will be a great advantage to me to be able to say that I have studied under Dudley Buck and would not probably find so much difficulty in procuring an organ. . . . This afternoon I take my first lesson. I will inform you that Mr. Buck charges $3.50 per lesson on the piano and $4.00 on the organ. We have obtained rooms where I think we will be very well treated. She charges $8.00 per week each. Fera has also obtained a teacher and commences his studies next Thursday."[5]

Brigham Young responded to the news of his sons' musical studies on June 28 and July 16.

Salt Lake City, June 28, 1877

Elders D. C. and F. L. Young
20 Pierrepont St.
Brooklyn, New York

My dear Sons,

Carlos's note of 19th and Fera's of 21st have both been received and read with interest and pleasure. I hope, as I believe, that you will make good progress in your musical studies under the masters you have chosen. I would not advise you to take more lessons than you can thoroughly master. Be sure to practice sufficiently to become reasonably perfect in one lesson before you take another; to do otherwise will be to waste your means by paying for more than you can make use of. Your studies in engineering have no doubt demonstrated to you the value of being thorough in all things. So with your music lessons, lay a good foundation. It has been wisely said that he is the best builder who builds well from the foundation up. This is especially applicable to those who are striving to master any of the arts and sciences. The thorough man is almost always the successful man.

My letter today will not be a very long one as I have a number of communications to answer that have been accumulated during my absence in Cache Valley, from whence I returned in recuperated health last evening, and at seven tomorrow morning I start for Juab and Sanpete counties to organize stakes of Zion therein. I am happy to say I am feeling excellently, and all the rest of the family are all well. No change of importance has occurred in the family since last I wrote, except the return of Arta from his mission. He reached home safely with Bro. [Albert] Carrington. On Monday evening, 11th inst., myself and a number of the family went to Ogden to meet him.

Praying the Lord to bless you,

I remain, your affectionate father,
Brigham Young

Salt Lake City, July 16, 1877

Elders D. C. and F. L. Young
Brooklyn, New York

My dear Sons,

Fera's letter of the 2nd and 3rd was received a few days ago, and from its perusal I was pleased to learn of the diligent attention you were giving to your musical studies. I am also exceedingly happy to hear that you attend the meetings of the Saints whenever you have opportunity and bear your testimonies to the truth of the principles of the everlasting gospel when called upon to do so. Bro. [William C.] Staines writes to me very encouragingly of your efforts, and the pleasure he received in listening to your words. I am also gratified to find from Fera's letter that he is beginning to realize how foolish has been the policy that has prompted our young folks to exclude religion from their societies. True religion is the life of the soul; they who seek to live without it are more foolish than they who strive to maintain this natural life without eating natural food. The adversary has no craftier snare for the feet of the young of God's people than to persuade them they can be Latter-day Saints and bury the principles of their religion so deep out of sight that when wanted they never can find them. Whilst away from home I hope you will continue your present practice of associating as much as practicable with the elders and members of the Church. But, as this is not always possible, and you have to form acquaintances with those not of us, be prudent in the choice of your companions. Choose those whose characters are established for truthfulness and honor, whose pursuits are honorable, whose lives are temperate, and whose expenses are moderate. Studiously avoid all those whose lives are tinctured with looseness, prodigality or profanity, and even among the very best of your associates be sure and only imitate their virtues. Remember that however bright any character may be, however much he may shine mentally or intellectually, that if he has vices they are blemishes and should not be copied. It would be as foolish, yes more so, to copy a man's moral blemishes because he has the reputation of being a gentleman, a student, or a good fellow, as it would be to make an artificial wart upon one's face because some very handsome man had the misfortune to have a natural one on his. We all of us are subject to the influence of others, especially of those for whom we have regard, and from our companions both our character and disposition we'll receive a tincture, as water passing through minerals partakes of their taste and efficacy. How careful then ought we to be to associate only with the upright, the good, and the pure.

Fera tells me that he is suffering from lassitude. I presume it is simply the result of the very warm weather, and when the days get a little cooler he will feel livelier. Should he not do so, I hope he will let me know.

My health at the present and for some time past has been very good. Bro. [John] Rowberry who saw me for the first time yesterday since his return from his mission complimented me on looking ten years younger. By the way, Bro. John Druce spoke at a short time during Sunday afternoon's meeting, and in his remarks referred very kindly to you both. The health of the rest of the family is good; Brigham Jun. is not quite himself yet. He went down with us to Juab Co., and I advised him to return to Logan as his cough was again troubling him. All the rest of the boys and girls are, so far as I recollect, about the same as when I last wrote to you. The letters we receive from Lorenzo D. in England are quite encouraging. He is zealously laboring and traveling amongst the people, and I believe, doing much good.

You will show this letter to Willard, who must not consider himself forgotten, but accept as though written to himself what I have said herein to you.

May the Lord continue to have you in his watchcare and preserve you from every evil and guide you continually by His spirit is the prayer of

Your affectionate father,

Brigham Young

Letter of August 6, 1877

Writing to his father on July 19, one month after arriving in Brooklyn to begin his music studies, Carlos announced the sudden termination of his budding music career. "I am sorry to inform you that I took my last lesson from Professor Buck today. He has an engagement in Detroit that will necessitate his leaving Brooklyn next Sunday. He expects to return about two weeks before we leave for Troy and then, if I desire any more information he will give me all he can in that time free. He says that I do not possess much talent, but have done better than he expected I would do this warm weather. If he had me a year he thinks I would be a fair pianoforte performer. He did not give me any encouragement on the organ. I find it more difficult than I at first supposed, to overcome the stiffness in my fingers, as they are now pretty well 'set.' But probably practice will overcome all that. Mr. Buck has given me enough exercises to keep me busy for some time, but if you think best I will endeavor to procure another instructor, although first-class ones are scarce at this time of the year. Fera's teacher is very good, but being only sixteen years old he could not give a pupil the discipline Prof. Buck could." Carlos added that Professor Buck was very desirous to play the Salt Lake Tabernacle organ and give a concert there. "If it is possible, he would like to get a detailed discription of the organ, and if there is nothing printed about it, could you not have Brother Ridges, who is familiar with all the technical terms, write out a discription to oblige him?"[6]

The news of his son's musical demise received the attention of Brigham Young on August 6, less than a month before his death.

Salt Lake City, August 6, 1877

Elders D. C. Young and F. L. Young
Brooklyn, New York

My dear Sons,

Carlos's letter of July 19th reached me a few days ago, and was perused with very much interest. I am glad to hear from you, that you both are endeavoring so assiduously to improve yourselves in your music lessons. I am sorry that it should have so happened that Prof. Dudley Buck was compelled to leave Brooklyn, as I have not the slightest doubt that under his tuition Carlos would have rapidly improved, as I know he has a most excellent reputation. I will shortly send to you, for him, a detailed description of our organ, as Carlos requests in his letter. If ever Mr. Buck should be traveling through this western country, we should be most happy to see him and have his opinion of our organ. Mr. Heller, the magician, was here a few days ago, and as you know he is a most excellent performer on the pianoforte and organ; one of the best, indeed, I have ever heard. He went to the tabernacle one day, and played for a considerable length of time upon the organ there, and pronounced it a most excellent instrument, which only confirms the encomiums that have been passed upon it by those who have previously performed thereon. It was very interesting to me to hear him play on our organ, realizing how much could be done with it by a skillful and experienced performer. I often regret that the young man whom we have to play on it Sundays does not take more interest in bringing out its full powers. I have hoped that Carlos would attain sufficient skill in this art to enable him, at any rate, occasionally to play for us during our religious services; I still hope it will be so.

My health remains excellent. I have much joy in my labors amongst the brethren and sisters, and feel repaid for my endeavors when I notice the growing feeling and desire to serve God that is animating the hearts of many of the Latter-day Saints. The reorganization of the stakes of Zion[7] is doing its work. It was not commenced a moment too soon, but we have great satisfaction in knowing that it is, to a very great extent, awakening the Saints to the full understanding that with us it should ever be the kingdom of God and His righteousness, as we know full well from the scriptures and our own experience that all other things which are desirable shall be added unto us.

The young men, too, continue in the good cause that so many have espoused in the Mutual Improvement Societies; and we have lately changed the old style of the Retrenchment Societies of the young ladies to conform in name, as we also wish them to conform in spirit to the Mutual Improvement Societies.

We had a most excellent time on the 24th of July. The children did admirably in singing their pieces. The large tabernacle was very beautifully redecorated with evergreens and artificial flowers. To show you the extent of the redecoration, I may tell you that it took 18,800 feet of festoons to complete the work.

The boys and girls generally are in good health. Arta talks about commencing the life of a farmer, and I have given him the opportunity so to do. Ernest is in the Co-op; Heber is still working with Bro. [William A.] Rossiter around the premises; and the rest are engaged in the same occupations as when I last wrote you.

With love to yourselves and Willard, and with constant prayers for your prosperity and happiness, I am

> Your affectionate father,
> Brigham Young

LORENZO DOW YOUNG

Lorenzo Dow Young
1856-1905

Lorenzo Dow Young, second son of Emmeline Free and Brigham Young, was born in Salt Lake City, September 22, 1856. He was educated in the family school and the University of Deseret. Prior to leaving for England as a missionary in 1876, he was employed at ZCMI. Between the time of his return from England in 1878 and his death twenty-eight years later, Lorenzo was employed with several Salt Lake City firms, including the Caine and Hooper Insurance Company and Smith and Free, Mining and Stock Brokers. He was secretary of the Eutonia Mining Company and for a time was travel agent for the Salt Lake Hardware Company. Separated from his first wife, Eleanor Crouch, by whom he had one daughter, Lorenzo married Dora Williams on September 2, 1896. He had no other children. Lorenzo Dow Young died of pneumonia in Salt Lake City on May 18, 1905, at age forty-nine.

Letter dated October 21, 1876

When twenty-year-old Lorenzo Dow Young arrived in England on September 9, 1876, he was the eighth son of Brigham Young to enter that land as a missionary. Upon docking at Liverpool, he was greeted by his brother Arta, who had preceded him to England in a like capacity fifteen months earlier. Two months later, having been appointed a traveling elder in the Leeds Conference, Lorenzo was called to speak at the semiannual London conference. In his few remarks to the assembled Saints he lamented his inability as a public speaker and expressed regret that in his youth he had not more readily embraced the opportunities that would have prepared him for that moment. In the two years of his mission, all of which time he labored as a traveling elder, Lorenzo had numerous opportunities to improve his oratorical skill.

The first letter sent by Brigham Young to Lorenzo in England was addressed to him jointly with his brother Arta, dated October 21, 1876.

Salt Lake City, October 21, 1876

Elders Arta D. and Lorenzo D. Young
Liverpool, England

My dear Sons,

A few days ago I received two letters from Lorenzo D., one dated Queenstown giving me an account of a rather unpleasant voyage across the Atlantic, the second informing me of his safe arrival in Liverpool. I was happy to hear that he was himself in good health, and that he found Arta enjoying the same blessing and diligently attending to his duties in the office at 42 Islington. Since Lorenzo left here, nothing of especial importance has occurred to any of the members of the family. All are feeling well, and with the exception of the impotent efforts of our enemies to harass and annoy me, all is peace and general content. Nor have we any idea that they will be more successful in the future than they have in the past. The God in whom we have trusted still lives, and if we rely upon His arm we shall find that it is not shortened nor His ear heavy to hear the supplications of His faithful people. It was my intention to have left for St. George next Monday, but the attorneys and the judges having fixed things so that I am to be brought up to again show cause next Tuesday why I should not be committed for contempt in the Ann Eliza case, my journey is now indefinitely postponed. Her lawyers doubtless fancy that to put an end to this constant annoyance I shall finally give way and pay them the coveted alimony *pendente lite*. But they have mistaken their man. Without the Lord moves upon me far differently to what he has yet done, I will spend the remainder of my days in prison before I will pay them one cent,[1] though I trust that the days I shall spend in prison in such a frivolous case as this of Ann Eliza Webb at the hands of a mob court will be very few, if any. The lawyers and judges well know that under the law to which she has appealed she cannot be recognized as my wife, and if she is not my wife under the law of 1862, how can she be granted a divorce, or what claim has she upon me for alimony *pendente lite?* It is an example of the old saying "that you'll be damned if you do and you'll be damned if you don't." One day a man is threatened with fine and imprisonment for entering into what they term an illegal marriage, and the next day it is adjudged that he pay alimony to the woman who the day before, it was claimed, was no wife at all. Consistency is said to be a jewel, but it is certainly a treasure not possessed by the aiders and abettors of the anti-Mormon crusade. Still they find it hard work to kick against the pricks, and though they throw overboard truth, justice, law, and reason, they yet find their bark makes slow progress towards the haven where every Mormon will be robbed of his rights, despoiled of his property, deprived of his liberty, and his substance given to the spoiler to riot in, and his family turned over to the embraces of the corrupt. Zion still prospers, the kingdom of heaven still increases upon the earth, and as a proof that we are not dead, we shortly intend by the help of God to commence two more temples to His name, one in Manti, Sanpete Co., and the other in Logan, and all being well, we hope to finish them in three years. Notwithstanding the increase of the spirit of Babylon in the hearts of some who claim to be Latter-day Saints, yet there is many a man and many a woman who has never bowed the knee to Baal, or fainted in the service of their God.

These will do the work of the Father, and His work now commenced will never die; its progress will never end. Let me entreat of you, my sons, to so live in prayerful humility, yet with zealous courage that you will always be ready to fight valiantly for the faith delivered to the Saints, and so live that your father and all good men will rejoice in your course and the heavens delight to honor you. I have no greater joy connected with my family than to realize that my sons are seeking to serve God, are striving to keep His commandments, are endeavoring to overcome the weaknesses of the flesh and are toiling to improve themselves in everything commendable and worthy of the acceptation of those who aspire to eternal lives in the kingdom of the Eternal Father. To aid you in walking in this path you have my constant prayers and continued faith that you may ever be guided by the light of God's Spirit and preserved in His all powerful hand.

Ruth [Young] is going with me to spend the winter south as is also Mira. Susan (Arta's wife) will spend the winter in Salt Lake City.

May the Lord bless you, prosper you, guide you, inspire you, and bring you home in peace and safety when your missions are accomplished is the prayer of

Your affectionate father,
Brigham Young

Letter dated May 15, 1877

"Your most appreciative letter of October 21st directed to Arta and myself, came to hand this morning," Lorenzo wrote his father on November 14. "I have perused its contents carefully, and repeatedly, and with my earnest endeavors intend to improve, and be benefited by the good counsel which it contains." Upon arriving in England, Lorenzo had found the mission president, Albert Carrington, intent upon assigning him to Germany, "but I told him what you said about my labouring close by so as to be with Art what time he was here, so I was then sent to the Leeds Conference." Lorenzo found Leeds a very "dark, smoky, and dreary place." Writing his letter about noon on November 14, he found the atmosphere so dismal he could scarcely see to write.

During their months together in England Lorenzo and Arta found much satisfaction in their association. Occasionally they were invited to attend conferences together. In November 1876 they were permitted to spend a week together visiting the sights of London prior to the semiannual conference there. "Arta has improved very much and I enjoy being in his company," Lorenzo wrote to his father, "for he is so willing to give me items concerning missionary labours which he has gained by experience. It did seem very strange to me at first to go out among the Saints, and eat and talk, and enquire into family affairs, and as yet it is very difficult, but I am becoming more used to it."[2]

In January 1877 Lorenzo was transferred from Leeds to become a traveling elder in London. While there he received the two following letters from his father.

Salt Lake City, May 15, 1877

Elder Lorenzo D. Young
England

My dear Son,

Since my return from the south, I have been gladdened by the receipt of two of your very interesting and welcome communications. They did not reach me until a few days ago, having been directed to St. George, which place, however, they did not reach until after my departure thence. I am very much pleased to learn from your letters that you are so actively engaged in the fulfillment of the purposes of your mission, and traveling so extensively throughout the district to which you have been assigned. I sincerely trust that the experiences you now gain and the spiritual power you now obtain may remain with you to cast a pleasing shadow over the whole of the course of your future life not to be forgotten or cast aside, but to be cherished and developed through all your later years until you attain in faith and good works to the fulness of the stature of a man in Christ Jesus.

Myself and the family generally, with the exception of Brigham Jun., are well. John W. has been rather unwell but is now greatly improved and is here with me attending to the duties pertaining to his calling. Willard still remains at Willet's Point doing routine duty. Carlos and Fera are at Troy. Instead of returning home during the summer vacation, the two latter will probably spend their time improving themselves in the art of music. Mahonri and Oscar are at the woolen mills. Alfales has just returned from Ann Arbor, hearty in health and brimful of spirits. He has already been received a member of the Salt Lake bar. Heber and Ernest are more immediately helping me, the first in outdoor labors, the latter in the office. Alonzo still remains in ZCMI boot department. Your sister Ruth was with us through the winter in the south and very much enjoyed her visits there, especially her labors in the temple, but of all this she has doubtless before this informed you.

After leaving St. George, myself and party came up through the settlements by way of Iron County and Beaver to Cove Creek, and there we struck off for Richfield in Sevier Co., and thence to Manti, holding meetings by the way. As you well have seen by the papers, we dedicated the site for the temple at Manti and the labor of excavating the foundation has been commenced and is being prosecuted vigorously. From Manti we came directly home.

Brothers [John] Taylor, [Orson] Pratt, Lorenzo and Erastus Snow, with other brethren, went on their return by way of Kanab, the Sevier and Sanpete valleys, holding meetings at every settlement. They organized stakes of Zion at Kanab and Panguitch and selected a president and high council for these stakes. Your brother, Brigham Jun., had a very severe cold and fever before leaving St. George. He traveled with us as far as Parowan, but he was so enfeebled by disease when he reached there that he had to stop. Brother George Q. Cannon remained with him. They reached the city on Saturday evening, 5th inst. Brigham has suffered exceedingly in his lungs and for the want of sleep. He is now improving rapidly.

The First Presidency and Twelve intend to leave this city on Wednesday next, the 16th, for Logan for the purpose of selecting and dedicating a site for the temple to be built there, and we shall hold meetings there on the succeeding Saturday, Sunday, and Monday.

My own health is excellent. I have not for years endured the labor of speaking at conference and public meetings as well as I have done during the last conference and of late. The pain which I have so frequently suffered from, in my stomach, after speaking to large congregations has troubled me but very little of late. For this I have felt exceedingly thankful.

Our enemies here are not idle; they are doing everything in their power to give us trouble. But their acts should only have the effect to stir the Saints up to greater diligence in keeping the commandments of God.

Since the completion of the temple at St. George, the spirit to look after the dead and to officiate for them, and also to attend to the necessary ordinances for the living, has taken possession of the faithful members of the Church all through these valleys. The Saints probably have never felt such interest in these subjects since the organization of the Church as they do at the present. This will be attended with good results, and as the work of building temples progresses, this spirit will be felt with greater power through all the branches of the Church.

John W. joins me in love and with constant prayers for every blessing to attend you that it is your privilege to enjoy,

I remain,

Your affectionate father,
Brigham Young

Letter dated June 15, 1877

Acknowledging receipt of his father's "very interesting and welcome" letter of May 15, Lorenzo remarked, "your letters are always repeatedly read, for in them I find spiritual strength, encourageing words, and parental love, which spurs me on to more dilligence in executing my duties, and administering the word of the Lord to those with whom I am called to associate." Noting that he had just returned from Liverpool, where he had bid farewell to his brother Arta, who was returning home, and had met the new mission president, Joseph F. Smith, along with other newly arrived missionaries, Lorenzo raised the question of an assignment in Switzerland, a topic that had been previously considered in correspondence with his father. Lorenzo's motive in making the request reveals a strong desire for personal improvement. "I should have liked very much to have traveled there with Bro. Webber. He being a well educated man. In his company I could have obtained a great deal of important knowledge, and many gentele habits, and ways, that I do not find among the Saints in this country. Since I left home, I have had more of a desire and love for learning than ever before in my life. I try to study in my field of labour, but my associates are those who have but little if any taste for knowledge, and instead of learning from them I am drawn back into the same old groove. I then have to throw away my ambition, (to an extent) or feel dissatisfied with the company of my unlearned brethren—never submitting to the latter; but by living humble and prayerful, I am the recipient of many of God's blessings, for which I feel very greatful."[3]

Learning that his father had sent instructions encouraging the missionaries to extend their labors into new areas in which the gospel had never been preached in an effort to inject new life into the proselyting work in England, Lorenzo wrote that he and his companion, A. O. Smoot, Jr., were leaving soon for the Isle of Wight.

Lorenzo closed what was probably the last letter his father received from him with these words: "My eyes are now growing weary and I will draw to a close, praying the Lord bless you with long life and every desire of your heart, with kindest love to yourself and family, I am your affectionate son."[4]

Within two months Brigham Young was dead. And although the mission president, Joseph F. Smith, and Orson Pratt returned to Utah upon receiving news of the President's death, Lorenzo remained in England until the termination of his mission on June 29, 1878.

Salt Lake City, June 15, 1877

Elder Lorenzo D. Young
London, England

My dear Son,

Your very welcome letter containing the description of the London Conference meetings, and your labors amongst the Saints in the district in which you travel, reached me safely a few days ago. I am much pleased that you take so great an interest in the duties to which you have been called. It is the noblest, happiest life that a man can lead to be a minister of salvation to the people of the nations, who now sit in the shadow of the darkness of unbelief and ignorance.

Never neglect an opportunity to do good, to enlighten the ignorant, or strengthen the weak. Raise your voice wherever possible in defence of the truth in the meeting houses and homes of the Saints, in the streets of the cities, or in the fields, so that when you return home you may be satisfied with your labors and realize that you have not been an unprofitable servant to our Heavenly Master. If, when declaring the word of truth, you are attacked by the wicked, do not condescend to argue with them, much less to retaliate. Do not attempt to "repay them in their own coin," to use an old English adage; such is below the dignity of your calling. Recrimination proves no truth; it enlightens no man's mind, but it is one of the weapons used by the adversary to produce hatred and malice in the hearts of mankind, and should never be indulged in by a Latter-day Saint. When you may be assailed, heed it not, bear your testimony to the great work the Lord is doing on the earth, proclaim the truth in meekness, and if they will not listen, leave them to their own folly. We are not called to cavil with the world. Some of my brethren have felt as though I ought to answer all the falsehoods that have been put in circulation during the last few months against the Latter-day Saints, and which have swept over this nation like a flood. I have said to them, "Brethren, I have lived on this earth longer than most of you, and have perhaps a little more experience. When you get to be as old as I am you will learn to trust in God. This is His work, and He will take care of it. If He does not, we cannot." And in this faith I am already fully justified, as our enemies have gone to such lengths that their stories are desecrated [discredited], they have missed the mark they shot at, and have not accomplished the end for which they set out. Without our help God has made them the instruments of manifesting their own folly and wickedness. So will it always be if we put our trust in Him. In the scriptures it is said, "perfect love casteth out all fear," and so does perfect faith.

Since my last letter to you, dated May 15th, but very little has occurred of especial interest connected with the family. Brigham Jun. has continued to slowly, yet steadily, recover, and is now in moderate good health. John W. is in California for a few days on railroad business. Nelson Empey, Walter Beatie, and Alma B. Dunford expect to start on their missions to England early next month. We have released James Harris from going on a mission; he did not have the spirit of the appointment and we deemed it best to have him remain at the theatre. My own health is good. It has not been quite so robust during the past week or two, as I overtaxed myself in traveling, talking, and laboring in the organization of the various stakes of Zion, which is now claiming the principal attention of the First Presidency and Twelve. Next Saturday and Sunday we go to Davis County, next to Tooele, then to Juab and Sanpete.

You are at liberty to draw from Bro. Joseph F. Smith such

sums as you need from time to time to buy your clothes and purchase other actual necessities. Be prudent and economical with this means. We will advise Bro. Smith of this permission in our next letter to him, and when we learn the amount you have drawn we will remit the same to Bro. [William C.] Staines at New York to be placed to the credit of the Liverpool Office.

Since writing the above, I have had a call from a gentleman, named Ferguson, of London, who tells me he was in the neighborhood of the Sadlers Wells Theatre on the evening of the London Conference. He says that the crowd that surrounded the doors was a rabble of the lowest order, still he does not think there would have been any disturbance if the proprietor had permitted the evening's meeting to proceed.

May God bless you, my son, with every gift and grace necessary to make you an instrument of great good in His hands, and, when you have finished your mission, bring you in peace, safety and purity to your home and friends in Zion, is the prayer of

Your affectionate father,
Brigham Young

FERAMORZ LITTLE YOUNG

Feramorz Little Young
1858-1881

The third of October 1881 was a day of mourning in Salt Lake City. That day word came that Elder Orson Pratt, an apostle who was one of the Church's most erudite defenders, had died; William Pullen, a worker on the Salt Lake Temple, had fallen to his death from the walls of that unfinished edifice; and a telegram was received from Elder Moses Thatcher in New York City containing news that his missionary companion, Feramorz L. Young, the twenty-three-year-old son of Brigham Young, had died of typhoid fever while returning home from Mexico and had been buried at sea.

Feramorz Little Young was born September 16, 1858, in Salt Lake City, the youngest son of Brigham and Lucy Ann Decker Young. He was educated in his father's private school, and in his early teens was employed as a clerk at ZCMI. A diary covering two months of his thirteenth year reveals an articulate young man, well-schooled for his age in the art of writing and grammar. It also reveals something of his drive and determination. After being laid off from his work at ZCMI due to "dullness of business" in January 1872, Fera wrote that it was the "most miserable day I have had for a long time—out of employment and not knowing what to do. I feel lazy and would do most anything." Two days later he felt "yet uncomfortable owing to my distaste for 'loafing.' " By the time he enrolled in school with a private tutor, Ida Cook, on January 22, 1872, he had resolved to prepare himself for an appointment to the U.S. Naval Academy. And, although as school progressed he "nearly lost spirit, it being very dull," he was determined to continue—"that I may be prepared for *the* school."[1]

In 1874 Feramorz was appointed to the Naval Academy at Annapolis, Maryland, but a growing awareness that his naval experience would not lead to the goal he had set in life led him to resign after two years. He then entered upon a course of civil engineering at the Rensselaer Polytechnic Institute in Troy, New York, graduating in 1879 in the same class with his brother Don Carlos. Among his associates, Fera was highly respected for his scholastic ability, and he was elected a member of the Pi Eta Scientific Society. Two incidents during his course of study at RPI are indicative of his ability. In 1878 he was enrolled with Carlos in an engineering class taught by J. A. L. Waddell, who later became a world-renowned bridge builder and engineer. The text for the class was Weisbach's *Theoretical Mechanics with an Introduction to the Calculus*.[2] One day Professor Waddell assigned a lesson from the text but stated that a particular problem therein was in error, and he gave the students a corrected version of the problem. As Fera studied in his room that evening he suddenly remarked to Don Carlos that Weisbach was right after all, and that the professor had erred in his correction of the text. Fera explained his rationale to Don Carlos, and again later that evening to his professor—neither of whom seemed to grasp his point. However, the next day, when Fera reviewed the problem at length before the class, all became convinced that "Young, Jr.," as Feramorz was known at the school, was right. On another occasion, toward the end of his senior year, he worked all one night and assisted a classmate in completing his thesis, after efforts of friends had failed to solve the problem: calculating the safety factor of a large steel bridge over the Mohawk River. Fera's own graduating thesis was a structural review and analysis of the Erie Canal Aqueduct spanning the Genesee River at Rochester, New York.

In addition to his scholastic attainments, Feramorz Young excelled in several sports at RPI, including football, baseball, gymnastics, and rowing. At the meeting of the RPI Athletic Association at Rensselaer Park on May 29, 1879, he participated in two of the twelve athletic events, the running broad jump and the five-hundred-yard dash.

After returning home from the East, Feramorz was employed briefly on the Utah Southern Railroad and the Salt Lake and Jordan Canal. He also became a partner in the jewelry firm of J. D. Swaner and Company.

Feramorz was called on a mission to Mexico with his friend, Moses Thatcher of the Council of the Twelve, in November 1880. Traveling by way of Omaha, Chicago, and New Orleans, they arrived in Mexico City on December 5. In addition to proselyting, Fera helped with the publication of Church pamphlets and articles in the Spanish language. He attended the first LDS conference in the Republic of Mexico held on the 17,000-foot slopes of Mt. Popocatepetl, fifty miles southeast of Mexico City. During the time he was in Mexico sixty persons were baptized in that land.

Ill with what was believed to be malarial fever, Feramorz left Mexico with Moses Thatcher, en route for New York City, in August 1881. As his condition worsened, the ship's doctor diagnosed his illness as typhoid fever but did not regard his case as terminal. However, on September 27, one hundred miles out of Havana, Cuba, Feramorz Young died. Warm weather at that latitude, with insufficient ice on board the ship and no means of embalming, compelled his being buried at sea. At 1:50 P.M. on September 28, the engines of the steamer *Knickerbocker* were stopped as passengers and crew solemnly listened to Elder Thatcher eulogize his fallen companion. The flag-draped body was then consigned to the ocean twenty miles off the coast of Florida at latitude 27°9′ and longitude 79°47′.[3] Family and friends of Feramorz Young paid their final respects to him in a special memorial service in the Salt Lake Tabernacle on October 5, 1881, immediately following the funeral of Orson Pratt.

Letter dated October 15, 1874

On September 24, 1874, Brigham Young received a short but welcome telegram from the Church emigration agent in New York City, William C. Staines: "Your son Feramorz passed the examination at the Naval Academy today; he will enter the school tomorrow. He feels well."[4] Feramorz had just turned sixteen[5] eight days before completing the entrance test to the academy. He had been attending school in Salt Lake City when he received his appointment from the Utah delegate to Congress, George Q. Cannon.

Brigham Young's letter of October 15 was his first to Feramorz after the boy's official acceptance to the Naval Academy.

Salt Lake City, October 15, 1874

My dear son Feramorz,

Your very welcome letter of the 3d inst. came safely to hand, and we were all much gratified to learn of your continued good health, and of the flattering success thus far attending you.

I send you thanks for the detail of your studies, the employments of the several hours of the day, and your description of the buildings, their surroundings and location, and should judge you will be able to occupy your academic time very pleasantly and usefully.

In your associations with your classmates and members of other classes it may be well to mention, though you are already aware of it, that wisdom dictates a kind, courteous, forbearing and gentlemanly course under all circumstances, and a careful obedience to all the rules of the academy and the requirements of its officers. This mention is not penned as an item that will be new to you, or one that has not had the consideration expected from one of your years, but because youth is liable to be impulsive, and in haste commit acts or make expressions tending to regret.

Your parents and all your relatives and friends have full confidence that your course at the Naval Academy will be characterized by the same gentlemanly, studious, obedient, and upright conduct that marked your walk at home, and anticipate, from time to time, corresponding reports from those under whose charge and direction you now are.

In regard to attending Church services on the Sabbath, or at other times, you have my permission, and that of your mother, to use your own choice in the matter, so far as the regulations of the academy will admit of your so doing. At the same time, whenever your choice or the regulations cause your attendance, your own judgment will dictate care to derive such benefit as may be possible to one as yet but little acquainted with the various and conflicting religious views entertained in the world, while you are at all times diligent and careful to hold fast to the belief in and practice of the doctrines of the gospel as revealed to us by the ancient prophets, Jesus and the apostles, also by the Prophet Joseph Smith.

During a sudden change in the weather in the forepart of September, I took a severe cold, and at times have been and still am somewhat troubled with rheumatism. At present I feel pretty comfortable as to any pain, but I feel weary and a desire for rest.

I was unable to address the people during our last conference, though my anxiety to meet with them was so great that I ventured to be carefully conveyed in my carriage to the temple block and assisted to my seat in the new tabernacle, the first day in the morning, and the other four days to the afternoon meetings. The weather was very pleasant all the time during our conference. A large number were present from the different settlements, and an excellent spirit was enjoyed by both speakers and hearers.

Business affairs seem to be improving, but the plottings of a few evil disposed persons prevent as rapid an improvement in that direction as might otherwise transpire.

Operations in the United Order[6] are steadily progressing, and the people are increasing in their understanding of its proper workings and the great benefits to be derived therefrom when conducted in fairness and wisdom.

Please correspond freely, and as frequently as convenient, with your brother Willard at West Point, informing each other of your latest news from home, and such other items as may be interesting or beneficial.

We always remember you in our prayers, and feel assured you will be preserved from harm and evil, and I feel to bless you in the name of the Lord.

> Your affectionate father,
> Brigham Young

Letter dated September 20, 1875

Feramorz waited a few days before responding to his father's letter of October 15. "I thought it would please you more, and be more beneficial to me to tend to my studies," he reasoned in explaining the delay.

In the face of a severe case of homesickness and the rigid discipline of military life, the encouragement of his father and friends at home was about all that motivated Feramorz to remain after his initial introduction to the Naval Academy. "I am glad to hear that all have great confidence in me, and I shall strive not to destroy that confidence. It shall always be my aim to honor the position which I now occupy both for my people's and my own sake."[7] However, the emotional strain of his new environment had a drastic effect upon his scholastic performance, and threatened his continuance at the academy: "Mother, you must encourage me all you can," the sixteen-year-old pled in a letter home, "for I am afraid it is going to be very difficult for me to stay here. I have studied all the time during the day except at drills, and have arisen a number of times at 4 or 5 oclock in the morning [the cadets were required to arise at 6:15 a.m.], but still I was found unsatisfactory in Algebra this week. It may be that I can make it up during the rest of the month. I try to anyway. I will have to stay one year if I am not able to keep up. It would be an awful trial for me to go home after having been expelled from this place."[8]

One feature of life at the Naval Academy that was particularly bothersome to Feramorz was the attendance at a sectarian church service required of all cadets each Sunday, unless exempted by their parents. Having received tacit approval from his parents to miss the service, Fera wrote for a formal statement of release only to find that his father was away. He then suggested that Albert Carrington, the president's secretary, send a statement in his father's absence. "Please get it some way as [I] am in perfect misery while at church," he urged. In an effort to relieve his homesickness, Fera concluded his letter with a final plea: "Tell me all the news at home—every little thing. This place is completely devoid of everything except mental and physical work."[9]

Compared with those first trying weeks, the following four months of cadet life drastically changed Fera's outlook. "I have seen times when I have felt rather homesick, though I am not troubled with that ailing much now," he wrote his father in January 1875. "I hope that in case I ever write home again about being homesick, you will take no notice of it whatever. I shall try to overcome my feelings in case I ever should feel homesick again. . . . Father . . . while I was homesick, of course I did not have a very good opinion of the Academy, but now that I am over that, I have changed my mind. I think now that one who gets through this place will have one of the best of educations. And I think, one is a perfect gentleman. The rules here are very strick concerning the use of tobacco, intoxicating liquors, &c. Only last week two cadets of my class were expelled from the Academy for drinking. The use of profane language is not allowed here. I don't mean to say that because the rules prohibit the use of these different things, they are not used."[10]

As Fera's outlook improved, so did his scholastic standing. "You must not think that I am at the foot of my class if I do not stand a star,"[11] he wrote at the end of his first year at the academy. At that time he stood 23rd out of a class of 53. In order of merit he was 23rd in mathematics, 21st in English, 27th in history, 26th in French, and he had 42 demerits. In his second year he stood 15th overall, out of a class of 43. In individual subjects he was 8th in mathematics, 30th in chemistry and physics, 14th in history and rhetoric, 26th in French, 2nd in drawing,[12] and had 72 demerits.

Salt Lake City, September 20, 1875

Elder F. L. Young
Annapolis, Maryland

My dear Son,

It gives me great pleasure to hear of the prosperity and faithfulness of my sons, so many of whom are now in different parts of the country studying to make themselves efficient in the various branches of business or professions they have chosen.

In your last letter you mention having drawn $50.00 of Elder W[illiam] C. Staines in New York, but you do not tell me if you have received the $100.00 I sent you from here by express on 3rd August. Please tell me in your next if you received it safe.

There is no news of stirring interest in our mountain home; peace prevails notwithstanding the malice of our enemies. The brethren are busy in their harvest fields and workshops, and trade is improving in the city. ZCMI is doing a large and increasing business, and the walls of its new building are rapidly nearing completion.

With regard to your brothers, Willard left here on Monday to assume his duties at the station in the State of New York to which he has been assigned. Alfales is doing excellently at Ann Arbor and is progressing rapidly in his studies and growing in the faith and power of the gospel. Don Carlos has entered the engineers school at Troy, New York, whilst Lorenzo and Alonzo are here pursuing their studies at the University in this city very diligently.

I rejoice whenever I hear that my sons are taking hold of the principles of eternal truth and are applying them to their lives. The strength of Zion is in the virtue of her sons and daughters; her foundations are laid in the practical observance by her children of the principles of faith, humility, truth, justice and love. Each of us, my son, must cultivate these principles. It is the duty of every Latter-day Saint, young or old, to serve the Lord. None of us are excused from this duty as, also, none of us are shut out from the attainment of the blessings of eternal life. Never in all your associations forget that you are a Latter-day Saint, nor omit your prayers evening and morning, nor fail to lean upon the Lord, nor to put your trust in Him. Never be ashamed to do what is right, nor to acknowledge your faith, nor to resist temptation, no matter by whom and in what manner presented, so shall you enjoy the blessing of heaven, and increase in faith, knowledge, and power with the Lord.

I want my sons to realize, and would be glad if all the world could understand, that no matter whether a man is a lawyer, a doctor, a mechanic, or indeed be he engaged in any occupation whatever, that thorough honesty and integrity will always lead to success, influence, and respect. If a young man wishes to prosper in his profession, this is the only sure road to progress; on the other hand, if he allows himself to be led from the direct path of honesty, either through the desire to make money fast, or as appears to be the idea with some members of the legal profession, that in the advocacy of a cause or the defense of a client everything is proper that the law does not condemn. If he permits this feeling to guide him he will be looked upon with jealousy and distrust by those who are acquainted with his course, not to say anything about the sinfulness of being dishonest. There is no doubt but that Benjamin Franklin's motto is a true one that "honesty is the best policy." I wish to impress this truth firmly on your mind that you will not forget it through all the intercourse and associations of your life.

My health continues excellent with the exception of occasional attacks of rheumatism. Your mother and the rest of the family are well. We remember you constantly with much love and best wishes, and we pray that you may be preserved from every snare and be permitted to return home, having accomplished a good work in preparing yourself for a life of truth and usefulness.

Your affectionate father,
Brigham Young

Letters dated October 16 and November 24, 1875

Unlike the writings of some of his brothers, one characteristic of Feramorz Young's letters to his father was their brevity. Three short paragraphs constitute his answer to his father's letter of September 20.

In reflecting upon his first year at the Naval Academy, Fera admitted that he had not made a very good beginning to his career but explained that he had worked as hard as he could and had managed to keep a satisfactory grade. Part of his letter contained a special request: "Father, a cadet of the 2d Class wished me to ask you if you would be willing to let him have your autograph. He, or rather a friend of his has a collection of autographs and wished to obtain yours. I thought that I could do no more than make the request. If you would not like to let anyone have your autograph on account of not knowing the character of the same, I can say that I have been in the same crew with him all of the past year and have found nothing in him but that which characterizes a gentleman."[13]

In letters of October 16 and November 24, Brigham Young made no reference to this request.

Salt Lake City, October 16, 1875

Elder F. L. Young
Annapolis, Maryland

My dear Son,

Your very welcome letter of the 2nd reached me on the 11th inst. I am glad to hear therefrom of your good health and general prosperity.

If you find the regulations are such that they will not let you have the $100.00 I sent you in August you can hand the enclosed order to the paymaster for him to return the money to me, and you can draw $50.00 from Bro. [William C.] Staines, which, with the previous $50.00 drawn of him by you, I will make right with him.

We have had a long and very delightful conference. The spirit of instruction and counsel was copiously poured out upon the elders who spoke and a rich outflow of the Spirit of God was felt by every true Latter-day Saint present. About one hundred and fifty elders were called on various missions, many of them to the Eastern and Southern States and Canada, quite a few to the Lamanites, and others to England, Scotland, Denmark, Sweden, Germany, Australia, and New Zealand. Amongst those called with whom you are acquainted are Elders F[eramorz] Little, Theo[dore] McKean, Mark Croxall, James Sharp, Geo. Teasdale, Charles S. Burton, Douglas Swan and Isaac Groo. During the conference the new tabernacle was dedicated, the prayer being offered by Elder John Taylor.

I am very pleased to think that my sons who are now away from home are doing so well. I hear often from Willard, Alfales, and Don Carlos, all of whom are striving to make the most of their opportunities that they may grow to be useful men in our Father's kingdom. I also receive encouraging reports from Ernest and Arta in England; the former is engaged in the Liverpool Office, whilst the latter is laboring as a missionary in the midland counties. I am told he is very faithful and becoming quite bold in bearing his testimony to the restoration of the gospel in its fulness and powers in these days.

I wish to say to you, you must not try to answer all the letters you receive. Let your friends write to you as often as they please, but do not attempt to reply to them all. Let your studies be your first consideration, and then, if you have time to answer a letter occasionally, do so.

I am still a little troubled with rheumatism; otherwise my health is good. The weather is beautiful; we are enjoying all the pleasures of a delightful Indian summer. The family and your friends are in good health.

Before closing let me exhort you, my son, to live your religion day by day, be faithful, honest, and true to all your duties and in all your associations, and ever keep your trust bright in the Lord your God.

Your mother is well and received a letter from you a day or two ago.

With love, and ever praying for your welfare and happiness, I remain,

>Your affectionate father,
>Brigham Young

Salt Lake City, November 24, 1875

Elder F. L. Young,
Annapolis, Maryland

My dear Son,

Brother George Q. Cannon who will leave tomorrow morning for Washington will bring one hundred dollars ($100) cy. [currency] which I have handed him to convey to you. With this remittance I associate the hope that you will use it judiciously and economically, which indeed, I have no doubt but that you will do. Be prudent in all things, adopt the plan of keeping a strict account of all your expenses; by this you will not only understand what becomes of your money, but it will also induce business habits and method and correctness in financial dealings in after life. I am very much pleased to learn through your letter to your mother that you are progressing so satisfactorily in your studies and are improving your standing in the various classes. You will find that much of the happiness of this life consists in having something worthy to do and in doing it well. It has been wisely said that "that which is worth doing is worth doing well." If a man have to drive the plow let him do it well; if only to cut bolts, make good ones; if to blow the bellows, keep the iron hot. It is our attention to our daily duties that makes us men, and if we devote our lives to the service of heaven, our faithfulness therein will eventually fit us with our Heavenly Father in eternity to dwell. Aspire to acquire knowledge that you may be able to do more good and also to progress in your sphere of life; but remember that you will win only by trust in the Lord, by present contentment and by doing faithfully that which you have in hand. This I have confidence you will do. No one advances who imagines himself too good or too big for present duties. Such a one is apt to sink into a smaller and a smaller place. In the long run, and for the most part, men are found in the places they have fitted themselves to fill. It is one of the most cherished hopes of my life to see my sons by faithfulness, diligence, and devotion to God and their duties, fit themselves to be able ministers of salvation to the children of men. This should be the great object of our lives.

We have had a very unfortunate fire in this city this week, at which the machine shop of Bros. Davis, Howe & Co. was destroyed. The loss of the building, a frame structure, would be but an inconsiderable matter if no other damage had been done. But the injury to the machinery and the burning of patterns and tools have run up the total damage to twenty-three or four thousand dollars. There is a great feeling of sympathy expressed by the brethren and many will extend a helping hand to assist the firm to erect another building, their business having become a very important branch of home industry which we can ill spare. I think of giving $1000 myself to help them to make a fresh start.

I have no doubt but that you heard the tidings of my release from my unjust imprisonment with intense satisfaction. You will also be greatly gratified to learn that my health is very rapidly improving. Yesterday was a lovely day after a long continued spell of wet weather, and I availed myself of the opportunity of taking the first carriage ride since my release. Today it would seem as though another storm was nearing us. Nearly six inches of rain has already fallen here this month which is something out of the ordinary course of the weather.

The family are all well. Hyrum is still working on the railroad; he anticipates being called on a mission before very long. Mahonri and Lorenzo are at work at the ZCMI whilst Alonzo still continues his studies at the university. And we all, father, mother, brothers, sisters, friends, and brethren in the office, all join in love to you, and in prayers for your welfare.

                                              Your affectionate father,
                                              Brigham Young

Letters dated February 15 and March 14, 1876

On January 20, 1876, mid-way through Fera's second year at the Naval Academy, his older brother, Brigham Young, Jr., paid him a visit. Brigham's diary account of that meeting is instructive in its portrayal of the daily routine at the academy and also the congenial relationship that existed between these brothers: "Put up at the Maryland Hotel. Walked over to cadets quarters, asked for information at Admiral Ro[d]ger's office; directed to main building. Sent in my card. Ferry came in a few minutes. I huged and kissed him. I could scarcely keep from sheding tears to see him so far from home among strangers. He has grown taller and heavier and is in excellent health. Says he is unsatisfactory in chemistry and philosophy, well advanced in mathamatics. . . . Visited the colleges and grounds. Examined the Engineer department where many beautiful models were exhibeted. Saw the cadets march out of quarters in squads and run to the music of brass band, all keeping step which looked fine. It was Ferry's day on shipboard, where I saw them going through their practice. Others were out with guns in the field. Others were going the system of signaling. This lasted from 4 til 5 p.m., when Ferry joined [me]. We repaired to his room by permission of [the] officer, where we chatted until twenty five minutes past seven, when I bade him good bye at the gate. His labors are: not allowed to rise until 6.15 a.m., clean his room, make the bed. 6.45 inspecting officer of rooms comes round. Breakfast at 7 oclock. Studies begin at 8, continue until 1 oclock. Dinner. Studies again from 2 to 4 p.m. Drill from 4 to 5 p.m. Studies from 7.30 to 9.30 p.m., then bed. Not allowed to study out of hours. Saturdays from 8 to 12 oclock, rest of the day allowed to go into the town, but prohibited from entering a hotel, store, or tobaconists. The cadets are not allowed to smoke as formerly which has caused much disatisfaction among those accustomed to it. We talked of home and parents. . . . He has made voyages and always on sailing vessel where midshipmen have to clime the ropes and do seamen's duty. He also has foil practice and first class are permitted target practice, broad sword, and boxing. Fine laboratory, a marine department, and I saw an engine which was constructed by the cadets. They are taught to take the engines apart and put them together again."[14]

Just before writing the following letter, Brigham Young had received a progress report from the academy containing the news that the use of tobacco among the cadets at the Naval Academy had been entirely suppressed, a subject of comment in the President's letter.

Salt Lake City, February 15, 1876

Elder F. L. Young
Annapolis, Maryland

My dear Son,

    I was very much gratified yesterday, when, on the receipt of the usual monthly report for January I found you were gaining so admirably in your standing in your class. I noticed that out of six studies reported, in five you were in the upper half of the class. I can assure you that the constant good news I receive from and of yourself and my other boys out in the world is very gratifying, and I feel thankful at all times that my sons are doing so well, and that I have so little cause for complaint at the course taken by any of them.

    We have had two very interesting incidents occurring in the family within the past few days. On Sunday evening Morris had a daughter born to him, of which he is proportionately elated, and today Nabbie was married to Bro. Spencer Clawson. The newly married couple will start tomorrow for the East, where Spencer will have to go to attend to the spring purchases of ZCMI.

    Accompanying the usual monthly report was "a report on the use of tobacco by the cadets of the Naval Academy," from which I am much pleased to learn that the officers of the academy have decided to entirely suppress the use of tobacco amongst the cadets. The ideas expressed in the report entirely coincide with my views that you have so often heard me explain, that tobacco, whether used in smoking or chewing, is an unmitigated evil to young men, injuring their health, impairing their mental powers and unfitting them for their daily duties and studies. But I am gratified to know that you do not indulge in these pernicious habits, smoking or chewing. Some young men seem to entertain the idea that to smoke, to chew, or to use profane language makes them appear more manly. Never was a greater fallacy. [Real] manhood is manifested in serving God and keeping his commandments. The highest type of mankind is shown in such worthies as Enoch, Abraham, Joseph, Nephi, Alma, Joseph Smith, and others. If boys wish to be thought manly, let them copy the best men and their virtues, not inferior and vicious men and their follies and vices.

Brigham Jun. and John W. are now both with me, and I am thankful to say we are all in good health as is also your mother and the rest of her family. I propose, should nothing intervene to prevent me, to start for St. George within ten days. Bro. [Daniel H.] Wells, Brigham Jun., and other brethren will accompany me. If I find the temple there sufficiently near completion, I shall dedicate the lower portion and commence attending to some of the ordinances of the house of the Lord therein.

The brethren called for Arizona have almost all gone, and those from the north are passing through this city every day. The companies generally have first class fitouts and appear to be just the kind of men to build up a new country. It is possible that Bro. Wells and Brigham Jun. will visit the new settlements before they return north.

You will see by the peculiarities of this letter that we have a "type-writer"[15] in use in this office. By skill and practice some of the clerks expect to be able to write before long with this machine twice as quickly as they can with a pen. Besides this it has the advantage of great plainness, and no one will be able to find fault with the obscurity of the handwriting.

With much love, and with constant prayers for your progress, preservation and happiness,

I remain,

Your affectionate father,
Brigham Young

Salt Lake City, March 14, 1876

Elder F. L. Young
Annapolis, Maryland

My dear Son,

I have received two letters from you within the last few days, which I shall not attempt to answer now, but will simply say that you may expect to see your brother John W. in a few days, and he will tell you all the news. He will also bring you a little money from me, and your trunk. I am quite willing you and your companions should buy the boat, you paying your share of it. Take good care of the boat, and learn to handle it properly and to row. It is good healthful exercise.

Myself and the family are all well. May God continue to bless you always.

Your affectionate father,
Brigham Young

Letter of August 23, 1877

By the beginning of Feramorz Young's third year at Annapolis, a career in the U.S. Navy did not hold the promise for his future that it had held two years previous. He sought earnestly for permission from his father to resign, that he might pursue a more practical course in life. Writing on November 5, he weighed the matter for his father: "When I came here it was for the purpose of gaining knowledge, which knowledge was not only to be a benefit to myself but to my people as well. For two years have I studied hard, hoping to get this education, pursuing branches of importance not only to one profession, but to all—as Mathematics, English . . . and so on, and on this account have scarcely looked into the future. Now, having entered upon a second two years course, I find my studies to be those pertaining to one particular profession and to no other—that is, to a naval officer. I know that you do not wish me to follow the Navy, neither do I wish to. In order to graduate, I will have to spend four more years, and then two of service before I can leave honorably after graduating. Not only will this be six years of my life lost, but I will have been pursuing a life to which my whole mind will have to be attached and thereby cause me to forget what knowledge I have gained of other affairs, besides my being under the control of the United States government. In fact, when I will have left the Navy six years from now I will be totally unfit for anything else. And again, during four years of the six, I will be roaming from one country to another away from the influence of home, friends, and my religion, in which case one is very apt to forget his position. Or, to the point, I think that I can fit myself for a better and more beneficial life, to myself, to you, and to our people, elsewhere than here."

Upon discussing his feelings with Admiral Rodgers, superintendent of the academy, Fera was told that he could resign "and do so honorably," but that the matter lay entirely with himself and his father. In concluding his letter, Fera left the final decision as to his career at the academy with his father. "Please consider the above and think what your advice to me would be. If it be favorable then I request to resign; if not, then I am willing to remain here and do the best I can. In making your decision do not consider my feelings but your own alone. I desire to act as you wish and in no other way."[16]

Recalling the night he had received his father's permission to accept an appointment to the Naval Academy, Feramorz noted that the subject of his becoming a civil engineer had been discussed and that George A. Smith, who had been present on the occasion, had observed that the best civil engineers had been trained at the Naval Academy. "That was a mistake, as none are educated here," Fera concluded.[17] And now, fully realizing his mistake and believing himself better qualified for the profession of a civil engineer than any other (which coincided with his father's first counsel), Fera requested that he be permitted to join his brother Don Carlos, who was then studying at one of the nation's top engineering schools, the Rensselaer Polytechnic Institute at Troy, New York.

On December 1 Feramorz received his father's "most welcome" letter giving him permission to resign from the Naval Academy. "Today I took your letter to Adm. Rodgers," he wrote on December 2, "and told him what my plans were and why I wished to resign. I said that I did not think I would like a naval life, and if I did, I said that my associations being what they were, I wished to pass my life with my people. I asked him if he did not think that I could acquire knowledge that would be far more beneficial to me outside the Navy elsewhere than here. He confessed he did, but thought the name this place would give me would be a great thing in my favor. He spoke freely with me and I tried to with him. He concluded by saying that you were my best adviser and my best course is to act as you said. His opinion of the school at Troy was very high, and seemed to think that I had made a good choice of schools. Admiral Rodgers had assured me before that there could be nothing dishonorable in my resigning inasmuch as I was not leaving on account of some scrape or of having become deficient, which he felt sure I was not doing. After a short talk I wrote out my resignation which he approved and forwarded to the

Secretary of the Navy. He told me to tell you that he had recommended me to the Secretary as one having a high standing in my class, and good conduct. He further said that he would answer your letter and I presume at the same time will tell you his feelings. My resignation will most probably be accepted by next Saturday and then I shall go direct to Troy."[18]

The next letter Feramorz sent his father was sent from 176 Congress Street, Troy, New York, where he had joined his brother Don Carlos and William Sharp as a student at RPI. Fera explained that he had talked with Professor Adams about enrolling. "At first I did not intend to enter till the beginning of the summer session, the first of February. In this way I would save the tuition of one term. But Prof. Adams thought that it would be better for me to enter now, and then I would get the review of all this term's studies and would be better prepared to pass my examinations. And besides, he would allow me to be examined with the class by which I would only be examined on a very small part of each branch, whereas, if I wait till next term, I cannot be examined with the class, but will be examined alone on every subject of each branch. If I enter now, they will require me to pass no examination till next term. You no doubt will see the advantage in all these privileges, and rather than risk not passing some of my examinations, I think it better to enter this term. However, I am writing this letter to you to ask your consent to do this. If I do not receive an answer before January the second I shall enter anyway."[19] Interpreting his father's subsequent silence on the subject as at least tacit approval, Fera enrolled at the January term, 1876.

As the 1876-77 school year drew to a close at RPI, Feramorz and Don Carlos were advised by their father to stay in the East and study music instead of returning home during the summer recess. Brigham Young suggested that his sons study organ and piano at the Boston Conservatory, and he named Buck, Morgan, and Eichberg as among the leading teachers. In June 1877 Fera and Carlos went to Brooklyn, New York, where Dudley Buck, who had consented to instruct Carlos, was spending several weeks of the summer. While there, Feramorz studied piano from a teacher described as "very good, but being only sixteen years old he could not give . . . the discipline Professor Buck could."[20]

Shortly after their arrival in Brooklyn, Feramorz and Don Carlos visited a neighboring branch of the Church, where they were called upon to speak to a congregation of some thirty Saints. "It was the first time I ever addressed any kind of an audience," Fera informed his father. "I sometimes used to try to speak in school, but I generally cried before I got through my little piece. However, this time I succeeded differently. I spoke I thought with a great deal of freedom, and did not feel scared in the least. But after I had spoken, what Carl said was about fifteen minutes, I became very dizzy and, had I not sat down, I would have fallen. I think Carlos must have been mistaken as to the time for it did not seem longer than three minutes to me."[21]

Because they remained in the East during the summer of 1877, Feramorz and Don Carlos did not see their father again. Brigham Young died on August 29 that year. The following letter, dictated to his secretary, George Reynolds, and dated August 23—one week before his death—was the last sent by President Young to one of his children.

Salt Lake City, August 23, 1877

Elder F. L. Young
Annapolis, Maryland

My dear son Fera,

A day or two ago I received your letter acknowledging the receipt of mine of July 17th. As ever I was glad to hear from you. I trust, when next you write, you will feel more encouraged; possibly, the warm weather having moderated, you will feel more of your natural vigor and energy and the prospect will appear brighter before you. Nothing worthy of obtaining is ever engaged by us without perseverance. "There is no excellency without labor." You must, therefore, strive on. The experience you gain will be invaluable. Experience is a good schoolmaster though the "school fees are somewhat heavy."

You must permit me, my dear son, in the love that I bear for you and your brothers and sisters, to say that I do not esteem the perusal of novels a wise means of increasing your desire to read. I should be very foolish if because I had a poor appetite I took to making my meals of poisonous herbs or berries because they tasted sweet or were otherwise palatable. It would be better for my appetite to remain poor than that I should destroy my vitality.

Novel reading appears to me to be very much the same as swallowing poisonous herbs; it is a remedy that is worse than the complaint. I certainly wish you loved reading. I hope that taste will yet be developed in you, but developed by all means with good, healthy, mental food. Read all good books you can obtain, the revelations of God, the writings of His servants, descriptions of His works, as seen in the animal, vegetable and mineral kingdoms; peruse the lives of the good and great of various ages and nationalities; make yourself acquainted with art, science and manufacture, and before long you will find an interest growing in these things that it will be no longer any trouble to read, but you will read eagerly and whilst so doing you will be fitting yourself for future usefulness.

Some excuse novel reading on the grounds that it gives them insight into the ways of the world, its life and society, others on the ground that they thus become acquainted with the best authors, their various styles and peculiar beauties. To the first plea I would say that the views of life given in most works of fiction are greatly strained or entirely false, and every elder in the Church of Jesus Christ who performs his duty will have enough experience in the vicissitudes of real life to satisfy him by the time he grows old. To the second excuse I would answer that the Bible and many works of history &c. contain as good, graceful, grand, unadulterated English as any romance that was ever written. Avoid works of fiction; they engender mental carelessness and give a slipshod character to the workings of the mind. To strengthen the mind, increase its perceptions, develop its powers, we should read the true and the wise. The perusal of the rest is worse than time wasted, it is time abused. Sell your Dickens' works and get Stephens' & Catherwoods' *Travels in Central America,* or Josephus's or Mosheim's *History.* The Bible is a very interesting book when read as history, especially to those who believe the truths that it teaches.

We have not heard from Willard since he was in Philadelphia at the time of the great labor strikes, but have no doubt that he safely returned to the routine of his garrison life at Willet's Point. The accounts we have received of the scenes and circumstances which attended those few dark days in July have very vividly impressed us with a realizing sense of the near approach of the breakup of our present form of government. We take no joy in the misery of our fellowmen. We understand too well what the near future will bring upon the unrepentant. There may be people who talk about an impending bloody revolution in this country with a gusto that smacks of fond anticipation. We are not amongst them. We would rather that the evil should be averted by the people turning from their wickedness and living unto God. The revolution foreshadowed should be averted by all the effort the people could exert against plague or famine, for it means a common ruin for workingman and capitalist, which will be irretrievable if the people permit it. In fact, it means the fall of Babylon, or as much thereof as spreads over this fair land of Joseph. It can only be prevented by a complete change in the hearts and lives of the people and an obedience to the plan of salvation, revealed by God in this generation. But we fear it is too late, the masses have gone too far, the body politic too corrupt, the tree is too rotten, it is fit only for the burning.

Give my love to Willard and Don Carlos, tell them I am well, as are the rest of the family. All is peace, the Lord's hand is over us and we are safe if we keep the commandments.

May the Lord bless you, my son. I remain,

Your affectionate father,
Brigham Young
G.R. [George Reynolds]

ALONZO YOUNG

Alonzo Young
1858-1918

Alonzo Young was born in the Lion House December 20, 1858, a son of Brigham and Emmeline Free Young. Unlike most of his brothers, he lived all of his life almost within a stone's throw of his birthplace. He was educated in Salt Lake City and was one of the first students tutored by Dr. John R. Park of the Deseret University. In 1879 Alonzo married Anna Richards; to them were born seven children. Commencing in 1898 he labored successively as a clerk and travel agent for ZCMI, and finally became manager of the wholesale shoe department. An active Church worker, he served as a member of the Ensign Stake high council from 1906 until his death. He died at his home in Salt Lake City on March 31, 1918, at sixty years of age. No letters to Alonzo from his father are extant.

PHINEAS HOWE YOUNG

Phineas Howe Young
1862-1903

Phineas Howe Young was the only child of Harriet Barney and Brigham Young. Harriet also had four children by a previous marriage who were raised in the Young home. Phineas was born February 15, 1862. At age fifteen he became tragically addicted to drugs following the administration of morphine during hospitalization to relieve suffering from typhoid fever. He struggled all his life to overcome the habit and finally died at age forty-one. His father likely never knew of the addiction, since the illness occurred about the time of Brigham Young's death; hence he was not alive to help the young man cope with the problem.

Although he inherited enough property and means for his support from his father's estate, "Howe" Young was a partner with his half-brother Royal B. Sagers Young in the Young Music Company in Salt Lake City. As an artist and craftsman, Phineas was a skilled pianist and produced some masterful woodcarvings. Of particular note is a highly detailed replica of the Assembly Hall on Temple Square, carved as a housing for a mantlepiece clock and now displayed at the Daughters of the Utah Pioneers Museum in Salt Lake City. Although his drug addiction kept him from church attendance, Phineas diligently led his family in devotion to their religion. He married Margaret E. Wayman on October 21, 1886, in the Logan Temple; two children were born to them.

Upon completion in 1902 of a new house on 7th East and 2400 South in Salt Lake City, Phineas renewed his determination to break his drug habit and urged his family to refuse any requests for relief.

He died in the ensuing struggle, on February 15, 1903, his forty-first birthday. Since he was only fifteen at the time of his father's death, it is doubtful that the President had occasion to write to him, which may explain the absence of correspondence between them.

Appendixes

Notes

JOSEPH ANGELL YOUNG

[1] Joseph A. Young, Diary, 16 February to 8 April 1864, pp. 4-7. University of Utah.
[2] Joseph A. Young to Brigham Young, 14 June 1864.
[3] *Deseret News*, 4 August 1875.
[4] Brigham Young, Jr., Diary, 6 August 1875.
[5] Franklin D. Richards to Brigham Young, 7 July 1854.
[6] Joseph A. Young to Franklin D. Richards, 17 July 1856, in *Millennial Star* 18 (2 August 1856): 482.

[7] A Church wagon train loaded with badly needed merchandise was traveling west from Fort Leavenworth, Kansas, under the supervision of Horace S. Eldredge on August 5, 1854, when a stampede occurred, resulting in the loss of 120 head of cattle. So depleted was the supply of animals for teams that the train's progress was severely limited until cattle solicited from other immigrant companies were procured. The Church train finally arrived in Salt Lake City on October 3. See Journal History of the Church, 29 August 1854, p. 1. The Journal History is a daily scrapbook-like compilation of clippings and commentary by clerks in the Church Historical Department.

[8] The "precarious" nature of Indian relations at this time grew out of an incident that occurred on August 8 when two sons of Bishop Allen Weeks of Cedar Valley, thirty miles southwest of Salt Lake City, who had gone to a nearby canyon after a load of wood, were brutally murdered and their bodies mutilated by Indians. Recognizing this to be the act of bad Indians, Brigham Young issued a letter on August 14 to inform red men in general that they need not expect retaliation in consequence of the conduct of a few renegades among them. In this emotionally charged atmosphere white citizens were also informed that any effort to abuse the Indians or retaliate would be vigorously dealt with, "for the whites do know how to do right, having been often and plainly taught." *Deseret News*, 17 August 1854, p. 2.

[9] Reference is made to the Deseret Alphabet, begun in 1853, which was an effort to simplify the spelling and reading of the English language by use of phonetic symbols.

[10] Antelope Island in Great Salt Lake was a herd ground for Church cattle at this time.

[11] Joseph A. Young to Brigham Young, 30 November 1854, in *Deseret News* 5 (1854): 20. An acquaintance described Joseph A. shortly after his appointment to head the Bradfordshire Conference: "He can scarcely any longer be considered the Joseph he was while at home. He has become a reflecting, praying, faithful man, that begins to comprehend what he must become, and the great responsibilities which rest upon him." James A. Little to James McKnight, 24 January 1855, in *Deseret News* 5 (1855): 92.

[12] The event that precipitated the Indian difficulties near Fort Laramie in 1854 occurred on August 19 when a detachment of soldiers from the Fort entered a Sioux Indian village at Sarpy's Point, eight miles east of Laramie, to arrest an Indian who had killed a cow belonging to a Mormon immigrant. When the Indian refused to give himself up, the officer in charge of the twenty-seven men—in an act of brash courage—ordered his men to fire upon the Indians, who, some one thousand strong, promptly killed the small detachment of soldiers. The Indians continued to vent their displeasure by ransacking government and American Fur Company posts in the area, destroying some $50,000 worth of goods. In addition, the Sioux not only made travel through the area precarious, but also put a stop to all mail service across the plains for a time. See news clipping from the Council Bluffs *Bugle* in Journal History, 18 August 1854.

[13] The Lion House, Brigham Young's principal residence on Brigham Street, now South Temple Street, in Salt Lake City.
[14] Joseph A. Young to Mary Young, 18 January 1855, in *Deseret News* 5 (1855): 88.
[15] Joseph A. Young to Mary Young, 28 February 1855, in *Deseret News* 5 (1855): 143.

[16] Joseph A. Young to Mary Young, 18 January 1855, in *Deseret News* 5 (1855): 88.
[17] Machinery for the manufacture of sugar had been imported from Europe in 1852 and set up on the northeast corner of the temple block, where the feasibility of producing sugar in Utah was established. The plant was dismantled and moved four miles southeast of Salt Lake City, where the manufacture of molasses was begun on July 1, 1855.

BRIGHAM YOUNG, JR.

[1] Brigham Young, Jr., Diary, 25-26 August 1877.
[2] Brigham Young, Jr., Diary, 2 October 1887.
[3] Brigham Young to William H. Hooper, 30 May 1862.
[4] Attacks upon mail stations and travelers crossing the plains—especially in the area between Forts Bridger and Laramie in 1861-62—dictated the need for protection of travelers in that area. Consequently, when Hooper and West started for Washington, D.C., in April 1862, they were escorted by twenty mounted men under the command of Colonel Robert T. Burton of the Nauvoo Legion. Burton and his men returned to Salt Lake City on May 31.
[5] Brigham Young, Jr., Diary, 24 June 1862.
[6] Brigham Young, Jr., to Brigham Young, 24 June 1862.
[7] Brigham Young, Jr., Diary, 6 July 1862.
[8] Ibid., 4 July 1862.
[9] Brigham Young, Jr., to Brigham Young, 11 July 1862.
[10] Strained relations between England and America developed in 1862 in the wake of a series of Confederate victories in Virginia and talk that England might recognize the Confederacy and interfere in its behalf in the Civil War.
[11] In 1860 a change was made in the method of Church immigration. Prior to that time money had been sent east each year to purchase wagons and teams, which immigrants then drove to Salt Lake Valley. However, beginning in 1860 the Saints in Utah, being rich in cattle but poor in money, outfitted teams that were sent east loaded with merchandise that was sold in the eastern market and returned with the Church immigration. These "church trains" saved the Latter-day Saints from ten to thirty thousand dollars cash each year. See Leonard Arrington, *Great Basin Kingdom* (Cambridge, Massachusetts, 1958), pp. 205-211; also Brigham H. Roberts, *Comprehensive History of the Church* (Salt Lake City, 1930), 5:106-111.
[12] Brigham Young, Jr., to Brigham Young, 4 September 1862.
[13] Brigham Young, Jr., to Brigham Young, 13 October 1862.
[14] Ibid.
[15] Ibid.
[16] An effort by Brigham Jr. to avoid burdening the poor is suggested in his diary entry of September 9, 1862: "Sister Dawson brot up some dinner for T. O. King and me, I refused to eat, but she looked so pained that I did eat for I was hungry and I bless her for the food. It is not always that we get dinner, but when we do it tastes good. God bless the people; they are as kind to me as tho' I were their own relation, and nothing is too good for me, that their scanty means can get, so they think."
[17] Brigham Jr. did overcome the habit. It should be noted that interpretations and attitudes toward the Word of Wisdom have changed over the years. Brigham Young, for example, stressed the importance of adherence to the principle, both from an economic and spiritual standpoint, but did not make adherence a test of fellowship. Treatment of the subject may be found in Leonard J. Arrington, "An Economic Interpretation of the Word of Wisdom," *Brigham Young University Studies* 1 (Winter 1959): 37-49; and Paul H. Peterson, "An Historical Analysis of the Word of Wisdom" (Master's Thesis, Brigham Young University, 1972).
[18] Brigham Young, Jr., to Brigham Young, 13 October 1862.
[19] Brigham Young, Jr., to Brigham Young, 4 February 1863.

[20]Brigham Jr. had met Jules Remy, traveler and author of the book *Journey to Great Salt Lake City* on September 30, 1862, at the mission office in London: "Mr. Jules Remy came in the office wishing to get the *Star*. He is the same gentleman that has written a book on Utah. I handed him my card, and he professed himself very glad to have met me, inquired kindly after my father, and the general interest of Utah, and expressed himself decidedly in our favor. He took his departure leaving his address with me." Brigham Young, Jr., Diary.

[21]When Robert T. Burton's command of twenty men escorted William H. Hooper's party through the area of Indian troubles in Wyoming in April-May 1862, he was instructed by the Territorial Secretary, Frank Fuller, to extend his services to protect the mail route until relieved or the danger passed. Brigham Young, Jr., accompanied Burton as second in command for a short time, but becoming disabled, he was relieved of his duty and traveled to Washington, D.C., with Hooper instead. Hence the reference to pay in connection with Burton's command.

[22]When Congress enacted its first anti-polygamy legislation in 1862, the prevailing opinion in Utah was that the measure was unconstitutional, as it sought to regulate the Latter-day Saints in the practice of their religion, and therefore should be disregarded. With reference to this, Governor Stephen S. Harding in his message to the legislature on December 19, 1862, charged the people of Utah with lack of loyalty to the federal government.

[23]Due to Indian depredations and other complications, the incidence of mail not reaching its destination in pioneer Utah was high. Frequently more than one copy of a letter would be sent by different routes to guarantee its arrival in Utah.

[24]Brigham Young, Jr., Diary, 6 February 1863.
[25]Brigham Young, Jr., to Brigham Young, 6 February 1863.
[26]The circumstances in the 1863 arrest of Brigham Young were as follows: Rumor of an impending arrest of President Young by a military force from Camp Douglas for an alleged infringement of the anti-bigamy law of 1862 threatened a confrontation between civilian and military forces in Salt Lake City. To avoid this, a "friendly complaint" was filed against the Mormon leader, charging him with violation of the anti-bigamy law. The President was subsequently arrested and appeared in court, where his case was bound over for the next term. However, when the grand jury sat in 1864 it found no indictment against him and he was discharged. See B. H. Roberts, *Comprehensive History of the Church*, 5:28-30.

[27]Brigham Young, Jr., to Brigham Young, 22-25 April 1863.
[28]Florence, Nebraska, was the terminus of the railroad in 1863; from that point further travel west was by oxteam.
[29]Brigham Young, Jr., to Brigham Young, 23 May 1863.
[30]Brigham Young, Jr., to Brigham Young, 14 March 1863.
[31]Brigham Young, Jr., Diary, 26 April 1863.
[32]Brigham Young, Jr., to Brigham Young, 28 November 1864.
[33]Brigham Young, Jr., Diary, 27 August 1863.
[34]Ibid., 6 July 1862.
[35]Brigham Young, Jr., to Brigham Young, 12 November 1862.
[36]Brigham Young, Jr., to Brigham Young, 4 February 1863.
[37]Brigham Young, Jr., to Brigham Young, 22 April 1863.
[38]Brigham Young, Jr., to Brigham Young, 21 June 1863.
[39]Brigham Young, Jr., to Brigham Young, 5 July 1863.
[40]Ibid.
[41]Brigham Young, Jr., to Brigham Young, 21 June 1864.
[42]Brigham Young, Jr., to Brigham Young, 25 November 1865.
[43]The *Union Vedette* was a non-Mormon newspaper published at Fort Douglas. The first issue appeared November 30, 1863. On January 5, 1864, the *Vedette* became the first daily newspaper in Utah.

NOTES

⁴⁴Men of General Patrick E. Connor's command from Camp Douglas had discovered gold- and silver-bearing ore in Bingham Canyon west of Salt Lake City in 1863.

⁴⁵Big Canyon, east of Salt Lake City, was later named Parley's Canyon after Parley P. Pratt.

⁴⁶Brigham Young, Jr., Diary, 2 October 1862.

⁴⁷Address at general council of European Mission held in Birmingham, England, in January 1866. British Mission History, 5 January 1866. MS.

⁴⁸Brigham Young, Jr., to Brigham Young, 4 September 1862.
⁴⁹Brigham Young, Jr., Diary, 5 October 1862.
⁵⁰Brigham Young, Jr., to Brigham Young, 13 October 1862.
⁵¹Brigham Young, Jr., to Brigham Young, 18 May 1865.
⁵²Brigham Young, Jr., to Brigham Young, 7 June 1865.
⁵³Brigham Young, Jr., to Brigham Young, 19 September 1865.
⁵⁴Brigham Young, Jr., to Brigham Young, 7 March 1866.
⁵⁵Brigham Young, Jr., to Brigham Young, 19 September 1865.
⁵⁶Brigham Young, Jr., to Brigham Young, 20 February 1866.
⁵⁷Brigham Young, Jr., to Brigham Young, 16 March 1866.

⁵⁸At the time of its inception in 1856, the Republican Party announced as one of the planks in its platform the eradication of those twin relics of barbarism—slavery and polygamy. Following the U.S. Civil War, which terminated slavery, the nation's lawmakers turned their attention to the "strangling of the remaining twin." The best treatment of the subject is Richard Poll's "The Twin Relic: a Study of Mormon Polygamy and the Campaign by the Government of the United States for Its Abolition, 1852-1890" (Master's Thesis, Texas Christian University, 1939).

⁵⁹Brigham Young, Jr., to Brigham Young, 3 April 1866.

⁶⁰At this time, Utah was embroiled in its costliest Indian war. The Black Hawk War commenced in April 1865 in Sanpete County. When the conflict ended three years later, seventy-five settlers had been killed and twenty-five settlements abandoned in five counties. At one time some 2500 men of the territorial militia were in the field, and expenses were incurred in excess of one and a half million dollars.

⁶¹Brigham Young, Jr., to Brigham Young, 8 May 1866.
⁶²Brigham Young, Jr., to Brigham Young, 27 March 1866.
⁶³Brigham Young, Jr., Diary, 17 January 1866, 26 March 1866.
⁶⁴Brigham Young, Jr., to Brigham Young, 9 June 1866. Faced with the prospect of sending one company of emigrants on the *Constitution*—an inferior vessel—Brigham approached Guion and Company seeking to charter a better ship, the *John Bright*. At first the company "utterly refused" to consider his request, stating that they already had 700 passengers booked for the *John Bright*. "I went from their office feeling that if the Lord wanted our people to sail on the 'Constitution' (for I had found out that she was what they call a very wet ship) that He would temper the winds and the waves. I had scarcely got out of sight before Mr. Norris—Guion's business man—overtook me, stating that I might have the ship 'John Bright' . . . as fine a vessel as sails out of the port of L-pool." Brigham Young, Jr., to Brigham Young, 8 May 1866.

⁶⁵Brigham Young, Jr., to Brigham Young, 3 April 1866.
⁶⁶Brigham Young, Jr., Diary, 21 June 1866.
⁶⁷Brigham Young, Jr., to Brigham Young, 19 September 1866.
⁶⁸Brigham Young, Jr., to Brigham Young, 28 August 1866.
⁶⁹Brigham Young, Jr., Diary, 24-25 September 1866.
⁷⁰Ibid., 25 October 1866.
⁷¹Ibid., 15 February 1867.
⁷²Brigham Young, Jr., Diary, 5 May 1867.
⁷³Ibid., 5 June 1867.
⁷⁴Brigham Young, Jr., to Brigham Young, 5 June 1867.
⁷⁵Ibid., 6 June 1867.

JOHN WILLARD YOUNG

[1] Thomas L. Kane to Brigham Young, 12 October 1871. Brigham Young University, Provo, Utah.

[2] Wilford Woodruff, George Q. Cannon to Charles W. Penrose, 25 April 1888, Woodruff Letter Book, pp. 253-57.

[3] Although his methods of building Zion occasionally ran counter to those of his associates, and he ultimately fell short of his goal, John W. Young undeviatingly affirmed his dedication to the cause. To the First Presidency in 1887 he wrote, "I know I am plain spoken, and at times may seem ultra in expressions, and perhaps say things in a way that may not always be agreeable; but underneath these superficial expressions I have a most intense desire to serve the cause we love so well, and to labor for it in that way and manner that will best subserve the interest of our Heavenly Father." John W. Young to John Taylor and George Q. Cannon, 11 July 1887. John W.'s private secretary noted, "He often explained many things of the past, of his great love for this great work and this people how that all he was doing for it and them, and he wanted to place this great work in a better light to the people of the world." John M. Whitaker, Diary, 15 September 1888. University of Utah, Salt Lake City, Utah.

[4] John W. Young to Lorenzo Snow, 23 September 1898.

[5] Blessing given to John W. Young by Brigham Young, Heber C. Kimball, and Daniel H. Wells, reported by George D. Watt. John W. Young Papers.

[6] John W. Young to Brigham Young, 21 April 1863.

[7] John W. Young to Brigham Young, 24 June 1863.

[8] John W. Young to Brigham Young, 13 March 1864.

[9] John W. Young to Brigham Young, 11 April 1864.

[10] Instructions regarding the labors of John W. in England are noted in the letter of Brigham Young to Brigham Young, Jr., 22 January 1866.

[11] John W. Young to Brigham Young 9 May 1866. Even at the end of his life, living in near poverty, John W. appeared in public meticulously dressed in his frock coat and pin stripes.

[12] John W. Young to Brigham Young, 9 May 1866. Not a holograph, probably dictated to John T. Caine.

[13] Ibid.

[14] Ibid. See also Journal History, 27 March 1866.

[15] John W. Young to Brigham Young, 9 May 1866.

[16] Undated newsclipping from the Auburn *Advertiser* accompanying John W. Young's letter to Brigham Young, 9 May 1866. John W.'s errand in Auburn also received notice in a Cincinnati newspaper. See Journal History, 25 April 1866.

[17] John W. Young to Brigham Young, 9 May 1866.

[18] John W. Young to Brigham Young, 18 September 1866.

[19] John W. Young to Brigham Young, 15 December 1866.

[20] Ibid. Shortly before the end of his mission, while in France with his brothers Brigham Jr. and Oscar, John W. saw the French monarch Napoleon at the Paris Exhibition. In a letter to his father he gave his impressions of the king: "The more I see of the world and those that call themselves the wise and great of the earth, the more my heart beats with joy to know that there is something on the earth that is really and truly worth living for, for outside of the Kingdom it seems worse than dros to me. I must say tho' that the first person I thought of while looking at Napoleon was my dear Father, for the bearing and form were so much like yours that it brought immediately your form before me. Napoleon seemed much care-worn and looked to me as if he could not bear up the cares of state much longer, unless there should be a change for the better." John W. Young to Brigham Young, 18 April 1867.

[21] "John W. Young Interviewed," *Millennial Star* 35 (9 September 1873): 566.

[22] John W. Young to Brigham Young, 30 August 1873.

[23] Brigham Young to John W. Young, 13 November 1874. John W. Young Papers.

[24] John W. Young to Brigham Young, 21 August 1875. Sentiments of love and

esteem characterize John W. Young's writings to his parents. During his mission to England in 1866 he wrote to his father after a long delay: "I seat myself to write to you and it is with great pleasure that I do so because I not only love you as a Father but, respect and honor you as a Prophet of God. . . . I know that you have a great amount of business to continually tax your mind, therefore I do not wish to thrust my communications upon you any oftener than they will be acceptable; if I do not write often enough, all you have to do is to say the word and I will write more frequently than I have done for I always esteem it a great privilege to do so." John W. Young to Brigham Young, 22 August 1866. From New York City in June 1871 John W. penned these lines on the eve of his father's birthday: "I seat myself to pen a few lines in commemoration of the day and to show, although in a far distant city, my thoughts fly back to my dear mountain home to my father whom I honor, love, and desire to obey. The day has been crowded with business but nevertheless my remembrance of you has been in the foreground of everything for I reverence the anniversary of the day that gave you birth, and if my sincere prayers avail anything, your days will yet be many on the earth." John W. Young to Brigham Young, 1 June 1871.

[25] John W. Young to Brigham Young, 22 November 1875.
[26] John M. Whitaker, Diary, 11 February 1889. University of Utah. Those who knew John W. Young were impressed with his striking personality. Seven workers who had labored under him laying track for the Utah Central Railroad in 1869 publicly acknowledged him in the pages of the *Deseret News:* "We take this opportunity of making known to you the admiration we feel for you, as a brother and a gentleman, and for the devotion and gentlemanly manner in which you have looked after our comfort and happiness, and also for the example you have set us as a servant of God." *Deseret News,* 27 January 1870. John M. Whitaker wrote, "He is a wonderful man, kind, considerate, lovable, gracious, never knows defeat, takes his problems to the Lord, prays about them, seeks divine aid, and is always saying, 'Brother Whitaker, all is for the Kingdom of God.' At other times when aroused, he is like a lion, courageous, brave, fearless, proud, persuasive and very much misunderstood. It seems his great incentive is for human advancement and happiness. . . . He moves among great men with an ease I have seldom seen. One day while we were waiting at the elevator at Exchange Place, it happened to be full and as it passed by him, President Bell, Manager of the Manhatten Club, one of the most exclusive in New York, was asked by another gentleman, 'Mr. Bell, who was that gentleman waiting at the door of the elevator?' Mr. Bell answered, 'That was President Brigham Young's oldest son, and a more perfect gentleman I have never known.' " John M. Whitaker, Diary, 29 March 1889.
[27] John W. Young to Brigham Young, 22 November 1875.
[28] Brigham Young, Jr., Diary, 29 December 1875; 3 January 1876.
[29] Brigham Young, Jr., Diary, 14-15 March 1876.
[30] John W. Young to Brigham Young, 21 March 1876.
[31] This holograph letter is dated April 7, 1875, which is undoubtedly an error as to the year, since reference to the death of Joseph A. Young, who died August 5, 1875, would require a date after that event.
[32] John W. Young to Brigham Young, 10 November 1876.

BRIGHAM HEBER YOUNG

[1] Dennis Michael Quinn, "Organizational Development and Social Origins of the Mormon Hierarchy, 1832-1932: A Prosopographical Study" (Master's Thesis, University of Utah, 1973), p. 289.
[2] Heber Young, Diary, p. 9.
[3] Heber Young, Diary, 24 May 1867.
[4] Ibid., 26 June 1867.
[5] Ibid., 26-27 July 1867.
[6] Heber Young to George Q. Cannon, *Deseret News* 17:239.
[7] Journal History, 12 December 1868.

[8]Heber Young to Albert Carrington, 1 August 1869, *Millennial Star* 31:550.
[9]Heber Young to Brigham Young, 9 February 1870.
[10]The Godbeite movement in Utah had its beginnings as early as 1864, when a group of prominent Utah merchants and intellectuals became critical of temporal and economic policies of Brigham Young. After its leaders, Elias L. T. Harrison, William S. Godbe, Edward Tullidge, and Eli Kelsey, were excommunicated in 1869, they formed the Church of Zion, which sought to revitalize Mormonism but which, by the late 1870s, had dissipated itself in spiritualism and contention. The movement provided the initial thrust for the main nineteenth century anti-Mormon vehicles of dissent: the Liberal Institute, the Salt Lake *Tribune*, and the Liberal Party. See Ronald W. Walker, "The Godbeite Church of Zion" and "The Origins of the Godbeite Protest: Another View," Typescripts, Church Archives; and Grant H. Palmer, "The Godbeite Movement" (Master's Thesis, BYU, 1968).

OSCAR BRIGHAM YOUNG

[1]Oscar Brigham Young to Brigham Young, 29 April 1873.

ERNEST IRVING YOUNG

[1]Ernest I. Young to Brigham Young, 27 December 1876.
[2]On the settlement of the Brigham Young estate see Leonard J. Arrington, "The Settlement of the Brigham Young Estate, 1877-1879," *Pacific Historical Review*, XXI (February 1952), 1-20.
[3]Manuscript History of the British Mission, 31 March 1875.
[4]Ernest Young to Brigham Young, 19 March 1875.

WILLARD YOUNG

[1]Willard Young, address at the semicentennial celebration of Brigham Young University, October 15, 1925, *The Utah Genealogical and Historical Magazine*, 17 (January 1926):10-11.
[2]*Deseret News*, 20 (8 June 1871):220.
[3]Willard Young, address at the semicentennial celebration of Brigham Young University, October 15, 1925, *The Utah Genealogical and Historical Magazine*, 17 (January 1926):11. See also Leonard Arrington, "Willard Young: The Prophet's Son at West Point," *Dialogue* 4 (Winter, 1969):39.

[4]Willard Young, p. 13.
[5]Chicago *Evening Post*, as cited in Deseret News 20 (14 June 1871):234.
[6]Willard Young to Brigham Young, 3 June 1871.
[7]George Q. Cannon had been editor and publisher of the *Deseret News* since 1867.
[8]The "ring" mentioned here was the term applied by Mormons to some federal appointees, ex-officers of the California volunteers who had remained in Utah, lawyers, government employees, merchants, and government contractors, who sought to incite conflict between Mormons and the United States. Some of those who were particularly offensive to the Mormon community at this time were James B. McKean, U.S. judge; R. N. Baskin, U.S. district attorney; O. J. Hollister, U.S. revenue collector; J. P. Taggart, U.S. assessor; and Dennis J. Toohy, editor of the Corinne *Reporter*.
[9]The Utah Southern Railroad was a southern extension of the Utah Central line that linked Salt Lake City with the transcontinental line at Ogden. The Utah Southern was commenced May 1, 1871, and the first track was laid in June.

NOTES

¹⁰A Methodist camp meeting, the first of its kind held in Utah Territory, was opened in Salt Lake City on June 10, 1871. Directed by the Reverends Inskip, Boole, Macdonald, and Searles, meetings were held in a large tent every evening for eight days. Brigham Young advised the Latter-day Saints, particularly the young people who had never witnessed such a meeting, to attend. See Journal History, 8-11 June 1871.

¹¹Willard Young to Brigham Young, 11 June 1871.

¹²Willard Young to Brigham Young, 19 June 1871.

¹³Preparations for the Independence Day celebration in Salt Lake City in July 1871 took on a volatile atmosphere when the non-Mormon residents of the city announced their determination "to maintain their independence of priestly dictation" by celebrating the day separate from the Mormon community. As the Latter-day Saints proceeded with plans for the day, Daniel H. Wells, commander of the Utah militia, issued orders to the martial brass bands, one company of artillery with ordnance to fire salutes, a company of cavalry, and three companies of infantry to render such service during the day as assigned by the committee of arrangements. In response to this action, George S. Black, acting governor of the Territory, forbade "all persons except United States troops" from participating in "any military drill, muster, or parade of any kind," and directed General De Trobriand at Fort Douglas, east of the city, to enforce his order with the United States troops. As more temperate counsel prevailed, the companies of militia marched, but without arms, the artillery fired salutes, the bands played, and the U.S. troops were present, but only as spectators and the day passed without violence. Brigham H. Roberts, *Comprehensive History of the Church*, 5:357-60.

¹⁴Willard Young to Brigham Young, 9 December 1871. Holograph, Brigham Young University.

¹⁵One episode in the long Mormon-gentile conflict in Utah that brought charges of ecclesiastical domination on one hand and carpetbaggery on the other was the accusation of murder made against Brigham Young in 1871 during the term of James B. McKean, who had been appointed chief justice of Utah's Supreme Court in July 1870. The charge against Brigham Young was made by U.S. Acting District Attorney R. N. Baskin, on the strength of a confession by the notorious William Hickman, who had admitted numerous killings and sought to implicate others, including Brigham Young. However flimsy the evidence, there were those in Utah at the time who were eager to grasp at an opportunity to involve the Mormon Church leader in crime. The accusation against Brigham Young never came to trial due to the decision of the United States Supreme Court in the Englebrecht case, which overturned and invalidated the proceedings of the federal courts in Utah for a period of nearly two years prior to December 1871. See B. H. Roberts, *Comprehensive History of the Church*, 5:399-417; also Thomas G. Alexander, "Federal Authority Versus Polygamic Theocracy," *Dialogue* I (Autumn 1966): 85-100.

¹⁶Willard Young to Brigham Young, 9 March 1872.

¹⁷Willard Young to Brigham Young, 7 April 1872.

¹⁸Willard Young to Brigham Young, 12 May 1872.

¹⁹Willard Young to Brigham Young, 23 June 1872.

²⁰Willard Young to Brigham Young, 17 January 1873.

²¹Willard Young to Brigham Young, 5 April 1873.

²²Ibid.

²³Willard Young to Brigham Young, 21 May 1873.

²⁴Willard Young to Brigham Young, 16 November 1873.

²⁵Willard Young to Brigham Young, 22 May 1875.

²⁶On June 28, 1875, the Chicago *Times* commented on Willard Young's graduation: "A son of Brigham Young has graduated from the military academy at West Point, standing third in his class. It has been said that polygamy results in the impairment of the mental faculties of the offspring, but this does not seem to prove the theory." Cited in Journal History, 2 July 1875.

²⁷Willard Young to Brigham Young, 3 November 1875.

²⁸Brigham Young's "imprisonment" was an incident in the divorce case then being litigated between the President and Ann Eliza Young. In 1873 Ann Eliza Webb Dee

Young, a plural wife of Brigham Young—married April 6, 1868—had brought a suit for divorce against him. Evidence indicates that the case was instigated and prosecuted more in a spirit of extortion and persecution than to satisfy justice. When the case came before Judge James McKean on February 25, 1875, Brigham Young was ordered to pay the plaintiff $3,000 to defray legal expenses and $500 per month alimony, the legal fee to be paid within ten days and the alimony within twenty. Upon refusing to pay the amounts directed, Brigham Young was cited in contempt of court, fined $25, and imprisoned for twenty-four hours. Judge McKean was subsequently deposed from office for fanatical and extreme conduct, and the case of Young vs. Young was reviewed in November 1875 before Judge David B. Lowe, McKean's successor as chief justice. After hearing the case, Judge Lowe ruled that alimony could not be awarded unless a valid marriage existed, noting that plural marriages were not regarded as valid by the laws of the land. Soon after this, Judge Lowe resigned and was succeeded by J. Alexander White; but before White arrived in Utah, Judge Jacob Boreman reversed the Lowe decision and ordered Brigham Young imprisoned until the sum of $9,500 was paid. Since the court did not specify confinement in a jail, Brigham Young was placed under the custody of a U.S. marshal in his own home. On November 12, 1875, on a writ of *habeas corpus*, Judge White voided the action of Judge Boreman and Brigham Young was freed. However, since White had not been confirmed by the U.S. Senate, his appointment was voided after three months in Utah. His successor, Michael Schaeffer, reviewed the matter of alimony, which had accumulated to $18,000 by that time, and reduced it to $3,600 *pendente lite* (while the litigation continued). This amount was paid by Brigham Young in July 1876, in the face of an order for attachment of his property. The divorce case was finally tried in April 1877, when it was decreed that the polygamous marriage between the parties was null and void under the law of the land, and all orders of alimony not already paid were revoked. Brigham H. Roberts, *Comprehensive History of the Church*, 5:442-54. Also, Thomas G. Alexander, "Federal Authority Versus Polygamic Theocracy," *Dialogue* I (Autumn 1966): 85-100.

[29]Willard Young to Brigham Young, 8 December 1875.

[30]Willard Young to Brigham Young, 29 October 1876.

[31]That Brigham Young had already pursued a less rigid course in this matter is suggested by Brigham Young, Jr.'s diary entry of March 12, 1875: "Found my father in excellent spirits confident in God and willing to submit to his providences. He paid the 3000 $ to Anne Eliza's lawyers. And assures me that he will pay the $9500. alimony if necessary without any fuss. He says the Lord has given me all I have, if He permits this why should I complain, it will come back again four fold, and disgrace them."

[32]On April 16, 1884, six years after his father's death, Alfales Young married an Episcopalian girl, Ada Cottle, in Salt Lake City.

[33]Willard Young to Brigham Young, 29 October 1876.

[34]Ibid.

[35]Ibid.

[36]Willard Young to Brigham Young, 25 December 1876.

[37]Willard Young to Brigham Young, 4 June 1877.

[38]Willard Young to Brigham Young, 18 July 1877.

[39]Willard Young to Brigham Young, 29 July 1877.

[40]In 1862 the Morrisites, comprising some 600 persons under the leadership of a Welshman, Joseph Morris, and two aides, Richard Cook and John Banks, had founded a church and established a colony at Kington Fort, near the mouth of Weber Canyon in Weber County, Utah. Practicing joint ownership of property, and expecting an imminent return of Christ, members of the sect were repeatedly disappointed when several announcements of Christ's coming failed to materialize. As disillusioned members sought to withdraw from the colony and insisted upon taking their property with them, they were imprisoned. Subsequently, Morrisite leaders were summoned to appear in court, together with their prisoners, to show cause for their actions. However, the summons was rejected and the officiating marshal was ridiculed and informed that any further resort to legal process would be met with armed force. A short time later, a posse led by Robert T. Burton was dispatched to arrest Morris, Cook, and Banks. Upon reaching the fort on June 13,

Burton's troop met defiance, and a three-day armed conflict ensued, which resulted in the death of several persons, including Joseph Morris and John Banks. The Morrisite affair was revived during the Mormon-gentile conflict of 1876 when Robert Burton and Dr. Jeter Clinton (who had attended the wounded John Banks before he died) were charged with murder—Burton for killing a woman in the fort, and Clinton for "poisoning" Banks. Burton was subsequently acquitted, and Clinton's case was dismissed for lack of evidence. Brigham H. Roberts, *op. cit.*, 5:39-59.

MAHONRI MORIANCUMER YOUNG

[1] Mahonri M. Young to Brigham Young, 16 December 1876.

ALFALES YOUNG

[1] J. Cecil Alter, *Early Utah Journalism* (Salt Lake City, 1938), p. 278.
[2] Mahonri Mackintosh Young Papers, Brigham Young University.
[3] Alfales Young to John W. Young, 21 October 1876.
[4] Alfales Young to Brigham Young, 18 November 1876.
[5] Three factors suggest that the April 6 date on this letter is in error and should read October 6: First, the letter appears in the Brigham Young letter book in the chronological setting of October. Second, the letter refers to President Ulysses S. Grant's visit to Salt Lake City "this week"; President Grant arrived in Utah on October 3, 1875. Third, there is no letter of Brigham Young to Alfales that predates April 6, 1875, as Brigham Young's comment in the first paragraph of this letter demands.
[6] Brigham Young, Jr., recorded the meeting of Brigham Young and President Grant: "Prest B.Y. and numerous company went to Ogden on special at 9.30 a.m. He met president Grant. His car was attached. Meeting was cordial enough. But to my mind there was a great contrast in the two men. Father looked noble, kind and good and self possessed. Grant, rather surly disipated and slightly confused. The interview lasted best part of an hour; father directing his conversation to Mrs. Grant I chatted with Gen. Babcock and Ex Sect. Borie. On arr. at SLC Prest. Grant and party went to Walker hotel." Brigham Young, Jr., Diary, 3 October 1875.

BRIGHAM MORRIS YOUNG

[1] B. Morris Young, Undated four-page manuscript detailing his part in the beginning of the YMMIA movement, B. Morris Young Papers.
[2] Lorenzo and Harriet Snow to Brigham and Margaret Young, 27 March 1875.
[3] B. Morris Young, Diary, 30 August-2 September 1877.

ARTA DE CHRISTA YOUNG

[1] Arta De Christa Young to Brigham Young, 18 May 1875.
[2] Arta Young to Brigham Young, 6 June 1875.
[3] Arta Young to Brigham Young, 12 October 1875.
[4] On April 5, 1876, four powder magazines constructed of rock, cement, and iron, located on the hill a mile northeast of the temple block, exploded, striking fear into the hearts of the people, many of whom thought the day of judgment had come. Owned by the Hazard, DuPont, Oriental and California Powder companies, with agents in Salt Lake City, the magazines contained forty tons of powder at the time of their ignition. In the

wake of the explosion people panicked, women fainted, and teams stampeded, as the earth shook, buildings swayed, doors were torn from hinges, plaster crumbled from walls, ceilings fell, windows shattered, and a wide area of the city was showered with chunks of rock, iron, and broken glass. One rock weighing 115 pounds was catapulted more than a mile and fell through the roof, ceiling, and floor of Shingleton's saloon, burying itself in the ground beneath. Many residences received extensive damage. Four persons were killed and scores wounded. One woman pumping water at a well was killed instantly when a careening boulder passed through her body. The explosion, according to witnesses, immediately followed a rifle shot in the vicinity of the magazines by one of two boys who were driving cattle from City Creek Canyon to the city at the time. Both boys were killed and their bodies scattered over a wide area. A group of young men playing baseball on a flat eighty rods from the magazine were prostrated by the concussion. The Arsenal Hill explosion was regarded as Salt Lake City's worst disaster to that time. See Journal History, 5 April 1876, pp. 1-3.

JOSEPH DON CARLOS YOUNG

[1] For both sides of this incident consult the *Deseret News* and Salt Lake *Tribune*, 9-11 March 1886.
[2] Joseph Don Carlos Young, Diary, 23 April 1895, 11 and 13 December 1895.
[3] See footnote No. 28 under Willard Young.
[4] Don Carlos Young to Brigham Young, 20 December 1876.
[5] Don Carlos Young to Brigham Young, 19 June 1877.
[6] Don Carlos Young to Brigham Young, 19 July 1877.
[7] Following the dedication of the St. George Temple in April 1877, Brigham Young called for "a more perfect order of the priesthood." This resulted in a general reorganization that saw the number of stakes and wards in the Church double, and a general perfecting of policy regarding priesthood and church government functions.

LORENZO DOW YOUNG

[1] See note 31 under Willard Young.
[2] Lorenzo D. Young to Brigham Young, 14 November 1876.
[3] Lorenzo D. Young to Brigham Young, 2 July 1877.
[4] Ibid.

FERAMORZ LITTLE YOUNG

[1] Feramorz L. Young, Diary, 13-26 January 1872.
[2] Don Carlos Young's copy of the Weisbach text, with his name and the date October 4, 1878, written in the front, is located in the Reception Hall bookcase in the Beehive House in Salt Lake City.
[3] Another witness of the burial of Feramorz Young was Frederick Ober of the Washington Museum of Natural History, later the Smithsonian Institute, who had been sent by Charles Hallock, editor of *Forest and Stream*, to explore the Caribbean area. In an article titled "Adios" in the March 16, 1882, issue of *Forest and Stream*, Ober noted, after describing his travels in Mexico, that much of Mexico and Cuba were disease-ridden. He added, "We were saddened and reminded that the climate of Mexico had some bad spots in it, by the death of one of our number, only one day out of Havana. We buried him next day at sea, almost within sight of the Florida coast, right abreast of Indian River,

NOTES

this young man, a son of Brigham Young; a right good young man, and whom we regretted should die such an untimely death."

[4]*Deseret News*, 23 (September 28, 1874): 556.

[5]Since the Navy, following the British precedent, preferred young midshipmen, sixteen was not an unusually young age for those entering the Naval Academy. Several of Fera's classmates were fourteen.

[6]The United Order established during the winter of 1873-74 was the Latter-day Saint answer to the national economic panic of 1873 and the depression that followed. The Orders that developed in Utah during the next decade were characterized by varying degrees of community cooperation. These ranged from complete consecration of private property and labor, such as practiced in Orderville, Utah, to community ownership and operation of cooperative enterprises, as practiced in larger cities of the Territory. See Leonard J. Arrington, *Great Basin Kingdom*, chapter 11.

[7]Feramorz L. Young to Brigham Young, 24 October 1874.

[8]Feramorz to Lucy Decker Young, 7 November 1874.

[9]Ibid.

[10]Feramorz to Brigham Young, 10 January 1875.

[11]Feramorz to Brigham Young, 24 October 1874.

[12]Fera's ability in drawing is reflected in a Deseret Agricultural and Manufacturing Society Diploma awarded to Feramorz L. Young for the "best line shaded drawing of machinery" at the annual fair held in Salt Lake City, October 4, 1879. The document is in the Church Archives.

[13]Feramorz L. Young to Brigham Young, 2 October 1875.

[14]Brigham Young Jr., Diary, 20 January 1876.

[15]The letter written with the new "type-writer" appears to be double spaced in all-capital, gothic face about the size of elite typewriter type.

[16]Feramorz Young to Brigham Young, 5 November 1876.

[17]Ibid.

[18]Feramorz Young to Brigham Young, 2 December 1876.

[19]Feramorz Young to Brigham Young, 11 December 1876.

[20]Joseph Don Carlos Young to Brigham Young, 19 July 1877.

[21]Feramorz to Brigham Young, 21 June 1877.

Biographical Appendix

The biographical data given here, intended to provide only minimal essential information, has been derived almost exclusively from the following sources: *Biographical Record of Salt Lake City and Vicinity* (Chicago: National Historical Record Company, 1902); Mark M. Boatner III, *The Civil War Dictionary* (New York: David McKay Co., 1961); H. C. Colles, ed., *Grove's Dictionary of Music and Musicians*, 6 vols. (New York: Macmillan Co., 1935); Frank Esshom, *Pioneers and Prominent Men of Utah* (Salt Lake City, 1913); Andrew Jenson, *Church Chronology*, 2nd ed. revised and enlarged (Salt Lake City: Deseret News, 1914); Andrew Jenson, *Latter-day Saint Biographical Encyclopedia*, 4 vols. (Salt Lake City: Deseret News, 1936); Allen Johnson, ed., *Dictionary of American Biography*, 11 vols. (New York: Charles Scribner's Sons, 1964); The Journal History of the Church of Jesus Christ of Latter-day Saints, 1830 to the present, Historical Department of the Church, Salt Lake City; *The National Cyclopedia of American Biography* (James T. White and Co., 1891); Brigham H. Roberts, *A Comprehensive History of The Church of Jesus Christ of Latter-day Saints*, 6 vols. (Salt Lake City: Deseret News, 1930); Orson F. Whitney, *History of Utah*, 4 vols. (Salt Lake City: George Q. Cannon and Sons, 1892-1904); and temple records and family genealogies filed in the Genealogical Society of The Church of Jesus Christ of Latter-day Saints, Salt Lake City, Utah.

ALLRED, JAMES (1784-1876), a native of North Carolina, was a member of Zion's Camp and served as a bodyguard of Joseph Smith. After coming to Utah in 1851, he was one of the founders of Spring City, Utah, and became presiding elder of that settlement.

ANGELL, TRUMAN O. (1810-1887), as Church architect, designed several important Utah buildings, including the Salt Lake Temple and the Lion House. A brother of Mary Ann Angell Young, Brigham Young's wife, he was born in Providence, Rhode Island.

ARNOLD, ORSON P. (1838-1912), was born in Amboy, New York. In 1849 he moved with his family to California and returned to Utah three years later. He was with Lot Smith's command in the Utah War and was accidentally shot, which resulted in his left leg being rigid at the knee joint the remainder of his life. A skilled horseman, he was employed by Brigham Young to drive his carriage. Arnold saw service in Sanpete and Sevier counties during the Black Hawk Indian War. He helped establish the Salt Lake City Street Railway and was its superintendent for many years.

ATKIN, GEORGE (1836-1899), was born in England and came to Utah in 1851. He was superintendent of the Tooele ZCMI for many years. As People's Party candidate for representative to the territorial legislature in 1874, Atkin won a contested election from Liberal candidate, Erastus S. Foote.

BIOGRAPHICAL APPENDIX

BANKS, JOHN (1806-1862), was born in England, where he held leading positions in the Church before he immigrated to America in 1850. After arriving in Utah he settled in Pleasant Grove. In 1862 he joined the Morrisites and was killed during the confrontation in Weber County in June that year.

BATES, GEORGE C. (? -1886), was born in New York and moved to Michigan in 1834. He was appointed U.S. district attorney for Utah and headed the defense in the 1875-76 trials of John D. Lee for complicity in the Mountain Meadows Massacre.

BEATIE, PHEBE YOUNG (1854-1931), youngest child of Brigham Young and Clarissa Ross, married Walter J. Beatie 7 January 1872.

BEATIE, WALTER J. (1850-1928), married Phebe Louisa Young, youngest child of Clarissa Ross and Brigham Young, on 7 January 1872. He was a missionary in England 1877-1879. After his return he was secretary-treasurer of ZCMI. He was Utah State bank examiner for eight years and bishop of the Salt Lake City 17th Ward.

BENEDICT, JOSEPH M. (1844-1896), a physician and surgeon, was born in Freeport, Long Island, New York. In 1870 he came to Utah, where he founded the Holy Cross Hospital in Salt Lake City.

BENSON, CHARLES A., a seventy, arrived in England as a missionary in July 1863. Ten years later he shot a man in Logan, Utah, during a drunken spree. On 18 February 1873, after eluding his pursuers four days, he was caught and lynched by an irate mob.

BERNHISEL, JOHN M. (1799-1881), was Utah's first delegate to Congress. He was born in Pennsylvania. After joining the Church he presided over the New York Branch before moving to Nauvoo, Illinois, in 1843. He came to Utah in 1851 and was territorial delegate to Congress eight years.

BLACK, GEORGE S., was private secretary of Utah's Governor J. Wilson Shaffer. Upon the death of the governor in 1870, Black was appointed territorial secretary.

BLACK HAWK (? -1870), Ute Indian chief, was the leading spirit behind the war bearing his name that commenced in Sanpete County, Utah, in April 1865. Before the termination of hostilities three years later, seventy-five settlers had been killed and twenty-five settlements abandoned in five Utah counties. Brigham Young regarded him as Utah's "most formidable foe among the redmen."

BOOLE, W. H., was one of seven Methodist ministers who held a camp meeting in Salt Lake City in June 1871.

BOREMAN, JACOB S. (1830-1913), born in West Virginia, was associate justice of Utah Territory from 1873 to 1880 and 1885 to 1889. Appointed to the Third Judicial District, he presided at both trials of John D. Lee at Beaver in 1875-76. In 1889 he moved to Ogden, where he resided until his death.

BRONSON, LEWIS, was appointed bishop of Fillmore, Utah, at the general conference in April 1855.

BUCK, DUDLEY (1839-1909), was born in Hartford, Connecticut. He studied music in Leipzig, Dresden, and Paris, 1858-1862. After returning to America, he established a remarkable reputation as an organist and composer and played in almost every city of importance in the country. He was organist at St. James Episcopal Church in Chicago, St. Paul's and the famous Music Hall in Boston, and the Holy Trinity Church in Brooklyn. He was a prolific composer, treating almost every class of composition.

BULLOCK, THOMAS (1816-1885), was born in Leeds, England. Two years after his conversion to the Church in 1841, he immigrated to America. An excellent penman, Bullock held several important church and civic clerical positions in Nauvoo and Salt Lake City. He was clerk of the Utah Territorial House of Representatives, Salt Lake County recorder, and chief clerk in the Church Historian's Office.

BURTON, CHARLES S. (1855- ?), was born in Salt Lake City, a son of Robert T. Burton.

He served as a missionary in Australia from 1875-1877 and subsequently was business manager of the Salt Lake *Herald,* manager of the Salt Lake Theater, and cashier of the State Bank of Utah.

BURTON, ROBERT T. (1821-1907), was born in Amersberg, Canada. After his arrival in Salt Lake Valley in 1848, he served in the Utah militia in early campaigns against hostile Indians. In 1856 he accompanied the relief force that rescued suffering handcart companies on the plains. As a captain of cavalry he participated in the Utah War and in 1862 was assigned to protect the mail route on the plains. Later that year he commanded the posse in the Morrisite conflict in Weber County. He served several terms of public office, including constable, deputy marshal, sheriff, assessor, collector of internal revenue, Salt Lake City councilman, territorial legislator and regent of the University of Deseret. He was also bishop of the 15th Ward in Salt Lake City. In 1884 he was named first counselor to the Presiding Bishop of the Church, William B. Preston.

CAINE, JOHN T. (1829-1911), was born on the Isle of Man and was converted to the Church in New York City in 1847. Arriving in Salt Lake City in 1852, he taught school and identified with the Deseret Dramatic Association. Following a mission to Hawaii in the early 1850s, he became one of Brigham Young's private clerks and assisted in the management of the President's business affairs. He played leading roles in the Salt Lake Theater and assisted Hiram B. Clawson in its management. In 1866 he went to New York to help with Church immigration. Subsequently, he was elected recorder of Salt Lake City, was a regent of the University of Deseret, and served on the Salt Lake Stake high council. Elected Utah's delegate to Congress in 1883, he served during the five succeeding sessions of Congress.

CALDER, DAVID O. (1823-1884), was converted to the Church in Scotland and immigrated to Utah in 1853. He was employed as a bookkeeper in the office of the Trustee-in-Trust of the Church in 1855 and two years later became chief clerk, a position he held until 1867. While in the Trustee's office he organized the accounting and record system of the Church. He was territorial treasurer from 1859-1870; freight and passenger agent for the Utah Central Railroad; and after a mission to Scotland, business manager and managing editor of the *Deseret News.* He later served as a director and secretary-treasurer of ZCMI.

CANNON, GEORGE Q. (1827-1901), was born in Liverpool, England. Converted to the Church in 1840, he immigrated to America two years later. As a missionary in 1850 he translated the Book of Mormon into the Hawaiian language. At various times he edited the *Western Standard, Deseret News, Juvenile Instructor,* and *Millennial Star.* In 1859 he was called to the Council of Twelve. He presided over the European Mission from 1860 to 1862 and after his return was private secretary to Brigham Young. During most of the 1870s he was Utah's delegate to Congress. After the death of Brigham Young he was appointed a counselor in the First Presidency. In addition to his Church assignments, he directed or administered several businesses, including the Union Pacific Railroad, ZCMI, Utah Sugar Company, and Zion's Savings Bank and Trust.

CARELESS, GEORGE E. P. (1839-1932), was born in London, England. After joining the Church, he immigrated to Utah in 1864 and became director of the Salt Lake Theater orchestra and the Tabernacle Choir. He was a partner with David O. Calder in a Salt Lake City music business and assisted in the publication of the *Musical Times.* In 1879 he organized a private orchestra; he later taught vocal and instrumental music at the University of Deseret.

CARRINGTON, ALBERT (1813-1889), was a native of Royalton, Vermont. A graduate of Dartmouth College, he subsequently taught school and studied law in Pennsylvania. He joined the Church in 1841 and was secretary to Brigham Young for twenty years; he also edited the *Deseret News.* He presided over the European Mission on four occasions: 1868-1870, 1871-1873, 1875-1877, and 1880-1882.

CARRINGTON, BRIGHAM W., son of Albert Carrington, was a missionary in England from 1872-1876.

CLAWSON, ALICE YOUNG (1839-1874), daughter of Brigham Young and Mary Ann Angell, was married to Hiram B. Clawson 26 October 1856 and became the mother of four children.

CLAWSON, HIRAM B. (1826-1912), was born in Utica, New York. After joining the Church he moved to Nauvoo, Illinois, in 1841. As a young man of twenty-two he had charge of the first construction work done by the Church in Salt Lake Valley. He was employed as private secretary and office manager for Brigham Young and was eventually entrusted with the management of the President's entire private business affairs. He directed the construction and management of the Salt Lake Theater and performed as an actor on its stage. In 1865 he assisted in founding the merchant firm of Eldredge and Clawson. A few years later he accepted the management of ZCMI. In addition to his business activities, he was bishop of the Salt Lake City 12th Ward and financial agent of the Church. Two of his four wives, Alice and Emily, were daughters of Brigham Young.

CLAWSON, NABBIE HOWE YOUNG (1852-1894), daughter of Brigham Young and Clara Decker Young, was married to Orson Spencer Clawson 15 February 1876.

CLAWSON, ORSON SPENCER (1852-1916), married Nabbie Howe Young, daughter of Brigham Young, 15 February 1876. He was the eastern buyer for ZCMI and ran a large wholesale dry goods establishment in Salt Lake City.

CLAWSON, RUDGER (1857-1943), was a member of the Council of the Twelve from 1898 until his death. At eighteen years of age he became private secretary to John W. Young. While laboring as a missionary in Georgia in 1879, he witnessed the shooting of his missionary companion by a mob. During the plural marriage crusade of the 1880s, he was convicted and served three years in the Utah penitentiary. He was president of the Box Elder Stake prior to his appointment to the apostleship in 1898.

CLINTON, JETER (? -1892), a doctor and druggist, arrived in Utah in 1850. For many years he served as a Salt Lake City councilor and alderman. Beginning in 1869 he operated a resort on the south shore of Great Salt Lake, which later became a stopping place of the overland stage.

COBB, CHARLOTTE, was a sister of James T. Cobb. A pianist, she entertained Brigham Young and guests at a special dinner honoring John M. Bernhisel in Salt Lake City 31 August 1855.

COBB, JAMES T. (1833-1910), was born in Massachusetts and educated at Dartmouth College. A newspaperman and writer, he was a personal friend of Oliver Wendell Holmes. He came to Utah in 1858 with his mother, who was a Mormon. His daughter, Luella, married John W. Young in 1877, and later, Nathaniel M. Brigham.

CONNOR, PATRICK E. (1820-1891), born in Ireland, was a veteran of the Mexican War and was wounded at Buena Vista. Upon the outbreak of the Civil War he organized the 3rd California Volunteers and was assigned to Utah, where he arrived in 1862 at the head of three companies of infantry and two of cavalry. Sent to guard the telegraph line and mail route from Indians, Connor was regarded locally as a spy for the government. In January 1863 he led an expedition against marauding Indians along the overland trail, which resulted in the killing of some three hundred Bannock and Snake Indians near Franklin, Washington Territory (now Idaho). Breveted brigadier general in 1863, Connor retired three years later and engaged in mining in Utah.

CROXALL, CAROLINE YOUNG (1851-1903), third child of Brigham Young and Emily Dow Partridge, was married to Mark Croxall 7 October 1868.

CROXALL, MARK (1844-1887), was born in Gresley, England, and came to Utah in 1860. He married Caroline Young, daughter of Brigham Young and Emily Dow Partridge, on 7 October 1868. Croxall was a missionary to Australia in 1876; he was employed as telegrapher for the Deseret Telegraph Company and as a merchant and bookkeeper at ZCMI.

CUSHING, JAMES A. (1844-1912), a native of England, was employed in Brigham Young's office for many years. In October 1874, when Deputy U.S. Marshal Arthur Pratt served a summons requesting Brigham Young to appear as a witness before the grand jury, he learned that the President was ill; however, Pratt persisted in an effort to personally serve the summons and obtained the assistance of U.S. Marshal George Maxwell. When the officers arrived at Brigham Young's residence, the gatekeeper, Joseph Shaw, refused them entrance. An altercation ensued in which James Cushing and Shaw forcibly "assisted Maxwell off the porch." Subsequently, both men were arrested for resisting the U.S. marshal.

DE TROBRIAND, PHILIP REGIS DENIS DE KERENDERN (1816-1897), was born in France and was a veteran of the U.S. Civil War. General De Trobriand was acting commander at Fort Douglas, Utah, in 1870-71.

DECKER, VILATE YOUNG (1830-1902), daughter of Brigham Young and Miriam Works, was married to Charles F. Decker 4 February 1847.

DRAKE, THOMAS J., a resident of Michigan, was appointed associate justice of Utah Territory in 1862. In 1863, along with Governor Stephen Hardy and Judge Charles Waite, he was the subject of a petition for removal from office for malfeasance.

DRUCE, JOHN (1818-1897), was counselor in the Salt Lake City 12th Ward for twenty years beginning in 1877. As a carpenter, he was employed on the temple block and assisted in construction of the Salt Lake Theater. In 1876-77 he was sent to the eastern states, where he presided over the Church units in New York, New Jersey, and Connecticut.

DUNFORD, ALMA B. (1850-1919), was born in Trowbridge, England, and immigrated to the United States as a child. A prominent Utah pioneer dentist, he married Susa Young, daughter of Brigham Young and Lucy Bigelow, on 1 December 1872. They were divorced in 1877.

DUNFORD, SUSA AMELIA YOUNG (1856-1933), oldest of three daughters born to Brigham Young and Lucy Bigelow Young, was married to Alma B. Dunford on 1 December 1872; they were divorced in 1877. She was married to Jacob F. Gates on 5 January 1880.

DURRANT, THOMAS C. (1820-1885), was vice-president and principal promoter of the Union Pacific Railroad.

EICHBERG, JULIUS (1824-1898), composer, was born in Duesseldorf, Germany. He studied the violin at Wuerzburg and Brussels and in 1846 was appointed professor of the violin in Geneva. He immigrated to America in 1856 and three years later settled in Boston. He subsequently founded the Boston Conservatory of Music, which for many years was the foremost violin school in America. His compositions include four operettas.

ELDREDGE, HORACE (1816-1888), was a member of the First Council of the Seventy from 1854-1888. Born in Brutus, New York, he joined the Church in 1836. After arriving in the Salt Lake Valley in 1848, he served as marshal of Utah Territory, assessor and collector of taxes, and brigadier general in the militia. In 1852 he was appointed general Church immigration agent. Four years later he joined with William H. Hooper in a Salt Lake City mercantile business. He was regarded as one of the community's most able businessmen. He helped establish ZCMI and became a director of that institution, as well as the Deseret National Bank and the First National Bank of Ogden.

ELLERBECK, THOMAS W. (1829-1895), was born in Pendleton, England, and immigrated to Utah in 1851. He was a talented penman, bookkeeper, and mathematician whose services were used extensively by Brigham Young. He had charge of all business affairs attendant to Brigham Young's railroad contracts and directed the construction of the first

BIOGRAPHICAL APPENDIX

Salt Lake City waterworks and gas company. He contributed to early Utah horticulture and agriculture by establishing the first nursery for the sale of plants and trees.

ELLSWORTH, ELIZABETH YOUNG (1825-1903), oldest child of Brigham Young, was married to Edmund Ellsworth 10 July 1842.

EMERSON, PHILIP H., from Michigan, was appointed associate justice of Utah Territory in 1873. He was judge of the third district court in Utah during the Ann Eliza Young divorce case and litigation of the Brigham Young estate.

EMERY, GEORGE W. (1833-1909), was Utah governor from 1875-1880.

EMPEY, NELSON (1837-1904), was bishop of the Salt Lake City 13th Ward from 1890-1904. He was a bodyguard of Brigham Young during the Utah War, was a missionary to the Indians, and engaged in military campaigns involving Indians of the Territory. In March 1865 he married Ella Elizabeth Young, oldest daughter of Brigham Young and Emmeline Free. He was a missionary to Canada and Great Britain. He contracted a section of the transcontinental railroad through Utah and was president of the Deseret Agricultural and Manufacturing Society.

FELT, NATHANIEL H. (1816-1887), was born in Salem, Massachusetts, where he became president of the branch after joining the Church in the early 1840s. Prior to his arrival in Salt Lake City in 1850, he directed affairs of the Church in St. Louis. In Utah he served as a Salt Lake City alderman, territorial legislator, and chaplain of the Utah militia. He directed Church immigration in New York in 1854-55, and a decade later was laboring as a missionary in England. For many years he managed a grain and produce business in Utah.

FERGUSON, JAMES F. (1828-1863), soldier, actor, orator, and lawyer, was born in Belfast, Ireland. He served in the Mormon Battalion and eventually became adjutant-general of the Utah militia. He was sheriff of Salt Lake County and provided military escort service for Brigham Young in his travels. He guarded the Beehive House during the President's absence at the time of the arrival of Johnston's army in 1858. Ferguson was a member of the Utah legislature and the Deseret Dramatic Association and assisted in founding and publishing the *Mountaineer*. He was a missionary in England 1854-1856.

FIELDING, AMOS (1792-1875), was an ink manufacturer in Salt Lake City beginning in 1869. He was also a member of the Salt Lake City School of the Prophets.

FLINT, KATE, operated a Salt Lake City house of ill-fame, which was abated in 1874 by order of city alderman Jeter Clinton. The resulting court case, Flint vs. Clinton, was the last adjudicated by Judge James B. McKean prior to his dismissal.

FOOTE, ERASTUS S., was Liberal Party candidate for Tooele County representative to the Territorial Legislature in 1874; he lost the contested election to George Atkin. In October 1874 he was appointed probate judge of Tooele County by acting governor George Black.

FOX, JESSE W. (1819-1894), surveyed several Utah cities, including Salt Lake City, Provo, Ogden, and Logan. He also located and surveyed the principal canals of Utah and accompanied Brigham Young on exploration trips to select sites for settlements. Fox was born in Adams, New York, where he taught school prior to moving west. In addition to his surveying work, he was chief engineer of the Utah Central and Utah Southern railroads.

FOX, JESSE W., JR. (1852-1928), was a surveyor, farmer, miner, and Salt Lake City businessman. He was counselor in the Salt Lake City 14th Ward bishopric, 1896-1906.

FREE, FINLEY C. (1838-1866), was a missionary in Europe from 1863-1865. After his return he joined the Salt Lake City police force.

FREEZE, JAMES P. (1834-1919), was born in Pennsylvania. He joined the Church in 1861 and that year came to Utah, where he became proprietor of the 13th Ward Co-op store.

He labored as a missionary in England and was a member of the Salt Lake Stake high council.

FULLER, FRANK, was appointed Utah territorial secretary by Abraham Lincoln in 1861 and removed from office by the same authority in 1863. Prior to the arrival of Governor John W. Dawson in the Territory in 1861, Fuller served as acting governor.

GIBBS, ISAAC L., from Nebraska, was appointed U.S. marshal for Utah Territory in 1862. He was the officiating officer in the 1863 arrest of Brigham Young on charges of violation of the federal anti-bigamy law of 1862.

GIBSON, DAVID, a seventy, arrived in England as a missionary in September 1862. For a time he was president of the Bedfordshire Conference.

GRANT, GEORGE D. (1812-1876), was a brother of Jedediah M. Grant. Born in Windsor, New York, he served as a bodyguard to Joseph Smith in Nauvoo. After coming to Utah in 1848, he was a captain of the Minute Men in early Utah Indian campaigns. Grant served as a missionary in England from 1854 to 1856. His daughter, Thalia Elizabeth, married Joseph A. Young.

GRANT, ULYSSES S. (1822-1885), Civil War general and president of the United States, visited Salt Lake City in October 1875. He was the only president of the United States whom Brigham Young personally met.

GREEN, ALPHONSO (1810-1875), was born in Brookfield, New York. He came to Utah with the Mormon pioneers of 1847 and settled in American Fork, where he was a cattleman.

GROESBECK, NICHOLAS, a seventy, arrived in England as a missionary in October 1865. He accompanied Oscar B. Young home from England in May 1867.

GROO, ISAAC (? -1895), was a missionary in Australia, 1875-1877. He was later a regent of the University of Deseret.

HARDING, STEPHEN S., an attorney from Indiana, was appointed governor of Utah Territory by President Abraham Lincoln in 1862 but was removed from office a year later.

HARDY, MILTON H. (1844-1905), was called by Brigham Young to assist in the organization of Young Men's Mutual Improvement Associations in Latter-day Saint settlements in 1875-76. During the last seven years of his life he was a member of the YMMIA general board.

HARRINGTON, LEONARD (1816-1883), was born in New Lisbon, New York. He was justice of the peace in Nauvoo, Illinois, and crossed the plains to Utah in 1847. Among the first settlers of American Fork, Utah, he served the community for thirty years as bishop, mayor, and postmaster.

HATCH, ABRAM (1830-1901), settled in Lehi, Utah, and operated a freighting business between Utah and the Missouri River. He served as presiding bishop of Wasatch County from 1867 to 1877 and as president of Wasatch Stake from 1877 to 1901.

HEMPSTEAD, CHARLES H. (? -1879), a Salt Lake City lawyer, was employed as an attorney for Brigham Young.

HILLS, LEWIS (1836-1915), was born in Massachusetts. After his conversion to Mormonism, he came to Utah in 1862. He was employed by Hooper, Eldredge and Company, and later the Deseret National Bank, where he became cashier, president, and chairman of the board of directors.

HOLLADAY, BEN (1819-1887), born in Kentucky, served under General Alexander W. Doniphan during the Mormon difficulties in Missouri. He freighted supplies to the army in Santa Fe during the Mexican War, and afterward to Utah, where he met Brigham Young. Holladay eventually bought out the Russell, Majors and Waddell Pony Express and Overland Stage line and expanded it to a 3300-mile business. Many of his superintendents, drivers, and riders were Mormons.

HOOPER, WILLIAM H. (1813-1882), was Utah's second territorial delegate to the U.S. Congress. Born in Maryland, he was engaged in the mercantile business and was a steamboat captain on the Mississippi River prior to moving to Utah. He represented Utah in four sessions of Congress beginning in 1859. His seat in the House of Representatives was contested by the Liberal candidate, William McGrorty, in 1867. Hooper was one of Utah's prominent bankers and became superintendent and president of ZCMI. His daughter Harriet married Brigham Young's son Willard.

HUNTER, EDWARD (1793-1883), was born in Newtown, Pennsylvania. After joining the Church in 1840 he moved to Nauvoo, where he provided substantial financial assistance to the Church and was a member of the city council and a bishop. After crossing the plains with the pioneers of 1847, he was appointed presiding bishop of the Church in 1851, a position he held until his death.

HUNTER, EDWARD (1821- ?), a son of William Hunter, served in the Mormon Battalion; he was bishop of the Grantsville (Utah) Ward from 1877 to 1888.

INGALLS, RUFUS (1820-1893), was a graduate of the United States Military Academy in 1843 and fought in the Mexican and Civil wars; in the latter war he was a Union general. In 1883 he retired from the army with the rank of brigadier general. He was with Colonel Edward J. Steptoe for eight months in 1854-55 in Salt Lake City, where he met Brigham Young. In 1866, during an inspection tour of the West for the Quartermaster Department of the Army, Ingalls again visited Salt Lake City and issued a report on Camp Douglas.

IVIE, JAMES (? -1866), was residing at Springville, Utah, when his interference in an Indian family quarrel, which resulted in a death, precipitated the Walker Indian War of 1853. Ivie was killed in 1866 near Fillmore, Utah, during the Black Hawk Indian War by Indians as they drove away some 300 head of cattle and horses.

JACK, JAMES (1829-1911), was born in Scotland and immigrated to Utah in 1853. He was employed as a clerk in the office of Brigham Young and succeeding Church presidents. He was also director of the Saltair resort west of Salt Lake City.

JENNINGS, THOMAS W. (1854-1908), was a son of William Jennings. While laboring as a missionary in England in 1872, he was invited to accompany George A. Smith and party to Palestine as a secretary. He was one of the founders of the Utah Commercial and Savings Bank.

JENNINGS, WILLIAM (1823-1886), Utah businessman and mayor of Salt Lake City from 1882-1885, was born in Yardley, England. He was baptized in 1852 after he had immigrated to America, married a Mormon girl, and moved to Salt Lake City. Beginning in Utah with a butchery shop and tannery, Jennings became one of the West's leading businessmen. In 1864 he built the Eagle Emporium in Salt Lake City, operating a merchandising business that eventually amounted to two million dollars annually. He assisted in organizing the Utah Central and Utah Southern railroads and was one of the founders and directors of the Deseret National Bank and ZCMI.

JONES, DANIEL W. (1830-1915), assisted in translating the Book of Mormon into the Spanish language in 1874-75. A veteran of the Mexican War, in 1875-76 he led an exploring party into south-central Arizona in search of a convenient access route to Mexico. He performed significant missionary service among the Indians.

KANE, THOMAS L. (1822-1883), was an ardent Free Soiler who wrote numerous newspaper articles advocating the abolition of slavery. Commissioned a lieutenant colonel, he fought in the Civil War and was wounded at Dranesville in December 1861. Promoted to brigadier general, he commanded a brigade at Chancellorsville. He contracted pneumonia just before Gettysburg but resumed his command on the second day of the battle, although too weak to sit on his horse. Due to ill health, he resigned from the army in November 1863. A close friend of Brigham Young and the Mormon people, Kane was instrumental in the peace negotiations that preceded the termination of the Utah War. Still convalescing from Civil War wounds, he visited Utah, accompanied by his wife and two sons, during the winter of 1872-73, part of which time he spent with Brigham Young in St. George.

KELSEY, ELI (1819-1885), was born in Ohio and taught school in Nauvoo, Illinois. While serving as a missionary in England in the late 1840s, he was assistant editor of the *Millennial Star*. In 1869 he joined the Godbeites and was excommunicated from the Church. During the remainder of his life he was engaged in a drugstore operation and mining in Ogden, Utah, and the real estate business in Salt Lake City. Having married plurally, he was under indictment for unlawful cohabitation at the time of his death.

KIMBALL, HEBER C. (1801-1868), was born in Sheldon, Vermont, and joined the Church in April 1832. He was a member of Zion's Camp in 1834 and performed extensive missionary labor for the Church, including a trip to England with the first missionaries to that land. He was called to the Quorum of the Twelve Apostles when that body was first organized in February 1835. From 1848 until his death twenty years later he was first counselor to Brigham Young in the First Presidency of the Church.

KIMBALL, HEBER P. (1835-1885), was a son of Heber C. Kimball and Vilate M. Kimball. A cattleman, stage operator, and freighter, he spent much of his life freighting between the Missouri River and California and assisting with Church immigration. He was a colonel in the territorial militia and led the first troops from Salt Lake City in 1866 against the Indians in the Black Hawk War.

KIMBALL, WILLIAM H. (1826-1907), a son of Heber C. Kimball, was born in Mendon, New York. He served as a missionary to England from 1854-1856. As an officer in the Utah militia, he led a company of Minute Men in early Utah Indian engagements.

KING, WILLIAM (1834-1892), a native of Cicero, New York, spent twelve years of his life as a missionary in the Hawaiian Islands, during four of which (1887-1890) he was president of the mission.

KINKEAD, CHARLES A. (?-1853), was a partner in the Salt Lake City merchandising firm of Livingston and Kinkead. He was engaged in freighting and mail delivery between Salt Lake City and the Missouri River outposts when he and three others were killed by Indians six miles from Fort Laramie.

KINNEY, JOHN F. (1816-1902), was born in New York and practiced law in Ohio and Iowa. He served as chief justice of Utah territory from 1854 to 1857 and 1860 to 1863. In 1863 he became Utah's third delegate to the U.S. Congress, succeeding John M. Bernhisel.

LITTLE, FERAMORZ (1820-1887), a son of James Little and Susannah Young (Brigham Young's sister), married Fannie Decker, sister of Lucy and Clara Decker, plural wives of Brigham Young. In 1850 Feramorz came to Utah, where he joined the Church. He delivered mail between Salt Lake City and the Missouri River and was engaged in Utah construction projects, including roads up Big Cottonwood and Provo Canyons, several sawmills, the first dam across the Jordan River, and the old Utah Penitentiary. He was prominent in the construction of Utah railroads and was a director of the Deseret National Bank. He served as a counselor in the Salt Lake City 13th Ward bishopric and served three consecutive terms as mayor of Salt Lake City beginning in 1876.

LITTLE, JAMES A. (1822-1908), brother of Feramorz Little and nephew of Brigham Young, labored as a missionary in England in 1854-56. He settled in St. George, Utah, in 1863 and helped survey and lay out the town of Kanab, Utah.

LITTLE, JAMES T. (1848-1898), son of Feramorz Little and Fannie Decker, was a prominent Salt Lake City banker.

LOWE, DAVID B., a Kansas jurist, was appointed chief justice of Utah Territory in 1875; he resigned that same year because of insufficient pay.

LYMAN, AMASA M. (1813-1877), was a member of the Council of Twelve from 1842 to 1867. His preaching of unorthodox doctrine pertaining to the atonement of Christ and his association with the Godbeites led to his excommunication from the Church in May 1870.

MACKINTOSH, DANIEL, was a clerk in Brigham Young's office; his daughter Agnes married Brigham Young's son Mahonri.

MAESER, KARL G. (1828-1901), was converted to Mormonism in Germany, where he taught school. He arrived in Utah in 1860 and four years later was appointed private tutor to Brigham Young's family. In 1867 he was called to preside over the Swiss and German Mission, and in 1875 he was sent to establish the Brigham Young Academy in Provo, Utah.

MAXWELL, GEORGE R. (? -1889), born in Michigan, was a veteran of the Civil War, in which he lost one leg. Prior to his removal from office in 1876, Maxwell was assistant U.S. attorney and U.S. marshal for the Territory of Utah. He opposed George Q. Cannon for the Utah delegate's seat in Washington and contested the election of Cannon in 1872.

McDONALD, ALEXANDER F. (1825-1903), a native of Scotland, was mayor of Springville, Utah, in the 1850s. During the decade 1862-72 he had charge of the tithing office in Provo, Utah. From there he was appointed to take charge of the tithing office and the construction of the temple and of Brigham Young's home in St. George, Utah. A Black Hawk War veteran, in 1882 he became president of the Maricopa Stake in Arizona.

McGRORTY, WILLIAM, a Salt Lake City merchant, opposed the election, and later contested the seat, of William H. Hooper as Utah's delegate to Washington in 1867.

McKEAN, JAMES B. (1821-1879), was born in Vermont and practiced law in New York, where he was elected to Congress in 1858. A veteran of the Civil War, he was appointed chief justice of Utah Territory by President U.S. Grant in 1870. He was on the Utah bench of the Third District Court during much of the litigation in the Ann Eliza Young vs. Brigham Young divorce case. It was his citation for contempt that resulted in Brigham Young's twenty-four-hour confinement in the penitentiary in March 1875. Removed from office in 1875 for what was termed "fanatical and extreme conduct," McKean practiced law in Salt Lake City until his death four years later.

McKEAN, THEODORE (1829-1897), was born in Allentown, New Jersey, joined the Church in 1851, and came to Salt Lake City in 1853. He was counselor to Bishop Frederick Kesler of the Salt Lake City 16th Ward and a member of the Salt Lake Stake high council. In the 1870s he completed two missionary assignments in the Eastern States. As a colonel in the Utah militia, he saw service in the Utah War of 1857-58 and in the Morrisite campaign of 1863. He later became a director of ZCMI.

McKENZIE, DAVID (1833-1912), a convert to the Church from Scotland, arrived in Salt Lake City in 1854 and was employed for a time as an engraver on Deseret currency. In 1868 he became private secretary to Brigham Young and subsequently became chief clerk in the President's office and bookkeeper for the Trustee-in-Trust and the Presiding Bishop's office.

MILES, WILLIAM H. (1810-1896), born in Southampton, Pennsylvania, presided over branches of the Church in Brooklyn and New York City before moving to Utah in 1861. He was president of the Eastern States Mission from 1865 to 1869.

MILLER, WILLIAM (1814-1875), was the actor in the famous "bogus Brigham" episode in Nauvoo, Illinois. When officers came to arrest Brigham Young in 1845, Miller, because of his resemblance to the Mormon leader, put on the President's coat and was taken into custody, only to be discovered too late as an imposter. He lived at Springville, Utah, where he was a counselor to Bishop Aaron Johnson. In 1860 he was called to preside over the Utah Stake.

MILLS, WILLIAM G., a high priest, arrived in England as a missionary in January 1861 and became president of the Birmingham District.

MITCHELL, FREDERICK A. H. F. (1835-1923), was counselor to Edwin Woolley of the

Salt Lake City 13th Ward for fifteen years, after which he served as president of the Hawaiian Mission from 1873 to 1875.

MORROW, HENRY A. (? -1891), a veteran of the Mexican and Civil wars, was commander of Camp Douglas from 1870 to 1874.

MUSSER, AMOS M. (1830-1909), was traveling bishop for the Church from 1858 to 1876. He directed the collection, forwarding, and reporting of tithing and collected money due the Perpetual Emigration Fund; he was also engaged in other Church business under the First Presidency and Presiding Bishopric. In 1873 he became an assistant trustee-in-trust for the Church.

NAISBITT, HENRY W. (1826-1908), joined the Church in England and came to Utah in 1854. He was a missionary in England from 1876 to 1878, part of which time he presided over the European Mission. He was employed at ZCMI.

NEBEKER, GEORGE (1827-1886), was sent to the Hawaiian Islands in 1864 and purchased the Laie plantation for $14,000. During his mission, which lasted nearly ten years, he established the sugar industry that formed the economic base for the mission.

NICHOLSON, JOHN (1830-1909), was born in Scotland and joined the Church in 1861. He was associate editor of the *Millennial Star* in England and the *Deseret News* in Utah; recorder in the Salt Lake Temple; and counselor to Lorenzo D. Young (Brigham Young's brother) in the Salt Lake City 18th Ward bishopric.

PACE, WILLIAM B. (1832-1907), was a member of the Mormon Battalion in the Mexican War and a colonel in the Utah militia in command of the Provo District. Payson, Utah, was named in his honor.

PARK, JOHN R. (1833-1900), came to Utah in 1861 from the East. In 1869 he was appointed president of the University of Deseret, a position he held for nearly twenty-five years. He became the first superintendent of public instruction in the State of Utah.

PATRICK, M. T., was appointed U.S. marshal for Utah in 1870; in October 1871 he delivered a writ for the arrest of Brigham Young on a charge of cohabitation with his plural wives. While the matter was being litigated, the President was "confined" to his home.

PEACOCK, GEORGE (1822-1878), was a farmer, legislator, probate judge, and resident of Manti, Utah, in whose home Joseph A. Young died.

PINNOCK, WILLIAM, was a British Army veteran who was converted to the Church and immigrated to Utah. A letter to the editor of the *Deseret News* in 1869 signed by Pinnock advocated rifle practice for members of the Utah militia.

POTTER, CARROL H., a colonel in the U.S. Army, was commander of the federal troops at Camp Douglas, Utah, at the outbreak of the Black Hawk Indian War in 1865. When federal troops were requested for service against the Indians, Potter wired General Dodge for permission to use troops at Camp Douglas against the Indians, which was refused. The burden of defense then devolved upon the Utah militia.

PRATT, ARTHUR, was deputy U.S. marshal involved in October 1874 in the altercation at the entrance to Brigham Young's residence that resulted in the arrest of Joseph Shaw and James Cushing for resisting an officer.

PRATT, ELEANOR (1817-1874), was a plural wife of Parley P. Pratt; she died in Salt Lake City on October 24, 1874.

PRATT, ORSON (1811-1881), a member of the Council of the Twelve from 1835 to 1881, had served missionary assignments in England on four previous occasions when he was called on a mission to Austria in 1864. Forbidden by the Austrian government to carry out his assignment in that land, he went to England, where he remained until August 1867. He was one of the most talented speakers and writers in the Church. In all, he crossed the Atlantic eight times in the interest of Church business and missionary work. He was Church Historian from 1874 until his death.

BIOGRAPHICAL APPENDIX

PRESTON, WILLIAM B. (1830-1908), was born in Virginia. As a young man he traveled to California, where he was converted to Mormonism in 1857. He assisted in the settlement of Cache Valley, Utah, and became bishop of Logan and a member of the Utah Legislative Assembly. In 1865 he accepted a missionary appointment to England, where he was business manager of the Liverpool office for three years. After returning to Utah, he engaged in railroad construction, was stake president at Logan, and in 1884 was appointed Presiding Bishop of the Church.

RANDALL, MILDRED E., was a schoolteacher who labored in Hawaii for the Church from 1873 to 1876, teaching English to the native Saints at Laie.

REYNOLDS, GEORGE (1842-1909), after arriving in Utah in 1865 from his birthplace in England, was employed as a clerk and secretary in Brigham Young's office. He provided the necessary evidence for the test case that eventually decided the constitutionality of federal anti-polygamy legislation. After the Supreme Court of the United States upheld Reynolds' conviction in January 1879, he was imprisoned for two years. From 1890 until his death he was a member of the First Council of Seventy.

REYNOLDS, WOOD J. (? -1863), was a teamster on the overland mail service. In January 1862 he and four others were arrested for the assault and robbery of ex-Governor John W. Dawson as he was leaving the territory. In June 1863, when Indians attacked the overland mail stage near the Jordan River ferry, Reynolds, the driver, was killed and his body was savagely mutilated.

RICHARDS, FRANKLIN D. (1821-1899), was president of the British Mission, 1850-52 and 1854-56. Born in Richmond, Massachusetts, he was converted to Mormonism by Brigham and Joseph Young in 1836. He was a member of the Council of the Twelve from 1849 to 1899. He also served in the Utah Legislature and was a regent of the University of Deseret, brigadier general in the Utah militia, probate judge of Weber County, and Church Historian.

RICHARDS, HEBER JOHN (1840-1919), a son of Willard Richards, was born in England, where he returned as a missionary from 1863-66. He studied medicine at Bellevue Hospital in New York and became one of Utah's foremost medical doctors.

RICHARDS, SAMUEL P., was a missionary in Hawaii from July 1863 to February 1866.

RICHARDS, SAMUEL W. (1824-1909), a brother of Franklin D. Richards, was born in Richmond, Massachusetts. He was president of the British Mission, 1852-54.

RICHARDS, WILLARD B. (1847-1942), a son of Willard Richards, was born at Winter Quarters, Nebraska. He was employed on the William H. Hooper ranch in Skull Valley, Utah, prior to his call to Europe as a missionary in 1867. He later became one of the leading stock raisers in the West.

RICKS, THOMAS E. (1828-1901), a native of Kentucky, accompanied Parley P. Pratt on the southern Utah exploring expedition of 1849-50. Six years later he assisted in establishing the Las Vegas Mission. He aided in the rescue of the Mormon handcart pioneers of 1856 and the Salmon River missionaries two years later. He was among the pioneer settlers of Cache Valley, Utah-Idaho, in 1859 and led Mormon colonization in the upper Snake River country of Idaho, where he became the first bishop and stake president there.

RITER, WILLIAM (1838-1922), played a leading role in the construction of railroads in Utah. He was president of the Swiss, Italian, and German Mission in 1864-65.

RODGERS, CHRISTOPHER R. P. (1819-1892), a Civil War veteran, was superintendent of the U.S. Naval Academy, 1874-78 and 1880-81. He was commissioned a rear admiral in 1874.

ROSSITER, WILLIAM A. (1843-1913), was born in London, England, and joined the Church at age seventeen. After immigrating to Utah, he was employed as a teamster by Brigham Young and became his private coachman and financial adviser; he was also appraiser and director of Zion's Savings Bank and Trust. He married Brigham Young's daughter Shemira.

ROWBERRY, JOHN (1823-1884), was presiding bishop of Tooele County, Utah. He accepted Mormonism in 1840 in England and returned there as a missionary in 1876-77.

SCHAEFFER, MICHAEL, succeeded J. Alexander White as chief justice of Utah Territory on May 31, 1876. He gave the final decision in the Ann Eliza Young vs. Brigham Young divorce case in April 1877.

SEEGMILLER, WILLIAM H. (1843-1923), was baptized in Florence, Nebraska, while en route from Canada to California in 1861. After arriving in Utah, he worked for Brigham Young and assisted with Church immigration and colonization. In 1873 he was persuaded by Joseph A. Young to settle in Richfield, Utah, where he became bishop, stake counselor, and eventually president of the stake from 1888 to 1910.

SHARP, JAMES (1843-1904), a son of Bishop John Sharp, was born in Scotland and came to Utah in 1850. He assisted his father in Utah railroad construction and succeeded him on the board of directors of the Union Pacific Railroad. He was mayor of Salt Lake City from 1884-1886; he completed two missionary assignments in Great Britain and was a director of the Deseret National Bank and Deseret Savings Bank.

SHARP, JOHN (1820-1891), was born in Scotland and immigrated to Utah in 1850. In 1854 he was appointed bishop of the Salt Lake City 20th Ward. A decade later he was named assistant superintendent of the Salt Lake City public works. He subcontracted a section of the Union Pacific Railroad through Weber Canyon, Utah; and when that company defaulted in its contract payment, he was among those sent to Boston to negotiate a settlement. He later was named to the Union Pacific board of directors.

SHARP, WILLIAM G. (1857-1919), a son of Bishop John Sharp, worked as a telegraph operator on the Utah Central Railroad. He studied at the Deseret University and with Brigham Young's son Don Carlos at Rensselaer Polytechnic Institute, Troy, New York, where he received a degree in civil engineering. He became superintendent of the Pleasant Valley Coal Company and was president of the United States Smelting and Refining Company.

SHAW, JOSEPH (1815-1876), was born in England; after coming to Utah he was employed as gatekeeper of Brigham Young's residence. He was arrested, along with James Cushing, in October 1874 after an altercation with U.S. marshal George Maxwell. He was the husband of Mary Ann Taylor, a daughter of John Taylor.

SHEETS, ELIJAH F. (1821-1904), was the bishop of the Salt Lake City Eighth Ward for half a century. In 1871 he was appointed traveling bishop in central Utah and had charge of all Church livestock and pastures for sixteen years.

SHERMAN, WILLIAM T. (1820-1891), Union general in the Civil War, visited Salt Lake City several times before his death. He called on Brigham Young on October 3 and 4, 1876.

SHIPP, MILFORD B. (1836-1918), was born in Indiana and moved to Utah about 1850. A graduate of Jefferson Medical College in Pennsylvania, he was well-known in Utah as a physician and later as an attorney. He completed several missionary assignments for the Church.

SIMS, GEORGE (1822-1865), a native of London, England, was converted to the Church in 1848 and immigrated to Utah in 1853. An excellent penman, Sims was employed as a clerk in Brigham Young's office. As a seventy he went on a mission to England in 1862. While en route home he drowned in the Platte River in October 1865.

SMITH, ALMA L. (1831-1887), a missionary in Hawaii from 1856-58, served as president of that mission in 1864-65 and 1874-75.

SMITH, ELIAS (1804-1888), a cousin of Joseph Smith, was born in Royalton, Vermont. He joined the Church at age thirty-one, taught school in Kirtland, Ohio, and was a leader of the Kirtland Camp, which moved Latter-day Saints from Ohio to Missouri in 1838. After coming to Utah in 1851, he was probate judge of Salt Lake County, business manager and editor of the *Deseret News,* and postmaster of Salt Lake City.

SMITH, GEORGE A. (1817-1875), was born in Potsdam, New York. A cousin of Joseph Smith, he joined the Latter-day Saints in 1832. He was named to the Council of the Twelve Apostles in 1839. In Utah he was a member of the militia and the territorial legislature. He became Church Historian in 1854 and in 1868 succeeded Heber C. Kimball as counselor in the First Presidency.

SMITH, JESSE N. (1834-1906), a cousin of Joseph Smith, was born in Stockholm, New York. After crossing the plains to Utah, he settled in Parowan in 1851 and was counselor in the stake presidency. After two missions to Scandinavia in the 1860s, he was called to preside over the Church in eastern Arizona. Smith was instrumental in establishing the Church colonies in Mexico.

SMITH, JOB (1828-1913), pioneer basketmaker and farmer in Salt Lake City, was born in England, where he returned as a missionary in 1849. He led a company of immigrants across the plains upon his return in 1854.

SMITH, JOHN E., of Pennsylvania, was a Civil War veteran and came to Utah in 1866 as U.S. assessor of internal revenue. After an assignment on the Indian frontier in 1870, he returned to Utah four years later when he was appointed to succeed Henry A. Morrow as commander at Camp Douglas.

SMITH, JOHN L. (1828-1898), took part in Utah Indian wars and was president of the Swiss and Italian Mission in 1856-1857.

SMITH, JOSEPH F. (1838-1918), was born in Missouri during the Mormon difficulties of 1838. After his father, Hyrum, was killed at Carthage, Illinois, in 1844, young Joseph assisted his widowed mother in crossing the plains with the Mormon pioneers. He was named to the Council of the Twelve in 1866 and was president of the European Mission in 1874-75. He returned on another assignment in 1877 and had been in England four months when he was called home following the death of Brigham Young. He became sixth president of the Church in 1901.

SMITH, ROBERT H., was called to accompany the Daniel Jones expedition to Mexico in 1875 but received permission to labor with Ammon Tenney among the Pueblo and Zuni Indians of New Mexico instead. Their success was phenomenal for they baptized more than a hundred in a few weeks.

SMOOT, ABRAHAM O. (1815-1895), was mayor of Salt Lake City and Provo, Utah, and president of the Utah Stake from 1868-1895. At Provo, Smoot was a banker, president of the Provo Woolen Mills, and a trustee of the Brigham Young Academy.

SNOW, ELIZA R. (See Eliza R. Snow Young)

SNOW, ERASTUS (1818-1888), born in Vermont, was a member of the Council of the Twelve from 1849-1888. He performed extensive missionary work for the Church in the eastern United States and pioneered that work in Scandinavia. In 1854 he was sent to direct Church immigration and publish the *Luminary* at St. Louis, Missouri. For many years he presided over the Latter-day Saints in southern Utah.

SNOW, LORENZO (1814-1901), joined the Latter-day Saints in Ohio in 1836. He was frequently engaged as a missionary prior to his call to the Council of the Twelve in 1849. In Utah he assisted in the colonization of Box Elder County and was a member of the Territorial Legislature for twenty-nine years. In 1898 he became the fifth president of the Church.

STAINES, WILLIAM C. (1818-1881), was born in England, where he returned as a missionary from 1860-1863. An expert gardener, he superintended Brigham Young's orchards and gardens. He was appointed territorial librarian and was a partner in the mercantile firm of Staines, Needham, and Company. During the last eighteen years of his life he was immigration agent for the Church.

STENHOUSE, THOMAS B. H. (1824-1882), assisted Lorenzo Snow in establishing the Swiss and Italian Mission in 1850. After joining the Godbeites in 1869, he was excommunicated from the Church.

STEPTOE, EDWARD J., U.S. army colonel, arrived in Utah on August 31, 1854, at the head of two companies of artillery and one of infantry, numbering about two hundred men. He was sent to Utah for the purpose of examining a route from Salt Lake City to California and investigating the Gunnison massacre.

SWAN, DOUGLAS A. (1849-1907), came to Utah from Scotland in 1863 and engaged in the railroad and banking business. As an accountant he worked for Utah Light and Power Company for many years.

TAYLOR, JOHN (1808-1887) emigrated from England to Canada prior to joining the Church. He was appointed to the Council of the Twelve in 1838 and eventually succeeded Brigham Young as president of the Church. In 1844 he was with Joseph and Hyrum Smith when they were killed in the jail at Carthage, Illinois, and was himself wounded. He published extensively for the Church and was a missionary in England and France. He was present at the dedication of the St. George Temple in 1877 and assisted in the stake reorganization that occurred that year.

TAYLOR, RICHARD J. (1848-1905), was a son of Church President John Taylor and a prominent Ogden, Utah, businessman. He was director of the First National Bank, Boyle Furniture Company, and a member of the city council. He served as a missionary in Hawaii in 1873.

TAYLOR, THOMAS (1826-1900), was the bishop of the Salt Lake City 14th Ward from 1871-1886. A native of England, he returned there as a missionary from 1862 to 1865 and was immigration agent for the Church in New York City in 1866. He succeeded in getting the large Church immigration through to Utah that year despite efforts of railway companies to raise prices. In Utah he was engaged in business and railroading.

TEASDALE, GEORGE (1831-1907), was born in London, England, accepted Mormonism in 1852, and immigrated to Utah in 1861. He was appointed to the Council of the Twelve in 1882. Employed in Brigham Young's merchandise store, he later took charge of the General Tithing Store and ZCMI. He performed extensive missionary service in Europe and the United States and was president of the European Mission from 1887-1890.

TENNEY, AMMON M. (1844-1925), born in Lee County, Iowa, learned Spanish while living in San Bernardino, California. For fifteen years he labored among the Indians as a missionary and interpreter in Utah and Arizona; he was president of the Mexican Mission, 1887-1889. Originally called to accompany the Daniel Jones expedition to Mexico in 1875, he was sent instead with Robert H. Smith to labor among the Pueblo and Zuni Indians in New Mexico.

THATCHER, FANNY YOUNG (1849-1892), a daughter of Brigham Young and Lucy Ann Decker, was married to George W. Thatcher.

THATCHER, GEORGE W. (1840-1902), Salt Lake City banker and businessman, married Luna and Fanny Young, daughters of Brigham Young. He was born in Illinois, served with Lot Smith in the Utah War, was a Pony Express rider and superintendent of the Utah Western and Utah Northern railroads, and was a missionary in England, 1873-74.

THATCHER, LUNA YOUNG (1842-1922), a daughter of Brigham Young and Mary Ann Angell, married George W. Thatcher on 4 April 1861 and reared ten children.

THATCHER, LUTIE (1868-1945), was the oldest child of George W. and Fanny Young Thatcher.

THATCHER, MOSES (1842-1909), was a member of the Council of the Twelve from 1879 to 1896. He was a missionary for the Church in Mexico and was chairman of a com-

BIOGRAPHICAL APPENDIX

mittee for the exploring and purchasing of land for the Church in Mexico. He was disfellowshiped in 1896.

THURBER, ALBERT K. (1826-1888), while en route with gold-seekers to California in 1849, was converted to Mormonism in Salt Lake City. He eventually settled in Spanish Fork, Utah, where he was mayor of the town for eight years and a delegate to the territorial legislative assembly for seventeen terms. In 1874 he moved to Richfield and was named first counselor to Joseph A. Young in the Sevier Stake presidency. Following Young's death, Thurber served successively as president pro-tem, first counselor, and in 1887 as president of the stake.

URSENBACH, OCTAVE (1832-1871), was born in Geneva, Switzerland. He was living in Salt Lake City when he was called as a missionary to the Swiss and German Mission, 1867-1869.

VAN COTT, JOHN (1814-1883), served in the presidency of the Scandinavian Mission and received a special assignment to work among the Scandinavian Saints in Utah. He was a member of the First Council of the Seventy, 1862-1883.

WAITE, CHARLES B., of Illinois, was appointed associate justice of Utah Territory in 1862. A year later he was the subject of a petition for removal from office.

WALKER, (? -1855), Ute Indian chief, died at Meadow Creek, near Fillmore, Utah. He had been baptized in Sanpete Valley in 1850.

WASHAKIE (1804-1900), was a Shoshone Indian chief from about 1850 to 1900.

WATT, GEORGE D. (1815-1881), joined the Church in England in 1837. He taught phonography (shorthand) in Nauvoo and Salt Lake City and worked for Brigham Young as reporter and secretary for sixteen years. Associating with the Godbeites, he was excommunicated from the Church in 1874.

WELLS, DANIEL H. (1814-1891), was born in Trenton, New York, and moved to Commerce, Illinois, in 1833; he was living there when the Latter-day Saints moved there six years later. He served the people of Nauvoo as councilman, alderman, university regent, and brigadier general in the Nauvoo Legion before joining the Church in 1846. In Utah he was ordained an apostle, and he served as second counselor to Brigham Young from 1857-1877. He was superintendent of public works in Salt Lake City, lieutenant general of the Nauvoo Legion, and mayor of Salt Lake City.

WEST, CHAUNCEY W. (1827-1870), was an Ogden, Utah, businessman and presiding bishop of Weber County from 1855-1870. A native of Pennsylvania, he was ordained a seventy at age sixteen and was a missionary to India in the early 1850s. He presided over the European Mission in the absence of George Q. Cannon in 1862-63. Together with Ezra T. Benson and Lorin Farr, he contracted to grade two hundred miles of the transcontinental railroad west of Ogden in 1868.

WHITE, J. ALEXANDER, of Alabama, was appointed chief justice of Utah Territory, succeeding David B. Lowe, in 1875. He remained in Utah only three months, having been called to testify before the Senate Judiciary Committee in Washington.

WHITNEY, NEWEL K. (1795-1850), a veteran of the War of 1812, was born in Vermont. He was a partner in the firm of Gilbert and Whitney in Kirtland, Ohio, when he joined the Latter-day Saints. After serving as a bishop in Kirtland and Nauvoo, he was appointed Presiding Bishop and Trustee-in-Trust for the Church at Winter Quarters, Nebraska, during the Mormon exodus west.

WILLIAMS, THOMAS (? -1874), married Zina Young, a daughter of Brigham and Zina D. H. Young, on 12 October 1868.

WILLIAMS, ZINA YOUNG (1850-1931), a daughter of Brigham Young, was married to Thomas Williams on 12 October 1868; after his death, she was married to Charles O. Card, 17 June 1884.

WILLIS, WILLIAM S. S., was in charge of a Mormon immigrant train crossing the plains in the late summer of 1865. The company, consisting of about 250 persons, left Wyoming, Nebraska, on August 15. The lateness of their start west and the exhausted condition of their livestock raised concern in Utah for their safety and necessitated the sending of a relief train from the Salt Lake Valley to meet them. The Willis company arrived in Salt Lake City on November 29.

WOODRUFF, WILFORD (1807-1898), was born in Connecticut. In 1839, six years after he joined the Church, he was called to the Council of the Twelve. He engaged in extensive missionary work for the Church in the United States and England. In Utah he served several terms on the territorial legislature and was president of the Horticultural Society. He was assistant Church historian and then Church Historian for many years prior to his ordination as president of the Church in 1889.

YOUNG, ALBERT CARRINGTON, was a son of Brigham Young, Jr., and Jane Carrington.

YOUNG, ALICE (See Alice Young Clawson)

YOUNG, ANN ELIZA (1844- ?), became a plural wife of Brigham Young on 6 April 1868. She brought a divorce suit against the President, which attracted much national attention in the later years of his life.

YOUNG, BRIGHAM S. (1857-1945), was a son of Brigham Young, Jr., and Catherine Curtis Spencer.

YOUNG, BRIGHAM T., was the oldest son of Joseph A. Young.

YOUNG, CAROLINE (See Caroline Young Croxall)

YOUNG, CATHERINE DAMCKE (1859-1924), was married to John W. Young, 2 January 1879; they were divorced 25 March 1890.

YOUNG, CATHERINE SPENCER (1836-1922), daughter of Orson Spencer and Catherine Curtis, was married to Brigham Young, Jr., 14 November 1855.

YOUNG, CLARA LUCINDA JONES (1845-1885), became a plural wife of John W. Young 26 March 1865.

YOUNG, CLARA STENHOUSE (1850-1893), a daughter of Thomas B. H. Stenhouse, became a plural wife of Joseph A. Young 4 March 1867.

YOUNG, EDWARD (1823- ?), was a half-brother of Brigham Young (Abigail Howe Young, Brigham Young's mother, died of tuberculosis on 11 June 1815 at age forty-nine, leaving five sons and six daughters). In 1817 John Young, Brigham's father, married a widow, Hannah Brown. Edward Young, born in 1823, was a son of this second marriage.

YOUNG, ELIZA R. SNOW (1804-1887), became a plural wife of Joseph Smith in 1842. After Joseph's death in 1844, Eliza was sealed to Brigham Young. She was president of the Relief Societies of the Church from 1867 until her death.

YOUNG, ELIZABETH (See Elizabeth Young Ellsworth)

YOUNG, ELIZABETH FENTON (1837- ?), became a plural wife of Brigham Young, Jr., 7 March 1868.

YOUNG, EMMELINE FREE (1826-1875), became a plural wife of Brigham Young 14 January 1846.

YOUNG, HARRIET AMELIA FOLSOM (1830-1910), became a plural wife of Brigham Young 24 January 1863.

YOUNG, HOWARD O. (1859-1922), was a son of Brigham Young, Jr., and Catherine Spencer.

YOUNG, JANE CARRINGTON (1840- ?), became a plural wife of Brigham Young, Jr., 15 March 1857.

BIOGRAPHICAL APPENDIX

YOUNG, JOSEPH W. (1829-1873), a son of Lorenzo Dow Young (Brigham Young's brother), was born in Mendon, New York. For many years he directed the Church immigration from the eastern frontier to Utah. In 1869 he was named president of the St. George Stake; he became mayor of the town in 1870.

YOUNG, JULIA ANN VILATE (1845-1928), was a daughter of Joseph Young, Brigham Young's brother.

YOUNG, LE GRAND (1840-1921), was a son of Joseph Young (Brigham Young's brother). As a young man he was tollkeeper on the road from Salt Lake City through Parley's Canyon. He studied law at the University of Michigan, graduating in 1871. A prominent Utah attorney, he served as legal counsel to Brigham Young. He was elected judge of the Third Judicial District after Utah was admitted to statehood. He was also a member of the Liberty Stake high council in Salt Lake City.

YOUNG, LORENZO DOW (1807-1895), younger brother of Brigham Young, was bishop of the Salt Lake City 18th Ward, 1851-1876.

YOUNG, LUCY BIGELOW (1830-1905), became a plural wife of Brigham Young 20 March 1847.

YOUNG, LUCY MARIA CANFIELD (1846-1915), became a plural wife of John W. Young 16 February 1864; they were divorced 12 June 1873.

YOUNG, MARGARET WHITEHEAD (1838-1916), became a plural wife of Joseph A. Young 19 February 1857.

YOUNG, MARY ANN ANGELL (1803-1882), was married to Brigham Young 18 February 1834.

YOUNG, MARY ANN AYERS (1834- ?), was married to Joseph A. Young 9 September 1852.

YOUNG, NABBIE (See Nabbie Howe Young Clawson)

YOUNG, PARALEE RUSSELL, wife of Oscar Brigham Young, was divorced from him about 1865.

YOUNG, PHEBE LOUISE (See Phebe Young Beatie)

YOUNG, RICHARD W. (1858-1919), oldest son of Joseph A. and Margaret Whitehead Young, was a West Point graduate and brigadier general in the U.S. Army.

YOUNG, RUTH (1861-1944), a daughter of Brigham Young and Emmeline Free, was married to Charles E. Johnson.

YOUNG, SUSA AMELIA (See Susa Amelia Young Dunford)

YOUNG, SUSAN SNOW, a daughter of Erastus Snow, was married to Arta De Christa Young 11 April 1875.

YOUNG, VILATE (See Vilate Young Decker)

YOUNG, WILLIAM G. (1827-1883), son of Brigham Young's brother, Lorenzo D. Young, was born in Ontario, New York. He was a missionary in England from June 1854 to February 1857, and bishop of the Big Cottonwood Ward, 1874-1877.

YOUNG, ZINA (See Zina Young Williams)

Appendix A
Chronology of Events in the Life of Brigham Young

1801	June 1	Born in Whitingham, Vermont.
1804		Family moves to Sherburne, New York.
1813		Family moves to Auburn, New York.
1815	June 11	Mother dies of tuberculosis.
1824	October 8	Marries Miriam Works in Aurilius, New York. Employed as carpenter, joiner, painter, glazier.
1829		Moves to Mendon, New York.
1830	Spring	First sees the Book of Mormon.
1831	Fall	Converted to Mormonism.
1832	April 14	Baptized by Eleazer Miller at Mendon, New York. Ordained an elder.
	September 8	Wife, Miriam Works Young, dies of tuberculosis.
	Sept.-Oct.	Travels to Kirtland, Ohio, to meet Joseph Smith.
	December	Leaves on mission to Canada with brother, Joseph Young.
1833	February	Returns to Mendon.
	April-August	Second mission to Canada.
	September	Moves family from Mendon, New York, to Kirtland, Ohio.
1834	February 18	Marries Mary Ann Angell.
	May-July	Travels to Missouri and back with Zion's Camp.
	Summer-Fall	Labors on construction of Kirtland Temple, printing office, etc.
1835	February 14	Appointed to Quorum of Twelve Apostles.
	May-September	Mission to eastern states with Twelve.
	Fall	Attends Hebrew school in Kirtland.
1836	March 27	Attends Kirtland Temple dedication.
	Summer	Mission to eastern states and New England.
1837	March-June	Business mission to eastern states with Willard Richards.
	June-August	Mission to New York and Massachusetts.
	Fall	Failure of Kirtland Bank.
	December 22	Forced to leave Kirtland, Ohio, for safety.
1838	March 14	Arrives at Far West, Missouri.
	Fall	Organizes Mormon evacuation of Missouri.

1839	February	Moves family to Quincy, Illinois.
	April	Travels to Far West, Missouri, with Twelve.
	May	Moves family to Montrose, Iowa.
	September 14	Very ill. Departs for mission to England.
	October 12	Father, John Young, dies.
1840	March 9	Leaves New York City on *Patrick Henry* for England.
	April 6	Arrives in England.
1841	January 19	Appointed president of the Twelve.
	April 21	Leaves England to return home.
	July 1	Arrives in Nauvoo, Illinois.
	September 4	Elected to Nauvoo City Council.
1843	July-September	Mission to eastern states to collect funds for Nauvoo House and temple.
1844	May 21	Mission to East to solicit support for Joseph Smith's presidential candidacy.
	June 27	Joseph and Hyrum Smith killed at Carthage, Illinois.
	August 6	Arrives in Nauvoo from the East.
	August 8	Asserts right of the Twelve to lead the Church in opposition to claims of Sidney Rigdon. Sustained by vote of conference.
	August 31	Elected lieutenant general of Nauvoo Legion.
1845		Directs Mormon preparations to leave Nauvoo.
1846	February 15	Leaves Nauvoo to lead Mormon exodus west.
	Fall	Establishes Winter Quarters on Missouri River.
1847	April 14	Leaves Winter Quarters, at head of pioneer company, for the Rocky Mountains.
	July 24	Arrives in Salt Lake Valley.
	August 18	Commences return to Winter Quarters.
	December 5	Ordained president of the Church at Kanesville.
1848	May 26	Leaves Winter Quarters for Salt Lake Valley with company of 1,229 persons.
	September 20	Arrives in Salt Lake Valley.
1849	March 12	Elected governor of provisional State of Deseret
1850	August 28-31	Selects site for city of Ogden [Utah].
	September 15	Chosen president of Perpetual Emigrating Fund Company.
	September 20	Appointed governor of Utah Territory by U.S. President Millard Fillmore.
1851	January 20-28	Visits settlements in Davis, Weber counties. Organizes Weber Stake.
	March 17-26	Visits Utah County. Organizes Utah Stake.
	April 22-May 24	Travels south to Parowan, organizing settlements. Explores Sevier Valley.

	July 21	Organizes three Indian agencies in Utah.
	August 8	Organizes three judicial districts in Utah.
	October 21-Nov. 7	Travels south. Locates territorial capital at Fillmore on October 29.
1852	April 22-May 21	Takes exploring trip to southern Utah, visits Indian tribes.
1853	February 14	Breaks ground for construction of Salt Lake Temple.
	July 18	Walker Indian war commences in Utah.
	October 26	John W. Gunnison and party of U.S. topographical engineers killed by Indians on Sevier River.
1854	May 4-30	Travels to southern settlements. Signs peace treaty with Ute chief ending Walker War.
1856	November	Organizes relief efforts to assist handcart pioneers stranded on plains.
1857	April 24-26	Visits settlements in Salmon River area of Oregon (now Idaho).
	July 24	Receives report of approaching army to Utah.
	September 11	Massacre at Mountain Meadows.
	September 15	Declares martial law in Utah. Forbids U.S. troops to enter Utah.
1858	March 21	Directs abandonment of northern Utah communities in face of approaching army.
	April	Moves family to Provo, Utah.
	April 12	Welcomes Alfred Cumming, his successor as governor, to Utah.
	Spring	Northern inhabitants of Utah abandon homes to avoid clash with army.
	June 11	Meets peace commissioners. Difficulties between United States and Mormons peaceably resolved.
	June 26	U.S. army passes through Salt Lake City en route to Cedar Valley.
	July	Family returns to Salt Lake City, along with other inhabitants of Territory.
1859	March	Rumors of arrest of Brigham Young with assistance of U.S. troops. Governor Cumming alerts Utah militia.
1860		Contracts to construct 500 miles of overland telegraph line.
1861	March 6	Dedicates Salt Lake Theatre.
	May 15-June 8	Visits southern Utah settlements.
	October 18	Sends first telegram over newly completed overland telegraph.

1862	June 12-15	"Morrisite War" in Weber County, Utah.
	September 1-25	Visits southern Utah settlements.
1863	January 29	Sixteen soldiers and more than two hundred Indians killed in battle at Bear River.
	March 10	Arrested on charges of bigamy under anti-bigamy law of 1862, placed under bond.
	April 20-May 19	Visits southern Utah settlements.
1864	September 1-29	Visits southern Utah settlements.
1865	April	Black Hawk Indian war begins.
	May 3-11	Visits settlements in Cache Valley.
	July 7-19	Visits settlements in Sanpete County.
	August 1-10	Visits Cache Valley.
	September 4-29	Visits southern Utah settlements.
1866		Settlements in central and southern Utah broken up because of Indian war. Inhabitants move to larger towns.
1867	March 21	Deseret Telegraph Company established, with Brigham Young as president.
	April	More settlements in Sevier and Piute counties abandoned due to Indian difficulties.
	April 22-May 15	Visits southern Utah settlements.
	Fall	Reorganizes Women's Relief Society.
	December	Organizes the School of the Prophets.
1868	May 21	Contracts to grade 150 miles of Union Pacific Railroad through Utah.
	Summer	Visits Utah settlements.
	September 20	Organizes stake at Nephi, Utah.
	October	Elected president of Zion's Cooperative Mercantile Institution.
1869	March 8	Utah Central Railroad organized, with Brigham Young as president.
	May 10	Transcontinental railroad completed.
	May 17	Breaks ground for Utah Central Railroad from Ogden to Salt Lake City.
	June 1	Provo Woolen Mills organized, with Brigham Young as president.
	June 20	Organizes Bear Lake Stake.
	November	Organizes "Young Ladies Cooperative Retrenchment Association."
1870	January 10	Drives last spike in Utah Central rail line at Salt Lake City.
	Feb.-April	Visits settlements in southern Utah and Arizona.
	August-September	Travels to southern Utah. Locates town site at Kanab. Organizes ward.
	November 25	Travels to St. George for the winter.

1871	February 10	Returns to Salt Lake City.
	June 26-July	Visits settlements in northern Utah and Idaho.
	October 2	Arrested on charge of cohabitation and confined to his home.
	October 9	Admitted to bail.
	October 24	Leaves for St. George. Accused of fleeing from justice.
	November 9	Dedicates St. George Temple site.
	December 26	Case called to trial. Returns to Salt Lake City.
1872	January 2	Appears in Third District Court. Case continued until March. Bail refused. Guarded in his own home.
	April 25	Released from custody on writ of habeas corpus.
	December	Travels to St. George with Thomas L. Kane.
1873	February 27	Returns with Kane to Salt Lake City.
	April 6	Calls five additional counselors to assist in responsibility of First Presidency.
	July 5	Named president of Zion's Savings Bank and Trust.
	November 28	Leaves Salt Lake City for St. George. Organizes United Order in southern Utah settlements.
1874	April 20	Returns to Salt Lake City.
	May	Organizes United Order in Salt Lake City wards.
	October	In ill health. Travels to St. George, Utah.
1875	February	Returns to Salt Lake City. Ann Eliza Webb Young divorce case.
	Spring	Organizes Young Men's Mutual Improvement Association. Organizes Brigham Young Academy, Provo, Utah.
	October 3	Visits with President Ulysses S. Grant in Salt Lake City.
1876	May 1-July 1	Visits southern Utah.
	November 1	Leaves for St. George.
1877	April 6	Attends general conference in St. George. Dedicates temple. Commences more complete organization of stakes.
	April 25	Dedicates temple site at Manti, Utah.
	April 27	Returns to Salt Lake City.
	August 29	Dies at his residence in Salt Lake City.

Appendix B
Brigham Young's Family

(Listed here are the wives by whom Brigham Young had children)

MIRIAM WORKS, 1806-1832 (1824)*
    Elizabeth
    Vilate

MARY ANN ANGELL, 1803-1882 (1834)
    Joseph A.
    Brigham Jr.
    Mary Ann
    Alice
    Luna
    John W.

LUCY ANN DECKER, 1822-1890 (1842)
    Brigham Heber
    Fanny Caroline
    Ernest Irving
    Shemira
    Arta De Christa
    Feramorz Little
    Clarissa Hamilton

HARRIETT E. COOK, 1824-1898 (1843)
    Oscar Brigham

CLARISSA DECKER, 1828-1889 (1844)
    Jeannette
    Nabbie
    Jedediah Grant
    Albert Jeddie
    Charlotte

LOUISA BEAMAN, 1815-1850 (1846)
    Joseph
    Hyrum
    Moroni
    Alvah
    Alma

CLARISSA ROSS, 1814-1858 (1844)
    Mary Eliza
    Clarissa Maria
    Willard
    Phebe Louisa

*Marriage date is in parenthesis.

EMILY DOW PARTRIDGE, 1824-1899 (1844)
    Edward Partridge
    Emily Augusta
    Caroline
    Joseph Don Carlos
    Miriam
    Josephine
    Lura

MARGARET MARIA ALLEY, 1825-1852 (1846)
    Evelyn Louisa
    Mahonri Moriancumer

EMMELINE FREE, 1826-1875 (1846)
    Ella Elizabeth
    Marinda Hyde
    Hyrum Smith
    Emmeline Amanda
    Louise Nelle
    Lorenzo Dow
    Alonzo
    Ruth
    Daniel Wells
    Adelle Elwin

MARGARET PIERCE, 1823-1907 (1846)
    Brigham Morris

ZINA D. HUNTINGTON, 1821-1901 (1846)
    Zina Prescinda

LUCY BIGELOW, 1830-1905 (1847)
    Eudora Lovina
    Susa Amelia
    Rhoda Mabel

ELIZA BURGESS, 1827-1915 (1852)
    Alfales

HARRIET BARNEY, 1830-1911 (1856)
    Phineas Howe

MARY VAN COTT, 1844-1884 (1865)
    Fannie

Appendix C
Chronology of Brigham Young's Children

Name	Birth	Death
Elizabeth	1825	1903
Vilate	1830	1902
Joseph A.	1834	1875
Brigham Jr.	1836	1903
Mary Ann	1836	1843
Alice	1839	1874
Luna	1842	1922
John W.	1844	1924
Brigham Heber	1845	1928
Edward P.	1845	1852
Oscar Brigham	1846	1910
Joseph	?	
Hyrum	?	
Moroni	1847	1847
Mary Eliza	1847	1871
Ella Elizabeth	1847	1890
Alvah	1848	1848
Alma	1848	1848
Fanny	1849	1892
Emily	1849	1926
Marinda	1849	1926
Clarissa Maria	1849	1935
Jeanette	1849	1930
Zina	1850	1931
Evelyn Louisa	1850	1917
Hyrum S.	1851	1925
Caroline	1851	1903
Ernest Irving	1851	1879
Nabbie	1852	1894
Willard	1852	1936
Dora	1852	1922
Mahonri	1852	1884
Emmeline	1853	1895
Shemira	1853	1915
Alfales	1853	1920
B. Morris	1854	1931
Phebe Louise	1854	1931
Louise H.	1854	1908
Jedediah G.	1855?	1856
Arta De Christa	1855	1916
Joseph Don Carlos	1855	1938
Susa Amelia	1856	1933
Lorenzo D.	1856	1905
Miriam	1857	1919
Albert J.	1858	1864?
Feramorz	1858	1881
Alonzo	1858	1918
Josephine	1860	1912
Clarissa H.	1860	1939
Charlotte T.	1861	1892
Ruth	1861	1944
Lura	1862	1862
Phineas H.	1862	1903
Daniel W.	1863	1863
Rhoda Mabel	1863	1950
Ardelle	1864	1900
Fannie	1870	1950

Brigham Young's Death, 1877

Appendix D
Chronological Listing of Letters
Of Brigham Young to His Sons

Date	Letter to	Page
1854, August 31	Joseph A.	7
1854, September 30	Joseph A.	8
1854, December 1	Joseph A.	10
1855, February 3	Joseph A.	13
1855, February 7	Joseph A.	16
1862, June 5	Brigham Jr.	22
1862, August 6	Brigham Jr.	25
1862, August 30	Brigham Jr.	27
1862, October 11	Brigham Jr.	31
1863, January 3	Brigham Jr.	35
1863, March 26	Brigham Jr.	39
1863, June 3	Brigham Jr.	42
1863, June 13	John W.	97
1864, December 8	Brigham Jr., D. H. Wells	48
1865, October 18	Brigham Jr.	54
1865, November 17	Brigham Jr.	59
1866, January 22	Brigham Jr.	62
1866, February 7	John W.	100
1866, February 8	Brigham Jr.	66
1866, February 27	Brigham Jr.	68
1866, May 23	Brigham Jr.	71
1866, June 15	Brigham Jr.	76
1866, August 11	Brigham Jr., John W.	78
1867, February 5	John W.	105
1867, March 16	Oscar B.	145
1867, March 28	Brigham Jr.	84
1867, May 21	Brigham Jr., John W.	87
1867, September 30	Heber	129
1868, September 3	Heber	133
1868, October 22	Heber	135
1870, February 16	Heber	137
1871, May 19	Willard	164
1871, June 17	Willard	166
1871, July 25	Willard	169
1872, January 26	Willard	172
1872, August 14	Willard	177
1873, April 14	Willard	180
1873, July 24	Morris	244
1873, July 31	John W.	108
1873, October 23	Morris	246
1874, August 11	Willard	184
1874, September 7	Morris	249
1874, October 6	Morris	251
1874, October 15	Feramorz	298

1874, October 26	John W.	109
1875, February 4	Ernest	152
1875, February 6	Willard	185
1875, June 4	Willard	188
1875, August 7	John W.	111
1875, August 24	Ernest, Arta D.	155
1875, August 30	John W.	113
1875, September 2	Alfales	219
1875, September 20	Feramorz	301
1875, September 21	Alfales	220
1875, [October] 6	Alfales	222
1875, October 16	Feramorz	303
1875, October 20	Alfales	224
1875, October 21	Don Carlos	266
1875, November 11	Willard	190
1875, November 18	Alfales	226
1875, November 24	Feramorz	305
1875, December 13	Ernest, Arta D.	157
1875, December 17	John W.	115
1876, January 7	Alfales	227
1876, January 11	Brigham Jr., John W.	117
1876, February 15	Alfales	229
1876, February 15	Feramorz	308
1876, February 16	Don Carlos	268
1876, February 17	Willard	193
1876, March 14	Feramorz	309
1876, March 24	Alfales	231
1876, March 28	Willard	195
1876, March 29	John W.	119
1876, April 17	Don Carlos	270
1876, April 24	Arta D.	255
1876, April 26	Willard	196
1876, July 17	Arta D.	257
1876, August 17	Alfales	232
1876, September 25	Alfales	234
1876, October 19	Willard	198
1876, October 21	Arta D., Lorenzo	284
1876, October 26	Alfales	235
1876, October 27	Don Carlos	271
1876, November 23	John W.	122
1876, December 29	Alfales	237
1877, February 15	Arta D.	259
1877, May 11	Don Carlos, Feramorz	274
1877, May 15	Lorenzo	287
1877, May 23	Willard	204
1877, June 15	Lorenzo	290
1877, June 28	Don Carlos, Feramorz	276
1877, July 16	Don Carlos, Feramorz	277
1877, July 28	Willard	208
1877, August 6	Don Carlos, Feramorz	280
1877, August 23	Feramorz	313

Index

Adams, Professor, 312
Allred, James, 118, 334
America, 323
American Fork, Utah, 137
American Fork Canyon Railroad, 178
American Fur Company, 322
Angell, Truman O., 15, 334
Ann Arbor, Michigan, 218, 287
Antelope Island, 9, 322
Apache Indians, 181
Arizona, 194, 197, 230, 231, 269, 309
Arnold, Orson P., 60, 334
Arsenal Hill, 255-56, 331
Arthur, Charlotte, 232-33
Ashby, Nathaniel, 143
Atkin, George, 118, 334
Atlantic and Pacific Railroad, 92, 94
Atonement of Christ, 259
Auburn, New York, 23, 100, 103-104
Australia, 191, 194, 304
Aztec Cattle Company, 21

Babcock, Orville E., 331
Baltimore, Maryland, 207-208
Banks, John, 209, 330, 335
Barrett Hall, Salt Lake City, 264
Baskin, R. N., 328, 329
Bates, George C., 172, 173, 335
Beatie, Phebe Young, 273, 335
Beatie, Walter J., 206, 273, 291, 335
Beaver, Utah, 159, 288
Beaver Dam Creek, Arizona, 55
Bedford, England, 34
Beecher, H. K., 113
Beehive House, 50, 269
Bell, Mr., 327
Benedict, Joseph M., 111, 335
Benson, Charles A., 63, 335
Benson, Ezra T., 20
Bernhisel, John M., 39, 335
Betts, Colonel, 116
Bigamy, 40. *See also* Polygamy
Big Canyon Creek, 50
Big Cottonwood Canyon, 98
Black, George S., 118, 329, 335
Black Hawk (Ute Indian), 77, 335
Black Hawk War, 72-73, 76-77, 325
Bliss, Tasker H., 162
Book of Mormon, 70, 260
Boole, W. H., 167, 329, 335
Boreman, Jacob S., 191, 221, 335
  grants contempt order, 225, 267
  illegal decision of, 226
  ruling in Brigham Young case, 330
Borie, Adolph Edward, 331
Boston Conservatory of Music, 274, 312
Bowery, 56
Bradfordshire Conference, 12, 13
Brazil, Emperor of, 256
Brigham City, Utah, 32, 35
Brigham Young Academy, 19, 144, 199, 225, 264, 265
British Mission
  Joseph A. missionary in, 6, 10, 12-13
  Brigham Jr. missionary in, 24-89 *passim*
  moral conditions in, 47-48, 59
  Oscar missionary in, 78, 144
  Heber missionary in, 84, 87, 128, 129, 132
  John W. missionary in, 99-113 *passim*
  apathy of people in, 104
  Ernest missionary in, 152, 154, 254
  Ernest appointed mission clerk of, 152, 257
  missionary work in, 154
  Arta missionary in, 155, 200, 229, 254, 268, 304
  Albert Carrington released from, 247
  Joseph F. Smith president of, 247, 289
  Lorenzo missionary in, 196-97, 200, 206, 233, 256, 258, 271, 283
  Arta secretary of, 257
  See also European Mission
Bronson, Lewis, 29, 335
Brooklyn, New York, 312
Buck, Aholiah, 100
Buck, Dudley
  Don Carlos studies under, 264, 275-76, 312
  Brigham Young recommends, 274, 280
  on Don Carlos's musical ability, 279
  requests organ description, 279
  invited to play organ, 280
  biographical note on, 335
Bullock, Thomas, 61, 335
Burton, Charles S., 304, 335-36
Burton, Robert T.
  returns to Salt Lake City, 22
  funds to pay, 36
  elected major general, 61
  protects overland line, 92, 324
  charges against, 209, 331
  escort service, 323
  in Morrisite conflict, 330
  biographical note on, 336

INDEX

Cache Valley, 134, 156, 178
Caine, John T.
   appointed immigration clerk, 64, 67
   travels of, 66, 101, 103
   manages theater, 247
   biographical note on, 336
Caine and Hooper Insurance Company, 283
Calder, David O., 136, 199, 336
California Volunteers, 35-36
Canada, 304
Cannon, George Q.
   called to Washington, D.C., 22
   travels to England, 24, 25, 32, 37
   directed to aid Brigham Jr., 26, 28, 31
   watches Anglo-American situation, 29
   accompanies Brigham Jr., 32, 37
   advised on immigration, 40-41
   Brigham Young orders clothing for, 58
   with Brigham Young sons in New York, 117
   sends *Deseret News*, 166, 170
   delegate to Congress, 178
   counselor to Brigham Young, 182
   attends Brigham Jr., 205, 275, 288
   appoints Feramorz, 297
   delivers money to Feramorz, 305
   biographical note on, 336
Careless, George E. P., 274, 336
Carlisle, England, 34
Carrington, Albert
   presides in Europe, 134
   leaves for Europe, 155
   travels with Ernest and Arta, 157, 196, 255
   counselor to Brigham Young, 182
   advised to release Ernest, 195
   returns from England, 206, 277
   release of, 247
   accompanies Arta home, 257
   writes to Brigham Young about sons, 268
   assigns Lorenzo to Germany, 286
   biographical note on, 336
Carrington, Brigham W., 258, 337
Cedar Valley, Utah, 98
Central Pacific Railroad, 178
Central States Mission, 242
Chicago *Evening Post*, 165
Church of Zion, 328
Church trains, 26, 80, 322, 323
City Creek, 23
City Creek Canyon, 98
Civil War (U.S.), 24, 323

Clawson, Alice Young, 110, 111, 131, 337
Clawson, Hiram B., 66, 101, 247, 337
Clawson, Nabbie H. Young
   visits brothers, 120, 231
   marriage of, 193, 230, 269, 308
   biographical note on, 337
Clawson, Orson Spencer
   visits Brigham Young's sons, 120, 231
   marries Nabbie Young, 193, 230, 269, 308
   is buyer for ZCMI, 230, 269, 308
   biographical note on, 337
Clawson, Rudger, 120, 337
Clawson, Stanley, 263-64
Clayton, Vilate Ruth, 128
Clinton, Jeter, 147, 209, 227, 331, 337
Cobb, Charlotte, 41, 44, 337
Cobb, James T., 41, 44, 337
Colonization, 182, 269
Colorado River, 182
Columbia River, 162
Connor, Patrick E.
   arrives in Salt Lake City, 35-36
   Brigham Young on, 36, 39, 40
   engages in mining, 49-50, 81, 325
   anxious to leave Utah, 97
   biographical note on, 337
Cook, Ida, 295
Cook, Richard, 330
Copenhagen, Denmark, 58
Cottle, Ada, 218
Cotton industry, 40, 55
Coughlan, Judge, 120, 196
Council of Fifty, 83
Council of Twelve, 92, 204, 288, 291
Crouch, Eleanor, 283
Crow Indians, 92
Croxall, Caroline Young, 137, 337
Croxall, Mark, 137, 304, 337-38
Cushing, James, 233, 338

Dancing, 228
Darwin, Charles, 199
Davis County, Utah, 115, 134
Decker, Vilate Young, 131, 338
Denver Indians, 22
Deseret Agricultural and Manufacturing Society, 333
Deseret Alphabet, 8, 51, 73-74, 322
Deseret Museum and Menagerie, 93
Deseret National Bank, 149, 204, 229
Deseret News, 19, 35, 166, 168, 170, 218
Deseret University. *See* University of Deseret
Deseret Woolen Mill, 128, 144, 213

De Trobriand, Philip Regis, 171, 329, 338
Diaz, President Porfirio, 21
Drake, Thomas J., 39, 338
Druce, John, 278, 338
Dunford, Alma B., 291, 338
Dunford, Susa Amelia Young, 231, 338
Durrant, Thomas C., 136, 338
Dusenbury, Bro., 170

Eagle Gate, 264
East Canyon Coal Company, 19
Echo Canyon, 136
Edmunds Tucker Act, 93
Eichberg, Julius, 274, 312, 338
E. J. Swaner and Company, 128
Eldredge, Horace S.
    to deliver petition, 39
    starts for states, 40
    to accompany John W., 43, 98
    assists immigration, 92, 95
    leads church train, 322
    biographical note on, 338
Ellerbeck, Thomas W., 10-12, 98, 225, 267, 338-39
Ellsworth, Elizabeth Young, 23, 339
Emerson, Philip H., 120, 221, 224, 339
Emery, George W., 221, 339
Empey, Nelson, 195, 233, 291, 339
Endowment House, 11
England, 12, 31, 46, 323. *See also* British Mission, European Mission
European Mission, 20, 21, 46, 47-48, 71, 134
Eutonia Mining Company, 283
Evans, Captain, 173

Farmington, Utah, 137
Felt, Nathaniel H., 62, 339
Ferguson, Mr., 292
Ferguson, James F., 339
Fielding, Amos, 112, 339
First National Bank, 149
First Presidency
    John W. first counselor in, 92, 109, 122
    remarks on John W., 93
    sets Willard apart for mission, 163
    organizes stakes, 204, 291
    to dedicate Logan Temple site, 288
Flint, Kate, 227, 339
Florence, Nebraska, 26, 33, 40
Foote, Erastus S., 118, 339
Forest Farm, 134
Fort Bridger, 323
Fort Douglas, 71, 98

Fort Kearney, 79
Fort Laramie, 11, 15, 322, 324
Fort Leavenworth, 322
Fort Limhi, 91
Fox, Georgiana, 149
Fox, Jesse W., 50, 149, 339
Fox, Jesse W., Jr., 191, 339
Franklin, Benjamin, 302
Free, Finley C., 56, 339
Freeze, James P., 182, 339-40
Fuerstenau, Germany, 132
Fuller, Frank, 36, 324, 340

Gardo House, 256
Gates, Susa Young, xxiv. *See also* Susa Amelia Young Dunford
Georgetown, 103
Germany, 104, 304
Gibbs, George F., 243
Gibbs, Isaac L., 40, 340
Gibson, David, 48, 340
Godbe, William S., 328
Godbeites, 139, 328. *See also* Church of Zion
Goethals, George W., 162
Government, 247, 314-15
Granite quarry, 182
Grant, George D., 3, 6, 16, 61, 340
Grant, President Ulysses S.
    John W. meets, 103
    Willard attends inauguration of, 179
    Indian peace policy of, 181
    appoints Utah chief justice, 221
    meets Brigham Young, 223, 331
    biographical note on, 340
Great Western Iron Mining and Manufacturing Company, 93
Green, Alfonso, 112, 340
Green River, 136
Grimes, Captain, 72
Groesbeck, Nicholas, 78, 340
Groo, Isaac, 304, 340
Guion and Company, 75, 325

Hallock, Charles, 332
Harding, Stephen S.
    message to legislature, 37
    Brigham Jr. irritated with, 38
    actions condemned, 39
    efforts frustrated, 40
    removed from office, 43
    leaves Salt Lake City, 97
    charges disloyalty, 324
    biographical note on, 340
Hardy, Milton H., 195, 229, 241, 340
Harrington, Leonard E., 225, 340

INDEX

Harris, James, 291
Harrison, Elias L. T., 328
Hatch, Abram, 340, 369
Hawaiian Mission, 242, 243, 244, 245-46, 250
Heeley, John J., 234
Heller, Mr., 280
Hempstead, Charles H., 171, 340
Hickman, William, 329
Hickox, George, xxviii
Hills, Lewis, 40, 95, 340
History, 209
Hoagland, Sister, 263
Holladay, Ben, 37-38, 340
Holladay and Halsey, 100
Hollister, O. J., 328
Holy Ghost, 250
Hooper, Hattie, 162
Hooper, William H.
    in Washington, D.C., 22, 80, 84, 134, 173, 323, 324
    Brigham Young writes to, 22, 23
    notes anti-Mormon sentiment, 69
    John W.'s impressions of, 103
    elected to Congress, 107
    daughter of marries Willard Young, 162
    appoints Willard to West Point, 163
    released from Congress, 178
    biographical note on, 341
Hunter, Edward (Grantsville Bishop), 123, 341
Hunter, Edward (Presiding Bishop), 36, 341

Idaho Territory, 70
Immigration
    loss of cattle, 8
    report on, 9, 29, 33, 43, 79, 134, 136
    preparation for, 40, 56-57, 64-65
    Brigham Young on, 40-41, 50, 51, 57, 59-60, 64-65, 80, 81
    via Colorado River, 51
    detained, 59-60
    funds for, 67
    Brigham Jr. supervises, 74-75, 76
    cost of, 81
    change in method of, 136, 323
Indians
    troubles with, 8, 11, 72, 81, 92, 98, 129, 322
    missionary work among, 181, 187, 304
    See also specific tribes, Black Hawk War
Ingalls, Rufus, 168, 169, 341

Inskip, Reverend, 329
Ireland, 34, 39
Isaacson, Dr., 263
Isle of Wight, 290
Ivie, James, 77, 341

J. D. Swaner and Co., 296
Jack, James, 230, 231, 238, 271, 341
Jennings, Thomas W., 199, 341
Jennings, William, 66, 67, 101, 104, 341
John Bright, 76, 325
Johnson, ex-Governor, 169
Johnson, President Andrew, 103
Johnson, Sybella White, 151
Jones, Daniel W., 191, 197, 341
Jordan River (Utah), 76, 147, 263
Juab County, Utah, 277
Julesberg, Colorado, 80, 129

Kalakuana, King David, 243
Kane, Thomas L., 24-25, 44, 91, 110, 341-42
Kansas City, 163
Kate Flint vs. Jeter Clinton, 227
Kaysville, Utah, 35
Kelsey, Eli B., 139, 328, 342
Kent, George W., 51
Kimball, Heber C.
    education of, xii, xiii
    on liquor licenses, 11
    at New Year's party, 36
    travels of, 42, 54
    charged with debt, 80
    death of, 134
    vacancy filled, 137
    biographical note on, 342
Kimball, Heber P., 73, 77, 87, 342
Kimball, William H., 6, 15, 16, 342
King, William, 244, 342
Kingdom of God
    importance of, xix-xx
    Brigham Young on, 9, 16, 28, 61, 63, 80, 118, 138, 181, 195
    desire of sons to build, 30, 113, 192, 203
Kington Fort, 330
Kinkead, Charles, 11, 342
Kinney, John F., 39, 342
Kirtland, Ohio, 80
Knickerbocker, 297

Latter-day Saints University, 163, 264
Lawyers, 81, 222, 235, 302
Leeds Conference, 283, 286
Leeds, Utah, 144
Lees, S. J., 61

Lewis, Gertrude F., 85
Lincoln, President Abraham, 39
Lion House, 12, 322
Liquor, 11, 71, 300-301, 308
Little, Feramorz
  starts for states, 40
  assists with immigration, 95, 191
  elected SLC mayor, 194, 269
  called on mission, 304
  biographical note on, 342
Little, James, 16, 191, 342
Little, James T., 108, 342
Little Cottonwood Canyon, 182
Logan, Utah, 35, 128, 140, 147, 188, 205
Logan Temple, 163, 275, 285, 288
London, England, 27, 34, 46, 129, 144, 146, 154
Lowe, David B., 226, 330, 342
Lyman, Amasa M., 88, 342-43

MacDonald, Reverend, 329
McDonald, Alexander F., 110, 343
McGrorty, William, 107, 134, 343
McKean, James B.
  confines Brigham Young, 172-73
  charges Brigham Young with contempt, 225, 267
  offensive to Mormons, 328
  Brigham Young charged during term of, 329
  rules in divorce case, 330
  biographical note on, 343
McKean, Theodore, 304, 343
McKenzie, David, 174, 183, 343
Mackintosh, Agnes, 214
Mackintosh, Daniel, 272, 343
Maeser, Karl G., 132, 137, 140, 161, 263, 343
Manti, Utah, 111-12, 147, 155, 158, 288
Manti Temple, 156, 275, 285, 288
Maxwell, George R., 159, 178, 233, 343
Medina, Wisconsin, 101
Mendon, New York, 100
Methodist Camp Meeting, 167, 171, 329
Mexico, 93, 94, 297
Michigan University, 218
Miles, William H., 85, 343
Millennial Star, 68, 73, 154
Miller, William, 112, 343
Miller and Richards, Edinburgh, Scotland, 73-74
Mill Farm, 151
Mills, William G., 43, 343
Missionary work,
  Brigham Jr. on, 27, 30
  in England, 82, 104
  progress of, 191
  among Indians, 197
  proselyting, 254-55
Mitchell, Frederick A., 182, 247, 248, 250, 251, 343-44
Money, 250
Montana Territory, 70, 79
Moquis Indians, 181
Morgan, Washington, 274, 312
Morgan County, Utah, 134
Morris, Joseph, 330-31
Morrisites, 209, 330-31
Morrow, Henry A., 171, 344
Morton, Catherine, 85
Muddy River Valley, Nevada, 55, 137
Musser, Amos M., 55, 134, 182, 344
Mutual Improvement Association. *See* Young Men's Mutual Improvement Association

Naisbitt, Henry W., 344
Napoleon III, 86-87, 326
National Contracting Company, 162-63
Navajo Indians, 181
Nebeker, George, 244, 344
New York City, 47, 50, 94, 117, 191
New York *Herald*, 107, 167
New York *Saturday Evening Globe*, 93
Nicholson, John, 120, 344
North American Exchange Company, 93
Nottingham, England, 254
Nuttall, L. John, 154

Ober, Frederick, 332
Ogden, Utah, 170, 273
Olmstead, Mr., 113
Omaha *Herald*, 217

Pace, William B., 77, 344
Pacific Springs, 33
Panama, 51
Paris, France, 86, 144, 326
Paris, Idaho, 264
Park, Hamilton G., 263
Park, John R., 163, 184, 249, 317, 344
Parowan, Utah, 205, 275, 288
Parry, John, 123
Patrick, M. T., 171, 344
Peacock, George, 156, 344
Penrose, Charles W., 21, 219
People's Party, 194, 230, 269
Perpetual Emigrating Fund, 80
Philadelphia, Pennsylvania, 208
Pierce, Eli, 242
Pi Eta Scientific Society, 264, 296
Pima Indians, 181

INDEX

Pinnock, William, 36, 344
Piute County, Utah, 72
Pleasant Grove, Utah, 137
Polygamy, 69, 324, 325
Postal service, 15
Potter, Carrol H., 71, 72, 344
Pratt, Arthur, 233, 344
Pratt, Eleanor, 110, 344
Pratt, Orson
    mission business of, 73, 74, 81, 260
    named speaker of house, 118
    organizes stakes, 288
    returns to Utah, 290
    death of, 295, 297
    biographical note on, 344
Pratt, Parley P., 80
Pratt, Romania B., 263
Preston, William B., 62, 345
Price, Captain, 72
Protestant Episcopal services, 169, 171
Provo, Utah, 144
Pueblo Indians, 197
Pullen, William, 295

Railroad
    Joseph A. works on, 5, 136
    Brigham Jr. works on, 19, 136
    progress, 79-80, 134, 136, 140, 177
    John W. works on, 92-93, 178
    northern Mexico, 93
    advantageous to Zion, 105, 106
    Heber works on, 127
    Hyrum works on, 149
    Feramorz works on, 296
    See also specific railroads
Randall, Mildred E., 263, 345
Reed, Samuel B., 127
Remy, Jules, 36, 324
Rensselaer Polytechnic Institute
    Don Carlos attends, 204, 264, 266
    Feramorz attends, 204, 238, 273, 296, 311, 312
    Morris visits, 243
Retrenchment societies, 281
Reynolds, George, 118, 199, 229, 313, 345
Reynolds, Wood J., 98, 345
Richards, Franklin D., 6-7, 16, 55, 78, 81, 107, 345
Richards, Heber John, 62, 345
Richards, Samuel P., 245, 345
Richards, Samuel W., 6, 7, 345
Richards, Willard B., 132, 137, 345
Ricks, Thomas E., 79, 345
"Ring," 118, 159, 166, 184, 205, 221, 223, 328
Riter, William W., 114, 345

Rodgers, Christopher, 237, 311, 345
Rossiter, William A., 281, 345-46
Round Valley, Utah, 77
Rowberry, John, 278, 346
RPI. *See* Rensselaer Polytechnic Institute

Sagers, Royal B., 319
St. George, Utah
    Brigham Young visits, 54, 87, 154, 197, 230, 256, 272, 280
    improvements at, 55
    telegraph extended to, 147
    Susa Y. Dunford moves to, 231
    progress of United Order at, 249
St. George Temple
    volunteers for, 110-11
    construction progress on, 124, 234, 249, 254, 286
    Brigham Young supervises construction of, 185
    dedication of, 198, 238, 309
    satisfaction with, 204
    ordinances commenced in, 269
    completion of, 288-89
Salt Lake and Eastern Railroad, 92
Salt Lake and Fort Douglas Railway, 92
Salt Lake and Jordan Canal Co., 296
Salt Lake City
    liquor traffic in, 11, 71
    elections in, 67, 139-40, 194, 230, 269
    influx of lawyers in, 81
    business dull in, 88
    little unemployment in, 97
    improvements in, 116, 178-79, 225, 229, 267
    Heber moves to, 128
    men sent to Muddy, 137
    United Order in, 156
    Methodist camp meeting in, 167, 329
    July 4 celebration in, 171, 329
    child mortality rate of, 228
    Arsenal Hill explosion in, 255-56, 331
    machine shop destroyed in, 306
Salt Lake *Democrat*, 217
Salt Lake Hardware Company, 283
Salt Lake *Herald*, 217, 224
Salt Lake Rock Company, 93
Salt Lake Stake, 92, 151, 152
Salt Lake Street Car Railroad, 178, 204
Salt Lake Supply and Forwarding company, 93
Salt Lake Tabernacle
    construction progress on, 43, 58, 61, 81, 98

conference to be held in, 131
Brigham Young sons haul materials for, 263
dedication of, 304
Salt Lake Temple
construction progress on, 43, 110, 182, 233, 247
Oscar works on, 144
Morris employed at, 243
Don Carlos architect of, 264
Salt Lake Theatre
Joseph A. works on, 5
performances at, 36, 151-52
John W. works on, 92
construction progress on, 98, 247
lighted by gas, 178
Sandwich Islands. *See* Hawaiian Islands
Sanpete County, Utah, 72, 76, 77, 231, 277
Scandinavia, 78, 104, 157, 255, 304
Schaeffer, Michael, 272, 330, 346
Searles, Reverend, 329
Seegmiller, William H., 114, 346
Sevier County, Utah, 5, 55, 72, 156, 288
Sharp, James, 266, 304, 346
Sharp, John
railroad builder, 5, 137
given bonds, 109
travels east, 118, 220, 266
with Heber, 128
visits Willard, 168, 170
named assistant church trustee, 182
reports on Don Carlos, 268
reports money matters, 272
biographical note on, 346
Sharp, William G., 220, 266, 273, 312, 346
Shaw, Joseph, 233, 346
Sheets, Elijah F., 182, 346
Sheldon, Ezra, 100, 103
Sherman, William T., 198-99, 201, 209, 346
Shipp, Austin, 51
Shipp, Milford B., 51, 346
Sims, George, 62, 346
Sioux Indians, 15, 322
Smith, A. K., 225, 236, 267, 272
Smith, Alma, 250, 251, 346
Smith, Elias, 51, 346-47
Smith, Emma, 243
Smith, George A.
attends Young family prayer, xxvi
travels, 84-85, 134, 154, 186, 247
health of, 114, 156, 188
counselor to Brigham Young, 137, 182
named trustee-in-trust, 182
death of, 219-20

against outside schooling, 265
recommends Naval Academy, 311
biographical note on, 347
Smith, Jesse N., 21, 58, 347
Smith, Job, 9, 347
Smith, John E., 80, 81, 347
Smith, John Henry, 241
Smith, John L., 182, 347
Smith, Joseph, 56
Smith, Joseph F.
travels, 124, 134
named assistant church trustee, 182
Morris sent to visit, 243
is British Mission president, 247, 289
Lorenzo to draw money from, 291-92
returns to Utah, 290
biographical note on, 347
Smith, Lot, 52
Smith, Robert H., 197, 347
Smith and Free Mining and Stock Brokers, 283
Smoot, Abraham O., 225, 347
Smoot, Abraham O. Jr., 290
Snow, Celestia Armedia, 242
Snow, Eliza R. *See* Eliza R. Snow Young
Snow, Erastus, 123, 288, 347
Snow, Lorenzo, 118, 182, 242, 243, 288, 347
Snow, Susan, 253
Southern Pacific Railroad, 182
Southern States Mission, 265, 304
Spanish American War, 162
Spencer, Clarissa Young, xxiii-xxiv
Staines, William C.
presides in London, 27
directs immigration, 64, 92, 233
travels with John W., 115
with Brigham Young's sons in New York, 117
reports on Brigham Young's sons, 177, 221, 277, 297
administers funds, 292, 304, 310
biographical note on, 347-48
Stakes, 204-205, 277, 281, 288, 291
State of Deseret, 64
Steel, Richard, 100, 103
Stenhouse, Thomas B. H., 44, 61, 80, 348
Steptoe, Edward J., 11, 348
Sugar industry, 15, 323
Summit County, Utah, 72, 134
Sunset Crossing, Arizona, 197
Swan, Douglas A., 304, 348
Swearing, 30, 300-301, 308
Swiss-German Mission, 133
Switzerland, 132, 138, 289

368

INDEX

Taylor, A. Bruce, 223
Taylor, John, 288, 304, 348
Taylor, Richard J., 246, 348
Taylor, Thomas, 64, 65, 66, 67, 101, 182, 348
Teasdale, George, 304, 348
Telegraph, 79, 81, 106, 147
Templeton Building, Salt Lake City, 264
Tenney, Ammon M., 197, 348
Thatcher, Fanny Young, 136, 140, 348
Thatcher, George W., 32, 98, 140, 348
Thatcher, Luna Young, 32, 80, 110, 348
Thatcher, Lutie, 110, 348
Thatcher, Moses, 182, 295, 297, 348-49
Thurber, Albert K., 114, 349
Timely Gull, 10-11
Tithing, 57, 80
Tobacco, 32-33, 300-301, 308-309
Tooele, Utah, 54, 84-85, 118, 244
The Transit, 264
Trustee-in-trust, 57, 182
Tullidge, Edward, 328

Union Pacific Railroad, 92, 118, 123, 127
Union Vedette, 49, 324
United Order, 5, 156, 184, 249, 299, 333
United States Military Academy, 161, 166, 169, 175-76, 177
United States Naval Academy, 300-301, 307, 308
University of Deseret, 136, 143, 149, 161, 241, 253, 264, 265, 283, 317
Ursenbach, Octave, 137, 349
Utah Central Railroad
  constructed by Joseph A., 5
  Brigham Jr. director of, 19
  John W.'s involvement with, 92, 107, 327
  Brigham Young sells bonds of, 108
  success of, 140
  Hyrum paymaster, treasurer of, 149
Utah Legislative Assembly, 37, 64
Utah militia, 60-61, 91-92, 171, 323
Utah National Guard, 162
Utah Northern Railroad, 19, 92, 107, 178, 247
Utah Southern Railroad, 108, 167, 177, 182, 247, 296, 328
Utah Western Railroad, 93, 117

Van Cott, John, 182, 349
Victoria, Queen, 104-105

Waddell, J. A. L., 296
Wainwright, Robert P., 162

Waite, Charles B., 39, 349
Walker (Ute Indian chief), 15, 349
Walker Brothers, 57
Wasatch County, Utah, 72, 134
Washakie (Shoshone chief), 79, 349
Washington, D. C., 24, 46, 179
Washington, Utah, 55
Watt, George D., 105, 349
Weeks, Allen, 322
Wells, Daniel H.
  European Mission president, 20, 46
  at New Year's party, 36
  travels of, 40, 53, 56, 79, 84-85, 197, 224
  is troop commander, 61, 76
  edits *Millennial Star*, 68
  is counselor to Brigham Young, 182
  accompanies Brigham Young, 193, 230, 231, 269, 309
  organizes Independence Day celebration, 329
  biographical note on, 349
West, Chauncey, 22, 32, 33, 37, 323, 349
West Point. *See* United States Military Academy
White, J. Alexander
  leaves for California, 116
  illness of, 191
  appointed Utah chief justice, 221
  Brigham Young awaits arrival of, 225, 267
  discharges Brigham Young, 226
  ruling in divorce case, 330
  biographical note on, 349
Whitney, Newel K., 349
Willet's Point, New York, 162, 189, 192, 198, 207, 314
William I, King of Prussia, 86
Williams, Thomas, 7, 137, 184, 247, 349
Williams, Zina Young, 184, 349
Willis, William S. S., 60, 350
Winsor Castle, Utah, 181
Woman's suffrage, 140
Woodruff, Wilford, 134, 350
Woolley, Edwin D., 275
Woolley, Joseph, 275
Worden, Mr., 23
Worden, Angeline, 23
Word of Wisdom, 88, 323
Works, James, 23

Yaqui Indians, 20
Young, Albert Carrington, 32, 350
Young, Alfales
  studies at Michigan, 158-59, 218, 301

visited by brothers, 189, 234
writes father, 200, 218-19, 232, 304
completes law degree, 206
returns home, 206, 275, 287
biographical sketch of, 217-18
receives father's biography, 218-19
travels with Brigham Jr., 219
receives letters from brothers, 219
father pleased with, 227
cautioned on handwriting, 235
wants Feramorz to join him, 238
works with Don Carlos, 263
admitted to bar, 275, 287
Young, Alice, 15. *See also* Alice Young Clawson
Young, Alonzo, 206, 287, 301-302, 306, 317
Young, Ann Eliza Webb
    divorce case, 107, 120, 200, 224, 226, 234-35, 236, 267, 272, 284-85, 329, 330
    suit by father of, 233
    biographical note on, 350
Young, Arta De Christa
    with Heber in Idaho, 128
    attends Deseret University, 136
    is missionary to England, 155, 200, 229, 254, 257, 268, 283, 284, 286, 304
    father's letters to, 155-59
    travels on continent, 157, 196, 255
    returns home, 206, 277, 289
    biographical sketch on, 253
    visits Willard, Feramorz, 254
    writing style criticized, 255
    has leg ailment, 268
    commences farming, 281
Young, Brigham
    lacked formal schooling, xi, xii
    personal integrity of, xxvii
    practical philosophy of, xxviii
    contradictory image of, xxviii-xxxix
    importance of interviews to, xxxviii-xxxix
    exemplary life of, 7, 16, 201
    moves into new house, 12
    holographs, 12, 16, 116, 251
    last illness of, 20
    works in Auburn, New York, 23
    contrasts own mission with son's, 26, 79
    travels of, 32, 42, 54, 84-85, 87, 115, 123, 131, 134, 153, 169-70, 172, 186, 188, 193, 194, 197, 230, 233, 269, 271, 309

    discontinues tobacco use, 33
    arrest of, 38, 324
    on government officials, 43, 54
    orders Deseret Alphabet type, 51, 73-74
    on progress of kingdom of God, 61, 63, 69-70, 181, 194, 205, 291
    Colonel Potter visits, 72
    charged with indebtedness, 80
    compared with Napoleon, 86, 326
    chided by Auburn newspaper, 103-104
    on technology, 106
    sells railroad bonds, 108
    on "ring," 118, 159, 166, 184, 205, 221, 223
    on sale of Co-op stock, 123
    ridiculed by ministers, 132
    on Godbeites, 139
    contracts mumps, 140
    contentment of, 159, 204, 274, 280
    attends parties, 167, 228
    urges attendance at Methodist meeting, 167, 329
    notes Utah celebrations, 171, 209, 281
    imprisonment of, 172, 173, 174, 191, 306, 329-30
    murder charge against, 172-73, 329
    plans colonization, 193, 269
    on Ann Eliza divorce case, 200, 224, 226, 234-35, 236, 267, 272, 284-85, 330
    reviews responsibilities, 204
    trust of in God, 205, 272, 284, 291
    death of, 208
    rheumatic condition of, 221, 233, 268, 299, 302, 304
    meets Ulysses S. Grant, 223, 331
    deeds property for academy, 225
    notes Charlotte Arthur case, 232
    charges legal despotism, 232-33
    on U. S. political situation, 238
    attends railroad meeting, 244
    dedicates Provo courthouse, 247
    requests Hawaii specimens, 251
    devotion of to Latter-day Saints, 274
    organizes stakes, 277, 281, 291
    overtaxes strength, 291
    donates to machine shop, 306
    notes advent of typewriter, 309
    life chronology of, 352-56
    counsel of to sons

INDEX

importance of work, vii, 190-91, 305
shun novel reading, xiv, xv, 313-14
be observant, xv, 14, 79, 146, 158, 246, 255
be frugal, economical, xvi, 16, 25, 28, 32, 65, 124, 188, 220, 228, 292, 305
be courteous, xvii, 14, 168, 298
develop honesty, integrity, xvii, 193, 222, 228, 302, 304
on self-improvement, xvii, 14, 26, 28, 31, 85, 87, 235
on education, xxix, 164, 190-91, 191-92, 195, 199, 225, 265, 266-67, 270, 274, 276-77, 305
on missionary work, xxxi-xxxiii, 7, 13-14, 16, 25, 26, 28, 31-32, 35, 48-49, 57-58, 59, 61-62, 63, 69, 76, 79, 80, 81, 97, 129-30, 133, 135-36, 138, 146, 153, 158, 245, 246, 248, 249, 255, 257-58, 259, 290-91
on military service, xxxiii-xxxiv, 164-65, 167-68, 170-71, 190-91, 193, 200, 201, 221, 298, 302, 304-306, 308-309
on student responsibility, xxxv-xxxvi, 221, 222, 223, 227, 228, 266-67, 270, 274, 276, 278
purity invites Holy Spirit, 7, 62
improve social graces, 14
live exemplary life, 14, 35, 130-31, 135-36, 170-71, 223, 259, 267
keep a diary, 22
associate with poor, 25, 31-32
shun evil, 26
responsibility to build kingdom, 28, 80, 118, 195
buy books, 31
on temptation, 49, 153, 167, 227, 270, 302
on happiness, 49, 190, 290, 305
be not discouraged by wrongdoers, 61-62
have open mind to Spirit, 69
trust in God, 76, 135, 291, 304
learn from travel, 79, 133, 255
exertion increases ability, 81
on perseverance, 85, 87, 223, 249, 313
courteous treatment follows good conduct, 97
be wise and discreet, 108
knowledge obligates us to labor, 109

priesthood brings responsibility, 130
obtain self-mastery, 130
on habits, 130, 257-58, 260
be prayerful, 135, 164, 168, 245, 270, 285, 302
honor priesthood calling, 146, 260
good thoughts safeguard against evil, 153
on God's protecting power, 157
on present opportunities, 158, 193
on necessity of balanced life, 164
on choosing associates, 165, 168, 227, 257-58, 278
remedy of for homesickness, 165
avoid unvirtuous women, 170
acquire practical knowledge, 190, 195, 209, 267, 270, 305
daily toil part of worship, 191
make knowledge, talents subserve God's purposes, 191
value of time, 193
proselyte among associates, 200, 221
plan mission after military service, 201
marry in the faith, 201
give life of service, 219, 302
strength of Zion in practical obedience, 221, 302
religion not for clergy alone, 221, 277-78
avoid argument, recrimination, 223, 290-91
folly destroys character, 228
blessings follow obedience, 228
improve literary skills, 235, 255
privilege to know God, 245
on learning language, 246, 248-49
accept customs of people, 246
present acts determine progress, 248, 305-306
avoid disreputable places, 258
on character, 258, 278
duty to keep commandments, 259, 304
study music, 274, 276
be thorough in all things, 276
defend the faith, 285
be able ministers of salvation, 290, 306
obey all rules, 298
strength of Zion in virtue, 302
prepare for life of usefulness, 303
priority of study, 304
on evils of tobacco, 308-309

cultivate love for reading, 314
family
  love for, xxii
  size of, xxiii, 357-59
  patience toward children, xxiv, 45
  on child discipline, xxiv-xxv, xl-xli
  family prayer, xxv-xxvi
  contributions of children, xxix-xxx
  sons serve as missionaries, xxx
  sons in military, xxxiii
  sons study in East, xxxv
  esteem of children for, xxxvi-xxxvii, 36, 38, 45, 121, 145, 180, 187, 201-202, 203, 289, 327
  reticent to discuss family, xxxix
  satisfaction with sons, 12, 16, 31, 44, 76, 97, 106, 145-46, 147, 153, 156, 157, 190, 193, 196, 219, 220-21, 222-23, 224, 227, 229, 248, 256, 257, 259, 268, 270, 280, 285, 287, 298, 301, 302, 304, 306, 308
  concern for relatives, 66, 85
  blesses sons, 95, 163-64
Young, Brigham Heber
  missionary to England, 84, 87, 128, 129
  biographical sketch of, 127-28
  member of relief company, 127
  transferred to Switzerland, 132
  defends father, 132-33
  requests money for books, 133
  requests farm, 151
  works at Co-op, 195
  works for father, 206, 281, 287
Young, Brigham Jr.
  on death of Joseph A., 5-6
  receives letter from Joseph A., 8
  herds church cattle, 9
  expresses social inadequacy, 19-20, 34, 52-53
  biographical sketch on, 19-21
  presides over European Mission, 20, 53, 99-100
  presides in Cache Valley, 20
  on father's last illness, 20
  on "underground," 21
  in Washington, D.C., 21, 22, 24
  in Mexico, 21
  meets with Aztec Cattle Co., 21
  in British mission, 24, 25, 27, 30, 34, 44-45, 46, 71, 73, 82, 83, 84, 87, 105, 106, 131, 323
  visits Thomas L. Kane, 24-25
  visits continent, 29, 53, 78, 86-87, 104, 326
  desire of to build Kingdom, 30
  compares English and Americans, 30
  advised to stop tobacco use, 32-33
  travels as speaker, 34
  expresses gratitude for father, 34, 38, 45
  on arrest of father, 38
  father's confidence in, 44
  reflects on past wickedness, 45
  concerned at moral conditions, 46-48
  feels education neglected, 52, 68
  studies French, English, 53
  on misconduct of elders, 59
  on John W.'s mission call, 65, 66, 77-78
  edits *Millennial Star*, 68
  supervises emigration, 74-75
  describes Danish royalty, 78
  encounters severe storm, 82-83
  named to Council of Fifty, 83
  witnesses assassination attempt, 86-87
  health of, 98, 123, 205, 210, 274-75, 278, 287, 288, 291
  sorrows for John W., 117
  visits brothers in east, 117, 229, 230, 307
  works on railroad, 134, 136
  called to the Twelve, 137
  greets Oscar in England, 144
  instructs in United Order, 156
  assists father, 182
  named counselor to father, 182
  travels with father, 193, 231, 236, 269, 272, 275, 309
  visits Arizona settlements, 197, 269
  appointed trustee, 199
  travels with Alfales, 219
  describes Naval Academy, 307
  meets Jules Remy, 324
  with Robert Burton's command, 324
  charters vessels, 325
Young, Brigham Morris
  birth of daughter of, 193, 229, 269, 308
  organizes MIA, 195, 229
  missionary to states, 206
  biographical sketch on, 241-44
  missionary to Hawaii, 242, 243, 244, 250, 251
  notes death of father, 242
  visits brothers in east, 243
  humorist, 243-244
  difficulty with Hawaiian language, 246, 248
Young, Brigham S., 32, 350
Young, Brigham T., 114, 152, 221, 350
Young, Caroline, 137

INDEX

Young, Catherine Spencer, 46, 87, 131, 350
Young, Clara Lucinda Jones, 106, 350
Young, Clara Stenhouse, 80, 114, 350
Young, Don Carlos. *See* Joseph Don Carlos Young
Young, Edward, 66, 101-102, 350
Young, Elizabeth Fenton, 112, 350
Young, Eliza Burgess, 235, 237
Young, Eliza R. Snow, 167, 350
Young, Emmeline Free, 112, 350
Young, Ernest Irving
  directs forest farm, 134
  to meet immigration, 136
  biographical sketch on, 151-52
  letter of to father, 151-52
  requests farm, 151
  involved in suit against father's estate, 152
  is missionary to England, 152, 154-55, 157, 254, 257
  diffidence of, 155
  travels to continent, 157, 196, 255
  to accompany Feramorz, 195
  appointed trustee, 199
  at ZCMI, 206
  meets Arta in England, 254
  at home, 258
  Carrington reports on, 268
  in President's office, 275, 287
  in Co-op, 281
  report from, 304
Young, Feramorz Little
  visited by brothers, 109, 204, 230, 243, 254, 307
  writes father, 158, 200
  progresses in studies, 158, 249-50
  enters Naval Academy, 183, 184, 249-50, 251, 297, 311
  visits home, 195, 233, 258
  studies music, 206, 274, 275, 276, 279, 312
  returns from cruise, 221
  academic standing of, 229, 300, 301, 308
  visits Alfales, 234
  resigns from Naval Academy, 236, 237-38, 272, 273, 310-12
  enters RPI, 238, 273, 287, 311, 312
  unsuited for Navy, 272
  suffers from lassitude, 278
  biographical sketch of, 295-97
  buried at sea, 295, 297
  intellectual ability of, 296
  missionary to Mexico, 297
  dies of typhoid fever, 297, 332
  on release from church attendance, 298, 300
  homesickness of, 299, 300
  motivated by confidence of parents, 300
  pleads for encouragement, 300
  scholastic performance falls, 300
  opinion of Naval Academy, 300
  requests father's autograph, 303
  father pleased with progress of, 305
  daily routine of, 307
  purchases boat, 310
  reports Rodgers interview, 311-12
  speaking ability of, 312-13
  is away when father dies, 313
  receives award for drawing, 333
Young, Harriet Amelia Folsom, 231, 350
Young, Harriet Elizabeth Cook, 143
Young, Heber. *See* Brigham Heber Young
Young, Howard, 51-52, 350
Young, Hyrum Smith, 136, 149, 199, 306
Young, Jane Carrington, 32, 350
Young, John W.
  travels to England, 26, 108
  writes to father, 43, 44, 96
  father orders clothing for, 58
  is missionary to England, 65, 66-67, 73, 78, 84, 99, 101, 104, 105
  Brigham Jr. awaits arrival of, 77-78
  travels on continent, 78, 86, 104, 326
  father's interest in, 84
  biographical sketch on, 91-95
  personality of, 91, 327
  motivation of, 95, 113, 119, 122, 326
  assists church immigration, 95, 99
  blessed by Church Presidency, 95
  devotion of to missionary work, 99, 113
  settles debts in Auburn, New York, 100, 103
  explains extravagance, 101
  gives uncle money, 102-103
  meets President Andrew Johnson, 103
  meets Ulysses S. Grant, 103
  encounters severe storm, 104
  trusts in God, 105
  interviewed by reporter, 107
  third trip to England, 107
  appointed counselor, 109, 119, 122, 182
  on death of Joseph A., 111, 112
  concern of for mother, 112
  health of, 113, 275, 287

work habits of, 116
with brothers in New York, 117, 229
business affairs of, 117-18
visits home, 119, 122, 131, 193, 230, 309
esteem of for father, 121, 327
kindness of to Oscar, 145
appointed trustee, 199
notifies brothers of father's death, 242
writes Don Carlos, 273
visits Feramorz, 309-10
describes Napoleon, 326
Young, Joseph A.
biographical sketch on, 3-6
in handcart relief company, 3, 60
missionary to England, 3, 6, 10, 13
assists with Church immigration, 4, 92, 99
blessed by Church Presidency, 4
is in train wreck, 4
builds Salt Lake Theatre, 5
presides in Sevier District, 5
family, 5, 114
death of, 5, 111, 155-56
father's influence on, 10
letter of to wife, 12
oversees lumber business, 98
travels to Europe, 99
railroad work of, 134, 136
to superintend temple construction, 156
father's satisfaction with, 156
establishes United Order, 156
accompanies Willard, 165, 166
gives Willard gold watch, 169
description of, 322
Young, Joseph Don Carlos
with brothers in New York, 117
writes father, 158, 304
visited by brothers, 189, 204, 230, 243
studies music, 206, 274, 275, 276, 279, 280, 312
is teamster with Alfales, 217
writes to Alfales, 219
at RPI, 220, 266, 287, 296, 301
returns home, 233, 258
joined by Feramorz, 238, 312
pays Morris's train fare, 243
biographical sketch on, 263-65
works at ZCMI, 263-64
architectural accomplishments of, 264
Southern States mission, 265
hazing incident of, 266

father dies, 313
Young, Joseph W., 26, 182, 351
Young, Le Grand, 183, 237, 351
Young, Lorenzo Dow (1807-1895), 120, 351
Young, Lorenzo Dow (1856-1905)
works at Co-op, 158
accompanies father, 196-97
is missionary to England, 196-97, 200, 206, 233, 256, 258, 271, 283, 286, 287
studies hard, 221
is in Sanpete County, 258
writes to father, 275
biographical sketch on, 283
death of, 283
with Arta in England, 283, 286
has speaking difficulty, 283-84
expresses gratitude for father, 286, 289
requests transfer to Switzerland, 289
desires personal improvement, 289
attends Deseret University, 301-302
works at ZCMI, 306
Young, Lucy Bigelow, 231, 351
Young, Lucy Maria Canfield, 106, 351
Young, Mahonri Mackintosh, 214, 218
Young, Mahonri Moriancumer
at Co-op, 158, 221
learns woolen business, 195, 206, 236, 256, 272, 275, 287
biographical sketch on, 213-14
writes to father, 213
rheumatic condition of, 213-14
marries Agnes Mackintosh, 272
works at ZCMI, 306
Young, Margaret Whitehead, 114, 351
Young, Mary Ann (1836-1843), 19
Young, Mary Ann Angell, 16, 112, 351
Young, Mary Ann Ayers, 11, 12, 15, 114, 351
Young, Mira, 286
Young, Morris. *See* Brigham Morris Young
Young, Nabbie, 230, 269, 308
Young, Oscar Brigham, 78, 85, 143-44, 145, 206, 275, 287
Young, Paralee Russell, 143-44, 147, 351
Young, Phineas Howe, 319
Young, Richard W., 5, 158, 221-22, 351
Young, Ruth, 286, 287, 351
Young, Susan, 286, 351
Young, Willard
with brothers in New York, 117
duties of, 158, 230
biographical sketch on, 161-63

INDEX

teaches at West Point, 162
supervises Columbia River construction, 162
in Spanish American War, 162
is blessed by father, 163-64
at U.S. Military Academy, 165, 189, 329
admittance criticized, 165, 166
impressions of academy, 166, 169, 172, 176, 177
writes to father, 169, 231-32, 304
progress report of, 174
expresses gratitude for father, 175, 180, 183, 187, 192, 202, 203, 206
explains demerits, 175-76
desire of to build Kingdom, 177, 192, 203
at presidential inauguration, 179
parental training of, 179
visits home, 183, 189, 244
promoted to sergeant, 183
academic standing of, 186-87, 189
appointed to engineers, 189-90
stationed at Willet's Point, 189-90, 192, 198, 204, 287
visits brothers, 189
appointed trustee, 199, 202
visits Williamsburg, 200, 203
on education, 202
on choosing a wife, 202-203
has weakness in speaking, 203
considers resignation, 207
unit of called to quell strike, 207-208
writes to Alfales, 219
leaves for New York, 221, 301
exemplary life of, 223

visited by brothers, 230, 254
Young, William, 16, 351
Young Academy of Salt Lake, 199
Young and Fowler Company, 128
Young Men's Mutual Improvement Association, 195, 229, 241, 281
Young Music Company, 319
Young University, Salt Lake City, 162

ZCMI. *See* Zion's Cooperative Mercantile Institution
Zion
  to be strengthened, 55
  progress of, 64, 80-81, 194, 221, 247
  railroad advantageous to, 105
  knowledge should upbuild, 265
  strength of, 302
Zion's Cooperative Mercantile Institution
  description of, 116, 229, 271
  moves into new building, 120, 195
  Idaho branch of, 128
  Ernest employed at, 151
  additions made to, 178
  opening and dedication of, 195, 232
  Brigham Young meets with board, 204
  Mahonri works at, 213
  Don Carlos employed by, 263-64
  Lorenzo works at, 283
  Feramorz works at, 295
  construction progress on, 301
  Spencer Clawson buyer for, 308
  Alonzo employed at, 317
Zuni Indians, 197
Zurich District, Switzerland, 133

Letters of Brigham Young to His Sons
By Dean C. Jessee

This book was set in Fototronic Laurel, printed on Starbrite Laid Finish—Pattern 27", and bound in Columbia's Bolton Buckram by the Deseret Press. End papers are Strathmore Grandee Text. Design was by Keith Montague of Bailey-Montague & Associates. Editing and production supervision was by Eleanor Knowles of Deseret Book Co.